States of Discipline

Transforming Capitalism

Series Editors: Ian Bruff, University of Manchester;
Julie Cupples, University of Edinburgh; Gemma Edwards,
University of Manchester; Laura Horn, University of Roskilde;
Simon Springer, University of Victoria; Jacqui True, Monash University

This book series provides an open platform for the publication of path-breaking and interdisciplinary scholarship which seeks to understand and critique capitalism along four key lines: crisis, development, inequality, and resistance. At its core lies the assumption that the world is in various states of transformation, and that these transformations may build upon earlier paths of change and conflict while also potentially producing new forms of crisis, development, inequality, and resistance. Through this approach the series alerts us to how capitalism is always evolving and hints at how we could also transform capitalism itself through our own actions. It is rooted in the vibrant, broad and pluralistic debates spanning a range of approaches which are being practised in a number of fields and disciplines. As such, it will appeal to sociology, geography, cultural studies, international studies, development, social theory, politics, labour and welfare studies, economics, anthropology, law, and more.

Titles in the Series

The Radicalization of Pedagogy: Anarchism, Geography, and the Spirit of Revolt, edited by Simon Springer, Marcelo de Souza and Richard J. White

Theories of Resistance: Anarchism, Geography, and the Spirit of Revolt edited by Marcelo Lopes de Souza, Richard J. White and Simon Springer

The Practice of Freedom: Anarchism, Geography, and the Spirit of Revolt, edited by Richard J. White, Simon Springer and Marcelo Lopes de Souza

States of Discipline: Authoritarian Neoliberalism and the Contested Reproduction of Capitalist Order, edited by Cemal Burak Tansel

(Re)producing the Multiple Crises: Theorizing the Imperial Mode of Living, Ulrich Brand and Markus Wissen (forthcoming)

A Sense of Inequality, Wendy Bottero (forthcoming)

Workers Movements and Strikes: Global Perspectives in the 21st Century, edited by Jörg Nowak, Madhumita Dutta and Peter Birke

States of Discipline

Authoritarian Neoliberalism and the Contested Reproduction of Capitalist Order

Edited by
Cemal Burak Tansel

ROWMAN &
LITTLEFIELD
INTERNATIONAL

London • New York

Published by Rowman & Littlefield International Ltd
Unit A, Whitacre Mews, 26-34 Stannary Street, London SE11 4AB
www.rowmaninternational.com

Rowman & Littlefield International Ltd. is an affiliate of Rowman & Littlefield
4501 Forbes Boulevard, Suite 200, Lanham, Maryland 20706, USA
With additional offices in Boulder, New York, Toronto (Canada), and Plymouth (UK)
www.rowman.com

British Library Cataloguing in Publication Data

A catalogue record for this book is available from the British Library

ISBN: HB 978-1-7834-8618-2
         PB 978-1-7834-8619-9

Library of Congress Cataloging-in-Publication Data

ISBN 978-1-78348-618-2 (cloth: alk. paper)
ISBN 978-1-78348-619-9 (pbk: alk. paper)
ISBN 978-1-78348-620-5 (electronic)

♾™ The paper used in this publication meets the minimum requirements of
American National Standard for Information Sciences—Permanence of Paper
for Printed Library Materials, ANSI/NISO Z39.48-1992.

Printed in the United States of America

Contents

Acknowledgements

I would like to thank the *Transforming Capitalism* series editors Ian Bruff, Julie Cupples, Gemma Edwards, Laura Horn, Simon Springer and Jacqui True for the extremely helpful editorial input they provided throughout the preparation of this volume. At Rowman & Littlefield International, Dhara Patel, Anna Reeve and Michael Watson showed great care and patience in managing the book. I am grateful to Chun-yi Lee, Adam David Morton and my colleagues in the Department of Politics at the University of Sheffield for their feedback, support and involvement at various stages of this project. Finally, I would like to thank the contributors for their generous contributions and unwavering commitment to the book.

—**Cemal Burak Tansel**, Sheffield

Abbreviations

AFDC	Aid to Families with Dependent Children
AKP	Justice and Development Party (Turkey)
AMDH	Moroccan Association of Human Rights
ANAP	Motherland Party (Turkey)
ANCI	National Association of Italian Municipalities
ANDCM	Moroccan National Association of Unemployed Graduates
AST	Alternativa Sindical de Trabajadores
CARA	Hosting Centre for Asylum Seekers
CBPP	Center on Budget and Policy Priorities
CGT	Confederación General del Trabajo
CIRI	Civic Innovation Research Initiative
CNPA	Cambodian National Petroleum Authority
CoBas	Sindicato de Comisiones de Base
COESS	Confederation of European Security Services
CPC	Communist Party of China
CPP	Cambodian People's Party
CPPCC	Chinese People's Political Consultative Conference
CRI	Italian Red Cross
CTNE	Spanish National Telephone Company
CUP	*Candidatura d'Unitat Popular* (Popular Unity Candidacy)
ECB	European Central Bank
ECOC	European Capital of Culture Initiative
EES	European Employment Strategy
EMU	Economic and Monetary Union
ENA	Emergency North Africa
EPI	Economic Policy Institute
ERC	*Esquerra Republicana de Catalunya* (Republican Left of Catalonia)

ERE	*Expedientes de Regulación de Empleo* (Labour Force Adjustment Plans)
ERSAP	Economic Reform and Structural Adjustment Program
ERT	European Round Table of Industrialists
ESM	European Social Model
EU	European Union
FDI	Foreign Direct Investment
GDP	Gross Domestic Product
HDP	Peoples' Democratic Party (Turkey)
IACP	International Association of Chiefs of Police
IFI	International Financial Institution
IMF	International Monetary Fund
INDH	National Initiative for Human Development
IRP	Institute for Research on Poverty
ISI	Import Substitution Industrialization
KBE	Knowledge-based Economy
MENA	Middle East and North Africa
MÜSİAD	Independent Industrialists' and Businessmen's Association
NDP	National Democratic Party (Egypt)
NGO	Non-governmental Organization
NPC	National People's Congress (China)
NPM	New Police Management
OMC	Open Method of Coordination
OPCM	Presidency of the Council of Ministers in Italy
PCI	Italian Civil Protection
PJD	Party for Justice and Development (Morocco)
PKK	Kurdistan Workers' Party
PMSC	Private Military Security Company
POLISARIO	Popular Front for the Liberation of the Sahara and the Rio de Oro
PP	People's Party (Spain)
PRWORA	Personal Responsibility and Work Opportunity Reconciliation Act
PSOE	Spanish Socialist Workers' Party
PYD	Democratic Union Party (Syria)
RGC	Royal Government of Cambodia
SEZ	Special Economic Zone
SME	Small or Medium-Sized Enterprise
SNAP	Supplemental Nutrition Assistance Program
SOE	State-Owned Enterprise
SPRAR	Protection System for Asylum Seekers and Refugees
SRI	Sexuality Research Initiative
SSI	Supplemental Security Income

TANF	Temporary Assistance for Needy Families
TFP	Thrifty Food Plan
TNC	Transnational Corporation
TOKİ	Turkish Mass Housing Development Administration
TUSKON	Turkish Confederation of Businessmen and Industrialists
TÜSİAD	Turkish Industry and Business Association
TVE	Town-Village Enterprise
UNHCR	United Nations High Commissioner for Refugees
UNTAC	United Nations Transitional Authority in Cambodia
UPI	Union of Italian Regions
USDA	US Department of Agriculture
USDHHS	US Department of Health and Human Services
WIC	Special Supplemental Food Program for Women, Infants and Children

Chapter 1

Authoritarian Neoliberalism

Towards a New Research Agenda

Cemal Burak Tansel

For a brief period in the aftermath of the political and financial turmoil of the 2007–2008 economic crisis, the established patterns of global economic governance seemed exceptionally vulnerable to increased critical scrutiny. The crisis seemed to have undermined the legitimacy of the policies that are grouped under the rubric of 'neoliberalism' as the ultimate template of economic management for a world that had ostensibly reached the end of its history. Sanguine critics firmly pronounced the demise of neoliberalism by stating that 'the neoliberal era lasted until August 2008 when the liberalized system of global financial markets imploded' (Altvater 2009: 75), and its imminent disintegration was cautiously heralded as signalling 'a transition to a new social order, a new phase of modern capitalism beyond neoliberalism' (Duménil and Lévy 2011: 326). For some, the crisis fulfilled the crucial function of accelerating an extant push—especially in the global South—towards 'postneoliberal' models.[1] The resultant post-crisis image of neoliberalism as a mode of economic governance in its dying moments was augmented by the budding crisis of its political counterpart. Political parties that have stood at the forefront of neoliberal restructuring over the last three to four decades faced a continuous haemorrhaging of their voter base, while the authoritarian regimes with kindred neoliberal credentials were confronted by popular upheavals—often provoked by the questions of social reproduction, that is, the crises of household, employment, indebtedness and access to services and public spaces (Schäfer and Streeck 2013: 17–23; Hanieh 2013). Yet despite the severity of the crisis of social reproduction and the widespread aversion towards austerity policies which have been unleashed by fiscally disciplined governments across the heartlands of neoliberalism it is difficult to maintain that neoliberalism has lost its position as the dominant blueprint of global economic governance. As Miguel Centeno and Joseph Cohen stipulated in the

1

aftermath of the financial meltdown, 'The crisis and ensuing Great Recession may have shaken neoliberalism's supremacy, but it remains unchallenged by serious alternatives and continues to shape post-2008 policy' (2012: 312; Crouch 2011). Given the extent and scope of popular protests against the variegated products of neoliberalism as well as the rapid rise of anti-austerity parties and movements, the enduring hegemonic position of neoliberalism leaves us with a rather curious puzzle. While, as Nancy Fraser recently put it, the key political and economic 'institutions face legitimation deficits at every scale' (2015: 181), efforts to challenge and reform those institutions, as well as the broader ideas and practices that underpin them, seem to be facing insurmountable difficulties. This picture forces us to reconsider the strengths and weaknesses of neoliberalism and to take seriously the wide range of economic and political tools at the disposal of those who are committed to the survival of capital accumulation. In short, we need to revisit two fundamental questions: (1) What makes neoliberalism such a resilient mode of economic and political governance? (2) What are the mechanisms and processes with which the core components of neoliberalism effectively reproduce themselves in the face of popular opposition? In the light of the increasing recognition of the failure of neoliberal model of governance since the crisis—even by those responsible for the diffusion of neoliberal policies (Ostry, Loungani and Furceri 2016)—we also have to explore at which sites and areas neoliberalism is most fraught with contradictions, cracks and fissures.

This book responds to these questions by reasserting the exigency of understanding neoliberalism as a regime of capital accumulation and of recognizing the key role that states play in its protection and reproduction. Accordingly, we interrogate and unpack the modalities of 'authoritarian neoliberalism', a set of state strategies with which the variegated processes of neoliberalism are maintained and shielded from popular pressure. We argue that contemporary neoliberalism reinforces and increasingly relies upon (1) coercive state practices that discipline, marginalize and criminalize oppositional social forces and (2) the judicial and administrative state apparatuses which limit the avenues in which neoliberal policies can be challenged. This argument should *not* be read to the effect that the deployment of coercive state apparatuses for the protection of the circuits of capital accumulation is a *new* phenomenon, nor should it lead to the assumption that the pre-crisis trajectories of neoliberalization have been *exclusively consensual*. In advancing the analytical utility of authoritarian neoliberalism, we are not asserting that the violent, disciplinary and anti-democratic means with which the capitalist states remove the barriers to accumulation should be understood as an innovation of neoliberalism. Not only are authoritarian forms of governance and neoliberal management compatible, but, as Wendy Brown has asserted, neoliberalism is 'even *productive* of, authoritarian, despotic, paramilitaristic, and corrupt state forms as well as agents within civil society' (2005: 38, emphasis added).[2] We begin our exploration by recognizing the various ways in which the 'so-called free-market reforms and globalisation' have been 'accompanied by political repression' (Mitchell 1999: 465) and emphasize the immanent tendency of the capitalist state to deploy its coercive, legal and economic power if/when 'strategies for the reproduction of capital-in-general are being challenged in significant ways' (Ayers and Saad-Filho 2014: 4). While acknowledging these important criteria, we underscore two qualifiers of 'authoritarian neoliberalism' which highlight how its tendencies and techniques of governance represent (1) a transformation of the 'normal' operation of the capitalist state (cf. Poulantzas 1978/2014: 80) and (2) a qualitative shift from the intrinsic 'illiberal' propensities of neoliberalism. Accordingly, we posit that authoritarian neoliberalisms

1. operate through a preemptive discipline which simultaneously insulates neoliberal policies through a set of administrative, legal and coercive mechanisms and limits the spaces of popular resistance against neoliberalism (Bruff 2014: 116);
2. are marked by a significant escalation in the state's propensity to employ coercion and legal/extra-legal intimidation, which is complemented by 'intensified state control over every sphere of social life ... (and) draconian and multiform curtailment of so-called "formal" liberties' (Poulantzas 1978/2014: 203–204).

Building on these premises, the book aims to initiate a conversation defined not only by an intellectual motivation to identify more accurately the contemporary mechanisms of neoliberal governance, but also, and perhaps more so, by a *political* impetus necessitated by the exigencies of what Barry K. Gills (2010: 169) has called a 'unique conjecture of global crises' comprising socioeconomic, political and environmental fallouts. As such, we present the book as an initial step towards formulating a new research agenda underpinned by 'authoritarian neoliberalism' as a conceptual prism through which the institutionalization and employment of a number of state practices that invalidate or circumscribe public input and silence popular resistance can be illuminated. This vantage point renders possible the explanation of such practices as part of a broader strategy inherently linked to the reproduction of capitalist order and of its logics of exclusion and exploitation operating at the intersections of class, gender, race and ethnicity.

This orientation also provides the rationale for the two themes that constitute the book's title. As the following introductory discussion and the subsequent analyses will accentuate, the state—and more specifically the *capitalist state*—emerges as the key organizational structure through which the authoritarian enshrinement of neoliberal accumulation regimes is facilitated. Tracing the state's constitutive role in these processes is imperative for two reasons. First, this appreciation allows us to negate the still enduring view that neoliberalism signals an unconditional withdrawal of the state from the realm of the 'economy'.[3] Second, and more importantly, it brings into focus the necessity of confronting neoliberalism politically by devising concrete strategies to challenge its mechanisms at the various levels of state structures and interstate organizations as well as at the level of everyday life.

Accompanying this emphasis on the state as a political organization that acts as a custodian of capital accumulation, the usage of the term in the title also refers to an embodied condition whereby authoritarian neoliberalism subjects individuals, collectives and populations to economic, financial and corporeal discipline. As authoritarian neoliberal strategies are marked by an explicit predisposition to insulate policymaking from popular dissent through coercive, administrative and legal deployment of state power, we tentatively claim that these manoeuvres have a particular disciplinary effect, not only on those who actively struggle against such policies, but also on the broader polity in which they operate. As Ian Bruff has suggested, the governance techniques that comprise authoritarian neoliberal regimes are not merely 'reactive', but 'are also increasingly preemptive, locking in neoliberal governance mechanisms in the name of necessity, whatever the actual state of play' (2014: 123). In other words, the panoply of neoliberal policies enacted in different spatial and scalar contexts—for example, the imposition of austerity, restructuring of public spaces and services, technocratic shifts in macroeconomic policymaking—are increasingly geared towards protecting the pillars of neoliberal accumulation. To paraphrase Marx's comments on the English state's efforts to confront pauperism in the nineteenth century, authoritarian neoliberalism does not conjure policies to solve specific problems (e.g. fiscal deficit, the lack of affordable housing, failing public services), but it does so increasingly to 'discipline' those who confront such policies and 'perpetuate' the underlying conditions that give rise to these predicaments (cf. Marx 1975: 409). When analyzed together with the constitutive role of state power in maintaining capitalist order, these disciplinary effects do not signal the substitution of 'direct' (or physical) repression with 'indirect' forms of violence, nor do they emerge merely as the contemporary 'methods of power', which—borrowing from Poulantzas's critique of Foucault—'rest not on right but on technique, not on law but on normalization, not on punishment but on control' (Poulantzas 1978/2014: 77). On the contrary, such disciplinary effects complement and coexist with 'the repressive apparatuses (army, police, judicial system, etc.) ... that are located at the heart of the modern State' (Poulantzas 1978/2014: 77).

The book, thus, refocuses attention on the question of state power and highlights the preemptive discipline instilled by authoritarian neoliberalism not only as necessary qualifiers to the extant academic literature, but also as a step towards informing radical political practice. We contend that the recognition of the state's indispensable role allows us to move from a position of reacting against neoliberalization to proactively building mobilizations, strategies and policies to counteract not merely its symptoms but also the actors and processes that engender those through the active utilization of state apparatuses. This introductory chapter conceptually and empirically maps the emergent patterns of authoritarian neoliberalism and the signal continuities they represent vis-à-vis the structural and intersecting inequalities inherent in capitalist societies.

TRACING THE LINEAGES OF AUTHORITARIAN NEOLIBERALISM

Despite its widespread employment and its successful grafting onto the analytical vernacular of a broad spectrum of social sciences research, neoliberalism is a heavily contested term.[4] Branded as an 'oft-invoked but ill-defined concept' (Mudge 2008: 703), the theoretical status and utility of neoliberalism has been a subject of intense dispute and constant reassessment.[5] In its broadest sense, a comprehensive definition may be utilized to situate neoliberalism as both 'a form of political economy and a political ideology' (Gamble 2001: 127), yet the ambiguity regarding the specific content of this formulation—that is, to what extent and under which circumstances a disparate set of economic policies and political strategies constitutes a consciously driven project of neoliberalization—negates any one-size-fits-all solution to its definitional entanglement. Given its recognition as a somewhat nebulous construct by many scholars, one could challenge the urgency of further qualifying neoliberalism with an additional set of criteria, as we do in this book with the 'authoritarian' prefix.

This quandary leads us to the following question: What is the utility of the concept of authoritarian neoliberalism? Should the concept be deployed in a manner to highlight that the emergent/existing forms of illiberal governance in capitalist societies (notwithstanding their spatial and scalar divergences) represent a watershed, or herald a new dynamic in the history of the capitalist mode of production? Should we understand the current conjuncture as a radical mutation in the relationship between the state, (varying forms of) democracy and capitalism, a transfiguration that leads to a clear demarcation between prior modes of capitalist management and the current configuration defined by an authoritarian drift? Such demarcations always represent a degree of ambiguity, as the complex forms of human interactions and the socioeconomic contexts within which these relations appear are bound to defy clear-cut categorizations. Nor should any classifications based on the observation of such social phenomena be seen as ossified categories, incapable of undergoing revisions. With this proviso in mind, we position authoritarian neoliberalism as a historically specific set of capitalist accumulation strategies that both exacerbates the existing, structural trends in the political organization of capitalism and embodies distinct practices geared towards unshackling accumulation at the expense of democratic politics and popular participation. Nevertheless, we stress that it is imperative to perceive authoritarian neoliberalism as a *spectrum* of disciplinary strategies, ranging from the more explicit demonstrations of coercive state power (e.g. policing and surveillance) to more diffuse yet equally concrete manifestations of administrative and legal mechanisms that entrench extant power relations and inequalities.

The rationale for focusing on the 'authoritarian' dimension of neoliberalism becomes more evident once we move away from the conventional accounts that posit a gradual ascendancy of neoliberal *ideas*, starting with the advocacy of the Mont Pèlerin Society to their worldwide adoption by policymakers from the late 1970s onwards. The focus in this particular, what Raewyn Connell and Nour Dados (2014) have called, 'origin story' of neoliberalism is the formulation of a political will to undermine the post-war welfare states in the West with a blueprint devised explicitly on the precepts of a group of thinkers variously associated with the neoliberal doctrine. In Marxist versions of this particular narrative as best exemplified in the account of David Harvey, the focus on neoliberal ideas and their transplantation onto the policy realm are accompanied by the argument that the political dimension of neoliberalism— symbolized by the administrations of Margaret Thatcher in the United Kingdom and Ronald Reagan in the United States—materialized as a 'project to restore class power' (Harvey 2005: 62) which, among other things, targeted the socioeconomic power of the organized labour movement. In non-Marxist versions of the same narrative, the neoliberal triumph is attributed not necessarily to the conscious or latent class offensive of leading policymakers, but to the successful dissemination of neoliberal ideas by the 'neoliberal thought collective': an epistemic community that has 'carefully connected and combined key spheres and institutions for the contest over hegemony—academia, the media, politics, and business' (Plehwe 2009: 22).[6] The 'ideas-centred explanation' of neoliberalism (Cahill 2014: 44), thus, charts a through line from early neoliberal thinkers to the current dominant model of governance, a position which grants a causal significance to the *ideas and theories* of neo-/ordo-liberal thinkers for the emergence and popularization of concrete neoliberal *policies* (e.g. austerity, see Blyth 2013: 142).

While these accounts capture a number of important aspects related to the ideational trajectories of neoliberalism as well as the specific class interests towards which many neoliberal reforms are oriented, their explanatory powers diminish significantly once we shift our focus to the manifestations of neoliberal restructuring outside its North American and Western European heartland. As Connell and Dados (2014: 118) have suggested, the conventional accounts are 'grounded in the social experience of the global North, which is in fact only a fragment of the story'. Extrapolating neoliberalism as the global diffusion of market-oriented ideas and policies based on the particular North American and Western European trajectories of capitalist development significantly reduces the analytical value of these accounts in contexts where the building blocks of the Western post-war development (e.g. the welfare state) have been historically weak or non-existent (Connell and Dados 2014: 123).[7] Recognition of this variety in developmental trajectories should not lead to the conclusion that the concept of neoliberalism holds value only in the study of certain contexts (e.g. the West), nor should it lead to its abandonment as an object of inquiry. Yet the above-outlined accounts hit a significant barrier not only when they attempt to explain the localized instances of neoliberal restructuring beyond the West, but also when they retrace the connections between neoliberal ideas and *Western* policies that are supposedly designed to realize such theoretical claims. To borrow from Connell and Dados (2014: 120) once more:

> There is a tendency in this whole literature ... to separate neoliberal theory from neoliberal practice. The theory is treated as pure neoliberalism, the practice as its always-imperfect realization. No doubt this is partly because the theory is so easily available, in hardline texts such as Friedman's *Capitalism and Freedom* (1962). It is partly because neoliberal policy entrepreneurs themselves talked this way, frequently lambasting politicians who lacked the courage to implement the hard line. But this separation has the unfortunate effect of diverting our attention from the practical problems (possibly very different from those that preoccupied Friedman or Hayek) to which neoliberal practices seemed to offer solutions.

From the perspective of those who focus on the 'neoliberal thought collective' as the causal dynamic behind the universalization of neoliberal models, the dissonance between pure theory and messy practice could be interpreted as a sign of neoliberalism's ability to adapt and mutate in the face of change and adversity (see Mirowski 2013: 52–53). Such an incongruity might not even register as a problem for the proponents of this account since, as Mirowski (2013: 53) has argued, 'neoliberals do not navigate with a fixed static Utopia as the astrolabe for all their political strivings. They could not, since they don't even agree on such basic terms as "market" and "freedom" in all respects.' Yet, again, this account does not provide significant insights into non-Western cases of neoliberal restructuring where, in most contexts, it is difficult to find traces of local policymakers actively seeking neoliberal remedies *because* they are grounded in a much-coveted economic theory, hence the difficulty of elevating 'neoliberal ideas and think tanks as the chief causal variable driving processes of neoliberal state transformation' (Cahill 2015: 206).

The shortcomings of the above-discussed accounts accentuate the urgency of advancing alternative conceptions of neoliberalism that do not (1) assume an automatic translation of neoliberal ideas into policy and (2) prioritize specific (i.e. Western) transition to a neoliberal accumulation regime as a global blueprint adopted in each and every local context without modifications. In other words, such an account should be able to recognize and explain the universal—yet not uniform—manifestations of neoliberalism while taking into account the ways in which local trajectories of socioeconomic development, state power and class politics affect the implementation of neoliberal restructuring.

In line with these preconditions, a plausible alternative to the 'ideas-centred explanation' is to conceptualize neoliberalism as a contingent response to the recurring crises of the capitalist mode of production.[8] Such an account requires conceptualizing neoliberalism as a mode of accumulation in the 'path-dependent sequence of accumulation regimes' (Fraser 2015: 167n.13) that comprises the history of capitalism. Linked directly to the crises and contradictions of capitalism, neoliberalism could be understood as a structural response adopted by state managers to offset and minimize the impact thereof and, thus, not exclusively as a set of economic ideas that has diffused outwards from a particular geopolitical and economic setting *because* these ideas have been articulated and promoted by a powerful transnational elite bent on advancing their own class interests. In this perspective, the rise of neoliberalism as a viable accumulation strategy is linked to 'the internal problems encountered by different advanced capitalist states as a result of their participation in an interdependent world economy, and the repercussions that the solutions adopted by some would have for the managerial capacities and options of the others' (Germann 2014: 707). By following this logic, we can also reinterpret the adoption of neoliberal reforms in the global South as a response to the same pressures and crises tendencies that enabled neoliberal policies to supersede the institutional and ideational supremacy of the preceding Keynesian post-war compromise. In this account, the materialization of neoliberal policies across the global South ceases to be an act of diffusion crafted *exclusively* by Western states and international institutions, but it is understood as a strategy deployed by state managers to tackle extant or budding economic and/or political crises.[9] As Connell and Dados (2014: 123, original emphasis) illustrate vis-à-vis the paradigmatic Chilean case (cf. Klein 2007; Harvey 2005: 39–63):

> The Chicago Boys—and the other players in the making of the dictatorship's economic policy—were not offering General Pinochet a textbook of economic theory. They were offering a solution to his main political problem: how to get legitimacy by economic growth, satisfy his backers in the Chilean propertied class, and keep the diplomatic support of the United States, without giving an opening to his opponents in the political parties and labor movement. Neoliberalism *as a development strategy* met those needs.

The 'structural' account is, thus, not only capable of addressing variegated paths to neoliberalization as contingent responses to capitalist crises (in both their economic and political forms), it also helps us better contextualize and assess the degree to which neoliberal ideas, as well as the agency of advanced capitalist states and international institutions, have played a role in globalizing neoliberal governance. As such, the account does not downplay the often violent and constitutive role of international political, economic and financial organizations in imposing neoliberal reform in the global South—and, increasingly, in the North. It does, however, rebalance the effect of such organizations by recognizing the constitutive role of local state strategies, socioeconomic conditions and class struggles in shaping the trajectories of neoliberalizations.[10]

Our inquiry follows this sensitivity to the examination of 'actually existing neoliberalisms' so as to underscore more explicitly their constantly evolving character, which increasingly appropriates spheres of social production and reproduction (Brenner and Theodore 2002: 354). Neoliberalism, as employed in this book, thus refers to a specific mode of capital accumulation and political rule that instrumentalizes the extant state apparatuses to de/re-regulate economic activity in a manner that privileges the commodification of labour, environment and social reproduction in both a seemingly 'self-regulating' market domain and a 'competitive' public sphere. The policy routes that enable these processes of appropriation range from 'the transfer to "the markets" of several functions of the state, especially the intersectoral and intertemporal allocation of resources' to 'the elimination of strategic planning and the abolition of controls on most intermediate and consumer goods prices' (Mollo and Saad-Filho 2006: 101). It is for this central role played by the state in entrenching neoliberalism that we affirm that the state is 'a permanent and necessary part of neoliberal ideology, institutionalization and practice' (Bruff 2016: 115) and that neoliberalism does not dismantle but thrives upon the institutional infrastructure of the state apparatuses through their remodelling in a competitive orientation and (re)positioning them as custodians of accumulation.[11]

Understanding neoliberalism as a mode of accumulation and its adoption in different contexts as responses to capitalism's economic and political crises also offers a contextualization of why neoliberal governance increasingly embodies an authoritarian rule underpinned by the erosion of democratic politics and the deployment of coercive state power. The endeavour to unmask these authoritarian practices, as stated above, should be accompanied by the recognition that (1) the political organization of capitalism regularly clashes with democratic politics—that is, capitalism's non-democratic impulses are not new (Fraser 2015)—and (2) the concrete episodes of neoliberal restructurings across the world are often constructed through authoritarian state power. As the book will explore in depth, the shifts from Keynesian welfare regimes or import substitution industrialization (ISI) strategies to neoliberalism in the global South and North were often made possible and regularly reproduced by non-democratic, illiberal and, at times, outright violent means. Examples of the non-democratic or authoritarian constitution of neoliberalism exist at various levels. At the international level, the institutional and ideological hegemony of the Washington Consensus brought about what Stephen Gill has called 'new constitutionalism', a 'move towards construction of legal or constitutional devices to remove or insulate substantially the new economic institutions from popular scrutiny or democratic accountability' (Gill 1992: 165, 2015). Where the imposed market discipline maintained by the panoptic micromanagement of the states and international organizations has faced popular challenges—as hegemonic 'habitualization and internalization of social practices ... provokes acts of resistance' (Morton 2007: 171)—the disciplinary mechanisms have resorted to more aggressive forms of control, including 'strategies of incarceration, military surveillance, organized violence and intervention' (Gill 2008: 222, 221–232). At the national level, paths to neoliberalism in many countries have been paved by the direct involvement of the military (e.g. Turkey and Brazil) and through the deployment of authoritarian state power (e.g. Thailand and Egypt).[12]

Authoritarian neoliberalism, thus, neither signifies that spatio-temporally variegated processes of neoliberalization have all been underpinned exclusively by authoritarian state power, nor suggests that, in cases where authoritarian state power was a prevalent trigger, we can understand those processes as unfolding in a linear, predetermined trajectory dominated by the state but unperturbed by social struggles. Moreover, the concept, as we envision in this book, does not follow a definition of authoritarianism in which the coercive apparatuses of the state are privileged and understood as *external* to liberal democracy. Subscribing to a coercion-oriented understanding of authoritarianism risks not only obscuring the ways in which authoritarian state power is enmeshed with capital accumulation, but also reifying a Eurocentric North–South binary whereby a 'liberal' capitalism in the global North is positioned as a model to be emulated by the 'authoritarian' capitalisms/state socialisms of the global South.[13] As opposed to enshrining an ossified separation of liberal democracy and authoritarianism, we maintain that it is important to recognize that state responses to the economic and political crises of capitalism can—and increasingly do—assume similar forms both in formal democracies and in traditionally defined authoritarian regimes. Accordingly, the authoritarian bent in state practices can work in tandem with institutions and legal frameworks that sustain a 'minimalist' democracy, that is, a political regime defined by 'the less demanding criterion of electoral competition' (Møller and Skaaning 2010: 276).[14] The essential components of representative democracies themselves could be subverted to execute policies beyond the public purview. As Ahmet Bekmen has elaborated vis-à-vis the Turkish case:

> Rather than direct repression, though it may be employed from time to time as in the case of Turkey, authoritarian statism is inclined towards a gradual transformation that has critical effects on the functioning of the liberal democracy by incapacitating political parties, the parliament, the judiciary and some sections of the bureaucracy, and empowering the technocratic-minded elite within the executive branch. (Bekmen 2014: 47)

Such transformations at the state level are often accompanied with the suppression of popular opposition and resistance through a combination of draconian policing, lawmaking, surveillance and the 'exclusion of dissident social forces' from participating in established arenas of political representation (Amoore et al. 1997: 181). In this regard, authoritarian neoliberalism marks a significant shift away from consensus-based strategies to a model of governance in which 'dominant social groups are less interested in neutralizing resistance and dissent via concessions and forms of compromise' but, instead, opt for 'the explicit exclusion and marginalization' of oppositional political and social forces (Bruff 2014: 116). Yet while we highlight the increasing ubiquity and scope of such coercive and disciplining practices, the presence of authoritarian neoliberal strategies does not always correlate to a declining hegemonic leadership. As Brecht De Smet and Koenraad Bogaert explain in this book, 'The difference between domination and hegemony is not the quantitative *proportion* between coercion and consent needed to maintain class power, but the extent to which force is successfully *grounded* in popular consent.' It is, thus, important to recognize that authoritarian neoliberalisms can encompass cases where the interest-based alliances between social groups that constitute the lifeline of neoliberal hegemonies are maintained through excessive force and repression even by democratically elected governments.

Recognizing the spectrum of authoritarian neoliberal strategies, from the utilization of direct coercion to indirect legal, administrative and political reform, also accentuates the question of which social forces, communities and individuals find themselves at the receiving end of the disciplinary statecraft. While neoliberal reforms clearly advance specific class interests—while limiting the others—the concrete effects of state policies on individuals and collectives vary significantly based on sociopolitical markers of gender, race, ethnicity, age and (dis)ability. The effect of neoliberalization on women, minorities, LGBTQ and other marginalized communities has intensified considerably after the economic crisis of 2007–2008 as the downturn not only triggered a deepening of austerity programmes that had a disproportionate impact on these groups, but also aggravated the concomitant crisis of social reproduction, most acutely felt in households. Increasingly 'masculine' and competition-oriented state responses to the crisis have either fallen drastically short of alleviating women's deteriorating working conditions and job prospects, or actively helped further disadvantage racialized minorities, people with disabilities and the LGBTQ (Hozić and True 2016; Smith 2016; Cross 2013; Reed and Portes 2014).

Downscaling from a state-level analysis to studying the concrete effects of authoritarian neoliberalism on everyday lives helps us understand the manifold ways in which the enshrinement of a particular 'economic' discipline shapes subjectivities and defines the conditions of possibility for resistance and designing political alternatives. If, for example, we rethink the 'constitutionalisation of austerity' (de Witte 2013: 589; Oberndorfer 2015) across Europe not purely as an economic programme designed to meet fiscal demands but also as a way to reconfigure public participation and citizenship, we can disentangle the various threads through which neoliberalism has paved the way for the further marginalization of dissenting subjectivities (Tyler 2013). As Liam Stanley (forthcoming) argues, through austerity policies, 'those lives that deviate from [a] form of liberal life are devalorised, while the bodies that are associated with this deviation are disciplined'. Given the expanding scale of the crisis of social reproduction in Europe, it is no coincidence that we are witnessing a deployment of popular rhetorical devices that discipline and criminalize the working classes, minorities and, increasingly, the racialized figure of the 'migrant' to whitewash austerity policies—which further aggravate this crisis—and shift the blame onto already marginalized communities.[15] Recognizing the inherently political character of contemporary neoliberalism and the utilization of its disciplinary tools to neutralize dissent further helps us draw important parallels between the austerity programmes in the global North and the structural adjustment programmes imposed upon the global South by the IMF and World Bank. In many ways, European societies are now being subjected to the same pressures and disciplinary conditions that numerous countries in the global South have faced through conditions attached to their internationally sanctioned debt and bailout programmes. The emergent linkages between these cases expose the common strategies employed by states and international organizations, as well as the shared disciplinary experiences lived by the subjects of those strategies.

MAPPING THE REPERTOIRES OF AUTHORITARIAN NEOLIBERALISM

As the book is concerned with constructing a research agenda aimed at identifying and exposing the violence of neoliberal governance, the individual chapters are designed to offer overviews of the key themes and processes with which authoritarian neoliberalism is constituted as well as the specific spatial/governmental contexts in which these processes unfold. Given that the topics and concepts we engage with traverse disciplinary boundaries, the book hosts contributors whose research draws on interdisciplinary practices as well as those who are grounded in different branches of the social sciences. In addition to this rich disciplinary variety, the following analyses employ a wide range of methods, from the operationalization of more recent approaches in qualitative research such as 'facet methodology' to ethnography. As such, the book aims not only to establish a genuine interdisciplinary dialogue but also to highlight the value of different methodologies and research tools in examining, explaining and unmasking the mechanisms of authoritarian neoliberalism.

The first part of the book features thematic chapters on the key processes, sites and actors that both constitute and are shaped by authoritarian neoliberalism. Setting out the thematic analyses with an examination of contemporary labour struggles, Mònica Clua-Losada and Olatz Ribera-Almandoz reveal the key role of the state in disciplining the working classes through anti-labour legislations and the enforcement of 'wage discipline' through low-income, precarious jobs. Zeroing on the Spanish Telefónica/Movistar workers' mobilizations, the authors stress that, despite the wide-ranging disciplinary effects of authoritarian neoliberal regimes, the working-class agency is still capable of resisting and subverting the conditions of exploitation. While the authors discuss the ways in which extensive privatization efforts and anti-labour legislations have fragmented the collective power of labour movements, their account of the Spanish mobilizations highlight that workers continue to find innovative ways with which to build common organizational links and fronts to challenge neoliberalism.

Kendra Briken and Volker Eick expand our engagement with coercive state power by historicizing the modes of policing in capitalist states and demonstrating the unique reconfiguration of 'public' and 'private' policing under authoritarian neoliberalism. While stressing the fact that the commercialization of security provision has not resulted in a withdrawal of the state from providing means of pacification, Briken and Eick demonstrate that states increasingly 'rely upon private and commercial/corporate means' to uphold their coercive functions. As the discussion of new organizational models of policing signals, even the state's own coercive apparatuses are now subject to the discipline of neoliberal rationality as 'police forces are managed more or less like police companies or enterprises'. Inasmuch as contemporary forms of policing are built upon 'an intimate intertwining of the state and corporate security', the authors also bring to our attention the ways in which pacification strategies are increasingly reinforced by projecting individualized responsibility and by exhorting citizens to police themselves and each other.

Wendy Harcourt's curation of female researchers' experiences of working in/against authoritarian neoliberal regimes display the disciplinary effects on individuals in brutal detail. Refocusing our interrogation of authoritarian neoliberalism at the level of body politics, Harcourt invites us to unmask the disciplinary strategies of neoliberalism and authoritarian state power by focusing on resistance from 'the position of the intimate, personal and political'. Vignettes of five women's research experiences that constitute the narrative of the chapter not only reveal the particular gendered effects of neoliberalism but also, as Harcourt powerfully argues, 'open up space for a wider understanding of what constitutes valued and validated knowledge in academe'.

The impact of authoritarian neoliberalism on social forces and their reproduction is further investigated in Sébastien Rioux's chapter on welfare provisions and the management of hunger. Zooming in on the United States to chart the historical trajectory of state responses to the recurrent crises of social reproduction, Rioux offers a detailed analysis of how food insecurity is manufactured in wealthy capitalist countries through state (in)activities. Underscoring the inherent class character of neoliberal reforms, Rioux elucidates the linkages between declining profitability, wage stagnation and the state-led shift from welfare to workfare. As the chapter concludes grimly, neoliberal reforms have succeeded in restoring the key circuits of capital accumulation. This restoration, however, has resulted in the expansion of 'an army of working poor for whom food and economic insecurity have become the norm'.

The focus on the state's role in shaping the accumulation processes is further sharpened in Annalena Di Giovanni's chapter on urban transformation under authoritarian neoliberalism. In line with our broader emphasis on understanding neoliberalism as an accumulation regime, Di Giovanni carefully unpacks the contradictions of 'neoliberal urbanism' and reasserts that state apparatuses are increasingly monopolizing decision-making powers to commodify public spaces. Tracing the concrete manifestations of this trend in the case of Istanbul's urban restructuring, Di Giovanni reveals that 'a planning model of fragmentation, private contracting and the centralization of local decision-making' undermines independent auditing mechanisms and excludes the public from influencing key decisions made about their living spaces. Under authoritarian neoliberalism, cities are thus shaped by the state's 'juridically authorised (if not legitimised) administrative domination' (Davies 2014: 3225).

Echoing the hitherto discussed themes of the commercialization of pacification and space, Luca Manunza's ethnographic research into refugee camps demonstrates the extent to which the management of borders has become an extension of 'humanitarian warfare' abroad and the regulation of the labour market within the European Union. Unpacking how a nexus of private providers and local administrations controls the 'hospitality business' of asylum seekers in Italy, Manunza reveals that EU border management is increasingly shaped by the desire to prevent a 'surplus population' from accessing the labour market and operates on deeply racialized premises.

The second part of the book opens with two chapters that continue to focus on the European Union's role in maintaining and reinforcing disciplinary mechanisms across various socio-spatial levels. Ian Bruff interrogates the European Union's legal infrastructure and highlights its role in insulating key decision-making processes from the purview of the public and enforcing neoliberal discipline. While the criticism of the European Union's 'democratic deficit' and its role as 'a supranational anchor for the domestic pursuit of market freedom' (Bonefeld 2015: 869; van Apeldoorn 2009) is well established in the critical literature, Bruff brings into fresh focus how non-binding 'soft' laws have become crucial tools with which to disseminate, institutionalize and enforce neoliberal policies. The chapter employs insights from the emerging literature on 'facet methodology' and deconstructs the European Social Model, as well as a number of EU initiatives, to evaluate their role in enshrining neoliberal common sense.

Shifting the focus from the European Union's own architecture to the effects of its disciplinary policies, Panagiotis Sotiris delivers a powerful indictment of the Troika-enforced fiscal austerity in Greece and exposes the extent to which the Greek case signals the establishment of a new European-wide 'permanent economic emergency'. Reflecting the book's overall aim in redefining neoliberalism as a contingent response to capitalist crises, Sotiris reconceptualizes EU integration as a 'class strategy' to alleviate the crisis of the European 'social model' and retraces the ways in which the imposition of austerity in Greece has been accompanied by tactics that have short-circuited the 'normal' political organization of the capitalist state (e.g. parliamentary process) and silenced the popular will of the Greek people. Sotiris's wide-ranging critique of the European Union's structural deficiencies results in a call for a decisive rupture with the Union and a reimagining of national and international communities based on social alliances of subaltern classes.

The remaining case studies offered in the book reveal how a broadly de-fined neoliberal macroeconomic policy has been installed upon established political regimes and utilized the existing or emerging authoritarian ten-dencies—despite variations in state forms/political structures—to enshrine capital accumulation.[16] In the particular cases of Cambodia, China, Egypt, Morocco and Turkey, the chapters argue that the transitions to a neoliberal regime of accumulation were often encouraged by the state elites and policy-makers to address not only economic woes, but also political crises brought about by intensified class conflict and loss of legitimacy. As such, retracing the histories of neoliberalization in those cases through the lens of authoritar-ian neoliberalism becomes paramount to contextualize and understand more accurately 'how (authoritarian) modalities of government have changed over the years and how these changes have an impact on the government of par-ticular peoples and places' (Bogaert 2013: 216). This manoeuvre also allows us to move away from essentializing the nature and influence of authoritar-ian state power in the global South and retain a sharper analytical sensitivity to the economic processes through which such state forms have reproduced themselves.

The reconstitution of authoritarian state power in Turkey over the last de-cade arguably represents the archetypal case of authoritarian neoliberalism. Barış Alp Özden, İsmet Akça and Ahmet Bekmen unpack the modalities of authoritarian neoliberalism in Turkey and carefully retrace how the ruling Justice and Development Party (AKP) has risen upon a threefold strategy of enforcing neoliberal reforms, demobilizing the organized working classes and displaying an instrumentalist political activism against the military tute-lage. The authors bring together key aspects of the economic, political and social components of the party's hegemonic activities into a single narrative that charts the interplay between populist and disciplinary strategies that paved the way for the marginalization and criminalization of oppositional forces against the backdrop of an increasingly authoritarian, de facto single-party regime.[17]

If the Turkish case embodies the ease with which neoliberalism can transform democratic—however limited that democracy might be—variants of capitalist states, Brecht De Smet and Koenraad Bogaert remind us that authoritarianism is already latent in the political organization of capitalism and that authoritarian states have excelled at embracing neoliberal reforms. Providing a comparative overview of Egypt's and Morocco's paths to neoliberal restructuring, the authors argue that neoliberalism was adopted as a response to fiscal, political and social turbulences triggered by the particular postcolonial configuration of these countries and their relationship to the world economy. In both cases, the extent to which the ruling classes managed to exert hegemonic leadership over the subaltern classes shaped the trajectory of their neoliberal programmes and the scale of popular resistance to them.

In the final two chapters, the utilization of existing patterns of control and regulation appears as a key factor in reinforcing neoliberalism. Simon Springer underscores the ways in which patronage and cliental relations in Cambodia have been remodelled to justify the status quo of a ruling class that has benefitted tremendously from the country's transition to a 'free market economy'. Labelling the symbiosis of Cambodia's hierarchal patronage structures and the neoliberalization of its economy *nepoliberalism*, Springer unmasks the violence continuously perpetrated by 'a kleptocratic system of nepotism'. While Springer accentuates a particularly localized component in reproducing neoliberalism in Cambodia, his analysis reasserts the importance of 'retaining the abstraction of neoliberalism as a "global" project' to map out the commonalities between 'geographically diffuse phenomena like inequality and poverty'. Kean Fan Lim's discussion of the paths to variegated neoliberalism in China captures a similar dynamic by underscoring the extent to which the Communist Party of China (CPC), through neoliberal restructuring, has redefined and repurposed a plethora of existing institutions and policies to entrench its political power. Lim shows that 'the strategies to effect market-like rule in China are first and foremost a legacy of authoritarian capacities and policies instituted *prior* to the launch of marketization in the 1980s'.

The book is concluded with a postscript by Cynthia Enloe, who encourages us to remain attentive to the questions of agency. Complementing our focus on the state, Enloe draws attention to the questions of *how* and *why* those who occupy key positions within the state apparatuses have promoted authoritarian neoliberal policies, and thus offers a crucial new avenue within which to devise future research projects on authoritarian neoliberalism.

CONCLUSION

States of Discipline acts as an exploration into the increasingly visible and salient symbiosis of neoliberalism and authoritarian state power. As such, we present the book neither as a definitive statement nor as the culmination of a done-and-dusted research project, but as a step towards analyzing the reciprocal relationship between neoliberalism and the often overlooked authoritarian political power that co-constitutes it. Beyond the themes and spatial/governmental contexts we explore in the book, the particular gendered, racialized and localized effects of authoritarian neoliberalism, as well as their relationship with the contemporary forms of indebtedness, financialization, migration and globalized conflict, require greater scrutiny.[18] While chapters in this book engage with many of these topics, we believe that additional in-depth case studies that take authoritarian state power seriously can illuminate the specific constellation of neoliberalism and state strategies that exploit the existing gendered, racial and class-based hierarchies as well as strengthen the analytical purchase of the concept.

We hope that the analyses provided in this book will speak to and inform concrete political struggles currently waged against authoritarian neoliberal strategies across the world. The road from theoretically informed research to political practice is always uneven and offers no guarantees, but we do hope that the book will make constructive contributions to the ongoing debates on tactics and strategies to challenge neoliberalism.[19] Chief among these contributions is reasserting the importance of retaining state power as the focal point of critique and radical political practice. While our thematic and country/region-specific analyses demonstrate that the concrete forms in which social movements and communities confront neoliberalism are always shaped by their local context, histories and forms of mobilization, we maintain that struggles against authoritarian neoliberalism ultimately need to address the question of state power. This should not be read to the effect that we prioritize one form of political practice over another (e.g. we are not advocating a side in the well-trod debates on whether the 'horizontal' versus 'vertical' organizations offer the best tools to practice radical politics) but rather as a call for a critique of and disruptive engagement with state power to confront neoliberalism strategically, that is, at its political–organizational heart.

How best to construct such a strategic engagement with the state and mobilize grassroots responses is, once again, heavily contingent upon where the state in question lies in the spectrum of authoritarian neoliberalism. While the entrenched neoliberal economic rationality in the West continues to close off avenues for socioeconomic alternatives and manifests predominantly as 'a technocratic transfer of power' (Lowndes and Gardner 2016: 15), those struggling for alternatives in the global South often face a whole set of different challenges that originate not necessarily from neoliberal economic management itself but from its symbiosis with authoritarian statisms. We should, therefore, remain open to embracing a variety of political tactics and practices just as authoritarian neoliberalism operates on a spectrum of disciplinary strategies. Recognizing the importance of this strategic receptivity would allow us to mitigate some of the existing fault lines in radical politics and lead to the reinvention and utilization of 'traditional' organizations.[20] Such tactics and practices, however, need to be informed by the lessons of past struggles and organizations, as engaging with the state—however critical the terms of that engagement might be—often risks becoming 'entangled with, and within, the institutions of the state and ever more distant from the traditional social base' (Boito and Saad-Filho 2016: 204) from which movements emerge. Finally, notwithstanding our focus on the constitutive role of authoritarian state power and the utilization of state apparatuses in maintaining capital accumulation, consent-making activities and efforts by the states, policymakers and transnational organizations to (re)constitute neoliberal 'common sense' should still be seen as integral components of the hegemonic status neoliberalism continues to enjoy.[21]

This book has been conceived and prepared within a turbulent conjuncture at which the economic and political crises of capitalism resulted in both the resurfacing and extension of authoritarian statisms in the Middle East and Latin America, the disintegration of the established centrist politics in Europe and the fragmented, yet forceful, rise of the xenophobic right and populist left across crisis-stricken countries. The exigencies of this conjuncture force us to reconsider and challenge neoliberalism not as a set of economic policies, but as a regime of governance that continues to undermine democratic politics and amplify latent authoritarian tendencies of capitalist states. We present this book as a contribution to the struggles waged for a democratic future unshackled by the economic and political chains of neoliberalism.

NOTES

1. See Leiva (2008); *Development Dialogue* (2009); Grugel and Riggirozzi (2009); Macdonald and Ruchert (2009); Panizza (2009); Peck, Theodore and Brenner (2010); Schmalz and Ebenau (2012); Springer (2015).

2. For analogous articulations of this point in different disciplinary contexts, see Lovering and Türkmen (2011: 73); Topak (2013: 567); Aydın (2013: 106); Tansel (2015).

3. While the once-dominant state withdrawal thesis has lost its influence to a large extent, it is possible to detect a symptomatic reincarnation of the 'state/market dichotomy' (Bruff 2011) in the recent literature on the BRICS (Stephen 2014: 929–30). For refined discussions of the relationship between the state and neoliberalism, see Konings (2010); Delwaide (2011); Dardot and Laval (2013: 216); Cahill (2014: 141); Soederberg (2014: 46).

4. This chapter will not provide a thematic review of the different ways in which the concept has been defined, given that a significant portion of the literature has focused on historicizing and retracing the conceptual and intellectual trajectory of neoliberalism. See, *inter alia*, Harvey (2005); Mirowski and Plehwe (2009); Peck (2010); Burgin (2012); Stedman-Jones (2012); Mirowski (2013). For recent interventions in neoliberalism's theoretical boundaries and the definitional struggles around the concept, see Peck (2013); Flew (2014); Springer (2014).

5. See also Dean (2014: 153–157); Eriksen et al. (2015: 912–914).

6. Philip Mirowski further suggests that the Mont Pèlerin Society, the kernel of this collective, 'evolved into an exceptionally successful structure for the incubation of integrated political theory and political action outside of the more conventional structures of academic disciplines and political parties in the second half of the twentieth century' (2013: 42–43).

7. The absence/weakness of Western-style welfare states, of course, does not signal a corresponding absence/weakness of different types of poor relief and social welfare.

8. The word 'contingent' is used here to highlight that neoliberalism is but one response to the recurring economic and political crises of capitalism. While it has taken a universal quality over four decades of implementation and enforcement, its structural linkage to capitalist crises should not be understood as a trigger of uniform reactions across different countries and socioeconomic contexts.

9. As Henk Overbeek (2003: 25–26, original emphases) has correspondingly interjected, 'There is a complex and dialectical relationship between neo-liberalism as *process* and neo-liberalism as *project*. Certainly, there is such a thing as a neo-liberal project that is pushed consciously and purposefully by its protagonists (organic intellectuals, entrepreneurs and politicians, organizational representatives, etc.). ... But of course, as critics of this approach will quickly point out, these programmes have never been simply put into practice. A hegemonic project or comprehensive concept of control is shaped, and continuously reshaped, in the process of struggle, compromise and readjustment.'

10. For the various ways in which organizations such as the World Bank and IMF install and sanction the 'discipline of the market' (Overbeek 2002: 80), see Weller and Singleton (2006); Bedirhanoğlu (2007); Harrison (2010); Güven (2012); True (2012, chs. 5–6).

11. As Nancy Fraser (2015: 184.n42) clarifies: 'This intensification and enlargement of repressive state power proceeds even as other state functions are being

eliminated, downsized, outsourced to private firms, or kicked up to transnational governance structures. Thus, the recalibration of the polity/economy nexus in financialized capitalism is in no way tantamount to the "disappearance of the state". On the contrary, states continue to exercise their historic repressive functions and to monopolize the means of violence—indeed, they do so in ever new and creative ways.'

12. See, *inter alia*, Boratav, Türel and Yeldan (1996); Beinin (2009); Wurzel (2009); Connell and Dados (2014: 122–129); Tansel (forthcoming). The role played by the military regimes in such transitions signals the extent to which restoring the pillars of capital accumulation was perceived by the juntas as a key—if not *the* key—step towards securing order, stability and the survival of their respective nation states. Neoliberal policies offered exactly the type of expeditious remedy the regimes were looking for after protracted economic and political crises. As Poulantzas (1976: 92, 106) illustrated in his analyses of Portugal, Spain and Greece, in such major 'crises of hegemony', 'the role of political parties for the bourgeoisie is replaced by that of the military'.

13. The decoupling of violence and liberal democracy has a deep-rooted antecedent in social theory. As Karl von Holdt has stipulated, 'Western social theory assumes that overt violence declines with the formation of the modern state and democracy through a combination of the consolidation of the modern state and its monopoly of legitimate coercion identified by Weber, the political technologies of Foucault's governmentality, and Bourdieu's gentle violence of symbolic power, with the result that the study of violence is reduced to studies of deviance, criminality or war' (2014: 130).

14. Upholding the freedom of markets at the expense of democratic politics was not an idea anathema to early neoliberal thinkers, as Hayek (1978: 143) himself suggested that 'an authoritarian government might act on liberal principles'. See also Dean (2014: 155); Bonefeld (2015: 872–874).

15. This should not be read to the effect that neoliberalization simply results in the dismissal of progressive causes or marginalized groups and communities. On the contrary, emancipatory goals shared and advanced by progressive movements continue to be adopted and subsequently neutralized by powerful transnational organizations as well as nation states and companies. In such cases, as feminist political economists have incisively demonstrated, the co-optation of progressive ideals such as 'gender equality and women's empowerment' are repurposed to fit the requirements of neoliberal rationality and 'only understood in relation to [their] ability to serve the market' (Elias 2013: 166–167; Dauvergne and LeBaron 2014; Roberts 2015).

16. This is a trend that is also visible beyond the case studies we have covered in the book. See, for example, Jasmin Hristov's (2014) account of the 'parallel' development of paramilitary activities and neoliberal restructuring in Colombia.

17. Chapters 6 and 10, the two chapters that focus on the Turkish case, were completed before the coup attempt on 15 July 2016 and, thus, do not explore the dynamics of the post-coup period. Nevertheless, the analyses provided in the chapters hold up well even after the coup attempt, since the subsequent crackdown ordered by the government represents not a new and unprecedented course but a significant intensification of the existing practices highlighted in those chapters.

18. These issues and the concrete ways in which they manifest in and constitute neoliberal governance have, of course, been subjects of many important studies. See,

inter alia, Bakker (2003); Bakker and Gill (2008); Goldberg (2009); Roberts and Mahtani (2010); Elias (2011); LeBaron (2014, 2015); Soederberg (2014); Bruff and Wöhl (2016); Montgomerie and Tepe-Belfrage (2016).

19. For a small selection of the recent discussions on extant/proposed radical political practices against neoliberalism from different perspectives, see Hall, Massey and Rustin (2013); Hanieh (2015); Huke, Clua-Losada and Bailey (2015); Dean (2016); Varoufakis (2016); Vey (2016); and Wigger and Buch-Hansen (2013).

20. See Bieler, Lindberg and Sauerborn (2010: 257); Bieler (2015); Huke, Clua-Losada and Bailey (2015); Fraser (2015: 188); Wigger and Horn (2015); Teivainen and Trommer (2016); Hesketh (2016).

21. Martijn Konings (2015: 112), for example, invites us to take 'the cultural spirit of neoliberal capitalism' more seriously and warns us against '[focusing] on the role of neoconservative elites and [portraying] the spiritual and cultural aspects of contemporary capitalism as oddly irrational moments in a process fundamentally driven by market imperatives and instrumental rationality'. On the role of 'common sense' in building neoliberal hegemony, see Soederberg (2006); Bruff (2008); Stanley (2014); and Roberts (2015).

BIBLIOGRAPHY

Altvater E (2009) Postneoliberalism or postcapitalism? The failure of neoliberalism in the financial market crisis. *Development Dialogue* 51: 73–86.

Amoore L, Dodgson R, Gills BK, Langley P, Marshall D and Watson I (1997) Overturning 'globalization': resisting the teleological, reclaiming the 'political'. *New Political Economy* 2(1): 179–195.

Aydın Z (2013) Global crisis, Turkey and the regulation of economic crisis. *Capital & Class* 37(1): 95–109.

Ayers AJ and Saad-Filho A (2015) Democracy against neoliberalism: Paradoxes, limitations, transcendence. *Critical Sociology* 41(4/5): 597–618.

Bakker I (2003) Neo-liberal governance and the reprivatization of social reproduction: Social provisioning and shifting gender orders. In: Bakker I and Gill S (eds) *Power, Production and Social Reproduction: Human In/security in the Global Political Economy*. New York: Palgrave Macmillan, 66–82.

Bakker I and Gill S (2008) New constitutionalism and social reproduction. In: Bakker I and Silvey R (eds) *Beyond States and Markets: The Challenges of Social Reproduction*. Abingdon: Routledge. 19–33.

Bedirhanoğlu P (2007) The neoliberal discourse on corruption as a means of consent building: Reflections from post-crisis Turkey. *Third World Quarterly* 28(7): 1239–1254.

Beinin J (2009) Neo-liberal structural adjustment, political demobilization, and neo-authoritarianism in Egypt. In: Guazzone L and Pioppi D (eds) *The Arab State and Neo-liberal Globalization: The Restructuring of State Power in the Middle East*. Reading: Ithaca Press, 19–46.

Bekmen A (2014) State and capital in Turkey during the neoliberal era. In: Akça İ, Bekmen A and Özden BA (eds) *Turkey Reframed: Constituting Neoliberal Hegemony*. London: Pluto, 47–74.

Bieler A (2015) 'Sic vos non vobis' (for you, but not yours): The struggle for public water in Italy. *Monthly Review* 67(5): 35–50.

Bieler A, Lindberg I and Sauerborn W (2010) After 30 years of deadlock: Labour's possible strategies in the new global order. *Globalizations* 7(1–2): 247–260.

Blyth M (2013) *Austerity: History of a Dangerous Idea*. Oxford: Oxford University Press.

Bogaert K (2013) Contextualizing the Arab Revolts: The politics behind three decades of neoliberalism in the Arab World. *Middle East Critique* 22(3): 213–234.

Boito A and Saad-Filho A (2016) State, state institutions, and political power in Brazil. *Latin American Perspectives* 43(2): 190–206.

Bonefeld W (2015) European economic constitution and the transformation of democracy: On class and the state of law. *European Journal of International Relations* 21(4): 867–886.

Boratav K, Türel O and Yeldan E (1996) Dilemmas of structural adjustment and environmental policies under instability: Post-1980 Turkey. *World Development* 24(2): 373–393.

Brenner N and Theodore N (2002) Cities and the geographies of 'actually existing neoliberalism'. *Antipode: A Radical Journal of Geography* 34(3): 349–379.

Bruff I (2008) *Culture and Consensus in European Varieties of Capitalism: A 'Common Sense' Analysis*. Basingstoke: Palgrave Macmillan.

Bruff I (2014) The rise of authoritarian neoliberalism. *Rethinking Marxism: A Journal of Economics, Culture & Society* 26(1): 113–129.

Bruff I (2016) Neoliberalism and authoritarianism. In: Springer S, Birch K and Mac-Leavy J (eds) *The Routledge Handbook of Neoliberalism*. Abingdon: Routledge, 107–117.

Bruff I and Wöhl S (2016) Constitutionalizing austerity, disciplining the household: Masculine norms of competitiveness and the crisis of social reproduction in the Eurozone. In: Hozić AA and True J (eds) *Scandalous Economics: The Spectre of Gender and Global Financial Crisis*. Oxford: Oxford University Press.

Burgin A (2012) *The Great Persuasion: Reinventing Free Markets Since the Depression*. Cambridge, MA: Harvard University Press.

Cahill D (2014) *The End of Laissez-faire? On the Durability of Embedded Liberalism*. Cheltenham: Edward Elgar.

Cahill D (2015) Representations of neoliberalism. *Forum for Social Economics* 44(2): 201–210.

Centeno MA and Cohen JN (2012) The arc of neoliberalism. *Annual Review of Sociology* 38(1): 317–340.

Connell R and Dados N (2014) Where in the world does neoliberalism come from? The market agenda in Southern perspective. *Theory and Society* 43(2): 117–138.

Cross M (2013) Demonised, impoverished and now forced into isolation: the fate of disabled people under austerity. *Disability & Society* 28(5): 719–723.

Crouch C (2011) *The Strange Non-death of Neoliberalism*. Cambridge: Polity.

Dardot P and Laval C (2014) *The New Way of the World: On Neoliberal Society*. London: Verso.

Dauvergne P and LeBaron G (2014) *Protest Inc.: The Corporatization of Activism*. Cambridge: Polity.

Davies JS (2014) Rethinking urban power and the local state: Hegemony, domination and resistance in neoliberal cities. *Urban Studies* 51(15): 3215–3232.

de Witte F (2013) EU law, politics, and the social question. *German Law Journal* 14(5): 581–611.

Dean M (2104) Rethinking neoliberalism. *Journal of Sociology* 50(2): 150–163.

Dean J (2016) *Crowds and Party*. London: Verso.

Delwaide J (2011) The return of the state? *European Review* 19(1): 69–91.

Development Dialogue (2009) Special issue: Postneoliberalism—A beginning debate. 51 (January): 1–212.

Duménil G and Lévy D (2011) *The Crisis of Neoliberalism*. Cambridge, MA: Harvard University Press.

Elias J (2011) The gender politics of economic competitiveness in Malaysia's transition to a knowledge economy. *Pacific Review* 24(5): 529–552.

Elias J (2013) Davos woman to the rescue of global capitalism: Postfeminist politics and competitiveness promotion at the World Economic Forum. *International Political Sociology* 7(2): 152–169.

Eriksen TH, Laidlaw J, Mair J, Martin K and Venkatesan S (2015) Debate: 'The concept of neoliberalism has become an obstacle to the anthropological understanding of the twenty-first century'. *Journal of the Royal Anthropological Institute* 21(4): 911–923.

Flew T (2104) Six theories of neoliberalism. *Thesis Eleven* 122(1): 49–71.

Fraser N (2015) Legitimation crisis? On the political contradictions of financialized capitalism. *Critical Historical Studies* 2(2): 157–189.

Gamble A (2001) Neo-liberalism. *Capital & Class* 25(3): 127–134.

Germann J (2014) German 'Grand Strategy' and the rise of neoliberalism. *International Studies Quarterly* 58(4): 706–716.

Gill S (1992) The emerging world order and European change: the political economy of European Union. In: Miliband R and Panitch L (eds) *Socialist Register 1992: New World Order?* London: Merlin Press, 157–196.

Gill S (2008) *Power and Resistance in the New World Order*, 2nd edition. Basingstoke: Palgrave Macmillan.

Gill S (2015) Market civilization, new constitutionalism and world order. In: Gill S and Cutler AC (eds) *New Constitutionalism and World Order*. Cambridge: Cambridge University Press, 29–44.

Gills BK (2010) Going South: capitalist crisis, systemic crisis, civilisational crisis. *Third World Quarterly* 31(2): 169–184.

Goldberg DT (2009) *The Threat of Race: Reflections on Racial Neoliberalism*. Oxford: Wiley-Blackwell.

Grugel J and Riggirozzi P (eds) (2009) *Governance After Neoliberalism in Latin America*. New York: Palgrave Macmillan.

Güven AB (2012) The IMF, the World Bank, and the global economic crisis: Exploring paradigm continuity. *Development and Change* 43(4): 869–898.

Hall S, Massey D and Rustin M (2013) After neoliberalism: Analysing the present. *Soundings* 53: 8–22.

Hanieh A (2013) *Lineages of Revolt: Issues of Contemporary Capitalism in the Middle East*. Chicago: Haymarket.

Hanieh A (2015) Challenging neoliberalism in the Arab world. In: Pradella L and Marois T (eds) *Polarizing Development: Alternatives to the Neoliberalism and the Crisis*. London: Pluto, 226–236.

Harrison G (2010) *Neoliberal Africa: The Impact of Global Social Engineering*. London: Zed.

Harvey D (2005) *A Brief History of Neoliberalism*. Oxford: Oxford University Press.

Hayek FA (1978) *New Studies in Philosophy, Politics, Economics and the History of Ideas*. London: Routledge & Kegan Paul.

Hesketh C (2016) The survival of non-capitalism. *Environment and Planning D: Society and Space* (Online). DOI: 10.1177/0263775816639313.

Hozić AA and True J (2016) Making feminist sense of the global financial crisis. In: Hozić AA and True J (eds) *Scandalous Economics: Gender and the Politics of Financial Crises*. Oxford: Oxford University Press, 3–20.

Hristov J (2014) *Paramilitarism and Neoliberalism: Violent Systems of Capital Accumulation in Colombia and Beyond*. London: Pluto.

Huke N, Clua-Losada M and Bailey DJ (2015) Disrupting the European crisis: A critical political economy of contestation, subversion and escape. *New Political Economy* 20(5): 725–751.

Klein N (2007) *The Shock Doctrine: The Rise of Disaster Capitalism*. Harmondsworth: Penguin.

Konings M (2010) Neoliberalism and the American state. *Critical Sociology* 36(5): 741–765.

Konings M (2015) *The Emotional Logic of Capitalism: What Progressives Have Missed*. Stanford, CA: Stanford University Press.

LeBaron G (2014) Reconceptualizing debt bondage: Debt as a class-based form of labor discipline. *Critical Sociology* 40(5): 763–780.

LeBaron G (2015) Unfree labor beyond binaries: Insecurity, social hierarchy and labour market restructuring. *International Feminist Journal of Politics* 17(1): 1–19.

Leiva FI (2008) *Latin American Neostructuralism: The Contradictions of Post-Neoliberal Development*. Minneapolis: University of Minnesota Press.

Lovering J and Türkmen H (2011) Bulldozer neo-liberalism in Istanbul: the state-led construction of property markets and the displacement of the urban poor. *International Planning Studies* 16(1): 73–96.

Lowndes V and Gardner A (2016) Local governance under the Conservatives: Super-austerity, devolution and the 'smarter state'. *Local Government Studies* (Online). DOI: 10.1080/03003930.2016.1150837.

Macdonald L and Ruchert A (eds) (2009) *Post-Neoliberalism in the Americas*. Basingstoke: Palgrave Macmillan.

Marx K (1975) Critical notes on the article 'The King of Prussia and Social Reform. By a Prussian'. In: *Early Writings*, Livingstone R and Benton G (trans). London: Penguin, 401–420.

Mirowski P (2013) *Never Let a Serious Crisis Go to Waste: How Neoliberalism Survived the Financial Meltdown*. London: Verso.

Mirowski P and Plehwe D (eds) (2009) *The Road from Mont Pèlerin: The Making of the Neoliberal Thought Collective*. Cambridge, MA: Harvard University Press.

Mitchell T (1999) No factories, no problems: the logic of neo-liberalism in Egypt. *Review of African Political Economy* 26(82): 455–468.

Møller J and Skaaning SE (2010) Beyond the radial delusion: conceptualizing and measuring democracy and non-democracy. *International Political Science Review* 31(3): 261–283.

Mollo MLR and Saad-Filho A (2006) Neoliberal economic policies in Brazil (1994–2005): Cardoso, Lula and the need for a democratic alternative. *New Political Economy* 11(1): 99–123.

Montgomerie J and Tepe-Belfrage D (2016) A feminist moral-political economy of uneven reform in austerity Britain: Fostering financial and parental literacy. *Globalizations* (Online). DOI:10.1080/14747731.2016.1160605

Morton AD (2007) *Unravelling Gramsci: Hegemony and Passive Revolution in the Global Political Economy*. London: Pluto.

Mudge SL (2008) What is neo-liberalism? *Socio-Economic Review* 6(4): 703–731.

Ostry JD, Loungani P and Furceri D (2016) Neoliberalism: Oversold? *Finance & Development* 53(2): 38–41. Available at: http://www.imf.org/external/pubs/ft/fandd/2016/06/pdf/ostry.pdf

Panizza F (2009) *Contemporary Latin America: Development and Democracy beyond the Washington Consensus*. London: Zed.

Peck J (2010) *Constructions of Neoliberal Reason*. Oxford: Oxford University Press.

Peck J (2013) Explaining (with) neoliberalism. *Territory, Politics, Governance* 1(2): 132–157.

Peck J, Theodore N and Brenner N (2010) Postneoliberalism and its malcontents. *Antipode: A Radical Journal of Geography* 41(S1): 94–116.

Plehwe D (2009) Introduction. In: Mirowski P and Plehwe D (eds) *The Road from Mont Pèlerin: The Making of the Neoliberal Thought Collective*. Cambridge, MA: Harvard University Press, 1–42.

Poulantzas N (1976) *The Crisis of the Dictatorships: Portugal, Spain, Greece*, Fernbach D (trans). London: New Left Books.

Poulantzas N (1978/2014) *State, Power, Socialism*. London: Verso.

Oberndorfer L (2015) From new constitutionalism to authoritarian constitutionalism: New economic governance and the state of European democracy. In: Jäger J and Springler E (eds) *Asymmetric Governance and Possible Futures: Critical Political Economy and Post-Keynesian Perspectives*. Abingdon: Routledge, 186–207.

Overbeek H (2002) Neoliberalism and the regulation of global labor mobility. *The Annals of the American Academy of Political and Social Science* 581(1): 74–90.

Overbeek H (2003) Globalization, neo-liberalism and the employment question. In: Overbeek H (ed) *The Political Economy of European Employment: European Integration and the Transnationalization of the (Un)employment Question.* London: Routledge, 13–28.

Reed H and Portes J (2014) *Cumulative Impact Assessment: A Research Report by Landman Economics and the National Institute of Economic and Social Research (NIESR) for the Equality and Human Rights Commission.* Equality and Human Rights Commission Research Report 94. Available at: https://www.equalityhumanrights.com/sites/default/files/cumulative_impact_assessment_full_report_30-07-14.pdf

Roberts A (2015) The political economy of 'transnational business feminism': Problematizing the corporate-led gender equality agenda. *International Feminist Journal of Politics* 17(2): 209–231.

Roberts DJ and Mahtani M (2010) Neoliberalizing race, racing neoliberalism: Placing 'race' in neoliberal discourses. *Antipode: A Radical Journal of Geography* 42(2): 248–257.

Roberts P (2015) Passive revolution in Brazil: Struggles over hegemony, religion and development 1964–2007. *Third World Quarterly* 36(9): 1663–1681.

Schäfer A and Streeck W (2013) Introduction: Politics in the age of austerity. In: Schäfer A and Streeck W (eds) *Politics in the Age of Austerity.* Cambridge: Polity, 1–25.

Schmalz S and Ebenau M (2012) After neoliberalism? Brazil, India, and China in the global economic crisis. *Globalizations* 9(4): 487–501.

Smith N (2016) Towards a queer political economy of crisis. In: Hozić AA and True J (eds) *Scandalous Economics: Gender and the Politics of Financial Crises.* Oxford: Oxford University Press, 3–20.

Soederberg S (2006) *Global Governance in Question: Empire, Class, and the New Common Sense in Managing North–South Relations.* London: Pluto.

Soederberg S (2014) *Debtfare States and the Poverty Industry: Money, Discipline and the Surplus Population.* Abingdon: Routledge.

Springer S (2014) Neoliberalism in denial. *Dialogues in Human Geography* 4(2): 154–160.

Springer S (2015) Postneoliberalism? *Review of Radical Political Economics* 47(1): 5–17.

Stanley L (2014) 'We're reaping what we sowed': Everyday crisis narratives and acquiescence to the age of austerity. *New Political Economy* 19(6): 895–917.

Stanley L (forthcoming) Governing austerity in the UK: Anticipatory fiscal consolidation as a variety of austerity governance. *Economy & Society.*

Stedman-Jones D (2012) *Masters of the Universe: Hayek, Friedman and the Birth of Neoliberal Politics.* Princeton, NJ: Princeton University Press.

Stephen MD (2014) Rising powers, global capitalism and liberal global governance: A historical materialist account of the BRICs challenge. *European Journal of International Relations* 20(4): 912–938.

Tansel CB (2015) The politics of contemporary capitalism in Turkey (and the politics of its interlocutors). *Development and Change* 46(3): 570–584.

Tansel CB (forthcoming) Ties that bind: Popular uprisings and the politics of neoliberalism in the Middle East. In: Işıksal H and Göksel O (eds) *Turkey and the Middle East in an Age of Turbulence*. London: I.B. Tauris.

Teivainen T and Trommer S (2016) Representation beyond the state: Towards transnational democratic non-state politics. *Globalizations* (Online). DOI:10.1080/147 47731.2016.1160599

Topak ÖE (2013) Governing Turkey's information society. *Current Sociology* 61(5): 565–583.

True J (2012) *The Political Economy of Violence Against Women*. Oxford: Oxford University Press.

Tyler I (2013) *Revolting Subjects: Social Abjection and Resistance in Neoliberal Britain*. London: Zed.

van Apeldoorn B (2009) The contradictions of 'embedded neoliberalism' and Europe's multi-level legitimacy crisis: The European project and its limits. In: van Apeldoorn B, Drahokoupil J and Horn L (eds) *Contradictions and Limits of Neoliberal European Governance: From Lisbon to Lisbon*. Basingstoke: Palgrave Macmillan, 21–43.

Varoufakis Y (2016) *And the Weak Suffer What They Must? Europe, Austerity and the Threat to Global Stability*. London: Bodley Head.

Vey J (2016) Crisis protests in Germany, Occupy Wall Street, and Mietshäuser Syndikat: Antinomies of current Marxist- and anarchist-inspired movements and their convergence. *Capital & Class* 40(1): 59–74.

von Holdt K (2014) On violent democracy. *The Sociological Review* 62(S2): 129–151.

Weller CE and Singleton L (2006) Peddling reform: The role of think tanks in shaping the neoliberal policy agenda for the World Bank and International Monetary Fund. In: Plehwe D, Walpen B and Neunhöffer G (eds) *Neoliberal Hegemony: A Global Critique*. Abingdon: Routledge, 70–86.

Wigger A and Buch-Hansen H (2013) Competition, the global crisis, and alternatives to neoliberal capitalism: A critical engagement with anarchism. *New Political Science* 35(4): 604–626.

Wigger A and Horn L (2015) Uneven development and political resistance against EU austerity politics. In Pradella L and Marois T (eds) *Polarising Development: Alternatives to Neoliberalism and the Crisis*. London: Pluto, 348–359.

Wurzel UG (2009) The political economy of authoritarianism in Egypt: Insufficient structural reforms, limited outcomes and a lack of new actors. In: Guazzone L and Pioppi D (eds) *The Arab State and Neo-liberal Globalization: The Restructuring of State Power in the Middle East*. Reading: Ithaca Press, 97–123.

Chapter 2

Authoritarian Neoliberalism and the Disciplining of Labour

Mònica Clua-Losada and Olatz Ribera-Almandoz

The rise of authoritarian forms of neoliberalism is now well documented in the political economy literature even though the focus has been on various reforms that remove key decision-making arenas from democratic control.[1] As Ian Bruff (2014) skilfully highlights, this is not a new process but rather the continuation of a key characteristic of neoliberal governance. While recognizing the return of authoritarian forms to European states is crucial for understanding the current crisis management strategies of states and capital, we still need a deeper understanding of the concrete forms in which this authoritarian turn is being developed, deepened, and, more importantly, challenged and contested. In this chapter, we explore the ways in which authoritarian neoliberalism finds expression in and against labour and how labour's agency shapes, contests and subverts such strategies.

It has become clear that the last 40 years of neoliberal rule have brought about an international lowering of wage shares (see Bengtsson and Ryner 2015), leading to a rise in the amount of workers who, even after receiving a salary, cannot be lifted above the poverty line (Pradella 2015). This has been reinforced by a direct attack on corporatist structures and what some have already heralded as the crisis of 'working class politics' (Panitch 1986). These deep processes of change mean that there has been an increasing 'domination of the executive arm of the state over the legislature ... the objective "decline of Parliament" within the state system' (Panitch 1986: 229). This process of blinding the democratic decision-making arenas needs to be considered in relation to specific historical formations. The case used in this chapter, Spain, provides a fascinating example as it never truly developed a democratic welfare state (Navarro 2006). Furthermore, by focusing on the disciplining power of authoritarian neoliberalism on labour, we can understand how authoritarian neoliberalism has a deepening impact on what Poulantzas (1978) termed the *isolation effect*. Here, we understand the isolation effect as the atomization of the social body through 'the constitution of the legal-individual citizen' (Hall 1980: 62). Authoritarian neoliberalism deepens the isolation effect in labour relations by further individualizing labour laws and weakening collective bargaining processes and institutions—a development that has been well documented in other cases of the European South.[2] A key characteristic of this isolation effect on labour has been the clear erosion of collective bargaining systems and labour legislation. As this chapter will show, this is a broad trend that encompasses not just legislative and regulatory changes but also the atomization of employment contractual relations. For instance, in the case of Telefónica, which we use as a paradigmatic example of these trends, there has been a division of tasks among a myriad of small companies as well as a company-level change, where previously employed workers have now been forced to become self-employed.

Labour in this chapter is utilized in a broad historical materialist sense.[3] We understand labour as both a social relation and the driver of class struggle. Within the context of this chapter, the disciplining of labour is considered to be occurring simultaneously in the arenas of production and reproduction. In other words, the disciplinary strategies devised against labour encompass both the curtailment of labour rights and the reduction in social rights. Therefore, we will consider the type of general disciplining of labour (the structural disciplining) as well as the organizational disciplining of labour (expressed in the attacks on the collective organizations of the working class, trade unions).

To fulfil this objective, the chapter develops two key sections. We first discuss the general disciplining of labour under authoritarian neoliberalism with reference to the Spanish context. Here, we trace three vital ways in which this process is being carried out: (1) the constitutionalization of previously democratic arenas, which has been extensively highlighted by the literature (e.g. Sandbeck and Schneider 2014 and Obendorfer 2015); (2) the growing judicialization of politics, with the use of the Constitutional Court as an additional parliamentary upper chamber primarily focused on recentralizing Spanish politics; (3) the elimination of parliamentary debates with the excessive use of royal decrees as a tool for creating new legislation. As we will show, this trend has been particularly acute in relation to both labour legislation and bills related to the imposition of austerity measures on welfare state services.

We then focus on a specific case study, which we maintain should help us disentangle the specific and concrete ways in which these processes are played out and, crucially, contested, resisted and subverted. We have chosen Telefónica (now Movistar) as it has been, historically, one of the largest employers in Spain. Telefónica was the state-owned telecommunications company that has consistently been one of the most profitable public companies in Spain.

It was a company that had been closely linked with the political economy of Spain. It underwent the longest privatization process in Spain—Franco had already started the sale of shares before his death—finally being privatized by the first Aznar government (People's Party, 1996–2000) by royal decree. It has been key to the, often failed, internationalization efforts of the Spanish economy to become a key global telecommunications player (e.g. it owned O2 in the United Kingdom until 2015). Currently, having changed its name to Movistar (the affiliate company dedicated to mobile technologies), it is at the forefront of developing new mobile technologies and hosts the annual Mobile World Congress in Barcelona, the largest event of its kind in the world.

It is in this last part of the chapter that we return to the key issues of contestation, resistance and subversion, which are often left out of discussions on authoritarian neoliberalism. The authoritarian attack is so overwhelming that we can be forgiven when we forget the types of contestation, subversion and resistance that occur from below. Yet, the case of Telefónica/Movistar, which in 2015 had one of its longest (and most economically damaging) workers' strike in their history, shows us that although the disciplining is fierce, the enduring class struggles prevent capital from fully subduing our human dignity.

UNDERSTANDING THE RISE OF AUTHORITARIAN NEOLIBERALISM IN SPAIN

We propose that to understand the rise of authoritarian neoliberalism in Spain, we need to conceptualize it as both an external and an internal process. Unlike other state contexts with stronger liberal-democratic traditions, the Spanish case presents a challenge to understanding the relationship between representative democracy, neoliberalism and authoritarianism that goes beyond the scope of this chapter. However, we can point out that in cases where transitions to democracy have not represented a break with the authoritarian structures of the state, as has been the case in Spain, neoliberalism has developed in a context of arrested democracy. Let us briefly expand on this. While representative democracy in Spain brought about the rolling out of political rights after 1978, it did little to entrench civil rights into Spanish political life and culture.[4] In fact, it was not until the Socialist Workers' Party (PSOE) government of 2004–2008 under the leadership of José Luis Rodríguez Zapatero that any attempt was made to redress this situation. The attempt was short lived and the economic crisis became a convenient excuse to hinder the advance of civil rights in Spain. Furthermore, the election of a People's Party (PP) government at the end of 2011, under strong Catholic influences, halted such efforts with an attempt to return to a not-so-distant past.

The key fields subjected to external pressures for reform—as identified by the IMF in their 2010 staff report, the first to highlight the dangerous extent of the crisis in Spain—were pension funds, the labour market and banking. As we will explore in this chapter, the choice of these policy areas is not a fortuitous coincidence. Rather, it represents the areas where the state has been unable to implement liberalization even after many years of continuous attempts to do so and despite the fact that these attempts were accentuated by the process of European integration (Clua-Losada 2015). In essence, the crisis has acted as the necessary catalyst to create a situation of impending reform. Furthermore, such a reform would have only ever been possible in a situation of weakened trade unions and a weakened institutional Left. The reason behind this is the fact that the 1978 elite pact, which secured the Spanish transition to democracy, had managed to neutralize leftist opposition by institutionalizing key Left parties and trade unions, while simultaneously depoliticizing civil society.

In this chapter, we are focusing on the internal forms of authoritarian neoliberalism and how they relate to labour. As Bruff (2014: 115) has argued, authoritarian neoliberalism can ultimately be observed in the processes that insulate policies and institutions from dissent. In the Spanish context, such tendencies can best be observed not just by focusing on authoritarian neoliberalism as an externally imposed practice but rather as a process often driven by internal developments and struggles. As is widely acknowledged, there is clear asymmetry in EU regulation in relation to how labour and welfare matters have been largely left to the mercy of member states and their internal political processes (Taylor-Gooby 2008). As many before us have pointed out (e.g. Grahl and Teague 2013), monetary union left member states with only one tool of macroeconomic management, that is, internal devaluation, the process whereby macroeconomic competitiveness is achieved by reducing wages (whether directly or indirectly) and a reduction of public expenditure.[5] By removing other monetary policy choices from member states, popular demands have been effectively isolated from previously democratic arenas of decision-making. If governments can no longer offer certain policy alternatives, the state is essentially divorced from popular demands. While this is not a new process, the current crisis has expanded the reach of issues that can be removed from the political arena.

There are three key internal forms of authoritarian neoliberalism in Spain which have become accentuated since 2010. First is the introduction of Article 135 into the 1978 Spanish Constitution by the PSOE, with the approval of the conservative PP. Article 135 transposes the deployment of structural deficit caps from the 2011 Fiscal Pact.[6] Essentially, this means that future public expenditure will be constitutionally curtailed, and therefore, future expansions of the welfare state will not be possible within the existing constitutional framework.

Second, there has been a growing judicialization of politics in the Spanish state, particularly since 2010. This has been particularly marked by the use of the Constitutional Court as a de facto upper chamber. This process was particularly evident during the PP government of Mariano Rajoy (2011–2015). It has become clear that the Constitutional Court has been used against the Autonomous Communities that have tried to go against the central government's political choices. In the Spanish context, Autonomous Communities have had the majority of welfare state services devolved to them (health, social care, education, etc.).[7] However, as they have limited tax-raising powers, most of their income comes from the state. This means that in a context of severe austerity, their ability to provide essential services is beyond their political will. The use of the Constitutional Court against decisions made in the Autonomous Parliaments shows a clear element of recentralization in Spanish politics.

Third, while the use of royal decrees as a way of passing controversial or urgent legislation in the Spanish Congress is neither new nor a tool used only by the PP,[8] it has been used consistently more often than before since 2011. The Rajoy government (2011–2015) approved 33.8 per cent of its legislation by royal decrees, thereby removing any possibility of parliamentary deliberation. Considering that the PP had an absolute majority in Congress, there was no actual need to overuse royal decrees unless the aim was to remove democratic deliberation from the public sphere.

The remainder of this section will focus on two key royal decrees which have drastically changed the shape of labour relations in Spain. First is the 2010 Royal Decree Law on Urgent Measures for Reforming the Labour Market. This royal decree law, promoted by the previous Socialist government, focuses on individualized labour relations by decentralizing collective bargaining. This was a big blow to the unions, as they had won in the 1980s the ability to set up collective bargaining at the sectoral level. Considering the productive structure of Spain, the obtainment of this right was crucial. In the Spanish case, the majority of workers are employed by small or medium-sized enterprises (SMEs), hence the ability to cover non-unionized workers under broad sector-level agreements increased the structural power of trade unions. By decentralizing collective bargaining to the company level, what was being done, in reality, was the destruction of the collective bargaining protections and institutions built up over the previous 30 years. Let us review the issues raised by the royal decree law step by step. The labour reform approved by the royal decree law in June 2010 stipulated (1) the reduction of severance pay to 33 days per year of tenure for unfair dismissal (previously 45 days was the norm) for almost all new permanent contracts; (2) financing eight days of all severance payments via a fund paid for by firms; (3) easing the criteria for 'fair' dismissal (which would entail 20 days' severance payment); and (4) broadening the conditions under which firms can opt out of collective wage agreements (IMF 2010). Other reforms included revising the conditions of temporary contracts, increasing internal flexibility of firms (e.g. working hours) and opening labour intermediation more broadly to private firms.

As already mentioned, this labour reform was a direct attack on the perceived power of trade unions in Spain. It reinforced the idea that employers are hampered by a legislation that disproportionately protects workers. The uneven relationship between the employers and workers, according to the IMF staff report, was due to the high union density among permanent workers in Spain, which was linked to the view that temporary employment is high in Spain due to the high costs of dismissal. However, it appears that although high dismissal costs have been created as an imperative for reform, they may not be the key to solving the unemployment crisis. It is compelling the way in which the IMF links dismissal costs with temporary employment, particularly as both Ireland and Sweden have much lower rates of temporary workers, yet they have higher severance payments for unfair dismissals.

Spain has a large and structural unemployment problem, which poses important challenges to trade unions (Campos Lima and Martín Artiles 2011). Throughout the crisis, Spain's unemployment rate has been more than double the EU27 rate and remained consistently above 20 per cent. The problem has worried international financial institutions for some time now, which brought about the advancement of labour market flexibilization as a solution. The Spanish labour market is characterized by what has often been termed a dual system of employment. An increasingly smaller proportion of permanent workers—who enjoy security of employment and wage increases linked to inflation—coexists with a growing majority of workers in temporary contracts.

Since the late 1980s, successive governments have attempted to deal with the perceived *rigidities* of the Spanish labour market. The first reforms led to the creation of temporary forms of employment, which have served governments well in periods of economic growth. However, in periods of crisis, unemployment spirals upwards more easily than in other countries as most temporary contracts are not renewed in such periods. Lowering permanent workers' dismissal costs is expected to reduce incentives to use temporary contracts. High levels of temporary, short-term contracts are seen as a key weakness of the Spanish labour market, together with having wage increases linked to inflation and low productivity.

Orthodox arguments about the Spanish economy reveal a basic contradiction. While the two key problems of unemployment and low labour productivity are widely acknowledged (with varying degrees of evidence being presented), the solution offered by most politicians, international organizations and mainstream economists is to move from a labour-intensive economy to a capital-intensive one, which would clearly provoke a rise in unemployment. This is particularly so in the case of Spain, as the industries which have typically absorbed such surplus labour in Northern and Western European countries are those related to the welfare state, in other words, the caring professions. In Spain, such work is still carried out largely in the domestic sphere, therefore lacking the required level of marketization necessary to absorb the redundant labour force.

The next problem identified by the IMF was that wages are linked to inflation rather than to productivity. The reform also touched upon this issue, allowing employers to opt out of collective agreements. This is considered a significant issue by many scholars too, and low productivity is attributed to labour (Royo 2009: 448). Interestingly, little evidence is produced for such arguments. In fact, there appears to be other public policy problems that contribute to low productivity, for example, problems in the education system as well as issues of low capital investment. The real issue, however, is the avoidance of real reform. The Spanish welfare state has been built around the heavy subsidization of employment creation. Subsidies take a large share of the public money destined for reductions in unemployment. A significant amount of these funds are used to subsidize employers (over 30 per cent), and yet unemployment remains a key problem.

The second labour reform we want to consider is a more recent one, also approved by a royal decree, this time by the PP government in 2012. This labour reform should be seen as the continuation of the one in 2010; however, in 2012, an the attack was far more direct on the workers as it stipulated the reduction of wages and projected an increased threat of unemployment. There were three key changes introduced by the reform which (1) allowed companies to reduce workers' salaries according to their profits, (2) increased the cases under which companies can utilize EREs,[9] and (3) emphasized an increase in the type of apprenticeship contracts that can be created, leading to a rise in mini-jobs and zero-hours contracts.

Having considered the ways in which the disciplining of labour has taken place in the Spanish context, we will now move to see how these processes are reproduced at the firm level. We are doing so to highlight that these processes not only produce disciplining effects that target labour, but are also contested and resisted by the workers themselves. Ultimately, in tracing the interactions at the firm level, we find capital's inability to fully discipline and control labour.

TELEFÓNICA/MOVISTAR: A TALE OF
PRIVATIZATION AND PREFIGURATIVE RESISTANCE

The process of privatizations in Spain consisted of a gradual divestment of public assets rather than a rapid mass sale of public companies. The first important phase of privatizations was launched by the Socialist Party government of Felipe González (1982–1996). Using the term 'public divestment process', the government closed small and medium-sized 'unprofitable' public companies, sold large industrial enterprises to transnational companies and sold block shares of large public companies, industries and financial institutions (Costas and Bel 2000: 233). This initial wave of partial privatizations was intensified under the Conservative government of José María Aznar (1996–2004). Through the Modernization Programme for the Public Business Sector (Programa de Modernización del Sector Público Empresarial), the cabinet completely privatized 43 public companies in key sectors of the Spanish economy, such as electricity, gas, oil, transport and telecommunications. This disposal of public property, which mainly affected large and profitable companies, entailed a drastic reduction in the importance of public sector enterprises in the economy and responded, at least in part, to the need to meet the convergence criteria established by the Maastricht Treaty signed in 1992 (Ortega and Sánchez 2002: 35).

In this context, the case of Telefónica is one of the most significant examples of the gradual privatization and labour disciplining processes in Spain, and it shows the crucial role that the state has played in restructuring capital–labour relations in the country over the last few decades. The company was created in 1924 under the name CTNE (Compañía Telefónica Nacional de España [Spanish National Telephone Company]), and it enjoyed a legal monopoly over telephone services in Spain until 1998 (Calvo 2010). In 1945, during Franco's dictatorship, the Spanish government acquired 79.6 per cent of CTNE shares (Telefónica 2016), an ownership percentage that was diluted over the following decades through subsequent share capital increases. Furthermore, like many other public companies, Telefónica experienced a partial privatization in 1995 under the Socialist government, although it was not entirely privatized until 1999, when the PP government sold the remaining 20.9 per cent of shares that the state still owned (Sociedad Estatal de Participaciones Industriales 2014; Telefónica 2016). Concomitantly, and using its linguistic advantage, Telefónica began a process of international expansion into the Latin American markets (Rodríguez-Ruiz 2014).

Despite its privatization, the state maintained close ties with the company. In 1996, Juan Villalonga was appointed CEO of Telefónica, a position he held until 2000. Villalonga was proposed by the main shareholders of the company (the banks Argentaria, Banco Bilbao and La Caixa), and with the endorsement of the Prime Minister of Spain José María Aznar, who was his schoolmate and childhood friend (Aznar 2012). This is not the only example of the political ties enjoyed by the firm, as several prominent political figures have been hired by the company or have been elected to its board of directors. These connections include Narcís Serra (member of PSOE, mayor of Barcelona 1979–1982, Minister of Defence 1982–1991 and vice president of the Spanish government 1991–1995), Javier de Paz (member of PSOE, general secretary of the Socialist Youth of Spain and member of the Executive Council of PSOE, 1984–1993), Trinidad Jiménez (member of PSOE, Minister of Health and Social Affairs 2009–2010, Minister of Foreign Affairs 2010–2011), Paloma Villa (Trinidad Jiménez's political consultant and spouse of the Socialist politician Eduardo Madina), Rodrigo Rato (member of PP, Minister of Economy 1996–2004, vice president of the Spanish government 2003–2004 and the 9th managing director of the IMF 2004–2007), Elvira Fernández Balboa (spouse of the current Prime Minister of Spain, Mariano Rajoy), Andrea Fabra (member of the PP), José Ivan Rosa (spouse of the current vice president, Soraya Sáenz de Santamaría), Eduardo Zaplana (member of the PP, president of the government of Valencia 1995–2002 and Minister of Employment and Social Affairs 2002–2004) and Yolanda Barcina (member of the Navarrese People's Union—a party with strong links to and recurrent coalitions with the PP—president of the government of Navarre 2011–2015). Furthermore, José Fernando Almansa (head of the Royal Household of Spain between 1993 and 2002) and Iñaki Urdangarín (member of the Royal Family and the brother-in-law of the current king of Spain) have held important positions in different international branches of the company. Similar cases of 'revolving doors' can be found in other privatized companies such as Endesa—for which the ex-Prime Minister José María Aznar worked as an external consultant—Repsol, Tabacalera, Argentaria or Gas Natural, the last of which included ex-Prime Minister Felipe González in its board of directors.

Before its complete privatization, Telefónica was one of the most consistently profitable public companies in Spain, with a net income of €551 million in 1994 and €1,804 million in 1999. In 1994, Telefónica employed a workforce of around 72,207 people, which made it one of the largest employers in the country (Telefónica 1994, 1999). As a result of privatization, however, the company initiated a process of workforce reduction through the launch of several consecutive dismissal programmes (EREs) and the outsourcing of key services such as sales, customer services and maintenance, which were formerly provided internally. Following the rationale of cutting labour costs, the workforce of Telefónica España was reduced within 20 years by nearly 60 per cent to 30,020 employees in 2014 (Telefónica 2014). At the same time, this contraction of the workforce had to be compensated with the use of the services of outsourced workers, including hundreds of contractors, subcontractors and self-employed workers. The restructuring of Spanish tele-communications was by no means an isolated case but was part of a broader international pattern of privatizations, corporate downsizing and deregulation of former state-owned companies carried out in the 1980s, 1990s and early 2000s. In countries such as the United States, the United Kingdom, Ireland and Germany, telecommunication companies adopted a business model based on the separation between, on the one hand, the management and running of the network infrastructure, and on the other, the provision of services (MacKenzie 2010). In all these cases and particularly in the case of Telefónica, by extending the use of subcontracted labour, an important share of the workforce was left outside existing collective bargaining agreements. Consequently, precariousness and the lack of secure employment in the sector increased while the bargaining power of traditionally highly coordinated trade unions was undermined and diluted (Rodríguez-Ruiz 2014).

Nevertheless, the workforce of Telefónica was not only the largest in the country, but also one of the most militant. It has been argued that the dismissal programmes in the 1990s and 2000s were carried out with the acceptance of both employers and workers since they offered 'favourable exit conditions', including early retirements and relocations (Rodríguez-Ruiz 2014). However, since Telefónica employees were replaced by subcontracted workers en masse, disputes were not reduced as expected, but transferred to the outsourced companies. One of the best-known cases was the Campamento de la Esperanza (the Camp of Hope), a campsite built between January and August 2001 by around 1,500 workers of the Telefónica network installer subcontractor Sintel. The firm had been part of Telefónica until 1996, when it was sold to the US company MasTec, owned by Cuban exile and anti-Castro leader Jorge Mas Canosa. In 2000, Sintel, which employed around 1,800 people, declared bankruptcy. After six months without receiving their salary and facing the threat of a redundancy programme—the first large-scale ERE executed in Spain—Sintel workers set out their tents in Paseo de la Castellana, one of the major avenues in Madrid. The location had an enormous symbolic resonance since there is a high concentration of important public and private buildings, such as the main ministries and embassies, financial institutions and the Real Madrid football stadium. Gradually, tents were replaced by handmade cabins, electricity and water were tapped and amenities—such as bathrooms, kitchens, a library, a museum, a meeting hall and portable swimming pools—were built (Tremlett 2001). In a display of creative organizing, workers used the occupation of public space not only as a form of protest against Sintel's owners, Telefónica or the Conservative government led at the time by José María Aznar, but also as a way of showing their technical skills to the passersby (Martínez Lucio 2011). The occupation demonstrated that the challenge produced by the lack of a fixed working location and therefore the impossibility of occupying a specific workplace and the related difficulties of coordination among workers could be overcome through a highly strategic and innovative struggle that gained great public and media recognition. Their organizational strength and the prefigurative aspects of the protest were, at that time, relatively rare within Spanish labour struggles.

After 187 days, an agreement was reached between Sintel's works council and the Spanish government, which led to the dismantling of the Camp of Hope. The deal included the reimbursement of unpaid salaries, early retirements and relocation of the majority of workers to other telecommunication companies. Years later, Sintel's former workers complained that the main points of the agreement were not only unfulfilled, but were also used as an excuse for creating new outsourced companies providing services to Telefónica. In the words of the union delegates and workers participating in the protest, 'the cause of this defeat was not the lack of will of [Sintel and Telefónica] workers, but the acceptance by trade union leaders of massive redundancies and the following outsourcing and labour precariousness that continues to this day' (quoted in Ubico 2016).

Consequently, after years promoting the atomization and territorial dispersion of the labour force, Telefónica currently hires the services of 10 different contractors—namely, Abentel, Cobra, Comfica, Cotronic, Dominion, Elecnor, Itete, Liteyca, Montelnor and Teleco—which, at the same time, receive services from more than 600 suppliers, including both subcontractors and self-employed workers. Furthermore, according to the Spanish Workers' Statute Law, companies with fewer than 50 workers are not entitled to have a works committee or to have workers' delegates if they have fewer than 10 workers, which limits workers' organizations in most of these smaller subcontractors and suppliers (Ley del Estatuto de los Trabajadores 1995, Articles 62 and 63). The law is effectively used as a means of hindering the workers' capacity of mobilization and coordination, as well as impeding the establishment of solidarity links between them. Although all these companies work directly or indirectly for Telefónica, the idea of being in competition against each other is used as a justification for reducing employees' salaries and imposing more precarious working conditions, which frequently leads to significant reductions in health and safety standards. As a member of Cotronic's workers' committee puts it, 'In qualitative terms, the precarity and contraction of [Telefónica's] labour force forces us to work from sunrise to sunset, to break the laws on labour risk prevention, and to lose fundamental rights, such as receiving overtime pay, having trade union representation in the workplace, or being covered by the collective agreement for the metal sector' (quoted in Ubico 2016).

In 2011, Telefónica was the fifth largest operator by total customers in the world (Rodríguez-Ruiz 2015). However, despite registering a record net income of more than €10,000 million in the previous accounting period (Telefónica 2011), the company used the economic crisis as an excuse to announce a new redundancy plan that would cause the dismissal of some 20 per cent of the workforce—around 8,500 employees, a number that was later reduced to 6,500—between 2011 and 2013. Concomitantly, the company has one of the biggest pay gaps between executives and median workers in Spain. In 2014, the then CEO of the firm, César Alierta, received €550,000 per month—that is, an annual payment of €6.6 million—whereas the average salary of a permanent employee was around €2,000–2,200 per month (Comisión Nacional del Mercado de Valores 2014). The difference is even more dramatic for the contract workers (e.g. Cotronic workers receive a maximum salary of €1,480 per month), subcontracted workers (with salaries of around €800 per month) and self-employed (€700–800 per month). The situation of the latter is even more precarious given that they have to deduct the vehicle and equipment expenses, taxes and social security contributions from their earnings. A self-employed technician explains the double exploitation they face as follows:

> Some years ago, being self-employed was a minority option, and only people who wanted to have more flexible schedules would choose it. However, the majority of the current self-employed are former employees of [Telefónica's] contractors. Back then, we had a company car, holidays. ... But they decided that this wasn't profitable enough, so we needed to be fired. They promised important compensations for our dismissals, and that we would keep working for them as self-employed with €2,500 per month salaries—until then, we earned €1,000 per month. We realized too late that, after discounting all the expenses and taxes we had to face, the €2,500 turned into €500. As self-employed, we had lost all labour rights. And if we wanted to negotiate with Telefónica, they told us 'you are an enterprise now!'[10]

In 2015, however, the increasing sense of frustration reached a turning point and Spain witnessed a wave of mobilizations comprising Telefónica's contractors, subcontractors and self-employed workers. Rallying around slogans such as 'They took so much from us that even fear was taken away' [*'Nos quitaron tanto, tanto, que nos quitaron el miedo'*], workers from Barcelona, Madrid, Bilbao, Seville and other Spanish cities began an indefinite strike to express their demands. The aim of the action was to denounce the deterioration of the existing working conditions, the workers' heightened sense of insecurity and their growing material needs, which were seen not only as a direct result of the socioeconomic crisis, but also as the outcome of the firm's privatization and restructuring which started in the 1990s. This was the first strike organized by self-employed workers in Spanish history. It was able to mobilize a large number of workers precisely because they had been employed by multiple contractors and subcontractors before the beginning of the crisis, and they had thus built strong networks that ultimately were used to coordinate the actions. The campaign was known as 'The Ladders Revolution' ['*Revolución de las escaleras*'] in reference to the ladders used by the telecommunications technicians to install and fix telephone and Internet wires (Sanz Sabido and Price 2016). This strike action was organized and coordinated outside of the established trade unions, which were perceived as incapable of representing the workers' interests. As a workers' delegate stated:

> If we ever reach any favourable agreement, it will be because of the grassroots mobilization [and] the trade union bureaucracies will be forced to accept them because of the workers' pressure. ... In Barcelona, our comrades organized protests and demonstrations in front of the trade unions' offices with the slogans 'We fight, we negotiate' and 'They don't represent us'. We are on strike in spite of the unions' manoeuvres to stop our mobilizations and to water down our demands. (quoted in Ubico 2016)

Nevertheless, conventional strike action and demonstrations were soon perceived as insufficient. Growing frustration with established channels, such as trade unions, that were traditionally used to express workers' demands led workers to combine the strike with other forms of disruptive actions and prefigurative practices. An assembly of subcontracted technicians coordinated by the grassroots trade unions CoBas (Sindicato de Comisiones de Base), AST (Alternativa Sindical de Trabajadores) and CGT (Confederación General del Trabajo) decided on direct action and occupied the Telefónica building that houses the headquarters of the Mobile World Centre, a key landmark in the heart of Barcelona. The occupation was used to attract the attention of the media, as well as to launch a campaign focused on damaging the reputation of the company's executives. Hence, the workers reproduced some of the practices and strategies developed during the Camp of Hope, together with taking advantage of the break that the 15-M cycle represented. As one participating worker explained:

> We had been accumulating a certain experience on the picket lines and in direct actions, and that's what people decided to do: we decided to enter the office in order to make visible our conflict and our social movement, and also to establish a continued alliance with other social movements, which was also opened up to all those parties that wanted to participate.[11]

The 15-M cycle of struggle had direct implications for how resistance was being perceived and organized by Spanish workers. The 15-M was a moment of rupture not just with the way the crisis was being managed in Spain, but also—and perhaps more importantly—with the established channels of political and social representation. Both trade unions and left-wing parties were the focus of vociferous criticism for having failed to provide an adequate response to the crisis. Furthermore, they were identified as also being part of the problem. The perceived lack of union opposition to the aforementioned 2010 Labour Reform (approved by the Socialist government)—despite a general strike—was seen as further evidence of the inability of the established organizations to provide a channel for resistance. The outcome has been an increased level of contention outside and within existing organizations. It could be argued that this was a positive outcome in workplaces where unionization was made difficult by structural conditions (such as the Telefónica subcontracting system), as the accumulated experience since the 15-M in community organizations and square occupations had been a great school of prefigurative action for many people, including some of the Movistar strike organizers.

Furthermore, a week before local elections were held in Spain, some candidates for mayor of Barcelona—Ada Colau from Barcelona en Comú, Alfred Bosch from *Esquerra Republicana de Catalunya* (ERC) and Maria José Lecha from *Candidatura d'Unitat Popular* (CUP), among other political leaders— entered into an agreement with the workers in which they committed not to contract services from companies that did not guarantee a maximum of 40 working hours per week, two weekly rest days and fair salaries. Thanks to this coordination with other social movements and political actors, direct negotiation was forced between the company's executives and the workers for the first time without the mediation of the established trade unions.

The case presented here shows the nexus between state disciplining, processes of privatization and the different moments of prefiguration that workers' struggles can establish. As such, it closely follows developments in Spain's authoritarian state project as well as the way in which each cycle of struggle materializes. The latest developments demonstrate that the current focus on occupying political institutions by many of the new 15-M-inspired political parties may also bring synergies with existing workers' struggles.

CONCLUSION

This chapter has focused on the effects of rising authoritarian neoliberalism on the disciplining of labour. It has done so by utilizing the Spanish case to uncover the legal and executive dynamics behind authoritarian neoliberalism and by considering the specific ways in which labour has been under direct attack in the management of the crisis. While the Spanish case has already been highlighted in the literature as a key example of authoritarian neoliberal strategies, we have not only identified 'the authoritarian turn' in Spain but also focused on how it is negated, resisted and subverted by labour. The chapter has investigated labour's relationship with authoritarian neoliberalism by tracing the process of privatization of Telefónica and the struggles this process has given birth to. Telefónica has been a useful example to explore authoritarian neoliberalism as it has provided us with a concrete nexus between authoritarianism, democracy and neoliberalism within the Spanish context. More importantly, and in line with our key argument, the case study reveals that authoritarian neoliberalism cannot be understood simply as a mode of domination but rather as the inability of the state to subdue and discipline labour. The Telefónica case demonstrates that even in the most difficult circumstances, workers find ways to resist and subvert the disciplining effects of authoritarian neoliberalism. It is in this sense that we hope that this chapter contributes to a critical political economy of emancipation rather than one focused on domination (Huke et al. 2015).

NOTES

1. See, for example, Bruff (2014) on authoritarian neoliberalism; Sandbeck and Schneider (2014) and Obendorfer (2015) for analyses of authoritarian constitutionalism.
2. See Campos Lima and Martín Artiles (2011); Koukiadaki and Kretsos (2012).
3. For more details on our conceptualization, see Clua-Losada and Horn (2014).
4. For more on the relationship between political and civil rights, see T. H. Marshall's (1997) classic work *Citizenship and Social Class*.
5. See also the chapters by Bruff and Sotiris in this book.
6. See Radice (2014) on the implications of structural deficit.
7. Autonomous Communities are the political and administrative divisions that comprise the Spanish state and have devolved powers. There are 17 Autonomous Communities, each with its own executive and legislative branch (Autonomous Parliament). They have asymmetrically devolved powers; in other words, not all Autonomous Communities have the same level of decentralized power. However, they all have responsibility over education, health and social services.
8. For example, the last PSOE government under Zapatero's premiership approved 56 royal decrees, which accounted for 29 per cent of approved legislation.
9. ERE (*Expedientes de Regulación de Empleo*) is a legal procedure utilized for redundancies, traditionally used when companies go bust. Under this reform, EREs can be used even in cases where the company requires only a temporary adjustment.
10. Interview with Ariel Paso, self-employed technician quoted in *La Directa*. Available at: https://directa.cat/sites/default/files/revolta_escales_suplement.pdf

11. Authors' interview with a worker, CoBas member and activist (3 November 2015).

BIBLIOGRAPHY

Aznar JM (2012) *Memorias I.* Barcelona: Planeta.
Bengtsson E and Ryner M (2015) The (international) political economy of falling wage shares: Situating working class agency. *New Political Economy* 20(3): 406–430.
Bruff I (2014) The rise of authoritarian neoliberalism. *Rethinking Marxism: A Journal of Economics, Culture & Society* 26(1): 113–129.
Calvo Á (2010) *Historia de Telefónica: 1924–1975. Primeras décadas: tecnología, economía y política.* Madrid: Ariel and Fundación Telefónica.
Campos Lima MP and Martín Artiles A (2011) Crisis and trade union challenges in Portugal and Spain: Between general strikes and social pacts. *Transfer* 17(3): 387–402.
Clua-Losada M and Horn L (2014) Analysing labour and the crisis: Challenges, responses and new avenues. *Global Labour Journal* 5(2): 102–113.
Clua-Losada M (2015) Tracing the competitiveness discourse in Spain: Social dumping in disguise? In: Bernaciak M (ed) *Social Dumping: Political Catchphrase or Threat to Labour Standards?* Abingdon: Routledge, 210–225.
Comisión Nacional del Mercado de Valores (2014) Estadísticas de Remuneraciones de los Consejeros de las sociedades cotizadas, Anexos estadísticos por sociedad. Madrid: Comisión Nacional del Mercado de Valores.
Costas A and Bel G (1999) Privatización y posprivatización de servicios públicos: Riesgos regulatorios e impuestos ocultos. El caso de España. *CEPAL: Serie Seminarios y conferencias* 3: 231–252.
Grahl J and Teague P (2013) Reconstructing the Eurozone: The role of EU social policy. *Cambridge Journal of Economics* 37(3): 677–692.
Hall S (1980) Nicos Poulantzas: State, Power, Socialism. *New Left Review* 119: 60–69.
Huke N, Clua-Losada M and Bailey DJ (2015) Disrupting the European crisis: A critical political economy of contestation, subversion and escape. *New Political Economy* 20(5): 725–751.
IMF (2010) Spain: Staff Report for the 2010 Article IV Consultation. IMF Country Report 10/254 (July). Available at: https://www.imf.org/external/pubs/ft/scr/2010/cr10254.pdf
Koukiadaki A and Kretsos L (2012) Opening Pandora's Box: The sovereign debt crisis and labour market regulation in Greece. *Industrial Law Journal* 41(3): 276–304.
Ley del Estatuto de los Trabajadores 1995 (Real Decreto Legislativo 1/1995) (24 March). *Boletín Oficial del Estado* 75: 9654.
MacKenzie R (2010) Why do contingent workers join a trade union? Evidence from the Irish Telecommunications sector. *European Journal of Industrial Relations* 16(2): 153–168.

Marshall TH (1997) *Citizenship and Social Class*. London: Pluto.

Martínez Lucio M (2011) From action to communication? *Employee Relations* 33(6): 654–669.

Navarro V (2006) *Bienestar Insuficiente, Democracia Incompleta*. Madrid: Anagrama.

Oberndorfer L (2015) From new constitutionalism to authoritarian constitutionalism: New economic governance and the state of European democracy. In: Jäger J and Springler E (eds) *Asymmetric Governance and Possible Futures: Critical Political Economy and Post-Keynesian Perspectives*. Abingdon: Routledge, 186–207.

Ortega MÁ and Sánchez MÁ (2002) La política de privatizaciones en España. *Momento Económico* 122: 32–40.

Panitch L (1986) *Working Class Politics in Crisis: Essays on Labour and the State*. London: Verso.

Poulantzas N (1978/2014) *State, Power, Socialism*. London: Verso.

Pradella L (2015) The working poor in Western Europe: Labour, poverty and global capitalism. *Comparative European Politics* 13(5): 596–613.

Radice H (2014) Enforcing austerity in Europe: The structural deficit as a policy target. *Journal of Contemporary European Studies* 22(3): 318–328.

Rodríguez-Ruiz Ó (2015) Unions' response to corporate restructuring in Telefónica: Locked into collective bargaining? *Employee Relations* 37(1): 83–101.

Royo S (2009) Reforms betrayed? Zapatero and continuities in economic policy. *South European Society and Politics* 14(4): 435–451.

Sandbeck S and Schneider E (2014) From the sovereign debt crisis to authoritarian statism: Contradictions of the European state project. *New Political Economy* 19(6): 847–871.

Sanz Sabido R and Price S (2016) The ladders revolution: Material struggle, social media and news coverage. *Critical Discourse Studies* 13(3): 247–260.

Sociedad Estatal de Participaciones Industriales (2014) Privatisations: Period from 1996 until the present. Available at: http://www.sepi.es/default.aspx?cmd=0001&IdContainer=50&idLanguage=_EN

Taylor-Gooby P (2008) The new welfare state settlement in Europe. *European Societies* 10(1): 3–24.

Telefónica (1994) *Annual Report*. Madrid: Telefónica.

Telefónica (1999) *Annual Report*. Madrid: Telefónica.

Telefónica (2011) *Annual Report*. Madrid: Telefónica.

Telefónica (2014) *Annual Report*. Madrid: Telefónica.

Telefónica (2016) History, 1924–2014. Available at: https://www.telefonica.com/en/web/about_telefonica/history

Tremlett G (2001) Shanty town pricks Spain's conscience. *The Guardian* (28 July). Available at: https://www.theguardian.com/world/2001/jul/28/gilestremlett

Ubico A (2016) 'La revolución en los sindicatos es llegar a esa masa de trabajadores sin representación'. *La Izquierda Diario* (9 April). Available at: http://www.laizquierdadiario.com/spip.php?page=movil-nota&id_article=36239

Chapter 3

Commodified Pacification
Police, Commercial Security and the State
Kendra Briken and Volker Eick

This chapter discusses the dialectical deepening of market relations within and around the most important pacifying organization of the state apparatus, the police, and its corporate counterpart, the commercial security industry. We start by introducing our theoretical approach to commodified pacification. It is widely agreed that policing today is a crucial part of authoritarian neoliberalism. However, in reframing the role of policing in line with the concept of pacification, we will reconnect critical security studies to the analysis of ongoing class struggles. We will do so by focusing on three different agents: corporate security, state police and non-profits (third-sector organizations). In line with Detlef Nogala (1995: 250), who points to the fact that 'commercial security companies ... owe their existence to a firmly profit mongering', we argue that security companies by definition are not 'private' but 'commercial', that is, concerned about profits and market shares. 'Private', to the contrary, refers to those initiatives that are not primarily interested in generating profits, such as militias, non-profits and crime-prevention schemes in all their shades (Eick 2013). In short, if there is talk about 'privatization' with regard to security, it is essentially about commercialization and commodification of 'security promises'.

In the following sections, we discuss the integration of corporate security (logics) into the various police organizations (part two); the commodification of policing through the deployment of commercial security companies (part three) and the extension of for-profit security providers into fields beyond the 'simple' provision of loss-prevention, guarding and patrolling—ranging from the local to the global scale (part four). We will focus on the consequences of commodification with regard to the (further) division, disciplining and sanctioning of the working classes and analyze how the 'poor policing the poor' (Eick 2003) turns into an integral part of commodified pacification. In the final part, we hold that the neoliberal pressure to use market-oriented competition within the realm of policing leads to intensified pacification, predominantly of the 'precarious classes'. While pacification is not limited to the nation state, as we will show in the remainder of this chapter, state/public entities and the corporate sector converge along competitive governance structures, thus creating a pacifying 'ring of steel' around the state monopoly of force.

COMMODIFIED PACIFICATION: THE LIVING THREAT

In the past few years, and increasingly after the crisis of 2007–2008, neoliberalism clearly underlined its potential to mobilize the ruling classes. In an unprecedented move, world leaders agreed to use public money to save the banking and, in large part, automotive sectors. For many, the aftermath of the crisis finally dismantled neoliberalism as dead (but dominant), with capitalism labelled as a zombie system (Smith 2008; Fisher 2009; Harman 2009; Peck 2010; Crouch 2011). We argue that what we are facing today is not yet another episode of the *Walking Dead*. Neoliberalism is alive and kicking and more effective than ever at reproducing itself. As tantalizing as the metaphor is, and as much as cultural studies read the current market-success of zombie-related movies and TV series as a reflection of this 'death', claiming the neoliberal brain to be dead would be a fatal misreading. It would amount to masking out the 'constant revolutionizing of production and uninterrupted disturbance of all social conditions'—as Marx and Engels (1969: 14) remind us in the *Communist Manifesto*, 'The history of all hitherto existing society is the history of class struggles.' Surprisingly, in most accounts on the rise of neoliberalism, violence and repression are widely neglected topics.

While neoliberalism is promoted by political think tanks like the Mont Pèlerin Society and many others (Mirowski and Plehwe 2009; Mirowski 2013), focusing only on the discursive and ideological levels of analysis obscures the less 'noble' spheres of capitalist modes of (re)production including state violence. Neoliberalism is not about a *laissez-faire* understanding of the state. On the contrary, the state reassures a coordinated set of governmental practices to overcome market exchange with market-led competition. The state might not be doing the actual legwork, but is running the show in implementing new forms of more direct evaluative governance. Just as lean management in the corporate world made continuous improvements in a critical part of (individual) performance management, neoliberalism calls for 'permanent vigilance, activity and intervention' as the only accepted forms of governance (Oksala 2011: 478). Thus, entrepreneurial state activities increasingly include evaluative loops that force institutions to prescribe and predict future outcomes. Neoliberalization includes the constant reconstruction of the legal, institutional and cultural potential to enable further competition. It is here where state violence and policing come into play. 'Securing' market conditions and class relations cannot be realized without policing. For this objective, extensive and efficient state violence is indispensable. The important point here is to understand policing as a *sine qua non* to 're-establish the conditions for capital accumulation and to restore the power of economic elites' (Harvey 2005: 19). The state sets the rules and, if necessary, utilizes coercive measures. And the state cannot allow people to opt out.

> For the economic rationality of market-mechanisms to extend maximally throughout society the possibilities for engaging in practices with alternative, non-economic rationalities must be restricted, by violent means if necessary. The occupation of empty buildings, streets and other urban spaces for activities with no economic aim has been one of the tactics of political activism against neoliberal hegemony. The violent suppression of such activism in Western democratic states must be seen not only as an attempt to protect private property—effective policing of the economic game—but also as an attempt to close off possibilities for opting out of it (Oksala 2011: 479).

'Securing' the markets becomes one of the main tasks for state activity, and the appraisal of security must be understood in this perspective. The 'securitization' of political discourses as analyzed by the Copenhagen School is one option to describe the move to silence or to deal with opposition. However, we are not convinced by the main premises of the securitization approach as such an interpretation tends to hide agency and (class) interests. Like with the concept of 'global security assemblages' (Williams 2016) or the idea of 'liquid security' (Zedner 2006), in the 'securitization' literature, the connection to the capitalist mode of production and 'actually existing neoliberalism' (Brenner and Theodore 2002) becomes blurred and power turns into a mere discursive matter. In line with Neocleous and others, we understand security 'not as some kind of universal or transcendental value but rather as a mode of governing or a political technology of liberal order building' (Neocleous 2011: 26). We align our analyses to the concept of pacification (Eick and Briken 2014). Although the term 'pacification' was coined for state practices abroad (e.g. British colonialism, Vietnam War), it is useful to understand states of discipline as internal affairs (McGovern 2015). The notion of pacification allows us, first, to analyze the triad of de/construction and reconstruction of 'security'. The use of politics and the use of force are not to be considered separately, and at the same time political ideology becomes social reality through military and/or police force. As Toscano (2007: 611) pointed out in his rereading of Gabriel Tarde's work, 'Pacification is not a mere social tendency, but a political project, borne by the multiple agencies of the state, driven by specific interests (e.g. the inventing classes) and aimed at neutralizing a form of oppositional politics.' The term 'pacification' highlights that 'security' needs to be seen as a constitutive power and a technique to allow for (re)constituting states of discipline. Second, pacification is a process and is not restricted to specific times or spaces, nor is policing restricted to, if at all concerned with, crime (Gordon 2005). Ackerman, Sacks and Furman (2014: 11) underline how this narrow understanding 'distracts us from the fact that ... the police power has long been a wide-ranging exercise in pacification'. In fact, pacification is the 'continuum of police violence upon which the fabrication of capitalist order is planned, enforced and resisted' (Rigakos and Ergul 2013: 169).

Under authoritarian neoliberalism the commodification of pacification intensifies, yet does not entail a retreat, or 'hollowing-out', of the state or its privatization, but builds upon an intimate intertwining of the state and corporate security. Loader and Walker (2001: 10) are almost right in claiming that we can see a move of policing technologies 'outwards to commercial security markets, downwards to municipalities and private organizations, and upwards to transnational institutions'.[1] However, this is decisively *not* the state abandoning policing, or, even more normatively loaded, the undermining of the '*monopoly* of the *legitimate* use of physical force' (Weber 1978: 54, original emphasis). On the contrary, we argue for an understanding of the *extension* of this very monopoly by means of state power. Furthermore, there is also an 'inward' move to privatize state tasks as entrustment (*Beleihung*) allows the state to devolve part of its competencies to the private sector and, hence, private bodies will act as quasi-public authorities (Baller 2014: 48–9).[2] Examples include the Special Police Officers in the United States, the *police spéciale* (*gardes particuliers, polices supplétives*) in France and the *Hilfspolizeien* and *Luftsicherheitsassistenten* (aviation security screeners) in Germany (O'Toole 1978: 10–1; Ocqueteau 1992: 60, 105–6; Nitz 2000: 57–66; Wissenschaftlicher Dienst 2007: 8–13).

In addition to and in line with the new mode of neoliberal governance, the state is creating market competition within its police forces (Gottschall et al. 2015: 231–65). Authoritarian neoliberalization intensively embeds policing activities in neocommunitarian belief systems including order and community (Eick 2010), and shapes them through politico-economic motivated cutbacks and privatization measures (Eick 2003), new socio-spatially oriented demands (Eick 2011), organization models such as New Public Management (Briken 2014) and a general trend from government to governance (Davies 2011). We argue that it is the politically encouraged and strengthened commodification of all spheres of social life, the *Landnahme*, or appropriation, in combination with the constant mode of reinvention and organizational innovation that ensures the resilience of the now authoritarian neoliberalism (Dörre et al. 2016).

In turn, and as we will show below, the growth and expansion of corporate security providers is dialectically linked to the ways by which neoliberalism is maintained politically by states of discipline. In referring to market mechanisms, the states enable the preemption and incapacitation of social forces contesting the very neoliberalizing state models. The ever-growing sphere of coercive practices that marginalize, discipline and control spaces, social groups and individuals are thus not limited to 'non-market' mechanisms such as state violence. To the contrary, states to a growing extent avail themselves of corporate logics to govern policing. This particular move to commodify policing is the main avenue allowing corporate security agencies to merge into one of the three—territoriality provided—roads of the nation state, namely, the legitimate use of physical force, or pacification by (the threat of) violent means.[3] Table 3.1 provides the areas within which commercial and non-profit policing emerged over the centuries, thus creating the 'ring of steel' that ostensibly provides the current form of commodified pacification.[4]

Table 3.1. Actually Existing Commodified Pacification

19th century *(origins)*		
Cash-in-transit	Labor disputes	Precinct control
Factory control	Market place control	Property protection
Guarding	Mercenaries	Train protection
20th century *(developments)*		
Administration	Event services (sports etc.)	Public transport
Airports	Factory fire departments	Reception services
Alarm control centers	Industrial safety	Shopping malls
Atomic plants	Military property protection	Sports stadia
Bodyguards	Parks & forests	Traffic control
City patrols	Patrol security (public space)	Video surveillance
Emergency call centers	Prisons	
21st century *('innovations')*		
Border control	Discothèques & pubs	Job Centers
City points	Electronic monitoring	Manhunt
Consulting (IT etc.)	Employment offices	Psychiatric clinics
Criminal investigation	Environmental safety	Riversides
Critical infrastructure	Facility management	Schools & universities
Deportation services	Forensics	Warfare
Detention centers	Hospitals	Workfare

Source: Eick and Briken (2014, updated).

NEW POLICE MANAGEMENT: CORPORATE CALLING

In Western European societies, the concept of police had already become
relevant in the Middle Ages. As Knemeyer and Trib (1980: 172–5) point
out, the term 'police', or *'polizey'*, had a broad meaning and was utilized
in three different ways—it reflected the condition of order in a community;
it described the regulatory system that ensured the order; and it was understood as a common good. This early phase is interpreted today in terms of
governmentality and can be understood as a move towards the pacification
of the population in an encompassing way. Such pacification strategies
include the control of family and civic morality, distribution of goods,
maintenance of infrastructures, suppression of ensuing protest and, last but
not least, economic and administrative regulation. In sum, police developed
into 'a grand intellectual project linked to state formation, prosperity and
security in Enlightenment thought' (Rigakos et al. 2009: 2). With the transition to the capitalist mode of production, we see the creation of the public
police pushed forward by nation states, and the police became, according to
an oft-quoted phrase, 'the last of the basic building blocks in the structure
of modern executive government' (Bittner 1970: 15). States focused on
'the fabrication of the reliable men' (Treiber and Steinert 1980), and state
regulation aimed at disciplining the poor to make them available as reserve
armies for the new labour markets.[5] The nineteenth-century emergence of
'the police' as a specialized authority with the primary formal responsibility
to safeguard against crime and insecurity is a feature of complex societies
(Reiner 2000: 7). Public policing was, of course, not restricted to the crime
control function, but had a clear mission statement towards the management
of 'folk devils' (Cohen 1972) and civil disorder.

In recent decades, policing as a state-provided and state-run 'service' has
re-emerged in different forms (Compare Tables 3.1 and 3.2). The police
forces extended their functions into social politics (Eick 2014), into the

Table 3.2. 'Traditional' Approach to Policing (1830s–1980s)

Modes and means	
public	state-provided
police	state-run
universal	indiscrete
reactive	repressive
citizen as 'objects'	subordinate

Source: Eick and Briken (2014, updated)

realm of commercial security (security partnerships, 'knowledge sharing' on advisory boards) and towards 'civil society' more generally—thus creating a veritable 'ring of steel'. New 'assemblages' of security providers continue to emerge and grow in scale and scope. We argue that to fully understand how this connects with authoritarian neoliberalism, these changes need to be attached to a more recent development, to the commodification of the police. Since the 1990s, and starting in the Anglo-Saxon world, the ideology and practice of New Public Management have significantly altered the police forces (Briken 2014; Gottschall et al. 2015: 231–68). The police forces are managed according to business rules, with accounting and controlling shifting the attention to a resource-led control of input, output and outcome. This new police governance model is characterized by a professionalized production of evaluative knowledge and by strategic targets. The chain of command must suit the police value chain, and rank-and-file officers are addressed no longer as 'street corner politicians' (Muir 1977) but as accountants. Police forces are managed more or less like police companies or enterprises. This is a fundamental break in how the state conceptualizes police forces, as they are now subjected to managerial policies. As in the private business, large parts of police work are now made quantifiable—condensed into measurable indices and records—and, more importantly, they can be benchmarked over time and space.

Today's performance indicators and target definitions do not simply offer a qualitatively different way of recording and measuring police action. They also affect police behaviour as the pressure to produce the prefigured results inclines officers to target specific types of crime and specific (potentially deviant) groups. Research on New Police Management (NPM) in Western European countries shows NPM's potential to fit into the means of states of discipline, while at the same time strengthening the resilience of neoliberalism in different ways. In the following discussion, we highlight the consequences of accountability models for the precarious and vulnerable populations and the new auctorial arrangements related to NPM.

Qualitative studies have unanimously found that NPM, *inter alia*, enforces social inequalities as police monitoring focuses on the (urban) poor and vulnerable parts of society as an inner-organizational routine by ticking performance boxes. Racial profiling, in this conception, turns into a rationale and even legitimate police practice to fulfil NPM expectations; and by the same token, 'creating' dangerous classes in order to pacify them is legitimized by NPM (Lange and Schenck 2004; Matelly and Mouhanna 2007; Loftus 2009; Fassin 2011). 'Cooking the books' to create more criminals and to solve crimes thus turns into common practice. The deliverance of comprehensive police services is no longer seen as a crucial state function. NPM's economic logic, thus, also fuels the outsourcing of policing tasks driven by the idea to focus on 'core police functions', which, in turn, are evaluated according to market mechanisms.

The police forces in England and Wales are but one example to showcase how public policing engages with commodified pacification. Strategies manufactured as a 'financial panic' (Collier 2006: 58) among the police forces in England and Wales have been on the reform agenda since the 1990s, thus long before the 'real' financial crises and cost-cuttings within the police emerged.[6] The concern about effectiveness (crime statistics, outcome) was more and more combined with concerns about efficiency (resources, input and output) and led towards an intensified centralized 'steering'[7] of the 43 police forces by means of inner-sectoral benchmarking exercises and constantly updated league tables (Gottschall et al. 2015: 234). Outsourcing is crucial for commodified pacification encompassing what Brodeur (2010) has referred to as high and low policing services. In the British report 'Private sector partnering in the police service', Her Majesty's Inspectorate of Constabulary (HMIC) and the National Audit Office (NAO) identify potential services for outsourcing on three scales:

> *Major business partnering*, where the force contracts a private sector partner to provide a significant area of policing (for example, by outsourcing business support services); *Custody partnering*, where the force contracts a private sector partner to provide either services (for example, detainee management, catering and cleaning), buildings or both. … *Consultancy support*, where forces purchase skills and expertise to help a transformation. (HMIC and NAO 2013: 5, original emphasis)

The different but interconnected police service delivery models include three different approaches: the 'police-led delivery', the so-called 'public–private delivery', and the 'third and private sector delivery' (HMIC and NAO 2013: 9). While the services can vary in terms of their connections to actual police forces and staff, there is clearly a new quality in collaboration regarding joint ventures and third-party delivery. The latter includes 'voluntary individuals or agencies to support policing services. For example, charitable and philanthropic organizations can assist forces with community-focused crime prevention or harm reduction activities' (HMIC and NAO 2013: 14). Joint ventures allow forces to form new bodies between 'two or more organisations to deliver agreed objectives' (ibid.). Usually, police staff and assets are transferred to the partnering organization. Take the example of the joint venture between West Mercia Police and Shropshire Libraries—the former delivering policing services to those rural and remote communities that are usually 'policed' by utilizing mobile library buses—both sharing responsibility for delivery, revenues, expenses, assets and control of the organizational procedures according to their agreement (Warrell 2016). Although this reads like a rather random case, it is one of many examples underlining the ways in which police forces today mesh up with different stakeholders (Briken and Eick 2011).

One crucial effect of this restructuring is that social politics and crime prevention appear as what they are: two sides of the same coin, thus quite literally merging 'the velvet glove and the iron fist' (Center for Research on Criminal Justice 1977). Commodified pacification includes a broadening of police work into all spheres of the social, thus speaking again to the ancient idea of '*polizey*'—but now with a commodified twist.

CAPITALIZING OUTSOURCING AND CONSULTANCY: SELLING SECURITY

This chapter is not meant to provide a comprehensive 'historical' account of the development of police and corporate security. Rather, we want to highlight some of the consistencies and current trends within the industry. By the late nineteenth and early twentieth century, corporate security providers emerged, both in North America and Europe, as for-profit 'protectors of privilege' while state policing was still in its infancy (Fogelson 1977; Monkkonen 1981; Knöbl 1998). This growth not only continued in parallel with the rise of state-salaried military and institutionalized police apparatuses, but was in particular fuelled by urbanization and industrialization processes. The respective demands led to the development of a core workforce in two main business areas: property protection—the watchman—and industrial dispute—the strike breaker—were here to stay (Nelken 1926; Shalloo 1933; cf. Rigakos et al. 2009).

As an example for the latter, think of Amazon's recent deployment of commercial security in their fulfilment centres in the United Kingdom. We know from recent research that Amazon uses its security staff to intimidate trade unionists who want to mobilize workers outside the fulfilment centre.[8] Although the local authorities maintain the streets and the parking space, Amazon acts as if its centres were private territory. Since the security staff is not part of the core workforce, Amazon exploits this division among employees. Belgium in late February 2012 would be another example. A German businessman running a metal factory there called a group of about twenty men equipped with batons and other weaponry on duty to the Belgian village of Sprimont. The men belonged to a security company regularly working in the southwest of Germany that was hired to confront striking metal workers in Belgium who had seized factory trucks to reinforce demands against the company owner (Deghaye and Dagonnier 2012; Gardner 2012).[9] Thus, the intervention of corporate security during labour disputes is still high on the agenda both in the global North and South (McMichael 2012; Ferus-Comelo 2014).

With the end of the Cold War—and the related dischargement of military and police forces to non-state labour markets—corporate security went global on a hitherto unprecedented scale and extended its scope by penetrating the formerly arcane realms of the state. Waging war (Singer 2003; Francioni and Ronzitti 2011), patrolling borders (Vallet 2014; Jansen et al. 2015) with the respective migration management (Gammeltoft-Hansen and Nyberg Sørensen 2013) and security consultancy (Walby and Lippert 2014; O'Reilly forthcoming) became transnational fields of expertise, while deploying detention services became popular business at the 'home front' (Moran, Gill and Conlon 2013). These are just five recently acquired fields of for-profit engagement (cf. Eick and Briken 2014). Such pacification services are provided in oligopolistic markets by transnational companies capable of serving the full security supply chain and delivering all the means of security production, including technology, manpower and expertise.

Consider, for instance, how the private and military security contractor (PMSC) formerly known as 'Blackwater' (today 'Academi') moved from the war theatre in Iraq to post-Katrina New Orleans with the authorization of the Department of Homeland Security to use lethal force against the citizenry (Scahill and Crespo 2005). Further in point, consider how the German government—notably, in contradiction to its constitutional law—decided to outsource the protection of its merchant fleet, the third-largest on the planet, to commercial security providers in 2011, as protection by the Federal Police—the constitutionally recognized authority to police German transnational logistics—was deemed to be too complicated and too costly (Knight 2011).

In a similar vein, commercial security providers protect borders in countries such as Austria, Denmark and Sweden (Eick 2016: 11), handle refugees and migrants, patrol detention and deportation centres as well as asylum application camps, and co-process asylum applications on behalf of the state (see Manunza in this book). In the United Kingdom, nearly half of all detained immigrants are held in the seven (out of eleven) privately managed facilities; the same applies to the United States, where, in 2010, 50 per cent of the 400,000 immigrants detained were held in for-profit amenities (Menz 2013: 118; Gammeltoft-Hansen 2013: 133). In both countries, as well as in Austria (Schenk 2015), deportation operations are also outsourced (Bernstein 2011; Lemberg-Pedersen 2013: 156; Nyberg Sørensen 2013: 248). The roughly one million refugees arriving in Germany in 2014–2015 were not detained but legally obliged to live in privately run refugee centres. Accordingly, the annual turnover of commercial security providers increased by 8.9 per cent and employment by 4.9 per cent—or 15,000 additional employees—in 2015 alone (Olschok 2016), among them a staggering number of neo-Nazis even torturing refugees Guantánamo-style, thus raising concerns about human rights standards (Komaromi 2016).

At the same time, while being high on the agenda already in the 1980s (e.g. Percy 1987), citizen-oriented projects aim at activating the population to participate in the co-production of security. We argue that, from its very beginning, such 'empowerment' of citizens was far from concerned with furthering democratic policing. To the contrary—though such programmes and projects follow multi-agency approaches and involve high levels of information gathering and sharing (Eick 2011)—police are the only organization and police officers the only people to fully oversee and control the process, thus turning the constant information into a resource for extending the state monopoly of violence. It is this way of pacification provision we now focus on.

PROFITEERING FROM NON-PROFIT POLICING: NEOLIBERALIZED NEIGHBOURS

Running states of discipline by private means includes policing provided by non-profit agencies. A list of these would include all kinds of 'sentinels' and militias, neighbourhood watch and crime-prevention schemes (with or without the support and/or participation of the police), civil wardens and organizations such as the 'Guardian Angels'. The emergence of such non-profit policing agencies, which grew significantly in scope and scale in the early to mid-1990s, can be explained by urban development strategies that seek to rejuvenate hitherto neglected parts of the respective cities and by workfare programmes targeting the urban poor (see Rioux in this book). As for the latter, so-called third-sector organizations deploy long-term unemployed in workfare schemes while instructing them on how to tackle what they and the local administrations perceive as disorder and incivilities (Eick 2011). In the United States, 'ending welfare as we know it' programmes began to mushroom from 1996 onwards. For example, non-profits such as 'Chrysalis' or 'Homeboy Industries' in Los Angeles started to provide downtown Business Improvement District associations with unemployed and homeless people to clean the streets. On Skid Row, non-profits helped the municipality to police the roads and also deployed former gangbangers as graffiti removal 'experts' capable of reading the respective tags (Eick 2007).

In Germany, workfare is based on the so-called Hartz IV laws deployed in 2004 (Knuth 2009), which stipulate that the long-term unemployed are to provide SOS services—acronym for *Sauberkeit, Ordnung* and *Sicherheit,* or cleanliness, order and security—as so-called One-Euro-Jobbers also supervised by non-profits.[10] Those workfare projects are deployed under fancy names, mirroring neocommunitarian endeavours, such as *Ortsdiener* (place servants), *Spielplatzkümmerer* (playground attendants), *Wohngebietsaufsichten* (residential neighbourhood supervisors), *Rote Teufel* (Red Devils) in Berlin, *Gelbe Engel* (Yellow Angels) in Stuttgart and *Grünpolizei* (Green Cops) in Frankfurt. Their tasks include notifying landlords and the police about graffiti, removal of graffiti, ensuring that dogs are kept on leashes in private and public city parks, enforcing the no-alcohol by-laws in parks and on squares and even the control of stationary traffic. Further, long-term unemployed are engaged as school and schoolyard attendants, as school-run escorts, as park inspectors, and as supervisors of residential areas and playgrounds; in addition, they control underground parking lots, enforce public green space by-laws and are available as contact persons in emergency and conflict situations, and pay heed to cleanliness (Eick 2011). This form of policing is meant, from the perspective of the public administration, to complement the state-led and commercial securitization of the city.

Finally, there is a trend of deploying urban poor as quasi-police forces to directly police themselves in their own residential areas (Eick 2003). As a group of leading German Christian Democrats made clear in 2011, a neocommunitarian approach to policing in 'disadvantaged' neighbourhoods and on 'superfluous' residents is still embraced:

> In neglected neighborhoods crime is more likely to grow than in neighborhoods where local residents feel at ease. Therefore, *district runners* or *neighborhood guards* should care for those parts of town identified as those with special developing needs [but] without holding sovereign powers. ... Ideally being at home in their operational area, they know the miseries of the local residents and enjoy far more trust compared to someone *from office.* (Gröhe et al. 2011: 26, original emphasis)

These are just a few examples of the many paradoxes that go along with the endeavour to create states of discipline on the local scale by 'empowering', 'activating', deploying and—where perceived as necessary—replacing the respective (unemployed) residents. Early on, Spitzer (1975: 645–646) described how the state distinguishes residents as 'social junk', that is, 'a costly yet relatively harmless burden to society', and potential troublemakers, that is, the 'social dynamite'. While 'social dynamite is normally processed through the legal system ... social junk is frequently (but not always) administered by the agencies and agents of the therapeutic and welfare state'.

Spitzer (1975: 649, original emphasis) reminds us that when the welfare state is dominant, 'potential troublemakers' might also be

> recruited as policemen, social workers and attendants, while confirmed deviants can be *rehabilitated* by becoming counsellors, psychiatric aides and parole officers. In other words, if a large number of the controlled can be converted into a first line of defence, threats to the system of class rule can be transformed into resources for its support.

In today's workfare environment within which pacification is extended to models of the 'poor policing the poor', authoritarian neoliberalism is individualized. For example, in 2007 the Berlin Senate created a workfare programme to deploy former gangbangers as non-profit pacifiers against other youth groups, while the state police provided hands-on training for non-profits' clients, youngsters aged between 17 and 20 years, given the task of graffiti removal in their respective neighbourhoods (Deggerich 2007; Eick 2011). Looking at such private, though state-induced, policing deployed on the local scale and keeping in mind the fact that state-induced commercial policing extends far beyond the local into the global realm, we conclude in the final section with some remarks on what might be called a glocalized form of 'authoritarian pacification' by commercial means.[11]

COMMODIFIED PACIFICATION:
A GLOCAL 'RING OF STEEL'?

Since the advent of rollback neoliberalism in the 1980s, its post-90s rollout has been coupled with intensified globalization which was fuelled by the end of the Cold War and the ensuing primitive accumulation in the 'European East'. It is also in this period that the for-profit solutions triumphed as the panacea against all Keynesian 'evils' on each and every scale. We can observe three different but connected processes in the realm of security provision, delivery and production: While most European nation states are still reluctant to cut the core police personnel (sworn officers, or other comparable notions of civil servants), the trend to centralize police governance and to shift organizational decision-making to NPM logics is obvious. Consequently, new arrangements bring together 'committed' actors and create new spatial arrangements beyond national soil (Fyfe, Terpstra and Tops 2013). From police training and protest policing to international peacekeeping and border control—the current militarization of the Mediterranean Sea just being one example (Eick 2016; Manunza in this book)—national police and military forces are co-working on the ground and via shared knowledge and infrastructure networks.

Such continuous 'improvement' aims at increasing effectiveness and efficiency and helps set the scene for cooperation with and co-optation of (but also competition with) corporate security.[12] In other words, (authoritarian) neoliberalism allowed for a second 'gold rush' within the corporate security world. As we have tried to highlight in this chapter, commercial security providers significantly extended their 'market share' in core areas of state sovereignty. The growth and expansion of the corporate security industry is dialectically linked to the ways in which neoliberalism is maintained politically by states of discipline that subject themselves to market mechanisms. Even in their core sovereign functions, states follow market logics and incorporate for-profit partners in order to allow for the preemption and incapacitation of social forces contesting—be it through the 'bare life' represented by 'the refugee'—the very neoliberalizing state models.

Last but not least, the state relies on its citizenry and a particular way of pacifying residents and 'guests' through consensus and 'integration'. Non-profit policing and the respective multi-agency networks—just like neighbourhood watch schemes or even militias—allow to steer rather than row on the ground while keeping in balance the 'ring of steel' surrounding the state monopoly of force and the populace living within (and resisting against) it. Inasmuch as we agree that authoritarian neoliberalism relies on coercive *state* practices and judicial and administrative *state* apparatuses, we hold that states of discipline heavily rely on *private* and *commercial/corporate* means to do so. The resilience of the authoritarian neoliberal nation state lies precisely in its ability to scale upwards and downwards, and to overcome its national limitations. We analyzed the dynamics of glocal security governance capacities in terms of commodified pacification to show how governments turned into enterprises in their own right, inventing market structures in areas as varied as welfare, workfare and warfare. In adding to Toscano's observation that pacification is not a mere social tendency (2007: 611), we end our chapter by concluding that pacification is a political and economic project, borne by the multiple agencies of the state, and ready, at all times, to neutralize all forms of opposition—where and whenever deemed necessary.

NOTES

1. For us, it is unconvincing to claim that policing moves 'downwards to... private organizations' as—whatever the term 'private' may entail—private bodies such as the *Deutscher Präventionsrat* (German Crime Prevention Council), the 'International Association of Chiefs of Police' (IACP), or the 'Confederation of European Security Services' (CoESS) clearly work beyond a local scale, or somewhere 'downwards'.

2. 'Entrusted persons or entrusted companies are private entities (natural or legal persons) entrusted by or on grounds of law with the independent sovereign perfor-

mance of certain public administrative duties... as a result, sovereign powers are exercised by private bodies' (Baller 2014: 48–49).

3. Besides the legitimate use of physical force, these monopolies encompass taxation and legislation.

4. We hold that only after (particular forms of) statehood emerged, it—in turn—makes sense to talk about the privatization and commodification of 'security'.

5. As Engels bluntly put it in *The Condition of the Working Class in England* in 1845: 'Because the English Bourgeois finds himself reproduced in his law, as he does in his God, the policeman's truncheon ... has for him a wonderfully soothing power. But for the workingman quite otherwise!" (Engels 2009: 186).

6. 'Police forces in England and Wales have contracted with the private sector for several decades. However, this activity has increased over the last two years as the service responds to the budget reductions required by the 2010 spending review, with more forces agreeing high value, long-term contracts' (HMIC and NAO 2013: 5).

7. The trend to centralize police governance applies to other countries as well, including Germany. Here, the only significant growth of officers and budgets during the last two decades occurred within the Federal Police, or *Bundespolizei* (Briken 2014).

8. This information stems from interviews that Kendra Briken, Phil Taylor and Kirsty Newsome (Universities of Strathclyde and Sheffield) conducted with Amazon workers and are confirmed by trade unionists and additional sources.

9. Only a few weeks earlier, in November 2011, intimidations by rent-a-cops occurred again, this time against hospital workers at the Charité, the largest public clinic in Berlin, where facility services personnel went on strike against low wages and the denial of collective bargaining (Schumacher 2011). When security workers themselves go on strike, they are confronted with similar contestations by their employers (Brigden 2011: 368).

10. One-Euro-Jobs are employment relationships for long-term unemployed that are not labour contracts but rather allowances. They are not subject to social insurance contributions; and only pay between one and two-and-a-half euros per hour. These jobs, according to the non-profit labour law, should not replace regular jobs and have to be complementary (cf. Eick 2011).

11. The term 'glocalization'—portmanteau of globalization and localization—originally referred to the adaptation of globally marketed products and services to local markets (cf. Robertson 1995; Swyngedouw 1997; Sharma 2009) and is here applied to the provision of commercial pacification to facilitate states of discipline.

12. Corporate pacification agencies compete in that they demand hitherto state-run businesses, and they clearly aim to exploit the willingness of states of discipline to cooperate by offering additional goods, services and 'expertise'.

BIBLIOGRAPHY

Ackerman AR, Sacks M and Furman R (2014) The new penology revisited: The criminalization of immigration as a pacification strategy. *Justice Policy Journal* 11(1): 1–20.

Baller O (2014) Legal powers in the performance of tasks of hazard defence by private security services—A case study. In: Baller O (ed) *Security Management International: Project Idea and Implementation*. Berlin: BWV, 47–56.

Bernstein N (2011) Companies use immigration crackdown to turn a profit. *The New York Times* (28 September). Available at: http://www.nytimes.com/2011/09/29/world/asia/getting-tough-on-immigrants-to-turn-a-profit.html?_r=0

Bittner E (1970) *The Functions of the Police in Modern Society*. Washington, DC: National Institute of Mental Health.

Brenner N and Theodore N (2002) Cities and the geographies of 'actually existing neoliberalism'. *Antipode: A Radical Journal of Geography* 34(3): 349–379.

Brigden C (2011) Unions and collective bargaining. *Journal of Industrial Relations* 54(3): 361–376.

Briken K (2014) Ein verbetriebswirtschaftlichtes Gewaltmonopol. *Kriminologisches Journal* 46(4): 213–230.

Briken K and Eick V (2011) Recht und billig? Wachschutz zwischen Niedriglohn und Ein-Euro-Jobs. *Kritische Justiz* 44(1): 34–42.

Brodeur J-P (2010) *The Policing Web*. Oxford: Oxford University Press.

Center for Research on Criminal Justice (1977) *The Iron Fist and the Velvet Glove*. San Francisco: Garrett Press.

Cohen S (1972) *Folk Devils and Moral Panics: The Creation of the Mods and Rockers*. London: MacGibbon & Kee.

Collier PM (2006) Costing police services: The politicization of accounting. *Critical Perspectives on Accounting* 1(17): 57–86.

Crouch C (2011) *The Strange Non-death of Neoliberalism*. Cambridge: Polity.

Davies JS (2011) *Challenging Governance Theory*. Bristol: Policy Press.

Deggerich M (2007) Drei Engel für Kreuzberg. *Der Spiegel* 61(38): 58.

Deghaye M-P and Dagonnier E (2012) *Milice privée allemande envoyée en Belgique par des patrons pour casser de l'ouvrier belge*. Sprimont: Ms.

Dörre K, Lessenich S and Rosa H (2016) *Sociology, Capitalism, Critique*. London: Verso.

Eick V (2003) New strategies of policing the poor: Berlin's neo-liberal security system. *Policing & Society* 4(13): 365–379.

Eick V (2007) 'Space Patrols': The new peace-keeping functions of nonprofits. In: Leitner H, Peck J and Sheppard E (eds) *Contesting Neoliberalism: Urban Frontiers*. New York: Guilford Press, 266–290.

Eick V (2010) Policing 'below the state' in Germany. *Contemporary Justice Review* 13(4): 21–41.

Eick V (2011) Lokale Kriminal- und Sicherheitspolitik. In: Dahme H-J and Wohlfahrt N (eds) *Handbuch Kommunale Sozialpolitik*. Wiesbaden: VS, 294–305.

Eick V (2013) Polychrome policing in Germany. In: Lippert RK and Walby K (eds) *Policing Cities: Urban Securitization and Regulation in a 21st Century World*. London: Routledge, 97–112.

Eick V (2014) Pazifizierungsprobleme: Polizei macht Schule. *Kriminologisches Journal* 46(4): 232–248.

Eick V (2016) Mediterrane Migrationsregime. *RAV-Infobrief* 38(118): 10–16.

Eick V and Briken K (eds) (2014) *Urban (In)Security: Policing the Neoliberal Crisis.* Ottawa: Red Quill.

Engels F (2009) *The Condition of the Working Class in England.* London: Penguin.

Fassin D (2011) *La Force de l'Ordre: Une anthropologie de la police des quartiers.* Paris: Seuil.

Ferus-Comelo A (2014) Private security, public insecurity: The casualization of employment and its effects in India. In: Eick V and Briken K (eds) *Urban (In) Security: Policing the Neoliberal Crisis.* Ottawa: Red Quill, 241–264.

Fisher M (2009) *Capitalist Realism: Is There No Alternative?* London: Zero.

Fogelson RM (1977) *Big-City Police.* New York: Harvard University Press.

Francioni F and Ronzitti N (eds) (2011) *War By Contract: Human Rights, Humanitarian Law, and Private Contractors.* Oxford: Oxford University Press.

Fyfe NR, Terpstra J and Tops P (2013) *Centralizing Forces? Comparative Perspectives on Contemporary Police Reforms in Northern and Western Europe.* The Hague: Eleven.

Gammeltoft-Hansen T (2013) The rise of the private border guard. In: Gammeltoft-Hansen T and Nyberg Sørensen N (eds) *The Migration Industry and the Commercialization of International Migration.* Abingdon: Routledge, 128–151.

Gammeltoft-Hansen T and Nyberg Sørensen N (eds) (2013) *The Migration Industry and the Commercialization of International Migration.* Abingdon: Routledge.

Gardner A (2012) Unions condemn violence at Meister Sprimont in Belgium. *Industriall Global Union* (1 March). Available at: http://www.industriall-union.org/ archive/imf/unions-condemn-violence-at-meister-sprimont-in-belgium

Gordon T (2005) The political economy of law-and-order policies. *Studies in Political Economy* 75(1): 53–77.

Gottschall K, Kittel B, Briken K, Heuer JO, Hils S, Streb S and Tepe M (2015) *Public Sector Employment Regimes: Transformations of the State as Employer.* Basingstoke: Palgrave Macmillan.

Gröhe H, Mohr-Lüllmann R, Henkel F, Roth P and Elbers D (2011) *Politik für die Stadt der Zukunft.* Berlin: CDU.

Harman C (2009) *Zombie Capitalism: Global Crisis and the Relevance of Marx.* Chicago: Haymarket.

Harvey D (2005) *A Brief History of Neoliberalism.* Oxford: Oxford University Press.

HMIC and NAO (2013) *Private Sector Partnering in the Police Service: A Practical Guide to Major Business Partnering, Custody Partnering and Consultancy Support.* London: National Audit Office.

Jansen Y, Celikates R and Bloois JD (eds) (2015) *The Irregularization of Migration in Contemporary Europe: Detention, Deportation, Drowning.* London: Rowman & Littlefield International.

Knemeyer F-L and Trib K (1980) Polizei. *Economy and Society* 9(2): 172–196.

Knight D (2011) Protection from piracy comes at a price. *Spiegel Online International* (26 August). Available at: http://www.spiegel.de/international/germany/the-world-from-berlin-protection-from-piracy-comes-at-a-price-a-782661.html

64   *Kendra Briken and Volker Eick*

Knöbl W (1998) *Polizei und Herrschaft im Modernisierungsprozess*. Frankfurt: Campus.

Knuth M (2009) Path shifting and path dependence. *International Journal of Public Administration* 32(12): 1048–1069.

Komaromi P (2016) Germany: neo-Nazis and the market in asylum reception. *Race & Class* 58(2): 79–86.

Lange H-J and Schenck JC (2004) *Polizei im kooperativen Staat: Verwaltungsreform und Neues Steuerungsmodell in der Sicherheitsverwaltung*. Wiesbaden: VS.

Lemberg-Pedersen M (2013) Private security companies and the European borderscapes. In: Gammeltoft-Hansen T and Nyberg Sørensen N (eds) *The Migration Industry and the Commercialization of International Migration*. Abingdon: Routledge, 152–172.

Loader I and Walker N (2001) Policing as a public good: Reconstituting the connections between policing and the state. *Theoretical Criminology* 5(1): 9–35.

Loftus B (2009) *Police Culture in a Changing World*. Oxford: Oxford University Press.

Marx K and Engels F (1969) *Selected Works*, Vol. 1. Moscow: Progress Publishers.

Matelly JH and Mouhanna C (2007) *Police: Des chiffres et des doutes*. Paris: Michalon.

McGovern M (2015) State violence and the colonial roots of collusion in Northern Ireland. *Race and Class* 57(2): 3–23.

McMichael C (2012) Hosting the world: The 2010 World Cup and the new military urbanism. *City: Analysis of Urban Trends, Culture, Theory, Policy, Action* 16(5): 519–534.

Menz G (2013) The neoliberalized state and the growth of the migration industry. In: Gammeltoft-Hansen T and Nyberg Sørensen N (eds) *The Migration Industry and the Commercialization of International Migration*. Abingdon: Routledge, 108–127.

Mirowski P (2013) *Never Let a Serious Crisis Go to Waste: How Neoliberalism Survived the Financial Meltdown*. London: Verso.

Mirowski P and Plehwe D (eds) (2009) *The Road from Mont Pèlerin: The Making of the Neoliberal Thought Collective*. Cambridge, MA: Harvard University Press.

Monkkonen EH (1981) *Police in Urban America, 1860–1920*. Cambridge: Cambridge University Press.

Moran D, Gill N and Conlon D (eds) (2013) *Carceral Spaces: Mobility and Agency in Imprisonment and Migrant Detention*. Farnham: Ashgate.

Muir WK (1977) *Police: Streetcorner Politicians*. Chicago: University of Chicago Press.

Nelken S (1926) *Das Bewachungsgewerbe*. Berlin: Verband der Wach- und Schließgesellschaften.

Neocleous M (2011) A brighter and nicer new life: Security as pacification. *Social and Legal Studies* 20(2): 191–208.

Nitz G (2000) *Private und öffentliche Sicherheit*. Berlin: Duncker & Humblot.

Nogala, D (1995) Was ist eigentlich so privat an der Privatisierung sozialer Kontrolle? In: Sack F, Voß M, Funk A and Reinke H (eds) *Privatisierung staatlicher Kontrolle*. Baden-Baden: Nomos, 234–260.

Nyberg Sørensen N (2013) Migration between social and criminal networks. In: Gammeltoft-Hansen T and Nyberg Sørensen N (eds) *The Migration Industry and the Commercialization of International Migration*. Abingdon: Routledge, 238–261.

Ocqueteau F (1992) *Gardiennage, surveillance et sécurité privée: Commerce de la peur et/ou peur du commerce?* Paris: CESDIP.

Oksala J (2011) Violence and neoliberal governmentality. *Constellations* 18(3): 474–486.

Olschok H (2016) Ein Schritt die die richtige Richtung. *Berliner Behörden Spiegel* 32(18): 45.

O'Reilly C (forthcoming) *Policing Global Risks: The Transnational Security Consultancy Industry*. Oxford: Hart.

O'Toole G (1978) *The Private Sector: Private Spies, Rent-A-Cops and the Police-Industrial Complex*. New York: WW Norton & Co.

Peck J (2010) Zombie neoliberalism and the ambidextrous state. *Theoretical Criminology* 14(1): 104–110.

Percy SL (1987) Citizen involvement in coproducing safety and security in the community. *Public Productivity Review* 10(4): 83–93.

Reiner R (2000) *The Politics of the Police*, third edition. Oxford: Oxford University Press.

Rigakos GS and Ergul A (2013) The pacification of the American working class: A time series analysis. *Socialist Studies / Études Socialistes* 9(2): 167–198.

Rigakos GS, McMullan JL, Johnson J and Özcan G (2009) *A General Police System: Political Economy and Security in the Age of Enlightenment*. Ottawa: Red Quill.

Robertson R (1995) Glocalization: Time-space and homogeneity-heterogeneity. In: Featherstone M, Lash S and Robertson R (eds) *Global Modernities*. London: Sage, 25–44.

Scahill J and Crespo D (2005) Overkill in New Orleans. *AlterNet* (12 September). Available at: http://www.alternet.org/story/25320/overkill_in_new_orleans

Schenk M (2015) 'Traiskirchen: Wir sind nur Dienstleister': Kommerzialisierung und Zähmung von Flüchtlings- und Sozialarbeit. *Kurswechsel* 30(4): 75–79.

Schumacher J (2011) Erfolg für Streikende bei Charité-Tochter. *Die Tageszeitung* (6 December). Available at: http://www.taz.de/!5106005

Shalloo JP (1933) *Private Police*. Philadelphia: Rumford Press.

Sharma CK (2009) Emerging dimensions of decentralization debate in the age of globalization. *Indian Journal of Federal Studies* 19(1): 47–65.

Singer PW (2003) *Corporate Warriors: The Rise of the Privatized Military Industry*. Ithaca, NY: Cornell University Press.

Smith N (2008) Neo-liberalism: Dead but dominant. *Focaal* 51(2): 155–157.

Spitzer S (1975) Toward a Marxian theory of deviance. *Social Problems* 22(5): 638–651.

Swyngedouw E (1997) Neither global nor local: 'Glocalization' and the politics of scale. In: Cox KR (ed) *Spaces of Globalization: Reasserting the Power of the Local*. New York: Guilford Press, 137–166.

Toscano A (2007) Powers of pacification: State and empire in Gabriel Tarde. *Economy and Society* 36(4): 597–613.

Treiber H and Steinert H (1980) *Die Fabrikation des zuverlässigen Menschen.* Münster: Westfälisches Dampfboot.

Vallet E (ed) (2014) *Borders, Fences and Walls: States of Insecurity?* Farnham: Ashgate.

Walby K and Lippert R (eds) (2014) *Corporate Security in the 21st Century: Theory and Practice in International Perspective.* Basingstoke: Palgrave Macmillan.

Warrell H (2016) West Mercia Police and Shropshire Libraries joint venture to deliver policing to the rural. *Financial Times* (11 January). Available at: www.ft.com/cms/s/0/681176b8-5c1c-11e2-bef7-00144feab49a.html#axzz49ZZJ676M

Weber M (1978) Economy and Society. In: Roth G and Wittich C (eds) *An Outline of Interpretive Sociology.* Berkeley, CA: University of California Press.

Williams MC (2016) Global security assemblages. In: Abrahamsen R and Leander A (eds) *Routledge Handbook of Private Security Studies.* Abingdon: Routledge, 131–139.

Wissenschaftlicher Dienst des Deutschen Bundestages (2007) *Privatisierung von staatlichen Sicherheitsaufgaben.* Berlin: Ms.

Zedner L (2006) Liquid security: Managing the market for crime control. *Criminology and Criminal Justice* 6(3): 267–288.

Chapter 4

Bodies in Resistance

Conversations on Gender, Body Politics and Authoritarian Neoliberalism

Wendy Harcourt

Gender politics under authoritarian neoliberalism is complex—it is often silent, often undercover, as making it visible through public resistance can lead to violent reprisals. Nevertheless, feminist research is working to ensure that women's knowledge, voices and actions are not erased from conversations around authoritarian neoliberalism, even if it has to be done in stealthy and careful ways, not always following academic convention. This essay is a contribution to those conversations with a reflection on the embodied experiences of resistance of activist researchers who identify as women and who are part of the network of scholars around the recently formed Sexuality Research Initiative (SRI) of the Civic Innovation Research Initiative (CIRI) at the International Institute of Social Studies, Erasmus University.[1]

It is important to be explicit about this research in the context of the aims of this chapter. The SRI undertakes research in order to create an open co-productive space that explores embodiment, gender and power relations in development practices. The research aims to look at how activists are involved in resisting dominant definitions of sexuality, body and gender relations in their different political struggles over sexual and reproductive rights and health (Harcourt, Heumann and Radjavi 2016). The research is conducted using feminist co-productive and reflexive methodologies incorporating insights from development studies as well as observations from the praxis of 'doing feminism' (Harding 1991; Rose 1997). One of the pivotal concepts of the research is body politics, defined as the political struggle of people to claim control over their own biological, social and cultural 'bodily' experiences. Bodies are understood as sites of cultural meaning, social experience and political resistance (Grosz 1994). The research, in particular, looks at where gendered and sexualized bodies are sites of political action.

Another key focus of the research is to understand sexuality from the point of view of the experiences, feelings and emotions of women engaged in resistance, where the lived body is a subject, not an object, of development discourses. In the tradition of earlier feminists writing on the body (Butler 1993; Grewal and Kaplan 1994; Shildrick 1997; Tamale 2011; Wieringa and Sivori 2012), the aim is to unpack the conceptual frameworks that are blind to how embodied experiences are embedded in dominant macro frameworks of politics, economics, culture and society, and to look at how experiences of female embodiment are informed by sexism, racism, misogyny and heterosexism (Spivak 1987, 1999; Mohanty 2003). Body politics is seen as a powerful form of resistance, linking the political dimension of the body with a radical form of democracy as women's movements aim to reclaim the lived experience of the female body as a vehicle for making and remaking the world (Petchesky 2002; Hartmann 1995; Vargas 2005).

In what follows, I continue this reflexive approach of the SRI by looking at 'embodied thinking' (Icaza and Vasquez 2016) in relation to experiences of women engaged with and writing about their resistance to authoritarian neoliberal states. I explore how their emotions and bodily experiences of political contestation are fleshly realities embedded in gender power relations informing neoliberal regimes. My interest is in how these women's lived experiences in various forms of resistance can be seen as cracks and fissures in neoliberalism's claim on 'how we think, what we know, how we claim to know' (Peterson 1992). In so doing, I understand neoliberalism as determined by more than abstract economic and financial imaginaries but as a product of organizations, actors, ideas, and the site of gendered/patriarchal norms, which can be known and, therefore, resisted. I look at 'bodies in resistance', through the concept of 'embodied thinking' in order to 'think through' the feelings, emotions and experiences of women writing about their struggles against the gendered violence (structural, physical and psychological) of neoliberalism.

In using the term authoritarian neoliberalism I take my cue from Centeno and Cohen (2012), quoted in the introduction to this book, that neoliberalism 'remains unchallenged by serious alternatives and continues to shape post-2008 policy' and that the resilience of neoliberalism as a mode of economic and political governance can be understood in the way that it 'reinforces and relies upon coercive practices that marginalize, discipline and control social groups' (Tansel in this volume). I explore how these practices are experienced and felt on the body by women engaged in and writing about resistance movements in their struggles against authoritarian state practices. I aim to reflect transparently on my personal as well as public engagement with the women who feature in this essay and the neoliberal context in which we are relating. I do so in order to look at how neoliberalism informs 'the principles, practices, cultures, subjects and institutions of democracy' of which doing university research is a part (Brown 2015: 9).

The main aim of the chapter is to contribute to a feminist critique of the neoliberal 'order of things' through embodied thinking on the experience of women activists' resistance against neoliberal forces. Part one discusses how I approach gendered understandings of the body in neoliberal discourse by explaining, in particular, the approach of civic innovation to understanding embodied thinking. Part two presents different conversations I have had over the last four years with five women engaged in the SRI research in order to explore their lived experiences of resistance in authoritarian neoliberal regimes. The concluding section reflects on the strategy of embodied thinking as a way to challenge state and neoliberal hegemonies.

GENDERED UNDERSTANDINGS OF THE BODY IN NEOLIBERAL DEVELOPMENT DISCOURSE

Body Politics and Neoliberalism

Body politics contains intimate, personal and public sites of struggle. These sites of struggle are connected in complex ways to dominant and changing neoliberal regimes, as our understanding of the body is 'irreducibly interwoven with other discourses, social, colonial, ethical and economic' (Shildrick and Price 1998: 3). In this approach to body politics, I conceptualize power as not only about what hegemonic forces determine what we think and do but also in relation to power at the everyday level. Doing research on body politics is about understanding and challenging the normative construction of gender and sexuality in everyday life through which our knowledge and our experiences of our bodies are formed. These constructions include the language and practices of intimacy, care, sexuality, health, medical and biological scientific processes.

Feminist theory has pointed to the body as the first place for resistance against neoliberalism (Bordo 1993; Underhill-Sem 2005). Understanding the body as a place underscores that bodies are not external to political processes but are firmly enmeshed in them. The lived experience of the body, the identity and definitions attached to bodies, inform and are connected in historically and geographically located political struggles (Harcourt 2009). By calling attention to the body as agent and subject of politics, feminists challenge the neoliberal 'order of things' (Carty and Mohanty 2015). Importantly, such politics is not only about resistance to domination but also about agency and the 'reappropriation, reconstruction, reinvention of bodies, places and place-based practices and the creation of new possibilities of being-in-place and being-in-networks' (Harcourt 2014: 1322).

In using embodied thinking as a way to understand women who are creating and writing about gender politics in authoritarian neoliberal regimes, I am trying to position women's experiences, emotions and bodily feelings as central, not peripheral, to understanding the impact of these regimes on women's lives. The dangers of writing about gendered bodies in these regimes are very real and there are strong responsibilities about doing such research that the academic feminist project needs to make apparent. These emotions and concerns are wiped away in the practices of the neoliberal university, which sees emotional difficulties as peripheral to the production of good, neutral research written for recognized academic journals dominated by neoliberal institutions and contexts. Sara Ahmed (2014: 5) invites us to think about the cultural politics of emotion in her reading of the emotionality of texts and the role of emotion in international terrorism, asylum and migration in the emergent field of affect studies. My chapter is inspired by her work, which explores how emotions shape individual and collective bodies. I am similarly inspired by scholars who speak about gender, race and displacement in studies on women in academia crossing North–South borders as part of their search for epistemic and political justice (Arashiro and Barahona 2015: 1).

Civic Innovation, Embodied Thinking and Resistance

As mentioned in the introduction, the concept of civic innovation has also been an entry point for this chapter in order to explore embodied thinking in development praxis. Civic innovation research looks at the 'creative forms of cultural, political and economic resistance' that are establishing 'pathways to social change' (Biekart, Harcourt and Knorringa 2016). Within this approach the SRI aims to understand 'lived experiences in the struggle for democratic power and to capture the fluidity of changing understandings of identities, bodies, emotions, networks, power relations and knowledge in today's "messy" world' (Harcourt, Icaza and Vargas 2016). The approach to 'think from the body' sees the body itself as a concrete place in which resistance takes place, with all the emotions, pain, confusion and 'mess' this implies.

In the research conducted by the SRI on 'bodies in resistance', the concept of civic innovation explores how gender and sexuality, together with other dimensions of inequality and discrimination, have become entwined in political struggles in the streets, in communities, in the silences, in the homes and in the 'in-between places'. Resistance is multiple and contradictory. What is seen as resistance depends on where people are positioned structurally, experientially and epistemologically. Resistance, therefore, refers not only to organized political defiance but also to everyday practice and emotions that are shaped and motivated by people's attempts to find their own political, social and cultural integrity. In this chapter I look at how research on gendered struggles in authoritarian neoliberal regimes is part of the feminist project of civic innovation.

By employing the term embodied thinking, I see resistance as an emotional and lived response to the dominant definitions of sexualized, gendered bodies. Resistance challenges indirectly or directly the oppressive effects/ disciplinary impacts of prevailing normative gender and body discourses and practices. In this understanding of resistance, not everyone deliberately challenges, or sets out to challenge, an oppressive force. Actions that expose by writing and communicating about those struggles for survival can also be seen as acts of resistance. Indeed, they can define the contours of the neoliberal system that oppresses and confines individuals (Harcourt, Heumann and Radjavi 2016). As we see below, supporting the publication of a gay magazine, writing about the erotic experience of breastfeeding, and acknowledging the need for silence and anonymity when organizing public demonstrations maps out the contours of where the visible becomes the invisible, and expression becomes sedition.

Methodological Note: Researching Bodies in Resistance

The research for this essay is based on private conversations, in person and in emails as well as in more public settings of workshop dialogues.[2] The oral and written exchanges have been about the research undertaken by the women whom I was supervising, and the 'other conversations' were the personal individual and collective narratives of deeply felt embodied experiences of resistance. In my chapter, I explore how those conversations were just as important a part of the process of embodied thinking about resistance as producing academic publications or popular writing and communiqués.

What is important to underline is that the chapter aims to recognize the embodied experience of the activists—the physical feelings and emotions that were happening alongside the academic analysis and observation. Taking such a methodological approach is important when looking at the complexities of gendered embodiment in relation to changing economies, geographies, cultures, networks of communications, experiences of pleasure and of visible and invisible interactions. Acknowledging emotions, feelings and fleshly realities enables us to look at how body politics is intimate and personal as well as political. By doing research, writing blogs, creating websites, speaking about pleasure and desire, and acknowledging specific pain, these activists are challenging how gender is played out in neoliberal regimes, including within academe. Their personal stories, in two cases leading to exile, reveal how body politics is integral to challenging authoritarian neoliberal regimes.

The stories I transcribe below are the ones shared in the in-between moments of doing research—the embodied and personal stories that are usually written out of academic discourse. They speak of emotion and pain in the doing of activism and research as the activists endeavoured to translate their passions and desires into academic language, rigour and discipline. Although I have permission to write about these experiences for this chapter, due to the sensitive nature of the conversations I have not used real names. Most of the information comes from private conversations and email correspondence between March 2012 and May 2016. I have where requested, due to safety, disguised some of the markers of the stories of Alya, Saba, Gita, Raha and Maria from Turkey, Bangladesh, Indonesia, Iran and Mexico, respectively. I selected these five women not only because I had the privilege of working with them as they prepared their academic writing, but also because of the close connection we made politically and personally. They were among the 50 or so scholars who have joined me in feminist reading groups (from 2013 to 2015) held at my house where we explored embodiment, movements, decoloniality and feminist ecologies via our own experiences. Such processes on the margins of university life allowed us to challenge the hierarchal disciplining imposed by universities as we spoke freely about our embodied lives and connected deeply as feminists travelling diverse but connecting paths. The conversations and stories we shared supported and encouraged my own journey as a feminist activist who had relatively recently joined academe in November 2011.

EMBODIED THINKING: FIVE NARRATIVES OF WOMEN'S RESISTANCE IN AUTHORITARIAN NEOLIBERAL REGIMES

Alya (Turkey)

In the three years I have known Alya, she has been involved in local activism while struggling to find time to do her PhD research on gendered experiences in environmental movements in coastal rural Turkey. The chequered nature of her research is due to not only her commitment to activism, but also her ill health as well as her need to find funding and time to do her research. She is also holding down a day job. As a result, our direct connection is intermittent, depending on her activities and on her health. Like her research subjects whom she sees as '*yılanın ağzında kuş gibi çığırıyoruz!*'—yelling like a bird in the mouth of a snake—she is overwhelmed by what is happening in Turkey. In an email to me in late 2015, she describes the emotional difficulties of living in an authoritarian neoliberal state:

> These days are hard times to ask if one is fine but I still hope that you are fine. We are living in such conditions that I feel ashamed of 'being fine' or 'being

happy' while people are murdered by the police-state especially in the Kurdish area [where] bodies of refugee children are found at the sea side. I feel ashamed of writing to you about my thesis or anything about me-myself while those things happen in the world and especially in Turkey. When we take some good news about our private lives, when we laugh, when we have fun with friends ... we all continue our daily lives but always with a deep feeling of guilt: While I am doing this, people are dying in the Kurdish area. Everyday we get used to receiving news of 'how many people, women, kids' are killed in Kurdish area; how a mother had to keep her daughter's dead body in the refrigerator as the special forces didn't let her bury. ... It was the first time we tasted hope after the June elections, but then everything got worse and worse.

I was planning to write you ... but as you know, that weekend I woke up with the news of [X] Massacre. Most of the activist people from X will carry this feeling of being guilty in the rest of our lives. ... The people who died at the massacre were mostly the ones coming from other cities; they came with buses from other cities for this protest and waiting for us at the beginning point of the march. ... I felt ashamed ... when I visited the wounded people. ... One of the men lost his leg however he was very strong and telling us that we should keep struggling, ... we met with a mother [of one who died] and she was smiling at us. ...

So within this context, I have been fighting with the ideas: Under these conditions am I selfish to think about the thesis? What is the meaning of getting a PhD while people are dying? Am I just thinking of my personal career while people are thinking of how to save their lives? On the other hand, I am thinking that keeping our daily lives is also a kind of struggle against what terrorism wants to steal from us. ...

With this confusion (of my body and soul) I will try to tell you more.[3]

The pain of her feelings and questioning of what her research is about is reflected in her writing and in her mental and physical uneasiness. Her email describes very poignantly how hard it is to be doing research in the face of authoritarian crackdowns.

In another email she writes:

During and after ... field work I was very depressed. ... This was the first time in my life that a field trip affected me very negatively. ... My feet stepped back. ... I pushed myself to meet with the people and speak with them. ...

And just recently I heard the voice of a bomb from my house where 28 people died. The place where the bomb exploded is a 10 minute walk from my house. ... This is the first time in my life that I began to be afraid to be in the crowded places, to be in the centre of the city. The fear entered into our daily lives.[4]

The pain and emotion is literally felt on her body, her feet dragging and the difficulty of engaging with the subjects of her research is poignant. One contribution Alya wrote for the CIRI research was a chapter for a book written with another colleague about women's organized resistance to abortion laws in the 2000s, a topic selected because they felt the discussion of current activities would be too dangerous. They were right.

In a third email sent in March 2016 she writes:

> When I was having an operation in October ... at the same time academics were issuing a press statement of the petition [Academics for Peace]. ... Now many are threatened. Some are fired, many are still under investigation by their universities.

One of her academic colleagues has contacted me at the ISS. She has been threatened with imprisonment and, worried about her son, now she wanted to leave Turkey. Alya writes about how these threats are having an impact on the bodies of her friends (activists and academics) around her:

> As I told you, the worst is losing our hope. Many of my friends began using anti-depressant pills. We wake up to a day where we are waiting for more bad news, what will happen today, how many kids will die, [wondering] will there be any explosion in the city.

There are many silences here too about her guilt at not being able to do research in these conditions:

> I will send you this e-mail without completing it. With this depressed and confused mood—I will continue to write you about my PhD.[5]

The sense of fear and confusion has not lifted, but has become embedded in the research process and also in our work together. These are very contradictory but real dilemmas for people doing research while living in conditions of crisis, fear and uncertainty.

Saba (Bangladesh)

Another brief but telling fragment from the life of a researcher where body politics in authoritarian regimes places her in direct danger comes from Saba in Bangladesh. I met her four years ago when she was completing her groundbreaking research on heteronormativity in Bangladesh and helped found the SRI group. She and I had many conversations over the last four years about sex, life, love and cats, and under the stories we swapped there was always the desire to go home, but also the awareness that the life she had led out of her country was not going to be possible as a single woman. Her conversations were always full of great passion and ability to describe and analyze the boundaries she was breaking in choosing to be sexually active as a single middle-class woman. Her research reflected this vibrant, intimate, personal and political approach to life. In these last years, my email inbox has filled with Saba's fun messages, selfies and teasing, along with candid worries about struggles with her ill health and social life. A typical missive in May 2015 (congratulating me on joining Facebook) was:

> Hello! long time and not much communication! how are you? freezing in the cold? ...
>
> I am doing alright, just my sugar level is way too high! I don't know how to manage my health and life! Sigh!
>
> Hey, I was wondering if you can send me (again, I know) the book proposal format ..., I seriously want to start that process.
>
> Secondly, any progress with the April plan? ...
>
> I am also very happy that you are on FB! Lovely!
>
> Love.[6]

In all the exuberance of her communication, there is always an edge of difficulty and worry—about her health, her political and home life, and wanting to use her research to make a difference, while recognizing the difficulty of navigating an area that was seen as morally transgressive in a conservative Muslim country. Despite these difficulties, she found success. My visit in 2014 attested that she was well recognized and in demand as a speaker and consultant. She commandeered an impressive number of contacts in professional networks among business and NGO circles and among LGBTQ activists. At a workshop on sexuality I attended, she invited her LGBTQ friends who had started the first (and only) gay magazine in Bangladesh.

That success crumpled in May 2016 when she had to flee within a week due to the brutal murder of those same LGBTQ friends and others in her closest circle. Saba, shaken and afraid, wrote the night her two friends were killed:

> The situation for people like me is very dangerous. My parents are panicked and so am I. I need to leave this country as soon as possible. I don't know what to do. ... Sorry, I am writing to you suddenly and like this, but the situation is really bad. I can't think straight.[7]

Her connections made during her studies and transnational activism enabled her to move quickly. In a letter she drafted, despite her anxiety and having to go into hiding, she describes her work on body politics and the difficulty she was facing:

> The focus of my work and activism is sexual rights and I am a publicly vocal supporter of the LGBTQ rights in Bangladesh. My PhD thesis was the first

one of its kind as I looked into the sexual non-normativities and their practices in Bangladesh, with focus on LGBTQ communities and their relation to the mainstream society. ... Whatever I do is in sharp contrast with social norms but [is] under the umbrella of human rights framework. ... In the past few weeks, LGBTQ community and its supporters (like me) have been living in fear as there is a strong backlash against us, and there has been an environment of fear. Last evening, two of my close friends, leading LGBTQ rights activists were brutally killed by unknown people at their home—and since then, most of us are either in hiding or restraining from all public activities. As a single woman, feminist activist and liberal academic I am in a particularly vulnerable position as my safety and security is in question. I am living in extreme fear, and my family is understandably worried about me. I have been cautioned by friends and people from the community to ... leave the country. ... I have had people from the police coming to my project events (last week) to monitor, which is highly alarming.

In this situation, I am feeling very unsafe and am reaching out to you to find some options to leave the country. ... I hope you can help me find some placement that can help me not only guarantee some safety, but where I can contribute significantly with my expertise.[8]

The Bangladesh government had done nothing to defend its LGBTQ citizens, already marginalized and invisible in the dominant heteronormative society where homosexuality is illegal and single unmarried women are considered social outcasts. Her life now is one of an exile directly due to her research, outspokenness, support and friendship with the LGBTQ community. The sense of responsibility of the ISS for her security is strong, as we are aware of how students like Saba who undertake research on body politics that challenge cultural norms in the apparent safety of the Netherlands can be placed in great danger when they return home.

Raha (Iran)

Another researcher activist based at the ISS who is now in exile is Raha from Iran, a feminist journalist and political activist who was imprisoned for her activism around women's rights. She describes herself as having for years

engaged in women's issues and published several books and many articles in women magazines and websites. My work has led to grave difficulties with the Iranian authorities. After the reformist period in Iran, I have received repeated warrants and notices from the authorities regarding my feminist activities and I was summoned on numerous occasions to various detention centers for investigation. In 2006, while trying to leave the country to attend a training workshop for journalists in X, I was arrested and imprisoned in the [X] Prison. In 2007, I was arrested and imprisoned in [XX] during a training workshop. In 2009, after publishing a critical report on police violence during the Green movement's demonstration, I was arrested and imprisoned in [XX] prison. Since leaving the country in 2010 I have received numerous summons. ... Despite these difficulties, I have continued writing and have published a book and several short stories along with several articles, essays, [and] interviews mostly published in Persian, [as well as] in German, English and French languages.[9]

She told me in harrowing detail her escape as she drove away from her husband and son, just in time to avoid the police and somehow managed to get a plane (not from her home city) to Germany with the help of friends and the support of a sister. She moved to the Netherlands in order to write up her experiences as a scholar, and for the two years that I have worked with her she has courageously faced the knowledge of continuous exile, as her trial was postponed and then held in absentia. She has thrown herself into her work, continuing to maintain a high online presence and also travelling around Europe to speak about the plight of women in Iran. She has engaged in some scholarly studies, hampered by her need to learn English, but has mostly continued her popular writing online in Persian. She defines her feminist body politics—her embodied struggle for women's justice in Iran—as a form of cyberactivism that connects feminists in Iran with those in exile outside the country. For several years her collectively edited website created a space to publish articles (in English and in Persian) on feminism, particularly ones that could not be published inside Iran. While she is physically safe in Europe, in cyberspace she continues to be in danger as the Iranian government frequently hacks into her Facebook account and infiltrates her website, while informing her lawyers that her writing continues to be seditious and harmful to the Iranian state. So while North American and European feminist audiences access her writings—for example, a recent piece on the erotic feelings of breastfeeding has been published in three languages—such pieces have led to the enforced closure of her website and more years added to her pending prison sentence (five years imprisonment on return to Iran).

She deeply misses her country and her compatriots. This sadness and her struggle to cope with it led to several illnesses including depression, and needing to have operations on both carpel muscles in her hands to combat repetitive strain injury due to her frequent typing. In the many conversations that we have had online and offline, she has shown untiring generosity, sharing her great skills in food, music and storytelling. Her conversations are full of this courage and deep sadness:

> I am wondering why several of my close friends have passed away one by one in the 4 years since I have left home. It's not due to our age but it is due to our time. ...

The last one was [a woman who studied at ISS]. ... She brought us all her modern capacities and experiences from western feminism. ... Finally she was one of the most beautiful women activist in our movement who has passed away on Saturday morning. ... It is heavy for me to tolerate this sadness far from my tribe.[10]

Reflecting on another loss of a young woman relative in Germany, she writes in an email about how lives in exile feel directly the impact of the authoritarian regime of Iran:

All of the disasters are related to the dictatorship of Iran, do you know why?

Let me tell you: My cousin is an artist. 14 years ago he left the art university in Iran to protest the governmental control and limitations of teaching art. ... They left so the daughter could have a good education, she was the best student in her gymnasium. ... Then she contracted cancer 3 years ago. ... Yesterday morning, she passed away in her father's arms. ... For me it is another story of exile. She knew that her father was not happy to live away from his homeland, he was always angry and his daughter felt it in her body. ... Anyway it's life and I am going tomorrow to her funeral rather than to her graduation party.[11]

In telling me about her activism for Iranian women's political rights around Europe, she has shared personal as well as political doubts and concerns. In her rooms full of the small items she could bring from Iran and the gifts from the diaspora, often over delicious meals, she speaks of the contradictions in her life. She poignantly describes her struggle to juggle her research on cyberfeminism; her journalistic writing, interviews and talks on the political situation in Iran; the estrangement from her family; and the outcome of her trial and ill health.

I have been thinking about my [current] identity, it has led to a lot of loss and pain. ... After 15 months, now I find myself as I am. I mean I am an emigrant diaspora feminist and activist who wants strongly to continue her activities now out of Iran. My new homeland is where I will be able to be independent, where I can develop my capacity, where I find a job, and [continue with] my writing and my activity as I did.

Now, with this new identity, everything is much clearer for me. ... I am willing to continue our research, I am proud of our collaboration. ... I came back this morning. Life is continuing as usual. This afternoon, I was interviewed by a ... radio and website about Iranian parliamentary election. ... There is a big discussion among Iranian feminists.[12]

She has consistently raised the problems of Iranian people while in the Netherlands, writing about women prisoners and mothers of small children, many of them her friends, trying to overcome the guilt of not being with them—she experienced this as both a personal and political dilemma, felt very clearly on her body, in her ill health and bouts of depression. In one email she wrote:

> Having an emotional and also rational conversation with you, I am improving my feelings regarding my situation. However I'm not sure about my psychological health but after talking with you, I am encouraged to focus on my main dilemma [loss of her family] even though it is a personal problem. However 'the personal is political'!

In Sisterhood.[13]

Gita (Indonesia)

'Personal is political' was also a phrase used often by Gita, an Indonesian student activist who did her master's at the ISS. While doing research she also found ways to continue her activism in the Netherlands, volunteering to help a women's abortion help service in Amsterdam, a connection she continues to cultivate after she has returned home to work in a legal rights NGO.

Her masters' thesis focused on embodied engagement of women, labour, LGBTQ and anti-corruption activists in the public protests around Bundaran Hotel Indonesia, Jakarta. The square was the only place protests were allowed officially at the time she was doing the research (now it is illegal again). She explored the experiences of four different groups of activists (women's rights, LGBTQ, anti-corruption and health groups) using Bundaran HI as a public space looking at subjectivities, gender relations and embodied experiences. She was interested in how, in an authoritarian neoliberal regime, activist groups saw Bundaran HI as an important place in their ongoing struggle for democracy, even if it was a constrained and monitored space. During the process of writing the thesis and since her return home, we have had some interesting exchanges about how to do embodied thinking as a methodological approach when writing about movement protests. One of her essays was a fascinating look at the billboard images of women around Jakarta and the ways those images related to the ability of young women to access different health services.

During her research on the activities of movements in Bundaran HI, she shared candidly the difficulty of being able to listen and learn from what her discussions and observations reveal, below the surface of what people described. In one email to me she writes:

> I am confused about how to understand the gender relations from the interviews. A question that comes often: 'Is it enough for a thesis?' Most of them said that each gender has the same opportunity and being treated equally.

On the other hand, she explored gendered differences in her observations:

> Gay, lesbian and HIV activist groups worry about security (using masks so they won't be recognized as people with AIDS). They also only invite their circle to come [to the protests in the square] just to be safe. Transgenders instead are highly public, they aim to entertain (with shows, carnivals, aerobic display) during the protest. LGBTQ are concerned about their safety in the square also because it is close to the base camp of the [right-wing] fundamentalists. Women rights protesters are concerned that they can be harassed in the square and don't feel protected as the security [from the government] are men.

As she went deeper into the research, she started to look at the different appearances and emotions—responses of families as well as other activists to what people are doing in the square. She also shared that many of the women found attending the protests intimidating:

> I want to include in the thesis reflective writing about intimidation. ... I feel it is important because it is not only me who has experienced similar things. When I have discussions with some of the activists, some of them told me that intimidation is an obstacle to women joining the movements. ... However, at the same time, I am also afraid that I take it too personally.[14]

This, we concluded together, was indeed gender power relations at play that were not acknowledged earlier. Personal feelings and emotions and the embodied thinking of the thesis led to a very rich piece of work full of insights about gender relations among mostly young 'progressive' people in Jakarta—yet it was difficult to shape this into a format that was considered valid knowledge in academe. In one of her last emails after having completed her MA successfully, she continues to bridge the academic and popular divide as part of a creative team of an NGO: 'I am trying to figure out how to bring my research to the public, [though] not in academic books'.[15] She is now collaborating with artists and networking with activists in Indonesia, writing short stories as well as doing research on abortion in Indonesia based on data she has access to from a Netherlands-based NGO.

Maria (Mexico)

Maria visited the ISS from Mexico while working on her dissertation on women defending their place in a rural area on the margins of the city of Guadalajara—an area marked by clan violence and environmental degradation. Using contextual, dialogical and auto-reflexive methodologies she analyzed how 'body, home, community and public social space are altered or re-configured in the women's activities in their cooperative'. The pollution of the rivers on which they depend is due to 'illegal discharges of heavy metals and other toxic substances from factories and agro-industries, that, combined with poor air quality and the lack of basic services as potable water, sewage system and garbage recollection services, are the causes of a variety of respiratory, skin, renal and cancerous diseases' (Unpublished paper 2015).

She was deeply concerned about the impact of the socio-environmental conflict experienced by the community due to government's and companies' neglect and disregard of environmental and health policies as well as the domination of drug cartels (who are closely linked to local police). Her work takes the body as the starting point for understanding the daily struggles of women and her connection to them as a researcher. She describes how the body is considered a political and central scenery that connects all the spheres of social life; it reflects and communicates, with visible and invisible marks, its experiences and the power relations, practices, discourses and institutions that shape it and its environment. Bodies as places talk about the objectified and subjectified forms of culture that construct them (Unpublished paper 2015).

She shares how embodied thinking led to the scrutiny of her own role as a researcher:

When I arrived [at the research site] and met the women I was shocked and partially disappointed because of their simple humanity. They did not resemble the heroines I read about or saw on documentary films. Now this first illusion shames me. They became my heroines exactly because of their humanity. Resisting is not easy, it is contradictory, conflictual. ... Resisting hurts. (Unpublished paper 2015)

We spent time discussing this difficulty of embodied thinking—made sharper by her former ambition to be a professional dancer where the demands on the body are great and by a diagnosis during her stay that she had a major health problem. We shared not only our different research approaches, but also different life experiences including the uncertainty and pressures of a neoliberal university environment while wanting to be responsible towards the people we write about.

Her emails on her return to Mexico have continued this conversation—oscillating between her own embodied existence, her diagnosis and its implications on her lifestyle and how to move into a competitive working environment after she was offered a job at her university while continuing to work in solidarity with the women of her research. She writes:

My health is better. ... It can be treated but it has been a little hard for me to process that it can't be cured. ... I decided to cool down this year so I have time to adjust to my new diet and exercise routine and to learn how to relax. ... It's harder than I imagined, most of all because of the institutional environment, the politics and the really tough competition involved.

Later she speaks of the increasing pressure and how she is learning to cope in an embodied and emotional way with the pressures of her new research work. A recent email states:

Currently I have two jobs and the responsibilities have increased so I'm always running from place to place. My project at the university is growing and I got a second job at a film studio. ... I was potentially facing around 4 months of unemployment a year because of vacation periods, and I was kind of terrified because in January the administration almost closed my project. ... The working conditions are getting worse and young people are the ones resenting it the most.
    ... I've had to make hard choices and try to decide what to do next in order to feel complete and to keep myself healthy; but I've been so busy trying to keep myself afloat that I've neglected some of the things that get me in touch with my essence. Maybe it's just the rhythm this system imposes on all of us. ... I don't like it.
    [My new research project] interweaves with our daily lives, and the fears and questions that emerge from them, especially because of the life stories. ... I have learned to bond [so] we can hear, see, feel, understand and support each other. ...
    [I am writing a] paper about the emotional and socio-affective dimension of the defense of places led by [the women in the earlier project].
    I also have to exercise every day and I'm doing yoga, which has helped me relax and 'live in the moment', it has been great for introspection and self-confidence.[16]

For Maria, doing research within an authoritarian neoliberal regime and the strain of competition have an immediate impact on her body as well as on her relations with others around her. As she wrote to me earlier about her experience with the women's collective:

My experience ... has led me to recognize my own humanity, my physical and emotional vulnerability, and to assume it with its imperfections, but also with its potentials. I have been able to strip myself from the masks I have had to put on according to the role I played and discovered that the mask I found hardest to take off is the one that helped me to hide, especially as a researcher: that of a vulnerable, emotional, mortal and human body. ... This is a major challenge because it demands assuming responsibilities, exposing and stripping oneself, being vulnerable, complex, and contradictory and embracing [thereof].[17]

These narratives speak of struggles of resistance against neoliberalism from the position of the intimate, personal and political. These are the unspoken 'obvious' truths of doing research, doing feminism, surviving and living in neoliberal regimes. The difficulty of sleeping, the feeling of guilt at survival, the pain of displacement, the emotion of compassion towards other, the push to keep going even as you find it hard to sleep, or experience ill health and the stress on your body. The continual questioning of whether bearing witness as an engaged activist and researcher is possible or safe is another part of the resistance against the disciplining of neoliberal regimes. In recording these 'in-between' conversations, we aim to break the silence in academic research over the discomforts felt when researchers challenge the dominant message that there is nothing to be done about the violence and the economic and political oppression of authoritarian neoliberal regimes. These fragments of embodied thinking help us understand better the depth of resistance to authoritarian neoliberalism, and open up space for a wider understanding of what constitutes valued and validated knowledge in academe.

CONCLUSION: CONTESTED PLACES OF
EMBODIED RESISTANCE—ACADEME

In conclusion, I reassert why embodied thinking in research on sexuality and gender can be seen as knowledge that helps us resist and redefine neoliberalism. Emotional engagement and connection, and commitments to activism are not rewarded in a neoliberal environment. Speaking about bodies across cultures and histories requires a different kind of research approach that is difficult to valorize within the disciplining process of academe. Embodied thinking helps us conceptualize an epistemology of resistance and emancipation that can counter the anatomies of dispossession and violence in the age of neoliberalism. Researching and acknowledging the particular and the connected challenges of feminists located in various geopolitical sites around the world opens up spaces that expose informational capitalism, the Walmartization of production, the informational state, surveillance and moral panic of the current neoliberal order. In seeking to recover subjugated knowledge, feminist writing is a political and epistemological challenge to neoliberal capitalist order. Praxis-based knowledge and reflexivity on their embedded position within the neoliberal regime enables feminists to generate embodied knowledge and interpretations of the world that make visible the struggles and violence they experience.

Making visible the intimate experiences of resistance and personal struggles in doing research can lead directly to violence and exile, as the stories above show. These stories directly confront the idea of research as neutral and apolitical product and show how research is part and parcel of a process of resistance. By recognizing that the subject of research has a body—and emotions, cares, particular histories, gendered life cycles, health, illness—we valorize the ordinary and everyday that can be recognized by all of us as determining our embodied and lived thinking. To bring the embodied experience back into research, we restore the sense that our fleshly intimate feelings of our bodies do count and shape our research processes. We position ourselves as researchers beyond the rational mind and, in a profound way, the actors of our own research and activism. We open the space for a deep critique of the objectivity of academic knowledge in neoliberal regimes and reclaim what has been produced as absent (non-normative knowledge, bodies, forms of being). It allows us to take the perspective of marginalized subjects, including feminist activists struggling to do research about their own activism and subjective experiences.

As Carty and Mohanty point out, 'The neoliberal state is pernicious for women's organizing because it is so adept at appropriating the discursive elements of those struggles and undermining the actual attempts to forge a politics of change' (Carty and Mohanty 2015: 84–5). Feminist 'counter vigilance' that recognizes the possibilities of discursive strategies to affect cultural and political change includes writing about the difficulties, contradictions and emotions felt on the body in different struggles. In such a 'productive acknowledgement of complicity' (Spivak 1999: XII), feminist writing positions women not as 'passive victims of neoliberal seductions' (Fraser 2013) but rather as subjects who are able to write about the difficulties of the struggles and contradictions of resistances. They have, as Sara Ahmed states, 'a great burden in re-positioning and reconciling' the imperfect and incomplete victories against neoliberal order of things (Ahmed quoted in Carty and Mohanty 2015: 88).

Neoliberalism and new developmentalism (Pradella and Marois 2015) continue to endure, but there are innovative ways of resisting, including ways in which activist researchers identify the cracks—even at the risk of their own liberty—and make changes at the everyday level. Embodied thinking is one strategy that can help us question and unmake the hegemonic worldview of neoliberal capitalism, via 'new narratives, new ways of thinking and doing' (Escobar 2012: 2).

NOTES

1. Thank you to the five women who agreed so readily for me to share our conversations in this chapter. Thank you also to my colleagues in the ISS Civic Innovation Research Initiative, in particular, Constance Dupuis, Silke Heumann, Rosalba Icaza, Karin Astrid Siegmann and Gina Vargas. The quoted conversations have been mildly edited for clarity.

2. Two large public events were held at the ISS in The Hague in 2013: Intercultural Dialogue (ICD) on Sexuality, Reproductive Health and Rights in Development: 'Going beyond the comfort zone' (June 2013) and the 'Theories and practice in civic innovation: Building bridges among politics, markets and gender/sexuality' (October 2013).

3. Personal correspondence (November 2015).

4. Personal correspondence (January 2015).

5. Personal correspondence (February 2016).

6. Personal correspondence (May 2015).

7. Personal correspondence (April 2016).

8. Personal correspondence (April 2016).

9. Personal correspondence (November 2014).

10. Personal correspondence (April 2015).

11. Personal correspondence (October 2015).

12. Personal correspondence (January 2016).

13. Personal correspondence (May 2015).

14. Personal correspondence (July 2014).

15. Personal correspondence (4 May 2016).

16. Personal correspondence (May 2016).

17. Personal correspondence (September 2015).

BIBLIOGRAPHY

Ahmed S (2014) *The Cultural Politics of Emotion*, second edition. Edinburgh: Edinburgh University Press.

Arashiro Z and Barahona M (eds) (2015) *Women in Academia Crossing North–South Borders: Gender, Race and Displacement*. Lanham, MD: Lexington Books.

Biekart K, Harcourt W and Knorringa P (eds) (2016) *Exploring Civic Innovation for Social and Economic Transformation*. Abingdon: Routledge.

Bordo S (1993) *Unbearable Weight: Feminism, Western Culture, and the Body*. Berkeley, CA: University of California Press.

Brown W (2015) *Undoing the Demos: Neoliberalism's Stealth Revolution*. New York: Zone.

Butler J (1993) *Bodies That Matter*. London: Routledge.

Carty L and Mohanty CT (2015) Mapping transnational feminist engagements: Neoliberalism and the politics of solidarity. In: Baksh R and Harcourt W (eds) *The Oxford Handbook on Transnational Feminist Movements*. Oxford: Oxford University Press, 82–115.

Centeno MA and Cohen JN (2012) The arc of neoliberalism. *Annual Review of Sociology* 38(1): 317–340.

Escobar A (2012) *Encountering Development: The Making and Unmaking of the Third World*. Princeton, NJ: Princeton University Press.

Fraser N (2013) *Fortunes of Feminism: From State-Managed Capitalism to Neoliberal Crisis*. London: Verso.

Grewal I and Kaplan C (1994) *Scattered Hegemonies: Postmodernity and Transnational Feminist Practices*. Minneapolis: University of Minnesota Press.

Grosz L (1994) *Volatile Bodies: Towards Corporeal Feminism*. Bloomington, IN: Indiana University Press.

Harcourt W (2009) *Body Politics in Development: Critical Debates in Gender and Development*. London: Zed.

Harcourt W (2014) The future of capitalism: A consideration of alternatives. *Cambridge Journal of Economics* 38(6): 1307–1328.

Harcourt W, Heumann S and Radjavi M (2016) Introduction. In: Harcourt W (ed) *Bodies in Resistance Gender Politics in the Age of Neoliberalism*. Basingstoke: Palgrave Macmillan.

Harcourt W, Icaza R and Vargas V (2016) Exploring embodiment and intersectionality in transnational feminist activist research. In: Biekart K, Harcourt W and Knorringa P (eds) *Exploring Civic Innovation for Social and Economic Transformation*. Abingdon: Routledge.

Harding S (1991) *Whose Science? Whose Knowledge? Thinking from Women's Lives*. Ithaca, NY: Cornell University Press.

Hartmann B (1995) *Reproductive Rights and Wrongs: The Global Politics of Population Control*, revised edition. Boston, MA: South End Press.

Icaza R and Vazquez R (2016) The coloniality of gender as a radical critique of developmentalism. In: Harcourt W (ed) *The Palgrave Handbook on Gender and Development: Critical Engagements in Feminist Theory and Practice*. Basingstoke: Palgrave Macmillan, 62–76.

Mohanty C (2003) *Feminism without Borders: Decolonizing Theory, Practicing Solidarity*. Durham, NC: Duke University Press.

Petchesky RP (2002) *Global Prescriptions: Gender Health and Human Rights*. London: Zed Books in association with UNRISD.

Peterson VS (1992) *Gendered States: Feminist (Re)visions of International Relations Theory*. Boulder, CO: Lynne Rienner.

Rose G (1997) Situating knowledges: positionality, reflexivities and other tactics. *Progress in Human Geography* 21(3): 305–320.

Shildrick M (1997) *Leaky Bodies and Boundaries: Feminism, Postmodernism and (Bio)ethics*. London: Routledge.

Shildrick M and Price J (1998) *Vital Signs: Feminist Reconfigurations of the Bio/logical Body*. Edinburgh: Edinburgh University Press.

Spivak G (1987) *In Other Worlds: Essays in Cultural Politics*. New York: Methuen.

Spivak G (1999) *A Critique of Postcolonial Reason: Toward a History of the Vanishing Present*. Cambridge, MA: Harvard University Press.

Tamale S (ed) (2011) *African Sexualities: A Reader*. Oxford: Pambazuka Press.

Underhill-Sem Y (2005) Bodies in places, places in bodies. In: Harcourt W and Escobar A (eds.) *Women and the Politics of Place*. Bloomfield, CT: Kumarian Press.

Vargas V (2005) Feminisms and the World Social Forum: Space for dialogue and confrontation. *Development* 48(2): 107–110.

Wieringa S and Sivori H (eds) (2012) *The Sexual History of the Global South: Sexual Politics in Africa, Asia and Latin America*. London: Zed Books.

Chapter 5

The Right to Starve

Hunger, Discipline and Labour Market Restructuring under Authoritarian Neoliberalism

Sébastien Rioux[1]

Hunger is at the core of capitalist social relations. It constitutes a key disciplinary moment in a system of exploitation based on the separation of direct producers from their means of subsistence. Labour struggles and social democratic parties have historically worked to reduce poverty, health inequalities and food insecurity by building up increasingly comprehensive welfare states designed to mitigate the fundamental contradiction between capital accumulation and progressive (let alone stable) conditions of social reproduction of the working classes. With nearly 800 million people suffering from chronic hunger globally in 2014–2016 (FAO 2015), growing food insecurity in advanced capitalist countries highlights the uneven, yet global, nature of the current subsistence crisis. In the United States, for instance, millions of American working class people are learning the hard way that the foundation of this brave new world is—and has always been—based on their freedom to starve.

The reality of 'want amid plenty' is perhaps one of the most painful ironies of the United States (Poppendieck 2000, 2014). While the United States stands as the most developed agricultural superpower, producing enough food to feed its entire population many times over, it has seen food insecurity rising at alarming rates over the last few years. Indeed, the financial crisis of 2007–2008 made visible contradictions that had been simmering for decades, showing the extent to which social and economic stability have been severely undermined during the period of neoliberal capitalism. Falling real wages as well as high rates of unemployment and underemployment have dramatically widened the gap between rich and poor, entrenching poverty and food insecurity even further, and severely weakening people's economic stability. The result has been a substantial rise in inequality, with total household wealth for the top 0.1 per cent increasing from 7 per cent in the late 1970s to 22 per cent in 2012. Indeed, 'the wealthiest 160,000 families [the top 0.1 per cent] own as much wealth as the poorest 145 million families, and that wealth is about 10 times as unequal as income' (Matthews 2014). By the time the financial meltdown happened in 2008, conditions were ripe for a major crisis in social reproduction to emerge. And as record numbers experienced the strong arms of poverty, the contradiction became increasingly harder to miss: widespread hunger and food insecurity in the country producing the cheapest food basket in the world's history.

Building on the work of Stuart Hall and Nicos Poulantzas, Ian Bruff has argued that we are witnessing the rise of authoritarian neoliberalism, which is not 'merely the exercise of brute coercive force' but also rooted in 'the increasing frequency with which constitutional and legal changes, in the name of economic "necessity", are seeking to reshape the purpose of the state and associated institutions' (Bruff 2014: 115). While Bruff does not deny that neoliberalism has always contained authoritarian tendencies, he argues that the latter have become more prominent since the global economic crisis of 2007–2008, especially in the European Union (Bruff 2016). Yet given that different countries or regional entities have different institutionalized histories of class struggles, authoritarian neoliberalism is by definition a deeply spatial concept whose history ultimately rests on a varied, uneven political geography, which is rooted in the ability of social and political forces to hamper, resist or repress the authoritarian tendencies of the neoliberal project. This chapter explores the uneven spatio-temporal development of authoritarian neoliberalism through a study of the restructuring of public welfare and food assistance programmes in the United States, as concrete manifestations of the state's ability to implement administrative and legal mechanisms designed to entrench class inequality through the creation, management and maintenance of a flexible labour market. More specifically, I argue that the disciplining effect of hunger and food insecurity has been, and remains, key to the imposition of neoliberal labour market restructuring in the United States.

The social dislocation of the post-war class compromise was accomplished at the price of a deep recession, soaring rates of unemployment, poverty and homelessness, and the decline of the nation's standard of living. Meanwhile, the crushing of organized resistance and the effective delinking between real wages and productivity—combined with waves of industrial delocalization abroad, new investments in labour-saving technology, deflationary measures and mechanization at home—paved the way to heightened capital accumulation. Neoliberalism is first and foremost a political project to restore class power and capital profitability (Duménil and Lévy 2004; Harvey 2005; Bellamy Foster and Magdoff 2009; Mattick 2011; McNally 2011; Panitch and Gindin 2012). Central to this political project was the restructuring of public welfare towards harsh and punitive workfare policies, designed to force a low-wage economy down the throat of an increasingly hungry American working class.

This chapter explores the management of domestic hunger in the post-war era and the production of a nationwide crisis in social reproduction. Part one documents the 'discovery' of poverty, hunger and malnutrition as national issues, and the ensuing expansion of public welfare institutions, including hunger-relief programmes, in the 1960s and 1970s. Part two considers the rise of neoliberalism as a set of disciplinary practices based on the enforcement of work norms and self-reliance through workfare policies. Part three explores the politics of hunger and malnutrition since the global economic crisis, and the dramatic rise in the depth and scope of food insecurity.

THE ROOTS OF PUBLIC WELFARE

The post-war industrial era has been celebrated for its remarkable social and economic achievements: high rates of economic growth, rising real wages linked to productivity growth, Keynesian macro-economic policies to secure countercyclical economic development, rising standards of living, low unemployment rates and a more interventionist welfare state. Liberal economist John Kenneth Galbraith praised these achievements in *The Affluent Society* (1958). Although Galbraith did not deny that poverty, hunger and malnutrition still existed, he argued that they belong to a past that was fast disappearing. They were remnants, pockets of misery soon to be eradicated by the objective forces of economic growth. Like many others, Galbraith did not seem to realize that this particular period of unprecedented prosperity was exceptional in capitalist history, and that rates of growth of this magnitude were premised upon the reconstruction of an industrial world so efficiently destroyed by the Second World War. In the United States, the triumphalist nature of this position was not only the necessary rhetorical arsenal behind Cold War propaganda, it was also based on the generalization of white suburban life as representative of the nation's standards of living (Galbraith 1976).

Against Galbraith's condescending and unfounded optimism, Michael Harrington's *The Other America* (1962) painted an entirely different canvas, where chronic poverty was the reality for some 40–50 million people. Like Dickens's vitriolic critique of the Victorian era, Harrington's depiction of a vast, 'invisible' economic underworld in the richest and most powerful nation on Earth made it clear that the rising tide of capitalist development was not lifting all boats. With hundreds of riots erupting in American cities between 1965 and 1968, 'the other America' made its presence felt and forced itself into mainstream politics. There was effectively something rotten in a system where two nations lived side-by-side, one celebrated and advertised, the other ignored and hidden. President Kennedy's more interventionist stance had already secured the expansion of food distribution and established a pilot Food Stamp Program in 1961. Yet it was Lyndon B. Johnson who would launch an 'unconditional war on poverty' during his 1964 State of the Union message. President Johnson's dream of a Great Society was constituted through an ambitious reform programme based on the elimination of poverty and racial injustice as its two main goals. The Civil Rights Act of 1964, the Economic Opportunity Act of 1964, the Social Security Act of 1965 (which authorized Medicare and allowed for the creation of Medicaid the following year) and the Housing and Urban Development Act of 1965 were key legislations supporting an emerging welfare state. In addition, the Food Stamp Act of 1964, the Child Nutrition Act of 1966 and the School Breakfast Program in 1966 proved essential to establishing an increasingly comprehensive food assistance programme.

While many had been shocked to learn about the existence of mass poverty, they could still feel reassured by Harrington's opinion that 'the other America is not impoverished in the same sense as those poor nations where millions cling to hunger as a defense against starvation. This country has escaped such extremes' (1971: 1). Arguably, America was ill-prepared for what was about to follow, as the country discovered the reality of chronic hunger and malnutrition. The scourge became a national issue in 1967 when senators Robert F. Kennedy of New York and Joseph Clark of Pennsylvania came to Mississippi to hold hearings as part of the Senate Subcommittee on Employment, Manpower, and Poverty. During these hearings the senators were eyewitnesses to the horrors of a starving nation. Following these revelations, the Field Foundation, which had already been involved in various projects to help the poor and hungry, decided to sponsor a trip to study the health and well-being of the population in seven counties in the state of Mississippi. 'The stark details of horribly diseased children, suffering from severe dietary deficiencies and hopelessly inadequate diets, were vividly captured in a report they presented in early June, on "Children in Mississippi"' (Kotz 1969: 9). The conditions of the children were so preoccupying that team members found it difficult to believe that they were examining American children.

The President's National Advisory Commission on Rural Poverty, which had been established in September 1966 by President Johnson, issued its report *The People Left Behind* in September 1967. Some 14 million Americans lived in the abyss of hunger and widespread malnutrition, unemployment and underemployment, low income, dilapidated housing, low educational levels and severely inadequate healthcare. The committee recognized in the opening lines of its report that the consequences of rural poverty 'have swept into our cities, violently. The urban riots during 1967 had their roots, in considerable part, in rural poverty. A high proportion of the people crowded into city slums today came there from rural slums' (Breathitt 1967: IX). While it might have been an agile political manoeuvre to bring attention to the issue, it failed to acknowledge that, whether rural or urban, the core problem was poverty on a mass scale. And the most dramatic report of the state of hunger in the United States had yet to come.

In 1968 the Citizens' Board of Inquiry into Hunger and Malnutrition in the United States published its report, *Hunger, U.S.A.*, which sought to ascertain whether earlier findings were prevalent at the national level. 'We have found concrete evidence of chronic hunger and malnutrition in every part of the United States where we have held hearings or conducted field trips,' the board reported (Citizen's Board 1968: 16). The report documented the effects of grossly inadequate diets on the prevalence of anaemia, growth retardation such as low heights and weights, protein deficiencies, parasitic infection, worms, viruses and bacterial diseases, low resistance to infection, high infant mortality, shortened life expectancy[2] and nutritional diseases such as scurvy, rickets, blindness and pellagra. The report also gave chilling evidence about the behavioural and psychological problems associated with hunger and malnutrition, including listlessness, apathy and permanent brain damage, and showed awareness of social issues associated with hunger and malnutrition, including distrust, frustration, alienation, withdrawal, social dislocation and a heightened sense of injustice and revolt. It conservatively estimated that at least 10 million Americans were affected by hunger and malnutrition, most of which were Native Americans, African Americans, Appalachian whites and Mexican Americans. The report also criticized the limitations of various food assistance programmes, including the Food Stamp Program, the National School Lunch Program, the School Breakfast Program and the School Milk Program. Yet it was truly with the 1968 CBS documentary *Hunger in America* that millions of Americans realized that hunger and starvation were alive and well in the most advanced capitalist society.

Shocked by these revelations, the Senate appointed a Select Committee on Nutrition and Human Needs in 1968. From 1968 to 1977, the committee played a key role in crafting legislation that expanded food assistance for families, children and the elderly. It was central in dramatically expanding and improving the Food Stamp Program in 1972, notably by making the programme mandatory on the states and establishing national eligibility standards. The committee was also responsible for the creation of the Special Supplemental Food Program for Women, Infants, and Children (WIC), as well as various child food assistance programmes and nutrition programmes for the elderly. Between 1969 and 1983, annual federal expenditures for food assistance increased from $1 billion to $19 billion (President's Task Force 1984: X). The

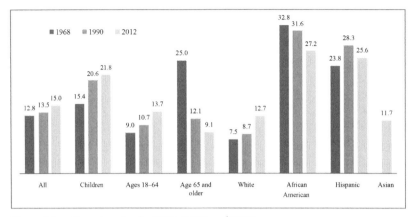

Figure 5.1.   Poverty rates in 1968, 1990 and 2012
Source: IRP 2016

Field Foundation's team revisited the question in 1977 and 'concluded that although some hunger remained evident, its manifestations had become more subtle and, therefore, more difficult to identify' (Nestle and Guttmacher 1992: 19S; see also Kotz 1979). Within the space of a decade, immense progress had been accomplished. The US poverty rate fell from 22.2 per cent in 1960 to 13 per cent in 1980 (Crooks 1995: 58). And although the painful reality of poverty and hunger remained all too real, a better future seemed to be on the horizon.

FROM WELFARE TO WORKFARE

If the election of Reagan in 1980 marked the end of Johnson's 'war on poverty' and Nixon's 'war on hunger', the Omnibus Budget Reconciliation Act of 1981 effectively declared war on welfare. In his first budget, Reagan managed to slash government spending and programmes 'designed to help the poor and the ill, young and old alike' (Trattner 1999: 365). By the mid-1980s the percentage of poverty-stricken Americans rose above 15 per cent, the highest rate since the mid-1960s. Reagan's significant reductions in public welfare contributed actively to the formation of a new class of poor that was visiting emergency food and shelter providers for the first time in their lives. Mounting inflation in the 1970s followed by neoliberal policies after 1980 undermined the working-class's purchasing power and standards of living. Average weekly earnings (in 1982–1984 dollars) fell from $341.73 in 1972 to $281.84 in 1982 to $266.43 in 1992, before reaching $288 in 2002 and $298.53 in 2014 (ERP 2015: 402). Figure 5.1 shows a secular trend towards rising poverty rates between 1968 and

2012. Of particular importance is the growing impoverishment of the working population and its direct impact on the number of children living in poverty. The increase of poverty between 1990 and 2012, in the context of rising average weekly earnings, highlights the extent to which economic inequalities are on the rise in the United States. As neoliberalism continues to increase the ranks of the working poor, it also concentrates wealth in the hands of a small economic elite of well-paid professionals.

Intended to be short-lived, the growth of emergency food systems proved to be anything but temporary, as the need for soup kitchens and food banks expanded dramatically in the 1980s (Brown and Pizer 1987; Clancy and Bowering 1992). Contemporaries knew all too well that the progress made in the 1970s to eliminate hunger 'through a combination of economic growth and expanded government program' was fast receding (Brown 1988: 99). 'The rapid increases in all program costs show the nation's growing dependence on these programs,' wrote Harrell R. Rodgers (1982: 57), 'a dependence brought about largely by the nation's economic problems in the 1970s and early 1980s. As inflation and unemployment increased simultaneously, the costs of social welfare expenditures increased greatly.' Indeed, 'federal programs for aiding the poor and the elderly absorbed less than 6 per cent of Gross National Product in 1962—roughly $100 billion in 1982 dollars. Today we spend roughly $430 billion on such programs, more than 12 per cent of the GNP' (President's Task Force 1984: 2). Reagan's cuts sought to limit the spiralling costs of existing welfare programmes at the very moment when they were most important.

In September 1983, Reagan established the President's Task Force on Food Assistance, an advisory committee whose function was to analyze existing food assistance programmes and make recommendations on how they could be improved. The task force issued its report in January 1984. It made an important distinction between two interpretations of hunger (President's Task Force 1984: XIV): 'The word hunger is used by health professionals to indicate physiological problems of undernutrition; it is used by most lay people to indicate also someone's inability—even occasionally—to obtain adequate amounts of food.' Regarding the first definition, the committee found 'little systematic evidence of widespread or increasing undernutrition in the U.S.'. Regarding the second definition, the report confirmed 'the continued existence of hunger', yet concluded that given current indicators and survey methods, the number of hungry individuals could not be documented.[3] Moreover, the report maintained that budget cuts had not fundamentally altered food assistance programmes, and that increasing funding levels would not succeed to eliminate the problems of hunger (President's Task Force 1984: 41). In addition, the report endorsed decentralized decision-making and argued for the importance of private and local solutions to the problems of hunger. While the President's Task Force might have been a failure for many progressive voices, it was a blessing for the Reagan administration, not only because it legitimized its course of action, but also because it revealed that the government was unable to document the problem it was creating.

Despite difficulties in measuring hunger, the impact of reductions in welfare spending was real enough (Brown and Allen 1988). The best-known study came from the Physician Task Force on Hunger in America, which issued its national report, *Hunger in America: The Growing Epidemic*, in 1985 as a response to the toothless report of the President's Task Force (Physician Task Force 1985). Defining food insufficiency in relation to economic indicators such as income and poverty, the report estimated that 20 million individuals (12 million children and 8 million adults) were suffering from hunger. As Marion Nestle and Sally Guttmacher (1989: 19S) made clear, however, the report of the Physician Task Force was part of a long series of hunger studies realized in the 1980s, with three subnational hunger studies conducted in 1981, 19 studies in 1982, 31 studies in 1983, 40 studies in 1984 and about 30 studies per year in 1985, 1986 and 1987. Based on their review of state hunger studies, Nestle and Guttmacher concluded that 'the numbers of people in need of welfare and food assistance have greatly increased', further noting that 'the time has come for anti-hunger advocates to assume the additional burden of anti-poverty advocacy and to demand that the federal government reclaim responsibility for the food and welfare of its citizens' (1989: 20S).

Welfare reforms remained firmly on the political agenda throughout the 1980s and the early 1990s. Meanwhile, growing rates of hunger and poverty, as well as the restructuring of the labour market towards greater flexibility amidst an anaemic economic recovery, translated into increased welfare dependency. Governor Bill Clinton's 1992 campaign promise to 'end welfare as we know it' made it clear that the welfare reform initiated by Reagan and pursued by George H. W. Bush was far from over. President Clinton's welfare reform law came in 1996 when he signed the Personal Responsibility and Work Opportunity Reconciliation Act (PRWORA). As the building block of an unapologetic workfare state (Peck 2001), the result of the law was a thorough 'restructuring of the nutritional and social safety nets' (Himmelgreen and Romero-Daza 2012: 107). PRWORA presided over the weakening of the social safety net by sanctioning more stringent eligibility requirements and requiring work in exchange for time-limited assistance. With few exceptions, the law forces recipients to work after two years on assistance. Moreover, the Temporary Assistance for Needy Families (TANF), which was created by the PRWORA to replace the Aid to Families with Dependent Children (AFDC), imposed a five-year lifetime limit for cash aid. The law also transformed people's access to Medicaid, as many in this new army of working poor no longer qualified for medical assistance.

Under the Welfare Indicators Act of 1994, the Department of Health and Human Services (USDHHS) must prepare annual reports to Congress on welfare dependence. Anyone living in a family receiving any amount from the AFDC/ TANF, the Supplemental Nutrition Assistance Program (SNAP) and/or the Supplemental Security Income (SSI) is considered a recipient. Anyone living in a family where AFDC/TANF, SNAP and/or SSI constitute more than 50 per cent of annual income is considered dependent. Figure 5.2 shows recipiency and dependency rates between 1993 and 2012. Three aspects are worth noting. First, it should be emphasized that the rise in recipiency rates after 2000 is taking place in spite of stricter conditions for food stamp eligibility and the 5-year limit placed on TANF. This suggests that recipiency rates systematically underestimate what they seek to measure, either because families are no longer eligible or because stricter conditions exclude them. Testifying on the effects of PRWORA on working families before the Committee on Education and the Workforce of the US House of Representatives in 2001, Heather Boushey (2002) concluded that 'even during the latter years of the boom, many families were unable to maintain stable, full-time employment', further noting that 'wages are too low to enable families to escape poverty and avoid material hardships'. Workfare provisions designed to force people to work for poverty wages have resulted in growing dependency rates, despite increasingly restrictive relief policies. The weakening of people's economic resilience is seen in the rapid growth of recipiency rates, following the financial crisis.

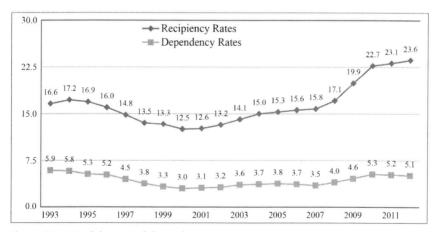

Figure 5.2. Recipiency and dependency rates 1993–2012
Source: USDHHS 2015

Second, TANF is a fixed block grant of money given to the states that have not changed over the years. 'In all but two states', the Center on Budget and Policy Priorities (CBPP) reported in 2015, 'the real (inflation-adjusted) value of TANF cash benefits has fallen since welfare reform's enactment and in the vast majority of states, TANF cash benefits today are worth at least 20 per cent less today [sic] than in 1996.' In addition, the five-year limit placed on TANF means that the programme is providing assistance to fewer and fewer needy families. According to the CBPP, average monthly caseload fell from 4.7 million families in 1996 to 1.7 million families in 2014 (CBPP 2015). If the five-year limit helps to explain relatively stable dependency rates, as people are effectively kicked out of the programme, it also suggests that part of the increase in recipiency rates after 2000—and a fortiori after the global economic crisis—comes from working families in need of TANF for the first time. This further suggests unmet needs on a growing scale amidst rising precarity.

Third and finally, recipiency and dependency rates are measured based on the presence of a limited number of programmes: TANF, SNAP and SSI. This means that key programmes such as the School Breakfast Program, the WIC Program and the National School Lunch Program are not included in determining recipiency and dependency rates. Together, these three observations suggest that recipiency and dependency rates, as measured by the US-DSSH, are both limited and limiting. What Figure 5.2 adequately measures, however, is PRWORA's effectiveness at forcing people off the welfare rolls (dependency rates) while producing a growing class of working poor that is increasingly dependent on restrictive and time-limited assistance programmes (recipiency rates). In this respect, the main achievement of President Clinton's welfare reform was to secure capital's expanded reproduction through workers' widespread economic vulnerability. If anything, the crisis of 2007–2008 brought forward contradictions that had been simmering for decades.

THE GLOBAL ECONOMIC
CRISIS AND ITS AFTERMATH

Growing disparities and market insecurity have been heightened by the global economic crisis, during which average annualized household wealth declined by 25 per cent for the bottom four-fifths, with disproportionally higher impact on the bottom two-fifths, overwhelmingly represented by single mothers and Black and Hispanic households (Allegretto 2011; DeNavas-Walt, Proctor and Smith 2011). Disparities are also shown in the overall share of wealth among every quintile. According to the 2009 American Community Survey from the US Census Bureau, working families in the lowest quintile received 4.8 per cent of total income, with the next four quintiles accounting for 9.9 per cent, 15.4 per cent, 22.6 per cent and 47.3 per cent. This represents an impressive redistribution of wealth at the top of US society, with 60 per cent of the population sharing less than one-third of the total income. Programmes designed during the expansion of the welfare rolls in the 1960s and 1970s have absorbed most of the dramatic rise in human insecurity, even though they have been severely limited by workfare policies.

While food security can be defined as the 'access at all times to enough food for an active, healthy life', food insecurity is conceptualized as an economic and social condition marked by 'the lack of consistent access to adequate food' (Nord 2009: 1, 3). Food insecurity thus refers to a situation whereby members of a household are unable to secure a normal diet. In its most extreme form, severe or prolonged food insecurity may result in hunger. Despite the fact that SNAP—the new federal Food Stamp Program—continues to be the main vector through which food assistance is provided, other programmes have also become increasingly solicited under neoliberalism. While the number of participants in the School Breakfast Program increased from 3.6 to 11.6 million children between 1980 and 2011 (USDA 2012b), the number of participants in the WIC Program grew from 1.9 to 9.0 million during the same period (USDA 2013a). The number of participating children in the National School Lunch Program has also grown rapidly: 7.1 million in 1946–1947, 22 million in 1970, 27 million in 1980, 24 million in 1990 and 31.6 million in 2012 (USDA 2013b). Despite these staggering figures, the US Department of Agriculture (USDA) estimated that 79 per cent of those eligible to participate in SNAP in 2011 were enrolled—compared with 72 per cent in 2009 and 54 per cent in 2002 (Leftin, Eslami and Strayer 2011: 15)—and that only 39 per cent of elderly and 42 per cent of individuals with incomes above the poverty line participated, thus suggesting a much deeper crisis in social reproduction (USDA 2014). Similarly, coverage rates for all participants in the WIC Program have remained relatively stable between 2000 and 2013, oscillating between 57 and 65 per cent (Johnson et al. 2015: D-3).

Meanwhile, Feeding America, a nationwide network of member food banks and emergency kitchens, estimated serving 37 million different people in 2009, an increase of 46 per cent since 2005 (Mabli et al. 2010). Based on a study of more than 62,000 in-person interviews, with clients from its national network as well as from over 37,000 completed questionnaires from its agencies, Feeding America reported that 36 per cent of its clients were from households with one or more adults employed. Among all adult clients, 60.8 per cent were women, 40.3 per cent were non-Hispanic white, 33.6 per cent were non-Hispanic black, 20.5 per cent were Latino or Hispanic, 3.9 per cent were American Indian or Alaskan Native, and 10.9 per cent were non-US citizens. The report also found that 45 per cent of those interviewed described their health as either 'poor' or 'fair', with 29 per cent of households reporting to have at least one household member in poor health. Many food-insecure households reported having to choose between food and other necessities, such as paying for utilities, heating fuel or rent. Of the 37 million people served in 2009, a staggering 14 million were children. One-fifth or more of the child population in 40 states and District of California lived in food-insecure households in 2009. This must be weighed against the fact that research on child health and development consistently indicates that children struggling with improper nutrition and living in food-insecure and food-insufficient households are more likely to experience difficulties such as lower academic achievement, stomachaches, headaches and colds, poorer health, higher hospitalization rates, anaemia, lower physical function, higher chronic health conditions, higher rates of anxiety and depression in school-age children, behavioural problems, depressive disorder and suicidal symptoms in adolescents (Simeon and Grantham-McGregor 1989; Chandler et al. 1995; Nord 2009: 7; Kesari, Handa and Prasad 2010).

Figure 5.3 shows the evolution of food insecurity in the United States between 1998 and 2014. The first part of the graph (left axis) is represented by two areas (very low food security and low food security) whose aggregate represents the total number of food-insecure individuals in the country, from 36.1 million in 1998 to 48.1 million in 2014. During this period, the number of individuals considered to be in a situation of very low food security almost

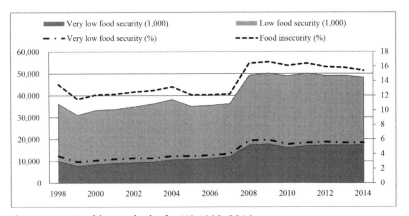

Figure 5.3.   Food insecurity in the US 1998–2014
Source: Coleman-Jensen et al. 2015: 6–7.

doubled, rising from 9.9 to 17.2 million, while those in a low food security state increased from 26.2 to 30.9 million. The second part of the graph (right axis) tackles the issue of food insecurity relative to the population. Food insecurity remained relatively stable, near 12 per cent between 1998 and 2007, and reached 16.6 per cent in 2009 before settling at 15.4 per cent in 2014. The growing prevalence of very low food security—from 3.7 per cent in 1998 to 5.5 per cent in 2014—suggests that food insecurity is becoming more entrenched and difficult to escape for a growing proportion of the population. As shown in Figure 5.3, food insecurity has increased both in absolute and relative terms since the late 1990s.

Another important trend to note is linked to the depth of poverty. Expressed as an income-to-poverty ratio, the depth of poverty measures how close individuals and households are from their poverty threshold. It is no secret that the rise of hunger in America is closely related to the growing number of working poor, which now forms the backbone of the US economy. In 2009, nearly one in three (30.1 per cent) working families earned less than 200 per cent of the official poverty line (Roberts, Povich and Mather 2010–2011). The Institute for Research on Poverty (IRP) estimates that in 2012, 6.6 per cent of all people lived with an income less than 50 per cent of the poverty threshold, 15 per cent under 100 per cent, 19.7 per cent less than 125 per cent, 24.6 per cent less than 150 per cent and 34.2 per cent less than 200 per cent (IRP 2016). Considering that 84 per cent of all client households served by Feeding America had incomes less than or equal to 130 per cent of the federal poverty line and that 16 per cent had an income equal or higher to 131 per cent (Mabli et al. 2010: 136), it seems more than reasonable to suggest that rates of poverty and food insecurity in the United States are underestimated. What this trend towards the ongoing impoverishment of the US society suggests therefore is that more and more people are only one economic downturn away from officially joining the ranks of the poor and food insecure. For about one-third of American families, unexpected expenses, sickness or temporary unemployment would be sufficient to dramatically undermine an already fragile financial situation.

In 2015, the US Census Bureau poverty threshold was $12,331 for one person under the age of 65, and $24,036 for a family unit of four people with two children under 18 years (US Census Bureau 2015). To put this into perspective, the Economic Policy Institute (EPI) has created a Family Budget Calculator to measure 'the income a family needs in order to attain a modest yet adequate standard of living'. Based on the institute's estimate of community-specific costs, one adult with no children would need $32,122 per year to live in Seattle/Bellevue, Washington, while an annual income of $72,274 would be required for a family of four. In Chicago, these amounts would, respectively, be $31,334 and $71,995 (EPI 2015). With 'a modest yet adequate standard of living' placed at almost three times what the federal government considers the poverty threshold, EPI's cost-of-living calculations demonstrate that those living with less than the poverty threshold are already substantially poor. It also suggests that the growing mass of working poor living with less than twice the poverty threshold already live in a chronic state of financial insecurity.

Furthermore, a recent overview of the SNAP by the Congressional Budget Office reveals that most participants in the programme in 2010 lived in households with very low incomes, on average $8,800 per year. The average monthly SNAP benefit per household was $287 or $4.30 per person per day (Congressional Budget Office 2012). In 2012, the maximum SNAP monthly benefit for a family of four amounted to $668 or less than $1.90 per person per meal. SNAP benefits are based on the Thrifty Food Plan (TFP), a minimal cost meal plan articulated around the idea that nutritious and healthy diets are compatible with cheap food. Although the TFP is remarkable for its effort at devising a comprehensive diet out of an unhealthy economic system, the reality is much less rosy as it stubbornly refuses to align itself with the ideals that animate the TFP. Indeed, Feeding America reported that 41 per cent of its client households are also participants in the SNAP. Among households with school-aged children, 62 per cent participate in the federal School Lunch Program and 54 per cent in the School Breakfast Program. Meanwhile, 54 per cent of households with children aged 0–3 year(s) participate in the WIC (Mabli et al. 2010).

In one of the many ironies emanating from the US food system, the USDA itself reported that 58 per cent of emergency kitchen users in 2010 were also participants in the SNAP, therefore undermining its own claim that it is possible to survive on a diet based on the TFP. Moreover, it reported that 80 per cent of SNAP participants had an insufficient intake of zinc and that 61 per cent showed a deficiency in vitamin C (USDA 2012a: 19). Moreover, the TFP is premised upon the rather difficult assumption that poor people have proper cookware and housing facilities to cook large quantities of cheap food. The reality is rather different. Poor people often live in less than appropriate houses or apartments because they cannot afford better housing. Under these circumstances, people often 'choose' to go hungry in order to avoid homelessness, preferring to skip a meal in order to pay for utilities and rent. They therefore submit themselves to the harsh and painful condition that is food deprivation in order to reconcile the contradictions of a system within which the only thing the disciplinary effect of the minimum wage can guarantee is precariousness and food insecurity.

Despite harsh welfare reforms to contain the spiralling costs of public welfare, welfare budgets have dramatically increased under neoliberalism. For instance, the costs associated with SNAP have skyrocketed over the years, rising from $17.1 billion in 2000 to $75.7 billion in 2011. Between 1980 and 2011, the costs of the School Breakfast Program have increased from $287.8 million to $2.9 billion (USDA 2012b), while those associated with the WIC Program rose from $727.7 million to $7.2 billion (USDA 2013a). Meanwhile, total costs for the National School Lunch Program increased from $3.2 billion in 1980 to $11.6 billion in 2012 (USDA 2013b). Given the growing fiscal crisis of the state, the pressure to enact policies contributing to reduce overall federal spending in social security programmes has resulted in the decision to not prolong the temporary Emergency Unemployment Compensation programme beyond 2013. This programme temporarily boosted SNAP benefits by implementing a state-wide waiver on the SNAP time limit.

One of the harshest provisions of the welfare law of 1996 was to limit unemployed childless adults aged 18–49 years without disabilities to three months of SNAP benefits in a 36-month period, unless they worked for at least 20 hours per week or were registered in a qualifying work or training programme. Given that the law did not require states to offer work or training programmes for 20 hours a week, most states simply do not offer such programmes because they are too expensive. In short, basic food assistance is denied to people who are actively searching for a job and will accept a spot in a training programme. The 1996 welfare law allowed states to request a temporary waiver of the three-month limit in areas with persistent high unemployment. Because of the effects of the global economic crisis, nearly every state qualified for a temporary suspension of the SNAP time limit. As a result, the number of able-bodied adults without dependents receiving SNAP benefits increased from 1.1 million in 2008, before the waivers became effective, to 3.9 million adults in 2010 (Zedlewski, Waxman and Gundersen 2012: 3). With unemployment rates now falling, fewer states qualify for the temporary waiver. As a result, the CBPP estimates that between half a million and one million recipients will be cut off in 2016 (Bolen et al. 2016).

The state is balancing its budget on the back of the poor and reinforcing further the neoliberal logic of wealth inequalities and economic hardships. Meanwhile, food banks and other private charities are increasingly solicited to provide hunger relief as the state is increasingly failing to fulfil its role as mediator between labour and capital. It is therefore not surprising that Feeding America, who as we saw, estimated serving 37 million different people in 2009, has come to rely extensively upon the help and contributions of its corporate partners. These partners include, among others, mammoth transnational corporations such as 7-Eleven, Bank of America, Campbell's, Cargill, The Cheesecake Factory, Coca-Cola, ConAgra Foods, Costco, Dannon, Del Monte, General Mills, JPMorgan Chase & Co., Kellogg's, Kraft, Kroger,

Ford Motor Company, Ikea, Monsanto, Morgan Stanley, Nestlé, Pepsico, The Safeway Foundation, Sam's Club, Starbucks Corporation, Sysco, Target, Unilever, Walmart and The Yum-O! Organization. These corporations are among the most powerful businesses worldwide. The corporatization of hunger-relief effort is a particularly troubling aspect of the twenty-first century 'hunger amid plenty'. Not only does it signal what feminist political economists call the privatization of social reproduction (Bakker and Gill 2003; Bakker and Silvey 2008; Bezanson and Luxton 2006; LeBaron and Roberts 2010), but also exposes the limits of the neoliberal state and its unwillingness to mediate the growing contradiction between the power of capital and progressive conditions for social reproduction.

CONCLUSION

For more than 50 years, the United States has tried to reconcile the contradiction between capital and labour through public welfare institutions and programmes. The expansion of the welfare rolls in the 1960s and 1970s, including the implementation of comprehensive food assistance programmes, was fundamental to the rapid fall in hunger and malnutrition rates. While food insecurity remained a considerable problem in the late 1970s, the nation seemed to be heading in a good direction as major progress was realized in mitigating the worst effects of food insecurity. The neoliberal restructuring of the economy was instrumental in reversing the trend towards the betterment of society. Today, food insecurity is a widespread phenomenon that is more costly than ever in spite of grossly underfunded and increasingly overstrained programmes and institutions. The neoliberal assault on the social safety net has restored the conditions of capital profitability, which produces an army of working poor for whom food and economic insecurity have become the norm.

This chapter has argued that the restructuring of the labour market under neoliberalism in the United States was premised upon welfare reforms designed to enforce work norms, restrictive relief policies and time-limited assistance. These measures were effective in large part because they reasserted the right to starve which had been muted by an expansive welfare roll in the 1960s and 1970s. The management of domestic hunger in the United States is a prime example 'that a state's own crisis intensifies at the same time as its strategies of displacement ... seek to stabilize the contradictions and dislocations emanating from socio-economic restructuring without granting material concessions to subordinate social groups' (Bruff 2014: 125). Indeed, the more the state is trying to resolve its own crisis through harsh, authoritarian welfare reforms, the more it creates the conditions for larger and more encompassing crises in social reproduction. The history of hunger, malnutrition and food insecurity in the United States is an embodied history of class power, of the extent to which capital's crises are first and foremost corporeal crises. That history is a litany of broken promises. If anything, it demonstrates that the right of the few to accumulate is ultimately rooted in the right of the many to starve.

NOTES

1. Many thanks to Cemal Burak Tansel for his thoughtful and helpful feedback. This research was funded by the Social Sciences and Humanities Research Council of Canada.
2. A recent study found that female mortality rates increased between 1992 and 2006 in nearly half of US counties (Wyler 2013).
3. USDA's annual surveys on food insecurity, which started in the 1990s, find their origins in the debate created by the President's Task Force on Food Assistance about how to construct reliable indicators to measure levels of food security. The federal government adopted the conceptual framework developed by Sue Ann Anderson (1990).

BIBLIOGRAPHY

Allegretto SA (2011) The state of working America's wealth, 2011. Economic Policy Institute Briefing Paper #292 (24 March). Available at: http://www.epi.org/publi cation/the_state_of_working_americas_wealth_2011/

Anderson SA (1990) Core indicators of nutritional state for difficult-to-sample popu- lations. *The Journal of Nutrition* 120(11S): 1555–1600.

Bakker I and Gill S (2003) *Power, Production and Social Reproduction: Human In/ security in the Global Political Economy.* New York: Palgrave Macmillan.

Bakker I and Silvey R (2008) *Beyond States and Markets: The Challenges of Social Reproduction.* London: Routledge.

Bellamy Foster J and Magdoff F (2009) *The Great Financial Crisis: Causes and Consequences.* New York: Monthly Review Press.

Bezanson K and Luxton M (2006) *Social Reproduction: Feminist Political Economy Challenges Neo-liberalism.* Montréal: McGill-Queen's University Press.

Bolen E, Rosenbaum D, Dean S and Keith-Jennings B (2016) More than 500,000 adults will lose SNAP benefits in 2016 as waivers expire. Center on Budget and Policy Priorities (18 March). Available at: http://www.cbpp.org/research/food-assistance/ more-than-500000-adults-will-lose-snap-benefits-in-2016-as-waivers-expire

Boushey H (2002) The effects of the Personal Responsibility and Work Opportunity Reconciliation Act on working families. Economic Policy Institute (4 March).

Available at: http://www.epi.org/publication/webfeatures_viewpoints_tanf_testimony/

Breathitt ET (1967) *The People Left Behind: A Report by the President's National Advisory Commission on Rural Poverty*. Washington, DC: Government Printing Office.

Brown JL (1988) Domestic hunger is no accident. *Social Work* 33(2): 99–100.

Brown JL and Allen D (1988) Hunger in America. *Annual Review of Public Health* 9: 503–526.

Brown JL and Pizer HF (1987) *Living Hungry in America*. New York: Macmillan.

Bruff I (2014) The rise of authoritarian neoliberalism. *Rethinking Marxism: A Journal of Economics, Culture & Society* 26(1): 113–129.

Bruff I (2016) Neoliberalism and authoritarianism. In: Springer S, Birch K and MacLeavy J (eds) *The Routledge Handbook of Neoliberalism*. Abingdon: Routledge, 107–117.

CBPP (2015) Chart book: TANF at 19. Center on Budget and Policy Priorities (20 August). Available at: http://www.cbpp.org/sites/default/files/atoms/files/8-22-12tanf-rev8-20-15tanf-chartbook.pdf

Chandler AK, Walker SP, Connolly K and Grantham-McGregor SM (1995) School breakfast improves verbal fluency in undernourished Jamaican children. *The Journal of Nutrition* 125: 894–900.

Citizen's Board of Inquiry into Hunger and Malnutrition in the United States (1968) *Hunger, U.S.A.* Boston: Beacon Press.

Clancy KL and Bowering J (1992) The need for emergency food: Poverty problems and policy responses. *Journal of Nutrition Education* 24(1S): 12S–17S.

Coleman-Jensen A, Rabbitt MP, Gregory C and Singh A (2015) *Household food security in the United States in 2014*, Economic Research Service ERR-194. US Department of Agriculture. Available at: https://www.ers.usda.gov/webdocs/publi cations/err194/53740_err194.pdf

Congressional Budget Office (2012) An overview of the Supplemental Nutrition Assistance Program (19 April). Available at: http://www.cbo.gov/publication/43175

Crooks DL (1995) American children at risk: Poverty and its consequences for children's health, growth, and school achievement. *Yearbook of Physical Anthropology* 38: 57–86.

DeNavas-Walt C, Proctor BD and Smith JC (2011) *Income, poverty, and health insurance coverage in the United States: 2010*, US Census Bureau Current Population Reports P60-239. Washington, DC: US Government Printing Office.

Duménil G and Lévy D (2004) *Capital Resurgent: Roots of the Neoliberal Revolution*. Cambridge, MA: Harvard University Press.

EPI (2015) Family budget calculator. Economic Policy Institute. Available at: http://www.epi.org/resources/budget/

ERP (2015) *Economic Report of the President*. Washington, DC: US Government Printing Office.

FAO (2015) *The state of food insecurity in the world 2015. Meeting the 2015 international hunger targets: taking stock of uneven progress*. Rome: Food and Agriculture Organization of the United Nations.

Galbraith JK (1976) *The Affluent Society*. Boston: Houghton Mifflin.

Harrington M (1971) *The Other America: Poverty in the United States*. Baltimore, MD: Penguin.

Harvey D (2005) *A Brief History of Neoliberalism*. Oxford: Oxford University Press.

Himmelgreen DA and Romero-Daza N (2012) Eliminating 'hunger' in the U.S.: Changes in policy regarding the measurement of food security. In: Markowitz L and Brett JA (eds) *U.S. Food Policy: Anthropology and Advocacy in the Public Interest*. Abingdon: Routledge, 103–120.

IRP (2016) How is poverty measured in the United States? Institute for Research on Poverty. Available at: http://www.irp.wisc.edu/faqs/faq2.htm

Johnson P, Huber E, Giannarelli L and Betson D (2015) *National and state-level estimates of Special Supplemental Nutrition Program for Women, Infants, and Children (WIC) eligibles and program reach, 2013*, Special Nutrition Programs Report No. WIC-15B-ELIG. Alexandria, VA: US Department of Agriculture.

Kesari KK, Handa R and Prasad R (2010) Effect of undernutrition on cognitive development of children. *International Journal of Food, Nutrition and Public Health* 3(2): 133–148.

Kotz N (1969) *Let Them Eat Promises: The Politics of Hunger in America*. Englewood Cliffs, NJ: Prentice-Hall.

Kotz N (1979) *Hunger in America: The Federal Response*. New York: Field Foundation.

LeBaron G and Roberts A (2010) Toward a feminist political economy of capitalism and carcerality. *Signs: Journal of Women in Culture and Society* 36(1): 19–44.

Leftin J, Eslami E and Strayer M (2011) *Trends in Supplemental Nutrition Assistance Program participation rates: Fiscal year 2002 to fiscal year 2009*. Washington, DC: US Department of Agriculture.

Mabli J, Cohen R, Potter F and Zhao Z (2010) *Hunger in America 2010*. Feeding America (January). Available at: http://www.feedingamerica.org/hunger-in-america/our-research/hunger-in-america/hunger-in-america-2010.html

Matthews C (2014) Wealth inequality in America: It's worse than you think. *Fortune* (19 August). Available at: http://fortune.com/2014/10/31/inequality-wealth-income-us/

Mattick P (2011) *Business as Usual: The Economic Crisis and the Failure of Capitalism*. London: Reaktion.

McNally D (2011) *Global Slump: The Economics and Politics of Crisis and Resistance*. Oakland, CA: PM Press.

Nestle M and Guttmacher S (1992) Hunger in the United States: Rationale, methods, and policy implications of state hunger surveys. *Journal of Nutrition Education* 24(1S): 18S–22S.

Nord M (2009) *Food insecurity in households with children: Prevalence, severity, and household characteristics*, Economic Research Service EIB-56. US Department of Agriculture. Available at: http://files.eric.ed.gov/fulltext/ED508211.pdf

Panitch L and Gindin S (2012) *The Making of Global Capitalism: The Political Economy of American Empire*. London: Verso.

Peck J (2001) *Workfare States*. New York: Guilford Press.

Physician Task Force on Hunger in America (1985) *Hunger in America: The Growing Epidemic*. Middletown, CT: Wesleyan University Press.

Poppendieck J (2000) Want amid plenty: From hunger to inequality. In: Magdoff M, Bellamy Foster J and Buttel FH (eds) *Hungry for Profit: The Agribusiness Threat to Farmers, Food, and the Environment*. New York: Monthly Review, 189–202.

Poppendieck J (2014) *Breadlines Knee-Deep in Wheat: Food Assistance in the Great Depression*. Berkeley, CA: University of California Press.

President's Task Force (1984) *Report of the President's Task Force on Food Assistance*. Washington, DC: Government Printing Office.

Roberts B, Povich D and Mather M (2010–2011) Great Recession hit hard at America's working poor: Nearly 1 in 3 working families in United States are low-income. The Working Poor Families Project. Available at: http://www.workingpoorfamilies.org/pdfs/policybrief-winter2011.pdf

Rodgers HR (1982) *The Cost of Human Neglect: America's Welfare Failure*. New York: M. E. Sharpe.

Simeon DT and Grantham-McGregor S (1989) Effects of missing breakfast on the cognitive functions of school children of differing nutritional status. *The American Journal of Clinical Nutrition* 49(4): 646–653.

Trattner WI (1999) *From Poor Law to Welfare State: A History of Social Welfare in America*. New York: The Free Press.

US Census Bureau (2015) Poverty thresholds. Available at: http://www.census.gov/hhes/www/poverty/data/threshld/index.html

USDA (2012a) Building a healthy America: A profile of the Supplemental Nutrition Assistance Program. Food and Nutrition Service, US Department of Agriculture. Available at: http://www.fns.usda.gov/sites/default/files/BuildingHealthyAmerica.pdf

USDA (2012b) The School Breakfast Program. Food and Nutrition Service, US Department of Agriculture. Available at: www.fns.usda.gov/sites/default/files/SBPFactSheet.pdf

USDA (2013a) WIC program participation and costs. Food and Nutrition Service, US Department of Agriculture. Available at: http://www.fns.usda.gov/sites/default/files/pd/wisummary.pdf

USDA (2013b) National School Lunch Program fact sheet. Food and Nutrition Service, US Department of Agriculture. Available at: http://www.fns.usda.gov/sites/default/files/NSLPFactSheet.pdf

USDA (2014) Supplemental Nutrition Assistance Program participation rates: Fiscal year 2010 and 2011—summary. Food and Nutrition Service, US Department of Agriculture. Available at: http://www.fns.usda.gov/sites/default/files/trends2010-2011_Summary.pdf

USDHHS (2015) Welfare indicators and risk factors: Fourteenth report to Congress, 2015. US Department of Health and Human Services. Available at: https://aspe.hhs.gov/report/welfare-indicators-and-risk-factors-fourteenth-report-congress

Wyler G (2013) U.S. Women Are Dying Younger Than Their Mothers, and No One Knows Why. *The Atlantic* (19 August). Available at: http://www.theatlantic.com/health/archive/2013/10/us-women-are-dying-younger-than-their-mothers-and-no-one-knows-why/280259/

Zedlewski S, Waxman E and Gundersen C (2012) SNAP's role in the Great Recession and beyond. Urban Institute (July). Available at: http://www.urban.org/sites/default/files/alfresco/publication-pdfs/412613-SNAP-s-Role-in-the-Great-Recession-and-Beyond.pdf

Chapter 6

Urban Transformation under Authoritarian Neoliberalism

Annalena Di Giovanni

Every crisis produces its own city. From 'austerity urbanism' in North America (Peck 2012) to 'asset-priced urbanism' in Ireland (Byrne 2016) passing by the 'New London Vernacular' (Hatherley 2016), the aftermath of the 2008 crash has affected how we afford a roof upon our head; where it is going to be located; who will be our neighbour; what will our outside routines be; and which services will still be there for us to move around, school our children, meet our social expectations and obtain care. Each instance of economic restructuring has confronted state institutions with the contradiction of having to step in to salvage markets; and almost invariably, new property and zoning regulations have been devised to displace overaccumulation through immovable assets. Each time the city has been turned into an agent of decompression versus the slowing down of financial investment, shrinking decision-making mechanisms in the name of economic necessity. Thus, each 'recovery' has disrupted our built environment and re-sold it to us as a financial product, a living space, an experience, a place in society and an identity.

The main case of urban transformation under authoritarian neoliberalism that I want to focus on, namely, 'Crazed' Istanbul, begins with an earlier crisis—that of 2000, followed by its IMF-induced 2001 rebound.[1] Sprawled between two seas and three coastal areas across a radius of 80 km and home to 80 per cent of Turkey's industrial activity as well as an estimated 15 million inhabitants, Istanbul seemingly presents all the grievances of a global city at the crossroads of neoliberalism: patterns of consumer-initiated gentrification, urban-focused economic governance, privatization of public services and the divestment of capital from industrial production to property development. And yet there is more to the case of Istanbul than just the pattern of a Fordist city meeting its end (Lever 2001). Ever since the 2000–2001 crash, and its subsequent thrusting onto power the Justice and Development Party (AKP), Istanbul has become both the engine and the signifier of an economic growth fuelled by real estate development, signature megaprojects and a reconfiguration of the urban commons. As the June 2013 protests against urban transformation in Gezi Park have proven, this political–economic process has been transformative of social relations, self-representations and forms of governance. Not only the 'crazing' of Istanbul has brought new social formations against the ruling establishment; the AKP itself has renegotiated the modalities and aesthetics of urban transformation.

What I therefore suggest is to look at urban transformation as a dialectical process comprising material forces, social pressure and negotiated representations. Without such a contextualization, 15 years of the AKP's 'crazing' of Istanbul would appear mercurial or risk being depoliticized as the product of a leadership of increasingly frenzied individuals. This is important given that, in its beginnings, President Recep Tayyip Erdoğan's neoconservative government debuted as a passive revolution of the marginalized political forces (Tuğal 2009) and rose to shine in the region as the champion of a consistently high economic growth. Once it secured a second mandate, the AKP successfully dismantled the legacy of military rule and civil conflict, crossing the decade as a torchbearer of both diversity and divestment. And yet such a seemingly steady tenure marked its first decade with a vertical fall into recession, war, repeated clampdowns on human rights and possibly the highest number of terrorism incidents since the 1980s. To this fall, a total breakdown of strategic alliances should be added.

Istanbul's skyline fully reflects this meandering trajectory. The city's body has wavered from TOKİ's (Turkish Mass Housing Development Administration) early ventures into public housing on the outskirts of the metropolis to the years of EU-modelled 'smart' planning and polycentric drive, up until the reinvention of heritage and tourism and the consequent crackdown on public spaces that has marked the post-2010 era. In fact, when looking at the transformation plans dotting Istanbul in 2016 and the sheer amount of court cases opened in order to push the projects through, one might even wonder if there is a viable political economic framework capable of explaining the AKP's transformation of Istanbul throughout 15 years. The AKP is certainly not the first political force to exploit Istanbul by means of renovation; and neither was it the first one to inaugurate the use of extreme means to enforce spatial changes. In this sense, the violent cleansing of Ülker Sokak behind Taksim Square in the 1990s (Selek 2001) and the string of megaprojects across Turkey pushed by the ANAP (Motherland Party) administration came only over a decade before the 'crazing' of Istanbul.

Notwithstanding the visibility and influence of the pre-AKP urban reforms, a conscious political and economic critique of Istanbul's transformation under the aegis of *neoliberal kent rejimi* (neoliberal urban regime) has entered parlance in the last 15 years. Even more so after the discursive production of the Gezi protests (and of earlier urban movements it was built on) the term 'neoliberal' permeates films, radio programmes, songs and social media. 'Neoliberal' is the term through which the AKP's transformation of Istanbul, in its unprecedented pace and scale, is made sense of and framed as a coherent political economy. And yet the contours of what makes urban transformation 'neoliberal' remain only partially satisfactory and somehow fail to explain how the neoliberal urban transformation process sustains itself and evolves across time. Scholarship has over time identified it either as a class-based project (Harvey 1989); a 'market without limits' utopia (Bourdieu 1998); a post-Keynesian rollback of state commitment vis-à-vis social security and provision of services (Jessop 2002); and a broadly defined 'market rationality' (Brown 2003). But when it comes to grounding the entrepreneurial logics of neoliberalism onto speculation and real estate development (Hackworth 2007; Harvey 1989; Ward 2003), accounts on what is *neoliberal* in this specific model of development—and if there is a model—are equally contradictory. Hackworth (2007: 13), for example, defines it as the 'aggressive promotion of real estate development, particularly spaces of consumption'. However, it is worth questioning when, in the past century, housing and commercial properties have not been a laboratory of exploitative practices. A more circumstantial summary comes from Harvey, who charts what he considers entrepreneurial logics of neoliberal urbanisms across three traits he finds distinctive: the first one is an overarching use of public–private partnerships, whereby speculation is financed though external, that is, non-state, sources of funding. The second is the speculative nature of transformation, as opposed to a tradition of rational planning. In other words, a *laissez-faire* planning culture, which bestows the realm of lived space to the fluctuations of free market demand, leaving inhabitants to bear the risks and costs of urban ventures. A third aspect is the focus on 'places and localities' rather than cognizance of the larger metropolitan fabric: as local development projects are cascaded discontinuously across the urban fabric under the spur of investment, so do polarization and inequality.

If we are to maintain the three facets Harvey marks as key characteristics of neoliberal urbanisms (how it is financed, who bears its price and risks, how it promotes an increasingly fragmented urban fabric due to *laissez-faire* planning), what Istanbul presents us with is a postlude of where it is eventually headed. In the long run, the contradictions of sustained urban growth are bound to jostle the tenets of liberal democracy; and holding the reins of both—as they continuously hinder each other—requires more relentless enforcement mechanisms. As I will demonstrate throughout the text, Istanbul's transformation has indeed operated as a power broker across small and medium developers, much in line with Harvey's three-pronged framework, while simultaneously financed through external funding that was artificially maintained by the government's monetary policies. Likewise, Istanbul's development projects are indeed fragmented, discontinuous and polarizing; yet still, planning functions have never been more centralized than now. And as neoliberal urbanisms unfold, who bears the risks of Istanbul's transformation? On this point in particular, the case of Istanbul suggests a rather uneven picture as its transformation has gradually escalated from punishing the poor to punishing more affluent classes. In fact, while the earlier stages of TOKİ and the crackdown on *gecekondu*[2] and unregistered housing follows a classic pattern of dispossession of the already dispossessed, the AKP's interventions on the urban space have progressively moved up from the economically dispossessed of the city's outskirts to those very classes it previously garnered consent from, such as the culturally hegemonic liberal middle class.[3]

This chapter will examine the transformation of Istanbul in the 2003–2013 decade as a case of urban development under authoritarian neoliberalism. Rather than extracting a continuous strategy out of the AKP's 'crazing' of Istanbul, we will examine polities and architectural discourses, together with social and political alliances, to chronicle how city-making—both as a political economy as well as a branding approach—has materialized as a chronically unstable, contradictory and increasingly despotic governance in order to sustain itself and its investment environment. Three arcs of urban planning will be singled out. The first one looks at the nexus between post-crisis restructuring and massive state intervention into the residential construction market. The second focuses on the transition from housing to place-branding during the preparation of Istanbul's European Capital of Culture Initiative bid and the 'crazy' megaprojects. The final arc traces a clamping down on public spaces and cultural heritage.

AUTHORITARIAN NEOLIBERALISM AND THE CITY

As a neoliberal project, the urban transformation of Istanbul under the AKP presents two distinct problems: its sustainability, and its changing types of intervention into the built environment. In other words, one problem is how the government has operationalized development in the long run; and the second, the forms that this model of development took. A response to the first issue is to locate the political economy of the AKP into the rubric of authoritarian neoliberalism; a second proposal is to examine the relations between this political economy and its spatial reproduction in terms of branding.

Framing the governance of the AKP over Istanbul's city-making in the years that followed the 2001 financial crisis as authoritarian neoliberalism means, first of all, putting an emphasis on the role of the state in the protection and reproduction of capital accumulation.[4] The 'crazing' of Istanbul is aligned with what Ian Bruff (2014: 115) identifies as a primary trait of 'authoritarian' neoliberalism: the increasing imbrication of market and non-market forces 'to the point that the separation of the two is a non-viable analytical tool'. A second distinctive aspect is the pace and frequency of constitutional changes to limit democratic fixtures. Policies not only change faster but must be also implemented at will by controlling any participatory process that might oppose them. In the case of urban planning, reducing uncertainty and delays through unilateral and expedited administrative authorizations accommodates a fundamental contradiction proper to estate development, that of being a traditionally slow-motion form of investment that resists frequent modification (Aalbers 2009, 2016). By virtue of its being located in highly mediated spaces such as cities, real estate is 'illiquid, entailing high transaction and operational costs upon sale, requires security, and is not easily divisible. Longer turnover periods create barriers to further accumulation, as capitals get tied up in situ until capable of generating high returns' (Weber 2002: 521). Overstepping stakeholders' appraisal not only enhances the marketability of a property asset (projects are guaranteed outside administrative approval and thus can be monetized at earlier stages) but also reduces its unyielding period. But pace and frequency are once again tightly related to a third distinctive feature of authoritarian forms of neoliberalism—coercion.

'Coercion' should not be understood only as sheer display of force and repressive mechanisms. Those too can be deployed, as they notably were in Istanbul during the June 2013 protests against the destruction of Gezi Park; but in the case of urban transformation, since it always entails the disruption of a quintessentially social domain, an element of encumbrance is almost inevitable as not all interests can be accommodated. From Haussman's Paris to London's Docklands, it is hard to locate a renovation process which has not tried to overstep certain stakeholders in order to favour more powerful others. In the case of urban transformation, I propose understanding coercion as a preemptive governance capable of legally restricting decision-making and auditing mechanisms. As polities must sustain the market of development investments and economic growth, policies are bound to restrict participation and accountability. Moreover, the ills of renovation are imposed onto dwellers as inevitable because they are sealed as part of larger restructuring fixtures. This narrative of 'inevitability' glossed over urban transformation corroborates Bruff's reflection on how 'frequent constitutional changes in the name of "economic necessity" are seeking to reshape the purpose of the state and associated institutions' (2014: 115).

By focusing on coercion, we move away from the understanding of neoliberal planning as a polity which has the withdrawal of central authorities from planning functions, and a subsequent fragmentation of decision-making across independent private interests, as its distinctive feature (cf. Hackworth 2007; Harvey 1989). On the contrary, even if construction awards are fragmented across private enterprises close to political power, and even if administrative reforms push towards 'going local', what we have is a retrenchment of government actors over decision-making powers in order to secure imbricated market and non-market interests. It is worth highlighting that such a planning model of fragmentation, private contracting and the centralization of local decision-making can be traced to planning under Thatcherism when the housing and property markets of London literally became a government business (Thornley 1991; Tewdwr Jones 2002). Therefore, by coercive mechanisms we imply the administrative restructuring of decision-making: if there is a pattern common to neoliberal cities showcasing a sudden spectacular growth, even more so after a period of recession (Istanbul but also Dubai, Qatar and London), it is that nothing is left to the chance of the markets' *laissez-faire*.

Even within a move from consensus to coercion, and even when its imbrication with the markets curtails any long-lasting strategy, the state is never separate from the social (Poulantzas 1978: 141; Bruff 2014: 118). Therefore, the state never ceases to negotiate its own imaginaries and representations through city-making. In the case of urban transformation, precisely because the political economy requires a continuous intervention into the built environment, spaces are marked by selected forms and self-narratives. As Gramsci (1971: 377) noted, 'Material forces would be inconceivable historically without form; and the ideologies would be individual fancies without the material forces.' No matter how fragmentary and fast-paced, or whether focused on property housing or large-scaled planning, transforming the urban directs the future through intervening on the past and reproduces social dispositions by managing everyday spaces. I label this reorientation of self-understandings and practices to sustain and direct market and non-market relations as 'branding the city' and emphasize it as an integral aspect of the political economy of urban transformation. In the marketing and place-branding literature, a brand is generalized as 'a product or a service made distinctive by its positioning relative to the competition and by ... a unique combination of functional attributes and symbolic values' (Hankinson and Cowking 1993: 10). Hence the intuition behind place-branding is that 'it's in the people's minds that the city takes form through the processing of perceptions and images about the city', and that these perceptions are part of the same process that 'follows the formation of images or of entities like products or corporations' (Ashworth and Kavaratzis 2010: 6). What positions and, therefore, 'brands' a place is the selection—or conversion—of a series of attributes which allow it to be marketed as unique: choosing the traits of a city brand implies laying claims to the control of which heritage, gestures, consumption routines, social dispositions and leisure patterns and even representations of the future are to be legitimized and to serve which economic aim. In tracing the branding of New York after the 1973 crisis, Greenberg (2010: 119) problematizes the use of marketing urban imaginaries by warning that 'the branding of cities and their politicians are now integrally intertwined'. In studying the combination of marketing and image-making with economic restructuring and austerity measures in the case of New York, Greenberg (2010: 116) comes to an understanding of branding as the realignment of a 'broader social formation, one in which an emphasis on image and media integration is tied to the extension of market priorities into new social and political realms'. We can, thus, argue that branding is not simply about selling the city.

What the case of 'crazed' Istanbul clearly brings to the fore is that urban transformation does not stop at 'branding' as a strategic positional choice within a competitive market. Urban transformation 'brands' the city in the sense that it imposes a specific mark on its spaces—an intention to make it more 'sellable' in view of certain market trends. A city brand is not just a discursive production inasmuch as it is an attempt (and an always risky one, in terms of sociopolitical costs) to 'associate the city with a desired category of urban development' (Anttiroiko 2014: 15). 'Branding' does not simply inform us about the recipient, that is, the potential buyer or the loyal citizen, it also refers to the maker, hence to the governance that seeks to alter its own item. As it will be seen in the case of Istanbul, under authoritarian neoliberalism these alterations can be made through increasingly undemocratic decision-making mechanisms; the projects are removed from the purview of accountability and relieved of lengthy auditing processes, and interventions scale up in size and pace. In short, under authoritarian neoliberalism cities are branded at a faster rhythm and on a wider scale.

Spaces are not simply selected from promotion and sale, they are also renovated or demolished. Branding is thus a very physical phenomenon: it transforms cities in its attempts to align markets and society under the same economics of loyalty and consumption. It is more than mobilizing the urban spectacle for the representation of power. As erratic as urban transformation might seem under the fast-paced, reactive and un-mediated conditions proper to authoritarian neoliberalism, it nonetheless always harbours a branding intention in producing its own materialities through distinct architectural languages, while trying to control the self-image of the city and the dispositions of its citizens. This language(s) is neither fixed nor necessarily consistent and, under authoritarian neoliberalism, it continuously falls short of achieving an even, hegemonic acceptance—and hence durability. Therefore, when looking at the 'crazing' of Istanbul under the AKP as a city-branding exercise contingent to an authoritarian neoliberal political economy, we are not making the case for a seamless strategy nor for a coherent aesthetic ideology.

The 'crazing' of Istanbul, thus, can be seen as a restructuring of capitalist alliances through coercive governance mechanisms aimed at serving a city-branding project. We propose that the political economy of city-making cannot be separated from how it is represented and marketed; and that, in a relational process, such branding informs planning polities through its economies and power relations. In other words, the marketing of a city's image—and the transformation of its spaces, its selection of memories, its visual narratives—is here advanced as dialectically constitutive within the economy it is designed to promote: necessity or growth, even when coerced, need to be reinforced symbolically in space.

'CRAZING' ISTANBUL

At the turn of the millennium, the Turkish economy crashed twice in four months. The first shock tolled in November 2000, after two decades of wayward government foreign currency loans borrowed on an overvalued Turkish lira (Özatay and Sak 2003; Alp and Elekdağ 2011; Candemir and Zalluhoğlu 2011; Yeldan 2006). The collapse of the markets in Asia, combined with the announcement of a coalition crisis inside a scandal-ridden government finally upset foreign investors' confidence, on which most of Turkey's current accounts—as well as the government budget—relied. As borrowed capitals withdrew rapidly and the lira fell by a third, Turkey defaulted and inflation hit a record 61 per cent. Four months later, in February 2001, the country experienced a second crash while following an IMF structural adjustment programme (Yeldan and Ünüvar 2016). Eventually, the IMF resolved to bail Turkey out of its liquidity shortage with an injection of $11.4 billion loan upon the condition of imposing harsh austerity measures aimed at curbing the inflation rate and thus attracting foreign capital back into Turkey. The government was to progressively privatize its major industrial assets, cut on public services expenditure and implement a contractionary monetary policy under the supervision of a newly restructured Central Bank (Yeldan and Ünüvar 2016).

The consequences of Turkey's austerity were to collapse entirely on the working class and lower middle classes, as their hard-earned savings dissolved in the space of a few days under the combined effects of insolvency and fiscal contraction. By the end of the year, 2 million workers had lost their jobs and hundreds of thousands were left waiting for due pay while interest rates skyrocketed to a record 3,000 per cent—making household borrowing impossible. When in November 2002 an enraged electorate was called to the polls, majority was awarded to the AKP, a new and the only party to emerge unscathed by scandals and crises. The party was established as a coalition of various conservative and Islamist groups led by the former mayor of Istanbul, Recep Tayyip Erdoğan.

Committed to a strict adherence to the IMF guidelines, the AKP agreed to undertake a recovery programme mostly aimed at tackling inflation through a contractionary monetary policy. In itself the programme embraced the same debt-ridden speculative growth of pre-crisis times (Yeldan and Ünüvar 2016) but with the added guarantee of IMF legitimacy and a privatization scheme for the largest state enterprises which was expected to pay off Turkey's debt in the short run. At a macroeconomic level, the Central Bank was to withhold currency reserves in order to maintain the lira artificially high and thus attract indirect foreign investments with the high interest rates of its state bonds. At the domestic level, the government was to profit from the liquidity offered by cash inflows as well as from the sales of industrial, resource and land assets. At a household level, despite losing their job security and a series of social provisions, workers would compensate the costs of the AKP's 'jobless growth' (Yeldan and Ercan 2011) by benefiting from easy credit access at reduced rates.

The crisis and IMF's bailout had in fact transformed Turkey from a debtor country into a borrowing country. Throughout the first decade of 2000s, the AKP's economic governance was blessed by an international inflow of liquidity contingent to all emerging markets in the pre-2008 years, due to foreign investors seeking to diversify their equity portfolios away from the stagnating global North stocks. Turkey was overtaken by a veritable gold rush which saw its economic growth index jump to a resounding 9 per cent between 2010 and 2011 as telecommunications, industries and at least 20 defaulted banks were securitized and the government was relieved of most of its public expenditures on industrial and public services. The long-term sustainability of such growth remained largely unquestioned even if it was financed through borrowings of 'hot money' (i.e. private portfolio investments) for up to 10 per cent of the yearly GDP. Thanks to an unprecedented and fast-paced inflow of capital at its disposal, a reputation as both a conservative and anti-establishment party with a broad electoral alliance and an electorate of households now able to spend above their means; the AKP's raising tide promised to lift all boats. But having dismantled the old industrial class through privatizations, the AKP still had the problem of setting large capital into motion again and of establishing its own capitalist class. The solution was to be found in the TOKİ's *housing leap*, and the 'constructocracy' doctrine behind it.

As the heir to a financial cataclysm, the AKP had ample manoeuvring space to restructure economy but remained at odds with the old military elite and as an outsider in the eyes of the old-established capitalist classes since Erdoğan's earlier political discourse had relied for years on populist rejections of IMF and consumerism.[5] Stepping in the vacuum left by the disappearance of an entire oligarchy, Erdoğan's party had won through showcasing a commitment to corporate responsibility, transparency, efficient management, individual freedoms and freedom of the markets. Hence, throughout the following decade—after securing a second (2007) and then a third (2014) electoral victory—the AKP governance shifted the core of production from industry to real estate development, and centred this new economy onto the transformation of Istanbul through a series of new administrative devices.

A fundamental step in this sense is AKP's revival of the TOKİ, originally founded by the Turgut Özal government in the aftermath of the 1980 military coup and then left dormant for most of the following two decades. During Erdoğan's first term in power, TOKİ was put under the direction of the prime ministry and provided with a new mandate to create quality low-cost housing and collaborate with local municipalities in urban renewal projects.[6] As early as January 2003, an Emergency Action Plan for Housing and Urban Development (law number 4966/2003) was passed by the parliament to allow TOKİ to act as the state contractor for the development and delivery of social housing complexes in order to meet 6 per cent of a national demand (estimated at around 6 million units). TOKİ was then given the *gecekondu* areas of the city, estimated to cover 65 per cent of Istanbul's larger metropolitan territory, as its primary area of intervention.

Gecekondu areas originate from a self-reliance model typical of Istanbul's industrial expansion throughout the 1960s and 1970s, whereby dwellers would build overnight shelters on public land and have authorities turn a blind eye over the act. This would effectively relieve the main employer of the country, the state, from having to provide wages commensurate to housing expenditure (Karpat 1976). Since then, some *gecekondus* have acquired a hybrid status of semi-legal neighbourhoods, and politicians have occasionally utilized them as an electoral pool which resulted in the buildings being recognized and registered officially; but the overall condition of private dwelling on public land retained the issue of property ownership open to dispute.

The uncertainty of *gecekondu* ownership was finally clarified by the momentum of economic necessity and the post-crisis wave of privatizations under the IMF guidance—particularly through the Directorate of the Land Office, whose public domains are now bequeathed to TOKİ (law number 5273/2004). Added to them are the assets of national real investment trust Emlak Konut (Karatepe 2016) and various funds that had failed with the recession. Moreover, a series of legal dispositions were created to expedite dispossession and implementation procedures.[7] Ultimately, with law number 5582/2007, TOKİ is now also entrusted with financial functions as it is authorized to securitize its own assets and issue mortgages (Karatepe 2016).

With the subsequent administrative reforms, zoning and planning decisions were centralized under the office of the prime ministry and the direction of TOKİ was entrusted to Erdoğan Bayraktar, who later acted as Minister of Urban and Environmental Planning. Consequently, local stakeholders such as municipalities and neighbourhood associations are not entitled to oppose projects anymore and as such, not only democratic spaces are curtailed, but also information can be withheld from concerned parties. Evicted dwellers are offered the chance to become house owners and undertake a mortgage under TOKİ's financial terms with no choice on the property location (often families find themselves relocated in outer city areas). Relocation and zoning are major indicators of TOKİ's speculative orientation as once privatized, upmarket areas inside the city are contracted to private developers close to the AKP—such as Ağaoğlu, Torunlar, Kuzu or İhlas—and reassigned for regeneration. At least 15 per cent of TOKİ's projects are destined to be luxury residential areas and shopping centres as they are presumed to further fund the construction of affordable complexes. This is a significant provision since under the IMF's fiscal consolidation guidelines the state is not allowed a housing provision budget. Hence, TOKİ's social housing is financed privately but its policies are under the sole control of the government.

Under the AKP direction of TOKİ, real estate development is de facto turned into a government business: land is an asset to be confiscated and re-sold by the state which, in turn, acts as another competitor, rather than as a regulator of markets. The state is now more than a competitor as it can generate demand through supply by coercively shaping the space at its disposal and exerting a significant control over all levels of the market—from the stage of primitive accumulation to the regulation of prices; from contracts to accessing building materials; from credit rates to strategic data. TOKİ is a state institution under the sole control of the prime ministry, financed largely, by foreign capital brought in by a monetary policy agreed between the government (once again) and an international organization (IMF). Further confusion comes from the fact that TOKİ's mandate on what is to be construed as 'social' and 'affordable' housing has no clear boundaries. TOKİ is only involved in property housing, leaving the rent markets largely unregulated. TOKİ also self-regulates its applications by allowing only the families that does not own a house to apply for its schemes. Hence the state short-circuits the property market through its own private agency. Notwithstanding these aspects, it is important not to see the AKP's 'housing leap' solely as a corrupted scheme of an otherwise potentially functioning property market. On the contrary, while instrumental to the ruling party and its business affiliates, TOKİ is also an aspect of fiscal consolidation where leaving the market unregulated has proved too risky, and central institutions are called to both accommodate as well as supervise the markets. In the long run, though, TOKİ proved insufficient to fulfil the state's growth policy on its own. In order to sustain Istanbul as a growth machine, the scope of transformation needed to scale up from fragmentary housing projects onto master planning; larger infrastructural interventions are required in order to generate a market of expectations and consumption habits compatible with the AKP's changes.

With law number 5216/2004, the government devolved master planning functions to metropolitan municipalities. Legal changes under the AKP appear in fact confusing, as most functions are seemingly decentralized into municipalities except for zoning and for the financing of municipalities themselves. In the case of Istanbul, this translated into the first master plan in decades and the creation of new ad hoc units to prepare large-scale strategic plans. The resultant Istanbul Metropolitan Planning unit functioned as a hub for young experts as well as academics and intellectuals (such as historians and sociologists) to convene on future interventions across the city and import the European Union's local governance principles such as polycentricity, sustainability and high-value-added enterprise. A first comprehensive plan at 1/25,000 scale was expected to be prepared by 2006 (subsequently rejected and re-submitted in 2009)—pompously defined by the mayor as Istanbul's 'constitution' among its citizens and councillors—as well as a second major 1/100,000 scale environmental plan. Both plans arouse enormous controversy once at least 50 special zones are declared exempt from municipal decision, and devolved to the government for transformation; both plans are also marked by the absence of so-called megaprojects such as the third bridge on the Bosphorus, the third airport or the second channel on the European side, all announced by the government and bound to bear enormous environmental and social consequences.

It is within this move towards comprehensive planning that the AKP utilized Istanbul's heritage for political aims and initiated the rebranding of the city's landmarks. The turning point can be identified as the preparations for the Istanbul's European Capital of Culture bid (ECOC). An earlier proposal to file Istanbul as one of the 2010 European Cultural Capitals originated as an independent project among NGOs, philanthropists and frontmen of the Istanbul's liberal elites (Karaca 2010) as a mean to promote the city's cosmopolitan heritage. But the focus on multiculturalism converged with, and eventually was shaped by, wider political concerns as Euro-American experts saw in the Turkish model, and particularly in then Prime Minister Recep Tayyip

Erdoğan's leadership, the West's stabilizing partner among an otherwise turbulent Middle East (Iğsız 2014). On the one hand, the AKP leadership was progressively locating Turkey towards the Middle East both through the use of unifying terms such as *ummah* (the transnational community of Muslims) and the Caliphate's legacy in the construction of its populist discourse—as well as by pursuing an active conciliatory role in the Arab region through then Minister of Foreign Affairs Ahmet Davutoğlu's so-called zero problems soft-power policy (Birdal 2014). On the other hand, this repositioning of Turkey towards a common legacy with its southern neighbours on the grounds of a unified Muslim framework coincided with the AKP's patronage of the small-to-medium entrepreneurial activity in Turkey by a business class expressly characterized as 'Islamic' and 'emerging' (see Özden, Akça and Bekmen in this book).[8]

It is interesting to notice how the two terms suggest a stably upwards economic trajectory and crystallize on the religious identity of its actors. On the grounds of a seemingly unstoppable 'business as usual' felicity, and with GDP growths matching a mediatized liberal commitment towards tactical issues such as coexistence with religious minorities and women's empowerment (Keyder 2010), the AKP marked a palatable Muslim neocon model to be promoted as opposed to an otherwise ailing Western involvement in the region.

Hence a series of actors' interests undoubtedly converged on marketing Istanbul as the 'cradle of civilization' at a time of disenchantment (Iğsız 2014) but aside from foreign concerns, the primary reason for the AKP was mostly an existential one. At the time of Istanbul's bid for ECOC 2010, Erdoğan's entourage was gambling on its political survival vis-à-vis the Turkish army in a bid to dismantle the legacy of previous military coup d'etats, and most notably the generals' control over government decisions via the Higher State Council (the so-called deep state). Tensions peaked during 2007—right after Istanbul had won its candidacy, together with Essen in German and Pecks in Hungary, to 'represent Europe's richness in diversity' (Rampton et al. 2011: II). Eventually, the government settled for the Turkish electorate to express its vote in a constitutional referendum called for 2010 (Istanbul's year as capital of European culture); a sizeable consensus among liberal and progressive elites to curb the army's oligarchs raised the AKP's chances to win a mandate for large institutional changes, advancing the prospect of a military retaliation given the Turkish Republic's record of previous military coups. The Prime Minister made no secret of his counting on the international spotlight provided by Istanbul European Cultural Capital to checkmate the military in case of showdown; this marked the nature and degree of investment in the Istanbul ECOC on behalf of the AKP leadership—and definitely its outcome.[9] Once the government rolled in, pushing the budget to an unprecedented €288.5 million that immediately sidelined any private donor's contribution, balance among stakeholders became problematic. AKP veterans were assigned leadership of the programme and special laws restructured the decision-making mechanisms of what had started as an independent initiative. Earlier high-profile promoters resigned in protest, and the opening ceremony of the Istanbul Capital of European Culture, held in Taksim Square on January 2010, culminated in the rather foreboding display of the Prime Minister elbowing other organizers away from the stage.[10]

Under the AKP's supervision and funding, Istanbul ECOC showcased 610 projects throughout 2010. Only 7.2 per cent of Istanbul's population reportedly attended any of the 2,725 performances or of the 763 exhibitions (Ozan and Ünver 2012), and no military intervention took place after Erdoğan's referendum victory; all in all a boost to tourism and investments were the two main payoffs of the costly initiative. But the most lasting outcome of Istanbul ECOC was undoubtedly the induction of the AKP's urban strategy to the branding of the city and its heritage. It was in fact on the preservation of urban heritage that at least 70 per cent of the €288.5 million budget was invested in the years between 2008 and 2010. Of these, the restoration of Islamic religious landmarks and ritual fountains clearly marked the boundary of what the government considered 'heritage'.[11] Performances and exhibitions stressed a cultural diversity devoid of uncomfortable historical narratives—such as the Armenian Genocide or the 1955 anti-Greek pogroms, not to mention the oppression of non-Turkish ethnic groups, primarily the Kurds—and tailored Istanbul's coexistence around selected heritages only, highlighting more marketable images of the past and deliberately repressing any representation of more uncomfortable unresolved issues.

Istanbul ECOC marks a passage from brute rentier speculation of the TOKİ years to a more attentive use of non-commodified spaces and of city branding. This is evident in the surge of a sort of 'neo-Seljuk' taste applied to renovation projects after 2008. Demolitions gave way to shopping malls and boutique hotels sporting a pastiche of early 1700s classicism (the so-called tulip period) mixed with a taste for soft-hued plastered facades and for street furniture that mimic Iznik ceramics motifs. At the same time, historical secular buildings have been progressively scheduled for demolition, often in order to make space for pre-existing Sunni Muslim religious landmarks.[12] The most renowned case is no doubt that of Taksim Square and Gezi Park which revolved around the razing of the square's green area to rebuild the Topçu Kışlası (army barracks), a complex of nineteenth-century blocks of no particular aesthetic merit other than the memory of a 1909 revolt conducted by conservative Muslims. Coupled with the municipality's intention to demolish the landmark Atatürk Cultural Centre to replace it with a new opera theatre; and to turn the historical Emek Cinema—site of the Istanbul Film Festival—

into a privately owned shopping mall; the AKP's plans to rebrand Taksim marked the *casus belli* for the June 2013 protests against the government and its 'crazed' Istanbul.

In parallel with the ECOC planning, the AKP begun to produce its own brand of signature megaprojects. These are consciously presented as bold, utopic gestures of spectacular size and cost. In 2011, a '2023 goals' campaign was announced, promising to mark the first century of the Turkish Republic. Promoted as 'crazy' and wheeled onto the public on account of their 'craziness' (*çılgınlık*) and economic ambitions, a wealth of megaprojects dictated by the government were announced. According to the plans, the city is to host the longest combined bridge across the sea ever built—the third of such kind on the Bosphorus—an artificial channel is to connect the Black Sea with the Mediterranean. Among other construction plans are a third airport, aimed at making Istanbul a primary destination for air traffic, the biggest mosque in the world and the largest shopping mall ever built in the city, all intended as signature gestures to celebrate the first century of the Turkish Republic with a 'New Turkey' outlook.

In terms of institutional enforcement, the TOKİ model of decision-making and hybrid financing have been extended to large infrastructural interventions, while demolition with subsequent reconstruction is still the favoured AKP approach to the preservation of heritage. Demolitions start even before plans have been drafted—and regardless of any court decisions on their feasibility or legality. Although the AKP never explicitly acknowledged a comprehensive cultural policy for Istanbul, at least in terms of planning patterns, a series of intentions appear to distinguish AKP's evolution in planning. There have clearly been changes, as it moved from a more property-oriented domain—such as housing and therefore interaction with households and tenants—onto retail and leisure and, hence, more short-term, rent-focused types of markets, but there have also been an effort to set increasingly coercive means to pull decision-making powers away from non-state actors. Effectively, regulatory institutions are no longer allowed to interfere with whatever is going to be built. This is particularly the case after the 2013 Omnibus law, passed in order to persecute the Chamber of Architects of Istanbul for organizing the Gezi protests in Taksim. The professional association has seen its members probed and trialled for performing their watchdog's duty against new 'crazy' projects. The post-2013 authoritarian clampdown against a constitutionally organized body is matched by the AKP's attempt to reform dispositions and aesthetics through a new class of architects and planners hired after being trained in private universities close to conservative AKP circles, once again matching coercion against dissent with the attempt to create an alternative disposition.

CONCLUSION

In 2013 the 'crazed' Istanbul finally revolted, and discontents of urban transformation served as the catalyst for millions of civilians depleted by an economic growth built on credit, precarization and authoritarianism. As for the AKP, urban transformation has been its undoing; and the failure to make it a hegemonic project has forced Erdoğan's party into a defensive position of increased coercion. It would be reductive to examine the discontent caused by the demolition of a few trees in Gezi Park without looking at years of mounting protests against the authoritarian neoliberalization of the industrial and public service workfare by means of increasingly coercive regulations over employment and union activity, as well as the breakdown of internal alliances on the neoconservative Islamic front.[13] Since 2010, the social and economic costs of the government's neoliberal policies have become openly unsustainable, forcing the AKP to move at a faster, and increasingly coercive, pace. Following Gezi, the AKP is also confronted by the challenge of the Kurdish peace process, never really advanced beyond some groundbreaking but ultimately demonstrative acts, and decidedly weakened by the party's ambiguous investment in the Syrian conflict. Above all, the payoffs of a decade of speculative growth and flexibilization confront the government with the first cracks of a new recession as loans are now due and the lira is back onto an inflation path. Following the June 2015 elections and the post-Gezi efforts of progressive forces to organize a common opposition, the AKP has lost its absolute majority in the parliament and the only mean to maintain power has been, once again, through increased authoritarianism. By July 2015, the Kurdish front had reopened through a series of military interventions in the southeast while the Turkish lira marked its second year of devaluation. And yet despite its freefall, or perhaps exactly because of it, the AKP's authoritarian neoliberal urbanism is far from reprieved, suggesting that the path from crisis of a neoliberal economy to that of social mobilization is not a guaranteed outcome (see also De Smet and Bogaert in this book). On the contrary, under ever-mounting economic and social pressures, the AKP has proceeded to 'militarize' its urban transformation as Kurdish areas shelled by the army have been scheduled for nationalization and subsequent renovation, while TOKİ is entrusted with the construction of 'refugee cities' for Syrian refugees. The government has also tightened its grip on the Central Bank through a series of key replacements, thus embracing the full control of both monetary and credit system policing and asserting its influence on key financial institutions. As of June 2016, President Recep Tayyip Erdoğan has celebrated his 15 years of urban transformation by raising the benchmark of 'necessary' demolitions to 6 million housing units.

The AKP's urban transformation begun under the gales of economic restructuring and fiscal consolidation, and secured a few years of consensus or at least compromise around the settlement of 'economic necessity'. Policies have unfolded as a seamless imbrication between planning institutions and markets where both decisions and capitals come through governments; and the liquidities to finance this accumulation regime were generated through bailout programmes which had already been imported to contain a previous crisis. What is necessarily marginalized within this ruling configuration is public input (Tansel in this book; Bruff 2014: 115). An increasingly centralized decision-making structure dramatically hastens the pace of capital circulation, and in looking at the case of Istanbul, we have demonstrated that precipitation (of decisions as well as the reactions and, therefore, new governmental adaptations) is the third distinguishing feature of authoritarian neoliberalism.

Situating 'authoritarian' neoliberalism in urban transformation also requires singling out the material and cultural forms that this regime of accumulation forces on the everyday lives of millions of citizens through renovated buildings, disrupted consumption routines and selection of memories. In transforming the city, the AKP has undoubtedly marked it with its very own brand of symbolic and aesthetic productions. I suggest to look at these forms as something else than a discursive reorientation: in an authoritarian neoliberal regime, neither consensus nor popular conviction are necessary at all times. There is no need for power to explain itself; and yet it does continue to 'change dispositions' (Tuğal 2016: 23), including aesthetic orientations. In the case of Istanbul, the preoccupation of manufacturing a new image of the city has walked hand in hand with the urge of whirling investments, although the contours of this image remained incomplete and often haphazard in line with the multifaceted and reactive nature of neoliberalism in its authoritarian stage. One only needs to look back to Turkey's first neoliberalization phase under ANAP (Yalman 2009) for proof that neither megaprojects nor forced urban renovation were introduced by the AKP. What AKP has tried to do though, at unprecedented scale, is to construct its own modernity (Ünsal 2015: 303).

During its years in power the AKP has changed its aims and objectives, its methods and its allies among organized political forces. Even more so, it has shifted from championing democracy to restricting democratic means in order to sustain its economic policies, as the vagaries of economic growth paved the way for a crisis of hegemony and eventually outward conflict (Tansel 2015). Meanwhile, the institutional reconfigurations that were required to accommodate the AKP's political economy have passed by means of increased coercion and faster-paced interventions. In this sense, the number of restrictions enacted in the years between 2012 and 2016 is paralleled only by those following the 12 September 1980 military coup; except that the AKP has its mandate from a series of electoral victories, and thus marks a compelling outline of neoliberalism's resilience both to the recurrent crises of accumulation as well as to the crises of hegemonic consensus. What 'crazed' Istanbul reminds us is how democratic forces cannot match authoritarianism on its very own terrain.

NOTES

1. The use of 'crazing' in the context of this chapter revolves around the buzzword *çılgın* (crazy) used by the AKP officers to promote their signature construction projects. However, it is worth noting that 'crazing' is also a term used in materials science to describe the slow and uneven cracking of certain materials under the stress of continuous force (Zhang et al. 2009).
2. Literally 'built overnight' unregulated dwellings typical of Istanbul's years of industrial expansion.
3. An example of such episodes of consent-making is the progressives' and Leftist endorsement of the AKP in its confrontation against the Turkish military before the 2010 referendum. The Kurdish conservative electorate voting for the AKP in the southeast of the country should also not be forgotten.
4. See Tansel in this book.
5. See Özden, Akça and Bekmen in this book.
6. See TOKİ's statute and history on its website: http://www.toki.gov.tr/kurulus-ve-tarihce. The mandate of TOKİ is also stated in law number 2985/1984.
7. Most notably law number 5162/2004, which enables TOKİ to expropriate buildings both from municipalities and from private owners. Law number 5302/2005 on provincial governorates is also emblematic as it muddles the issue of authority on zoning functions between locally elected municipalities and government-appointed provincial administrators.
8. See, for example, the two country reports from the European Stability Initiative (2005, 2007).
9. Author's interview with Korhan Gümüş (Human Settlements Association) (April 2016).
10. Author's interview with Korhan Gümüş (Human Settlements Association) (April 2016).
11. Certain legacies native to the region, such as the Kurdish and partly the Armenian culture, were explicitly left out of the ECOC discursive construction. Moreover, the minorities that were allowed to enter this 'multicultural' frame were characterized purely in religious terms, removing linguistic, political, gender and ethnic diversity.
12. An example is the suppression of the nineteenth-century bank buildings in Karaköy to reconstruct a seventeenth-century mosque. Streams of non-Sunni-Hanafi Islam are excluded from the AKP's selective heritage.
13. See Özden, Akça and Bekmen in this book.

BIBLIOGRAPHY

Aalbers M (2009) Geographies of the financial crisis. *Area* 41(1): 34–42.

Aalbers M (2016) *The Financialization of Housing: A Political Economy Approach.* Abingdon: Routledge.

Alp H and Elekdağ S (2011) *The Role of Monetary Policy in Turkey During the Global Financial Crisis.* Washington, DC: International Monetary Fund.

Anttiroiko A-V (2014) *The Political Economy of City Branding.* Abingdon: Routledge.

Ashworth GJ and Kavaratzis M (2010) *Towards Effective Place Brand Management: Branding European Cities and Regions.* Cheltenham: Edward Elgar.

Birdal MS (2014) The Davutoğlu Doctrine: The populist construction of the strategic subject. In: Bekmen A, Akça İ and Özden BA (eds) *Turkey Reframed: Constituting Neoliberal Hegemony.* London: Pluto Press, 92–106.

Bourdieu P (1998) *Acts of Resistance: Against the Tyranny of the Market.* New York: The New Press.

Brown W (2003) Neo-liberalism and the end of liberal democracy. *Theory & Event* 7(1). DOI: 10.1353/tae.2003.0020

Bruff I (2014) The rise of authoritarian neoliberalism. *Rethinking Marxism: A Journal of Economics, Culture & Society* 26(1): 113–129.

Byrne M (2016) 'Asset price urbanism' and financialization after the crisis: Ireland's national asset management agency. *International Journal of Urban and Regional Research* (Online). DOI: 10.1111/1468-2427.12331.

Candemir A and Zalluhoğlu AE (2011) The effect of marketing expenditures during financial crisis: The case of Turkey. *Procedia: Social and Behavioral Sciences* 24(1): 291–299.

European Stability Initiative (2005) *Islamic Calvinists, Change and Conservativism in Central Anatolia.* Istanbul: ESI. Available at: http://www.esiweb.org/pdf/esi_document_id_69.pdf

European Stability Initiative (2007) *Sex and Power in Turkey: Feminism, Islam and the Maturing of Turkish Democracy.* Istanbul: ESI. Available at: http://www.esiweb.org/pdf/esi_document_id_90.pdf

Gramsci A (1971) *Selections from the Prison Notebooks*, Hoare Q and Nowell-Smith G (eds and trans). London: Lawrence & Wishart.

Greenberg M (2010) Branding, crisis, and utopia: Representing New York in the age of Bloomberg. In: Aronczyk M and Powers D (eds) *Blowing Up the Brand: Critical Perspectives on Promotional Culture.* New York: Peter Lang, 115–144.

Hackworth JR (2007) *The Neoliberal City: Governance, Ideology, and Development in American Urbanism.* Ithaca, NY: Cornell University Press.

Hankinson G and Cowking P (1993) *Branding in Action: Cases and Strategies for Profitable Brand Management.* London: McGraw-Hill.

Harvey D (1989) From managerialism to entrepreneurialism: The transformation in urban governance in late capitalism. *Geografiska Annaler B* 71(1): 3–18.

Hatherley O (2016) *The Ministry of Nostalgia.* London: Verso.

Iğsız A (2014) From Alliance of Civilizations to branding the nation: Turkish Studies, image wars and politics of comparison in an age of neoliberalism. *Turkish Studies* 15(4): 689–704.

Jessop B (2002) Liberalism, neoliberalism, and urban governance: A state-theoretical perspective. *Antipode: A Radical Journal of Geography* 34(3): 452–472.

Karatepe İD (2016) The state, Islamists, discourses, and bourgeoisie: The construction industry in Turkey. *Research and Policy on Turkey* 1(1): 46–62.

Karpat KH (1976) *The Gecekondu: Rural Migration and Urbanization*. Cambridge: Cambridge University Press.

Keyder C (2010) Capital city resurgent: Istanbul since the 1980s. *New Perspectives on Turkey* 43: 177–186.

Lever WM (2001) The post-Fordist city. In: Paddison R (ed) *Handbook of Urban Studies*. London: Sage, 273–283.

Ozan B and Ünver C (2012) Exploring the impact for Istanbul of being a European Capital of Culture. *Performance* 4(4): 52–59.

Özatay F and Sak G (2003) Banking sector fragility and Turkey's 2000–01 financial crisis. *Brookings Trade Forum*: 121–172.

Peck J (2012) Austerity urbanism. *City: Analysis of Urban Trends, Culture, Theory, Policy, Action* 16(6): 626–655.

Poulantzas N (1978/2014) *State, Power, Socialism*. London: Verso.

Rampton J, McAteer N, Mozuraity N, Levai M and Açkalı S. (2011) Ex-Post Evaluation of 2010 European Capitals of Culture: Final report for the European Commission Directorate General for Education and Culture. London: ECORYS.

Selek P (2001) *Maskeler Süvariler Gacılar. Ülker Sokak: Bir Alt Kültürün Dışlanma Mekanı*. İstanbul: Aykırı.

Tansel CB (2015) The politics of contemporary capitalism in Turkey (and the politics of its interlocutors). *Development and Change* 46(3): 570–584.

Tewdwr-Jones M (2002) *The Planning Polity: Planning, Government, and the Policy Process*. London: Routledge.

Thornley A (1991) *Urban Planning Under Thatcherism: The Challenge of the Markets*. London: Routledge.

Tuğal C (2009) *Passive Revolution: Absorbing the Islamic Challenge to Capitalism*. Stanford, CA: Stanford University Press.

Tuğal C (2016) *The Fall of the Turkish Model: How the Arab Uprisings Brought Down Islamic Liberalism*. London: Verso.

Ünsal BÖ (2015) AKP dönemi kentleşme politikaları ve kentsel dönüşüm. In: Koray M and Çelik A (eds) *Himmet, Fıtrat, Piyasa: AKP Döneminde Sosyal Politika*. İstanbul: İletişim, 301–313.

Ward K (2003) Entrepreneurial urbanism, state restructuring and civilizing 'New' East Manchester. *Area* 35(2): 116–127.

Weber R (2002) Extracting value from the city: Neoliberalism and urban redevelopment. *Antipode: A Radical Journal of Geography* 34 (3): 519–540.

Yalman G (2009) *Transition to Neoliberalism: The Case of Turkey in the 1980s*. İstanbul: Bilgi University Press.

Yeldan E (2006) Neo-liberal global remedies: From speculative-led growth to IMF-led crisis in Turkey. *Review of Radical Political Economics* 38(2): 193–213.

Yeldan E and Ercan H (2011) Growth, Employment Policies and Economic Linkages: Turkey. Employment Working Paper No. 84. Geneva: ILO.

Yeldan E and Ünüvar B (2016) An assessment of the Turkish economy in the AKP Era. *Research and Policy on Turkey* 1(1): 11–28.

Zhang W, Srivastava I, Zhu YF, Picu CR and Koratkar NA (2009) Heterogeneity in epoxy nanocomposites initiates crazing: Significant improvements in fatigue resistance and toughening. *Small* 5(12): 1403–1407.

Chapter 7

From Mare Nostrum to Triton

Humanitarian Emergencies and Neoliberal Migration Management in the Mediterranean

Luca Manunza

The study of migration cannot be limited to the analysis of merely objective parameters and metrics, such as the number of migrants, their countries of origin and their tangible and/or perceived economic impact. Migration processes comprise a series of symbolic elements related to both the migrants and to their perception in the host country and the analysis of these elements provides us a more systematic reading of migration as a 'total social fact' (Sayad 1999). This chapter focuses on a key site of migration in contemporary Europe and investigates the main *dispositifs* of management adopted by the Italian government to address the arrival of thousands of migrants on the country's southern coasts. I utilize the term *dispositifs* to denote a complex strategic network that links police practices, laws, administrative measures, scientific statements and mechanisms formed in order to cope with an urgency (Foucault 1997). The commodification of migrants, the creation of a discourse that heavily emphasizes the notion of the 'victimhood', the technologization of border control and the implementation of control *dispositifs* such as electrified border fences have all become common practices in Western democracies' strategies of migration management. While particularities of the Italian context in migration management (e.g. corruption, private use of public finance, racism in high government positions) are important, these context-specific features should not obscure a common strategy that crosscuts an EU-level tendency to adopt practices of a 'securitarian management' of migration (Campesi 2011). One only needs to remember the new criminalization policies established in Germany after the events in Cologne, the legislative practices adopted in Denmark, the anti-migrant sentiments and wall-building in Bulgaria, Croatia and Austria to underscore the commonalities across different EU members vis-à-vis their perception and management of migration.

The chapter interrogates the role of the Italian government and the immediate effects of relevant specific operations—namely Emergency North Africa (ENA), Mare Nostrum and Triton—through ethnographic research by focusing on what I call the Italian business of hospitality. Part of this work attempts to spell out the functions, the operational and strategic aspects of what I am going to define as the 'business of hospitality' in Italy and in the specific and paradigmatic case of Naples. Processes and events analyzed here start in 2011, when the social and political upheaval in Tunisia and the subsequent humanitarian wars (Dal Lago 2010; Azzellini and Kanzleiter 2006) triggered an intensification of migration and an unstable rearrangement of the Mediterranean routes to access the European Union. It is in this period—besides Frontex and Eurosur[1]—that Emergency North Africa, Mare Nostrum and Triton—three important emergency *dispositifs* regarding the management of migratory flows—were employed in Italy.

Despite its current relevance and the attention it has garnered, migration is a recurring pattern in European history. The whole history of the twentieth century was linked to the displacement of populations caused by a series of wars. From the end of the Second World War to 1996, 70 wars took place in different countries which caused approximately 20 million deaths and 60 million injured civilians. In this context, migration remained a constant in the Mediterranean area and, starting from 1989, the situation intensified due to the presence of a low intensity 'war theatre' which regulates the relations between the *Western* societies and the rest of the world. Therefore, we should recognize that war and migration are not mutually exclusive social events. The intervention of Western forces in armed conflicts in Somalia, Iraq, Libya, Sudan, Syria, Lebanon and Afghanistan was never labelled as 'wars of aggression', which contributed to the normalization of armed conflict situations on a large scale in the region. During the recent Libyan War in 2011, when a journalist asked the Italian President Giorgio Napolitano if Italy was involved in a 'real war', he replied that nobody had ever declared war on Libya.[2] This is the context in which contemporary migration should be analyzed with all its implications concerning the implementation of emergency laws on an ethnic basis, the recruitment of a vulnerable and precarious workforce and the use of private agencies for border control. *Our wars*, as explained by Dal Lago (2010), are continually redesigned and constantly refinanced. In this context, the economic role of migrants is relevant as they are targeted by securitarian policies and identified as 'public enemies' (Maneri 2009). This could be interpreted as a performative mechanism of stigmatization (Harcourt 2009), which serves the urban economy and is functional to the economic structure of many European countries.

This argument will be expanded in two parts. The chapter will first examine the changing landscape of migration in the Mediterranean in the aftermath of the Arab Spring and Western interventions in the Middle East and North Africa. I will explore the ways in which the Italian state, in line with EU directives, encouraged a 'hospitality business' within which non-state actors were positioned to receive and accommodate migrants and asylum seekers. In the second part, I will take a closer look at the restructuring of European border protection programmes as exemplified by Mare Nostrum and Triton operations, and investigate how these operations increasingly securitized the Mediterranean migration flows.

THE ITALIAN BUSINESS OF HOSPITALITY

On 19 March 2011, the Odyssey Dawn military operation in Libya was initiated with the involvement of countries such as the United States, France, the United Kingdom and later on Italy, which performed air strikes not only against Muammar Gaddafi, but also against civilians and migrants in the area. These events went hand in hand with the Arab Spring in Tunisia, which resulted in a new conflict and increased migration flows on the border during a difficult phase of stabilization. Thus, the riots surrounding the so-called second democratic independence in Tunisia, the *liberation war* against the Libyan Rais and the worsening of the political situation in Sudan had a significant impact on the flow of migration. In 2011, in the war-affected Mediterranean area, more than 60,000 migrants arrived in Italy from the Tunisian and Egyptian coasts in an attempt to escape the conflict (see Figure 7.1). The efforts to stabilize the new governments in Tunisia and Libya through dubious international mediation

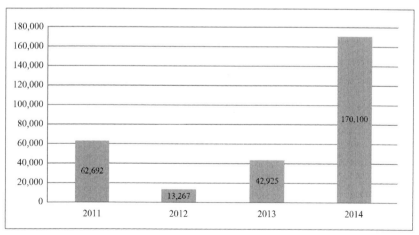

Figure 7.1.   Official immigration figures in Italy, 2011–2014
Source: Ministry of Interior (2015)

efforts aimed at controlling migration flows in 2012 and 2013. These efforts, however, failed to curb the migration flows: in 2014 the number of migrants who left their countries because of the conflicts in Syria and Libya increased significantly.

The arrival of numerous asylum seekers on southern Italian coasts between 2011 and 2012 is a testimony to the structural changes in the social and geopolitical structures triggered by the Arab Spring in the Mediterranean. The ongoing wars in North Africa prompted, beyond the internal political changes, new migration flows to surrounding countries, and particularly to Italy. In 2011, the number of migrants increased significantly, leading the Italian Prime Minister to declare, on 12 February 2011, the state of humanitarian emergency in the country due to the exceptional influx of citizens from Northern African countries. This was followed, on 30 March 2011, by the reception plan provided by the Department of Civil Protection (Dipartimento della Protezione Civile). On 18 February, the Council of Ministers of the Italian government appointed Giuseppe Caruso (Prefect of Palermo) as the 'Commissioner for the implementation of all actions to overcome the state of emergency'. The emergency *dispositif* (Petrillo 2009; Palidda 2011) conceived to deal with this cyclical social phenomenon was designed to implement a mere humanitarian reception and the newly appointed Commissioner was provided with significant economic and human resources—such as soldiers—to face this emergency. However, migrant arrivals in Lampedusa continued to increase, while repatriations and transfers to the mainland took place only sporadically. On 6 April 2011, a new agreement was signed in the context of a conference organized by the government with representatives of the Union of Italian Regions (UPI) and National Association of Italian Municipalities (ANCI) to discuss new ways to deal with the emergency plan. The key points of this agreement were designing a reception system to evenly distribute migrants throughout the country, implementing a welcome plan through the National System of Civil Protection, seeking the European Union's support to grant migrants temporary protection and create a special fund for the municipalities which take charge of migrant minors.

On 7 April 2011, the state of humanitarian emergency was officially declared in North Africa, allowing exceptions to normal operations in the area. The ENA (Emergency North Africa [*Emergenza Nord Africa*]) plan of reception was conceived on 6 April 2011 in the course of a joint conference between the government, regions and local institutions. It was characterized by three main objectives: (1) making provisions for the initial reception of migrants; (2) achieving an even distribution of migrants on the national territory; (3) providing basic assistance. Moreover, it envisaged a distribution of migrants in various Italian regions in accordance with the population density of each region. The implementation of this plan entailed the allocation of a conspicuous amount of money and resources to carry out the different typologies of intervention.

For instance, the budget section attributed to 'forces and means' included expenses to strengthen the staff of CRI (Italian Red Cross), firefighters, police, army and port authority as well as the costs of evaluation for all international protection applications. Moreover, it included the reimbursement of expenses for Red Cross' missions in Tunisia, in the UNHCR camp of Choucha on the border with Libya, and for waste management operations. However, the Italian government's intervention can be described as merely logistic as highlighted by a statement of the UNHCR's head of communications at the Choucha Camp:

> The role of Civil Protection is only logistical. They set up four tents for international organizations to coordinate different actors, allow them to get together and arrange meetings. Subsequently, this property was donated to Tunisia's interim government. Moreover, as far as I am aware, the Italian Government made a cash donation which was reinvested in a project of waste management.[3]

The role of the Italian Civil Protection (PCI) in Tunisia remains unknown for many UNHCR operators. Some of them, interviewed in February 2011, stated that the Italian camp and the operations of support to the management of the camp were financed through a donation previously made by the Italian government itself. But, the only tangible aspects of the Italian intervention in Tunisia are the aforementioned four tents in the 'Camp of Olives', which hosted, in the first week of March 2011, the UN operation centre in Choucha Camp.

Given this hollow presence and the alarming waste situation in the camp and surrounding areas, the intervention of the Italian Civil Protection could be described as inadequate, which does not come as a surprise, given the previous unsuccessful experiences of PCI in waste management and disposal in Italy (Petrillo 2009).

Equally present in the 'forces and means' section of the ENA emergency plan's budget was the removal and destruction costs of the boats used by migrants to reach Italian coasts. On 5 April 2011, an agreement was signed between Italy and Tunisia—respectively represented by Minister of Internal Affairs Roberto Maroni and his Tunisian counterpart Habib Essid—to strengthen border controls on people leaving from Tunisia to Italy and define the modalities of repatriation for Tunisian migrants illegally landed in Italy after 5 April 2011. As a consequence of this agreement, the Italian government provided Tunisia with six patrol boats, four patrol trucks and a hundred jeeps. The ENA budget plan also covered expenses for the detention of migrants who were not eligible for humanitarian protection and assistance, as well as the costs

Table 7.1.   Regional Distribution of Refugees in Italy

Region	Number of Refugees (2012)	Total Capacity
Piemonte	1.358	3.819
Valle d'Aosta	20	108
Lombardia	2.424	8.557
Trentino	282	882
Veneto	1.069	4.270
Friuli	335	1.057
Emilia Romagna	1.509	3.846
Toscana	972	3.221
Umbria	298	787
Marche	419	1.345
Lazio	1.709	4.892
Abruzzo	10	0
Molise	122	260
Campania	2.075	4.728
Puglia	1.182	3.300
Basilicata	164	476
Calabria	887	1.643
Sicilia	1.130	4.093
Sardegna	371	1.350
Liguria	488	1.367
Total	**16.844**	**50.000**

Source: Ministry of Interior (2015)

for the construction and maintenance of three new identification and hospitality centres in Italy, including the one in Santa Maria Capua Vetere in the province of Caserta. The latter was shut down by the judiciary only fifty days after its opening, due to the inadequacy of the facilities and the numerous complaints by activists and associations, who exposed the inhumane living conditions in the centre and its repeated violations of fundamental rights.

Of the total budget, 41.7 per cent consisted of 'assistance' expenses, which means that the management of emergencies was to be achieved through various steps which included first-aid measures, even distribution of migrants across the country, accommodation, and collaboration with associations and institutions in the framework of ENA. The scope of assistance also included the establishment of a supervisory board to monitor PCI's activities in providing various services to migrants, including cultural and linguistic mediation, legal consultancy, Italian language teaching and orientation to social and health care services.

On 20 June 2011, the Ordinance No. 3948 issued by the Presidency of the Council of Ministers (OPCM) appointed a series of officials to the ENA framework, who were responsible for working with PCI in order to identify adequate facilities to host migrants, and stipulate agreements or contracts with public and private entities to ensure reception in the regions. The facilities selected by the officials had to comply with the SPRAR (Protection System for Asylum Seekers and Refugees [*Sistema di Protezione per Richiedenti Asilo e Rifugiati*]) or CARA (Hosting Centre for Asylum Seekers [*Centro di Accoglienza per Richiedenti Asilo*]) regulations depending on the

Figure 7.2.   Choucha Refugee Camp
Luca Manunza, 2011

type of accommodation and services provided. For instance, the facilities that fell under the SPRAR umbrella had to supply courses for the promotion of the migrants' well-being and inclusion in the host community. On the contrary, the ones featured in the CARA category had to provide only basic forms of reception, which did not entail the integration of migrants in the local communities.

The same OPCM established the allocation of €46 per day for each adult refugee and €80 for unaccompanied minors. Moreover, in line with the 'state of emergency', officials could allow exceptions to the SPRAR or CARA regulations, with the implicit risk of compromising the quality of hospitality services. Hence, this ordinance, which reflected the wider securitarian trend that characterized the national approach to migration, defined the framework in which the Italian government developed its system of migrants and refugees reception.

The 'migrant question' is framed by a dreadful convergence: between an authoritarian neoliberalism and 'authoritarian emergency'. This presents itself not only as a set of military and violent practices, but like most of the authoritarian government models, it also requires a degree of legitimacy and consensus. Through the ethics of profit, this regime aimed at creating the necessary conditions of consent to undertake certain economic actions. Consent was necessary in the creation of such a dubious infrastructure. This is how the economic environment around the 'migrant question' was established. Waste management in the city of Naples, the experience of G8 in Italy, the construction of new prisons, the attempt to transform Civil Protection as a conduit for emergency intervention—those are only some of the most obvious examples of how the state shaped the moral and the economic climate. Migration was thus subjected to certain narratives where the 'human drama' (the refugees, the barges, the traffickers, etc.) and 'fear' (the desperate, criminals, etc.) were conjoined to pave the way for the creation of dedicated services, such as the 'residence of solidarity' (Saitta 2011). The result is the creation of immigration centres like the one in Mineo in Sicily, the operation costs of which amounted to about €20 million in 2011 (Mazzeo 2011).

As explained above, the number of migrants assigned to each Italian region was proportional to its population density. According to this principle, the three regions with the highest number of migrants were Lombardy, Campania and Piedmont. In Campania, for instance—given the high number of migrants assigned to the Neapolitan region—a high number of associations and NGOs were established with the purpose of participating in the allocation of funds for the accommodation of migrants. Many of them, however, did not meet the necessary requirements to be eligible for this kind of assistance. Also, due to the often-poor quality of the facilities that hosted migrants in the province of Naples, a series of activists and volunteers developed an informal system of control to monitor the provision of reception services. An activist who supervised the reception of Northern African refugees in one of the biggest local associations called 'Un'ala di riserva', described his experience as follows:

> Already in November 2011 we had teamed up with the Chamber of Labour in Naples and some non-profit organizations to monitor a number of associations that sheltered migrants. We filed a complaint to the prosecutor's office on the mismanagement of the emergency by the Civil Protection, which was the institution in charge of coordinating the network of organizations, hotels and community houses engaged in the provision of basic services. A clear example of mismanagement was 'Un'ala di riserva', an association which ran around thirteen hotels in the station area with only eight operators. Some of the main tasks of the operators were teaching Italian culture and language as well as supplying cultural mediation services, but they were totally unqualified to fulfil such duties. It was not clear how and why they had been employed, as there were no official selection procedures for both the associations and their operators, but we had the feeling that the whole process was absolutely discretional. Overall, the management of the hotels was completely inadequate because the staff was not trained to deal with migrants, while cultural mediators did not speak any foreign language. We also found that asylum seekers were left without documents for over a year, leading to situations of severe abuse and exploitation. For instance, some of them had sex in exchange for money in the hotels where they were staying; others were illegally hired to work in agriculture. At first, they didn't even have clothes, so we arranged the '5 cents' market, where they could buy or exchange clothes at a very cheap price.[4]

Under the supervision of the head of PCI Cincini, public funds for reception in Campania were handled through a network of private associations which did not meet any objective selection criteria. In this context, the case of the aforementioned 'Un'ala di riserva' association became sadly famous due to the investigation conducted by the Naples prosecutor, who exposed the misuse of public funds. It emerged from the investigation that €152,000 were spent for the purchase of a real estate property in Milan; €733,000 were employed to acquire a phone card service company; €15,000 were used to rent a café and €100,000 went into buying a real estate property in Naples. Lastly, €130,000 were appropriated by the heads of the association, who also stole €345,000 through the falsification of bills. Moreover, members of the regional administration were investigated for having drafting public contracts in exchange of money.

The list of unjustified purchases and fraudulent uses of public money for reception is much longer than the one that was made public by the prosecutor.[5]

Furthermore, as revealed in an interview with the representative of an important union in Campania, this money was often used to support mafia-run businesses:

> The Hobbit hotel in Scampia, where many migrants were housed, belonged to the mafia family of Marano, just like the Tifata resort in Salerno, where migrants were often given food once a day, like dogs. Or the Millennium hotel in Eboli, where migrants lived in a building without windows and doors, which was only later renovated.[6]

In addition, an interview conducted with a social worker revealed that migrants rarely received their €2.50 daily allowance for pocket money to which they were entitled. The money was instead stolen by the managers of the hosting facilities and used to run illegal activities like the one described below:

> Some managers did not give migrants pocket money for four to six months. On top of that, they came up with illegal ways to take advantage of that situation. The €2.5 bonus could be spent exclusively in a pre-established list of shops, which were quite far from the hotels and the city centre. For example, migrants had to make a real journey to buy phone cards to contact their families in their countries and they didn't even have money to buy bus tickets. The managers

Figure 7.3.   Choucha Refugee Camp
Luca Manunza, 2011

would offer to take the pocket money and buy the things migrants needed. Of course, this 'service' came with a high price, which sometimes amounted to 50 per cent of the pocket money that the managers would keep for themselves.[7]

Another interesting aspect about these actors is their racially biased and selective management of migrants. For example, a manager of one such hospitality association showed up at the landing of migrants but selected some specific nationalities of asylum seekers. This person discarded the Eritreans, Somalis and the Syrians based on the assumption that they would not want to stay in Italy and attempt to leave, thus they would not guarantee the monthly income for the association.

The *business* of migration has also produced mechanisms of urbanization and repopulation of urban and rural areas. This sector has played an important role in the transformation of existing social patterns. In the case of Italy, the population of national origin is declining (–0.1 per cent), while the population of international immigrants is increasing with an average rate of 7.8 per cent (Caritas 2015). The presence of migrants has a substantial impact on the urban space, as well as on the broader economic and social systems of the host countries or regions. Migrants play a significant role in the labour force of the hospitality industry—a staffing mechanism mostly implemented in large urban areas. In Italy, the hospitality industry acts as a nexus between different state and non-state actors, as it increases the profits of hotel companies in the absence of formal clients. It was after the tourism market crisis when hotels opened up to 'hospitality', lavishly remunerated by the government. Many of these hotels, pointed out by investigations from the magistracy, have used migrants for maintenance or portage. In other cases, they have been used as forced labour to work in the informal market of fruit and vegetable harvests—that is, low-cost workers for the owners of small and big local businesses (Perrotta 2014). However, for the public administration, the presence of immigrants in urban areas (often ghettoized and isolated in specific sectors) is both a resource and a problem to be managed. A relevant example can be found in the letters sent to the government of the City of Naples from district committees of Piazza Garibaldi, in which the committees complain about the presence of migrants and request more security:

Dear Dr A. S., we met Saturday at the Piazza Municipio, during the demonstration. I am writing you to expose the serious situation (that you already know) about the inhabitants of Garibaldi Sq. and Corso Umberto. The degraded conditions and dirt, disorder, lawlessness and absolute arrogance of the 'characters' that are settled there at every hour of the day. They are Napolitan, Slavs, immigrants and nomads, drunkards and mendicants. We are prisoners in our own home! The negotiations for paid sex take place in via Nolana, right in front of the eyes of children and adults. Thefts 'con pinza' take place peacefully because all warnings to the victim are followed by a warning from the accomplices which move in feline proximity. Buses are dirty, and there you can find a primitive and frightening 'court of miracles'. North Africans sell old shoes all along Corso Umberto and Piazza Garibaldi by day, and by night, they peddle by extracting from their mouths cocaine ovules. The entrance to the city is like a large carousel of rogues, crooks and ruffians. They piss over the walls even in daylight. They do vulgar gestures in front of women and young girls. The inhabitants of the area are tired, bitter, but, most of all, feel afraid and insecure. Dear Dr., we stay with our Mayor from the beginning. We believed and we still believe [that] ... having a different Napoli is possible![8]

Naples municipality receives a great amount of letters like this one which delineates how *dispositifs* of hospitality are perceived as a disastrous management idea. While hospitality encouraged the emergence of coexistence between migrants and natives, it also legitimized a muscular government programme to increase gentrification on the basis of establishing clean and orderly spaces.

Figure 7.4. Choucha Refugee Camp
Luca Manunza, 2011

My hypothesis is that Ordinance No. 3948 has generated a complex set of problems. The hospitality given to migrants in some hotels or residences included a series of paths and activities aimed at integration and interaction of migrants with local people. However, the push for integration was marred by parallel problems related to the management and supervision of funds. Local organizations, such as those managed by the Red Cross in Campania, hosted migrants in hotels, but only managed to provide food and accommodation without properly trained staff and without a social inclusion programme. Even charitable organizations related to the Church, such as the Cooperative Domus Caritatis, have not been exempt from harsh controversy. The latter decided exclusively to host minors instead of adults to receive the double bonus.

The North Africa Emergency, or Emergency North Africa (ENA), officially finished in December 2012. In the aftermath of the programme, the government offered each migrant registered in Italy during the emergency (ENA) a bonus of €500 to encourage them to leave the country (excluding some protected groups that continued the programme) and a special residence permit that would allow them to travel across Europe.

MARE NOSTRUM AND TRITON: THE LAST BORDER

Mare Nostrum was a Roman name for the Mediterranean Sea. The term originally was used by Romans to refer to the Tyrrhenian Sea. The term was again revived by Mussolini for use in fascist colonial propaganda. The Italian government, as in the colonial fascist propaganda, chose this name to be the title of the new operation against 'illegal' immigration in the Mediterranean. The Ministry of Interior Affairs exploited a disastrous event to allocate about €190 million for this new offshore police operation.[9]

On 3 October 2013, in proximity of the Sicilian island of Lampedusa, a boat coming from Libya sank, resulting in 336 deaths, 20 missing people and only 15 survivors. This tragic episode in the Mediterranean prompted Italian Prime Minister Enrico Letta to strengthen the national coastal patrol system, by authorizing the Mare Nostrum operation. The Ministry of Internal Affairs defined this mission as a 'military and humanitarian' one, which aimed at 'increasing and strengthening surveillance and rescue operations at sea to improve the safety of human lives', preventing the Mediterranean from becoming a 'sea of death'.[10]

Beyond any rhetoric, this mission led to the reinforcement of the Constant Vigilance operation, which the Italian Navy had been conducting since 2004 in the Channel of Sicily through permanent air and sea patrols of the coast.

The Mare Nostrum operation contained a double objective: it was presented simultaneously as a programme to ensure the safety of life at sea over 175 miles and fight illegal trafficking of migrants. The operation led to the rescue of some 13,000 migrants, the detention of 336 smugglers, the seizure of 9 vessels and the implementation of 439 actions concerning the search and the rescue of migrants. However, after the rescue missions, many migrants were transferred to the most important ship of the Italian Navy (*San Marco*) and identified there to unburden identification centres on the national territory. At the same time, many refugees refused to be identified for several days, in order to have the chance of applying for asylum in other European countries, as established by the Dublin II regulation.

This situation gave rise to harsh tensions on the *San Marco* ship, leading to some migrants being subject to violence during identification procedures and to violations of the Eurodac regulation on the transmission of asylum seekers' biometrical data. In particular, violations revolved around the lack of effective information provided to asylum seekers, which were not offered in a language they could understand and in a manner that recognized cultural and gender-based differences. In addition to these violations, the identification processes also infringed upon the fundamental rights of migrants as physical and psychological pressure were used against extremely vulnerable people such as recently rescued migrants. Hence, while the Eurodac regulation provides several tools to ensure the protection of migrants' fundamental rights, the actual procedures carried out on the *San Marco* ship during the first rescue operations and the role played by the representatives of other national and international bodies remained obscure. At the same time, the overall approach seems to be more oriented towards the containment of migration flows than the reception of refugees and asylum seekers. The estimated cost of the Mare Nostrum operation amounted to some €9 million per month—an unbearable cost for the Italian government, which declared the end of the operation at the beginning of October 2014.

Only a few weeks later, Italy announced its new strategy to face the migration emergency: the Triton operation. Triton was intended to replace Mare Nostrum and was presented by the Minister of Internal Affairs as follows:

> Yesterday the Council of Ministers decided that the start of the new Frontex mission should coincide with the end of the Mare Nostrum operation. ... Europe takes the sea for the first time. European countries will work together in defence of the Schengen borders and the Mediterranean borders.
>
> Over €100,000,000 was spent for the Mare Nostrum operation in a year, the new operation will have no cost for Italy. The Frontex agency is going to start a new operation called Triton that is expected to cost little more than €3,000,000 per month and will be covered by European funds. The new operation managed

by Frontex aims at patrolling Schengen borders within the range of 30 miles from the Italian coast. Hence, controls will be accomplished in Italian waters, while the rescue and search of migrants in international water will be the responsibility of North African countries.[11]

Notwithstanding the Minister's attempt to emphasize the alleged continuity between the two operations,[12] Frontex Executive director Gil Arias-Fernández has repeatedly underlined that Triton is extremely different from Mare Nostrum, not only in terms of resources, but also as to its aims and objectives: while the old Italian operation aimed at promoting rescue operations at sea, the new one is specifically framed as a border security operation, which delegates the responsibility of undertaking rescue operations to member countries.[13] Moreover, in contrast to the Italian Minister's statement, it has not been entirely financed by Frontex, but it involves contributions by fifteen member states. The assets provided by EU member states to help Italy control its borders consist of two surveillance aircraft, three ships and seven teams to conduct intelligence operations and run screening identification procedures.

Thus, Triton could be interpreted as a political redefinition of the borders, which transcends conventional geopolitical contingencies and is embodied by an extremely asymmetric conflict in which migrant vessels are opposed to a high-tech army. Italy's ambiguous attitude is highlighted by its attempts to hide from the public opinion the real aims of the operation and, at the same time, to represent its political role in EU foreign policy as crucial to the most important agreements in the field of migration. Moreover, Triton does not come without advantages for Italy—it effectively minimizes the economic and political burden of rescues at sea while significantly increasing controls in Italy's territorial waters.

However, in spite of the strengthening of security at the Schengen borders, in 2015 migrant landings on Italian coasts increased about a third compared to 2014, as shown by the data of the Italian Ministry of Internal Affairs.

More importantly, the number of deaths increased as well, leading to 3,000 deaths in the Channel of Sicily only in 2015. Italy's securitarian obsession brought about an approach to the migration emergency that is framed in terms of mere border control and is in line with the main trend that characterizes the current political direction of the European Union. In other words, the key to understanding the contemporary *dispositifs* of migration management and the practices of international actors such as Frontex is, as highlighted by Palidda (2009), to focus on the crucial distinction between citizens and non-citizens, which goes hand in hand with the separation between *productive classes* and *dangerous classes*. In this conception, the main purpose of Triton is to facilitate the collection of detailed data on migrants in order to identify the ones to let in and the ones to keep out.

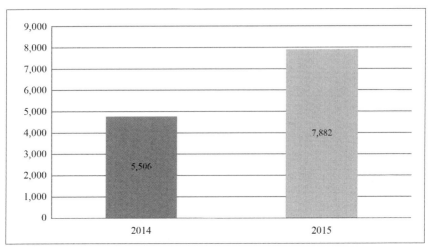

Figure 7.5. Arrivals on Italian coasts, 2014–2015
Source: Ministry of Interior (2015)

CONCLUSION

The chapter has evaluated the social costs and function of emergency operations revolved around the issues of migration in the Mediterranean and highlighted how increasingly privatized humanitarian agencies play a direct role in the management of migration and post-conflict settlements.[14] The trends highlighted in this chapter are embodied in the establishment of permanent/ temporary war zones, where the use of exceptional measures becomes the norm and migrants are not entitled to a legal, social and political status (Mirzoeff 2004; Dal Lago 2010). The construction of such places, which can be defined as modern camps, in Italy (e.g. CARA, SPRAR) and abroad reflects the fundamental principle of contemporary securitarian management which affirms that citizenship does not derive from the condition of being a human, but being a human is recognized exclusively in relation to an existing citizenship status. As to the ENA plan and the Mare Nostrum and Triton operations, the chapter has highlighted how humanitarian interventions and the use of military power in an emergency situation are intertwined in a complementary relationship, in which the rule and the exception coexist and thus the variable geometry of power is adjusted.

In this context, humanitarian intervention has become a tactical instrument and a strategic resource. The construction of detention centres for migrants, the establishment of special units of the army and private police, the clientelistic distribution of funds for basic assistance and the collusion between crime and politics are only some of the *dispositifs* adopted by the Italian state to deal with the migration emergency. Handling the ordinary through emergency practices has become a recurrent element in EU policies which respond to the neoliberal imperative of maximizing profits or, in other words, eliminating the human surplus (Koizumi and Hoffstaedeter 2015; Dardot and Laval 2014). The complex transition phase following the protests of 2011 in the Maghreb region continues to have an impact on the relationship between the two sides of the Mediterranean immigration and asylum nexus. The most recent bilateral agreements and practices of cooperation are exclusively directed at counteracting irregular immigration (Ozzano and Giorgi 2016) and building new, unreachable borders for those who want to cross the sea.[15]

With Mare Nostrum and, subsequently, Triton the European Union has failed to adopt a common policy to safeguard migrants' lives and their right to enter the Schengen area to apply for international protection. This, in conjunction with the worsening of several conflicts in countries like Syria, has led to a growing militarization of the Mediterranean. EU institutions have not yet programmed a legal access route to Europe for asylum seekers or those who seek jobs. Meanwhile, the number of migrants who lose their lives and remain unidentified in the attempt to reach Europe has sadly increased. These are the premises to reflect on the foundations and outcomes of the ongoing Triton operation and the wider approach to migration adopted by Italy and, to a large extent, the European Union. Securitarian management of migration continues to have a dramatic impact on thousands of lives that escape from wars and poverty to seek protection in ostensibly democratic Western countries.

NOTES

1. The European Border Surveillance System (commonly abbreviated Eurosur) is an EU-wide programme that uses drones, reconnaissance aircraft and satellite remote sensors to track migration. The programme was put into effect by the EU Parliament on 10 October 2013. On 2 December 2013, Eurosur was initiated in eighteen EU member states and Norway. Frontex is an agency of the European Union established in 2004 to manage the cooperation between national border guards securing its external borders.

2. President Giorgio Napolitano, interview during the official visit in Florence (21 May 2011). Available at: http://www.ilfattoquotidiano.it/2015/02/18/libia-napoli tano-litalia-non-puo-tirarsi-come-nel-2011/1436784/

3. Author's interview with Mohammed Abu Amra at Chucha Camp, Tunisia (14 February 2011).

4. Author's interview with F.E., Naples (30 May 2015).

5. Among other things, some €5,720 was spent on football match tickets and shamelessly expensive restaurant bills.

6. Author's interview with R.S., Naples (27 May 2015).
7. Author's interview with R.S., Naples (27 May 2015).
8. Letter sent to the Mayor of Naples and his staff in April 2012. Courtesy of an official member of the municipality of Naples.
9. For the detailed cost of the mission, see 'Mare Nostrum'. Available at: http://www.marina.difesa.it/cosa-facciamo/operazioni-concluse/Pagine/mare-nostrum.aspx
10. Angelino Alfano, 'Ministry of Internal Affairs, Press Conference, Palazzo Chigi, Roma' (14 October 2013). Available at: http://www.difesa.it/Primo_Piano/Pagine/Mare_Nostrum.aspx
11. Angelino Alfano, 'Ministry of Internal Affairs, Press Conference, Luxemburg' (9 October 2014). Available at: http://www.interno.gov.it/it/notizie/novembre-parte-triton-sostituira-mare-nostrum
12. Angelino Alfano, 'Ministry of Internal Affairs, Press Conference, Luxemburg' (9 October 2014). Available at: http://www.interno.gov.it/it/notizie/novembre-parte-triton-sostituira-mare-nostrum
13. The declaration of Gil Arias-Fernández can be found at: http://www.interno.gov.it/sites/default/files/camera_assemblea_informativa_alfano_16.10.2014.pdf
14. See also Cole (2005); Castles, Özkul and Cubas (2015); Pech and Padis (2004) and Zolo (2010).
15. In 2002, the Bossi-Fini Law was adopted to further limit the possibilities of legal immigration and employment and to reduce the presence of 'irregular and *clandestine*' immigrants in Italy. Since 2002, illegal immigration has been considered a criminal offence in Italy.

BIBLIOGRAPHY

Azzellini D and Kanzleiter B (2006) *Le business de la guerre*. Roubaix: Gatuzain.
Campesi G (2011) The Arab Spring and the crisis of the European border regime: Manufacturing emergency in the Lampedusa crisis. EUI Working Papers RS-CAS 2011/59. Available at: http://cadmus.eui.eu/bitstream/handle/1814/19375/rscas_2011_59.pdf?sequence=1
Caritas (2015) (ed) *XXIV Rapporto Immigrazione Caritas e Migrantes*. Rome: Caritas Italiana.
Castles S, Özkul D and Magdalena AC (eds) (2015) *Social Transformation and Migration: National and Local Experience in South Korea, Turkey, Mexico and Australia*. Basingstoke: Palgrave Macmillan.
Cole D (2005) *Enemy Aliens: Double Standards and Constitutional Freedoms in the War on Terrorism*. New York: The New Press.
Dal Lago A (2010) *Le nostre guerre: filosofia e sociologia dei conflitti armati*. Rome: Manifesto Libri.
Dardot P and Laval C (2014) *The New Way of the World: On Neoliberal Society*. London: Verso.
Foucault M (1997) *'Il faut défendre la société': Cours au Collège de France (1975–1976)*, Bertani M and Fontata A (eds). Paris: Seuil/Gallimard.

Harcourt EB (2009) La strada verso il profiling razziale è lastricata di immigrati. In Palidda S (ed) *Razzismo democratico: La persecuzione degli stranieri in Europa*. Milano: Agenzia X.

Knight P (2003) *Mussolini and Fascism*. New York: Routledge.

Koizumi K and Hoffstaedter G (eds) (2015) *Urban Refugees: Challenges in Protection, Service and Policy*. Abingdon: Routledge.

Mazzeo A (2011) Mineo, profughi SPA. *AgoraVox* (7 April). Available at: http://www.agoravox.it/Mineo-profughi-Spa.html

Ministry of Interior (2015) Presenze dei migranti nelle strutture di accoglienza in Italia. Available at: http://www.interno.gov.it/sites/default/files/dati_statistici_marzo_2015.pdf

Mirzoeff N (2004) *Guardare la guerra: Immagini del potere globale*, Bortolini M (trans). Rome: Meltemi.

Ozzano L and Giorgi A (2016) *European Culture Wars and the Italian Case: Which side are you on?* Abingdon: Routledge.

Palidda S (2009) Insertion, integration and rejection of immigration in Italy. In: Guild E, Groeneddijk K and Carrera S (eds) *Illiberal Liberal States: Immigration, Citizenship and Integration in the EU*. Farnham: Ashgate.

Palidda S (ed) (2011) *Racial Criminalisation of Migrants in the 21st Century*. Farnham: Ashgate.

Pech T and Padis M-O (2004) *Le Multinazionali del Cuore: Le Organizzazioni non Governatove tra politicha e mercato*, Valenti S (trans). Milano: Feltrinelli.

Perrotta D (2014) Ben oltre lo sfruttamento: lavorare da migranti in agricoltura. *Rivista il Mulino* 1(14). DOI: 10.1402/75749.

Petrillo A (ed) (2009) *Biopolitica di un rifiuto: Le rivolte anti-discarica a Napoli e in Campania*. Verona: Ombre Corte.

Saitta P (2011) Neoliberismo e controllo dell'immigrazione: Il fallimento della 'tolleranza zero' e i paradossali esiti dell'informalità. In: Carzo D (ed) *Narrare l'altro: Pratiche discorsive sull'immigrazione*. Rome: Aracne, 107–126.

Sayad A (1999) *La double absence: Des illusions de l'émigré aux souffrances de l'immigré*. Paris: Éditions du Seuil.

Zolo D (2010) *Tramonto globale: la fame, il patibolo, la guerra*. Firenze: Firenze University Press.

Chapter 8

Cease to Exist?

The European 'Social' Model and the Hardening of 'Soft' EU Law

Ian Bruff[1]

The ongoing and seemingly unending crises of the Eurozone, and of the European integration project more broadly, have dominated the headlines over the last decade. More recently, these have begun to have notable consequences for not just 'economic' questions related to budget deficits, sovereign debt and a possible lost decade in terms of economic stagnation but, increasingly, the social and political fabric of a range of European countries as well. As such, it is clear that Europe is now at a critical juncture in its contemporary history. Inspired by facet methodology, the chapter focuses on the fate of the much-discussed notion of a European 'social' model (ESM) in order to analyze the growing entanglements between economic and social policy in the European Union (EU) since the 1990s.

An important aspect of these developments has been what I call the hardening of 'soft' law. This has manifested itself in the gradual mutation of mechanisms such as the Open Method of Coordination (OMC), which was established in 2000 and initially concerned with the relatively voluntary and dialogical sharing of different examples of 'best practice' from across the EU on social themes such as unemployment and welfare policy. Since then, there has been a steady 'hardening' of these mechanisms towards more punitive and centralized processes based on the assumption that there is in fact a singular (neoliberal) best practice to be applied across the EU at the behest of the European Commission. However, there has not been the ignorance of 'social' goals, but their growing articulation-cum-subordination to 'necessary' economic objectives via increasingly hierarchical legal mechanisms. Hence, the chapter shows how even governance practices seemingly far removed from what we associate with the term 'authoritarianism' are part of the rise of authoritarian neoliberalism. Indeed, one could argue that the notion of an ESM is central to this development in Europe, whether one considers the emergence of more coercive legal apparatuses or the growing social and political instability which increasingly calls them into question.

Through the argument that the reconceptualization of the ESM is central to understanding the EU's sense of self and possible future(s), the chapter is structured as follows. The next section makes use of the recent emergence of the facet methodology approach to outline a method for making sense of the EU and especially for arriving at a set of core research concerns. This allows me to establish the notion of an ESM as crucial for understanding the EU. The subsequent sections elaborate, discussing firstly the re-interpretation of the ESM in the 1990s and secondly the establishment and gradual hardening of 'soft' law in the area of social policy, the latter coming to the fore from 2000 onwards. I then cover post-2010 developments, especially in relation to the new Economic Governance arrangements, and finally the latent fragility of the new regime. The chapter concludes with some comments on what this all means for the ESM's contemporary relevance.

MAKING SENSE OF THE EUROPEAN UNION

Full comprehension of the world in all of its complexity is highly unlikely, for 'some kind of assumptions (as to what we are thinking *about*) must be made before we can even begin to think' (Thompson 1995: 48, original emphasis). This is especially the case for the EU, which is a multilayered, multifaceted entity of considerable complexity and which has evolved radically since its beginnings in the 1950s. I often start my courses which cover the EU by stating to students that acquiring a full, comprehensive and in-depth knowledge of the EU is impossible, for both researchers and students. The time that would be needed to account for all aspects of the EU's complex, unique institutionalizations and practices makes it inevitable that, at the very moment that this process is completed, the EU would have evolved in one way or another, forcing us to start again in our task.

In the past, I have argued that 'the complexity of the world in which we live means that research has to be undertaken in a myriad of overlapping and interconnected social relations' (van Apeldoorn et al. 2010: 216; see also Bruff 2011). This means that 'even what is in principle a holistic perspective cannot say everything and must necessarily prioritise' (Dunn 2009: 318). That is, *all* researchers choose (implicitly or explicitly) to privilege certain ways of viewing the world over others. However, these declarations still left open the question of the doing of research (although see van Apeldoorn et al. 2010: 218–9), especially when the object of enquiry (i.e. the EU) is always in a state of complex evolution. Indeed, this is reflected in the EU literature itself, which even in its most enlightened forms still has a tendency to present different approaches as relatively self-contained yet also relatively universal in scope, making it difficult to envisage how dialogue can take place.[2]

So how can we make sense of the EU, and moreover of the EU's contribution to the emergence of distinctively European forms of authoritarian neoliberalism? As the quick-witted reader will have noted, I have already narrowed significantly the key set of research concerns and questions for this chapter, from the EU in general to authoritarian neoliberalism more specifically. Nevertheless, the two are related, for—as this book demonstrates—although authoritarian neoliberalism has some core tenets it is not simply a template conceptualization that is then uncritically applied across the world. It is here that I introduce the 'facet methodology' approach, which has emerged recently out of research projects housed within the Morgan Centre for Research into Everyday Lives at the University of Manchester.[3]

Up to now, facet methodology has been utilized for the study of the range of dynamics which constitute the lived experiences of personal relationships and relationalities, but the principles are relevant for other forms of research. This can be found in the visual metaphor and defining principles outlined by Jennifer Mason. For example, on the metaphor:

> The methodology we are developing involves envisioning research fields as constructed through combinations and constellations of *facets* as we might see in a cut gemstone. ... It is in the way the light is cast and plays in the facets that we come to perceive and appreciate the distinctive character of the gemstone. ... Now imagine that the gemstone encapsulates the thing we want to understand and explore. ... [The facets] will involve different lines of enquiry, and different ways of seeing. ... The aim of our facet methodology approach is to *create a strategically illuminating set of facets in relation to specific research concerns and questions*: not a random set, or an eclectic set, or a representative set, or a total set. The rigour of the approach comes ultimately from researcher skill, inventiveness, insight and imagination—in deciding how best to carve the facets so that they catch the light in the best possible way. (Mason 2011a: 76–7, original emphases)

This means that a key defining principle is what she calls a 'connective ontology', which instead of abstracting *from* the multidimensional, relational and entwined nature of the world—for example, through long lists of different layers or dimensions, or of dualisms such as micro/macro—abstracts *through* the entwinements, seeking out connections and relationalities. Hence, the facets are neither self-evident nor self-contained: they are 'purposefully created in relation to existing background knowledge and theoretical debate to create flashes of insight with striking or revealing effects' (ibid.: 80). As such, facets are not simply in the eye of the beholder creating them, but at the same time their (re)construction 'requires and celebrates researcher creativity, inventiveness, [and] a "playful" approach to epistemology' (ibid.: 76). Different lines of enquiry will be grounded in different entwinements, and moreover different conclusions could be drawn from analysis of the same entwinements. This artful understanding of research bears fruit when it comes to generating and substantiating knowledge: 'What we see is not the totality but instead a constellation or an association of flashes created by the facets, in which some elements shine particularly brightly or intensely. This helps us to perceive the distinctive character of what we are looking at' (ibid.: 81).

Therefore, it is impossible to specify 'this' or 'that' facet in a deterministic fashion, which would repeat the problems inherent to more typical social science approaches, namely the search for categorizability when studying a complex world. Nevertheless, 'everybody connects causes and effects ... [because] everybody thinks' (Gramsci 1985: 25), which means that 'even if the facts are always unique and changeable in the flux of movement of history, the concepts can [and must] be theorised' (Gramsci 1971: 427). Hence, a facet methodology approach does not deny the need to produce revealing insights and convincing arguments, but it does make researchers more aware of how they can employ 'concepts ... as expectations rather than as rules. ... [These concepts appear] in historical practice, not as ideal types fulfilled in historical evolution' (Thompson 1995: 62).

As noted in the introduction, key to the arguments made in this chapter is the assumption that the ESM is central to understanding the EU—that is, when examining the EU gemstone, the 'social' elements shine particularly brightly.[4] This set of research expectations is drawn from numerous claims made in relation to the ESM, both in academic publications and political discourses. The latter will be considered in the next section; on the former, Delanty and Rumford echo many when arguing that the notion of an ESM is 'central to the European Union's sense of self' (Delanty and Rumford 2005: 25). Furthermore, the term ESM 'resonates with debates on the fundamental values, shared history, and political identity to which Europe can lay claim' (ibid.: 106). In other words, it is not just the policy and institutional areas pertaining to social concerns that glow particularly intensely, but their broader, more intangible and in some ways more fundamental resonances. Indeed, it is not difficult to find various grand claims made on this point: see Rifkin's (2004) discussion of 'The European Dream', Hill's (2010) book on 'The European Way' and Vaughan-Whitehead's (2015: 3) claim that the ESM is the 'soul' of the EU. It is thus unsurprising to see Jepsen and Serrano Pascual (2005: 232) observe that, even if invoked in less encompassing ways, 'the concept of ESM is often taken for granted ... in a manner implying that all further discussion is superfluous'. In consequence:

The European Social Model is in fact a loosely defined normative concept and, as such, is used with differing meanings in accordance with rather ambiguous definitions. A clear definition of what constitutes its essence seems to be lacking in most documents on the subject, while a review of the most important of these documents reveals, furthermore, that, insofar as definitions are to be found, they do not necessarily converge. (ibid.)

For Jepsen and Serrano Pascual this means that 'the significance of the concept could be interpreted as one manifestation of a political struggle to push certain items onto the political agenda' (ibid.). Therefore, while it is fair to say that the ESM is 'best thought of as representing a cluster of policy priorities centring on welfare, social partnership and a mixed economy' (Delanty and Rumford 2005: 109) which place economic and social concerns on a par with one another, it is also true that the *invocation itself* is politically charged. As such, although it is logical and worthy for scholars to point to the decline of the ESM in recent decades,[5] this should not be the core of our critique. Instead, we ought to build on these observations and enquire into *the decline of the traditional conception of the ESM and the ways in which it is being reconceptualized*.

The next section elaborates, primarily with reference to developments in the EU from the 1990s onwards. Of particular relevance is how the reconceptualization of the ESM is inextricably bound up with the evolution of the EU's legal architecture. This is important because, as Brenner et al. (2010: 184–5, original emphasis) argue, neoliberalization processes have over time generated 'important *cumulative* impacts or sedimented patternings upon the uneven institutional landscapes of world capitalism', which gradually reshape not just specific domains or fields but also the landscapes themselves. As such, the reconceptualization of the ESM has ramifications which go well beyond just these facets of the EU gemstone, not least because of how they have become increasingly entwined with other (often economic) facets.

TRANSFORMING THE ESM, IN THE NAME OF THE ESM

Principally, three features are generally held to have distinguished Western Europe after 1945 from other middle- to high-income capitalist countries/ regions (see Albert 1993; Hay et al. 1999; Esping-Andersen 1990). These are relatively low levels of socioeconomic inequality, generous welfare states and a significant role for organized labour in the workplace and in policymaking—all of which were underpinned by a supportive political consensus that gave a prominent role to 'non-market' institutions in the political economy.

This forms the basis for what Jepsen and Serrano Pascual (2005: 232–3) view as the two assumptions which are common across different understandings and constructions of the ESM: (1) the binary opposition between the ESM and the US model, the latter of which is portrayed as individualistic, unequal and uncaring; (2) this superiority of the ESM being based on the interrelation of the goals of economic success and social cohesion, that is, of 'performance' and normative factors. These became points around which a wide range of social and political actors and opinions could rally, especially in light of ubiquitous discourses on 'globalization' in the 1990s and the contemporaneous broadening and deepening of the European integration project. During this decade, the idea of a pan-European social model (i.e. inclusive of post-socialist states readying themselves for entry into the EU) was so prominent that it became a dominant trope.

It is important to note that the rise of this discourse came after developments in EU institutionalizations and practices which would make the ESM, as traditionally conceived, harder to maintain. As noted by many critical political economy scholars, the revamping of the European integration process in the 1980s was predicated upon the rise to ascendancy of an alliance of transnational capital, principally in the form of the European Round Table of Industrialists (ERT), and elements of the European Commission, in articulating a 'competitiveness' discourse that arose out of the initial desire to improve economic performance and which became hegemonic.[6] This entailed the support for the European Single Market and, later, Economic and Monetary Union (EMU). Although the so-called Social Dimension was also introduced during this period, unlike 'economic' initiatives, it was on a voluntary and not statutory basis.

The subordination of social to economic concerns can be dated to this period, and during the 1990s the emphasis remained on unifying the Single Market rather than harmonizing regulations in line with traditional notions of the ESM. Hence, the dominant thrust was towards the elimination of 'distortions' to the market—for example, via directives to liberalize key sectors such as telecommunications and the significant reduction in the scope for national states to support industries—rather than the realization of social goals. In addition, it is true to say that the 1992 Maastricht Treaty was the first EU Treaty to contain text on social issues and thus could potentially form the basis for binding EU legislation. Nevertheless, it also mandated a series of criteria for member states to meet in order to be included in EMU (such as low budget deficits and low inflation), which by default took priority over alternative socioeconomic goals such as full employment and reduced inequality.

It is with the above in mind that one must read the striking declarations at the start of the European Commission's famous 1994 White Paper on European social policy. Here it is stated that 'there are a number of shared values which form the basis of the European social model. These include democracy and individual rights, free collective bargaining, the market economy, equality of opportunity for all and social welfare and solidarity ... economic and social progress must go hand in hand' (European Commission 1994: 2). So far, so traditional for the ESM. However, the language shifts thereafter, when the document goes into more detail. For instance, already by page 3, when referring to the earlier White Paper on growth, competitiveness and employment (European Commission, 1993), it is stated that the paper

> raised a number of fundamental questions which are central to the future development of social policy, notably that competitiveness is crucial for wealth and job creation and that labour market policies in particular need to be reoriented. The principles set out in the White Paper need to be borne in mind in the formulation of future Union social policy, as do the Union macro-economic guidelines. (European Commission 1994: 3)

And on page 4, when discussing guiding principles and objectives, the Commission argues that 'the accent has to be shifted from the objective of [welfare] assistance to the objective of employment generation'. In a few pages, the ESM as traditionally conceived is fundamentally challenged, despite the affirmative rhetoric at the start of the document. The ESM could continue to exist, but only if 'social' institutions and practices proved able to adapt successfully to the challenges of the contemporary period.

It is instructive to remind readers that during this period of widespread discussions of 'globalization' and its potential negative impact on social standards via a competitive 'race to the bottom', cross-country coordination via the EU was often attractive for those in favour of an ESM as traditionally conceived. While developments such as the above were acknowledged as fetters on the establishment and maintenance of an ESM at the EU level, the potential for these constraints to be replaced by more enabling mechanisms and regulations was stressed.[7] The major problem for these optimistic perspectives was how the ESM was being reconceptualized via the ongoing institutionalizations of EU-level practices in the opposite direction of travel. These made it increasingly difficult for social concerns to have anything resembling parity with the objectives of unifying the Single Market and establishing EMU.

It is worth restating here that, despite appearances to the contrary in this section, it is precisely the articulation-cum-subordination of social policy goals to objectives such as competitiveness and macroeconomic guidelines such as low budget deficits that makes it so important to explore the EU through its social facets. As will be discussed in the next two sections, it helps

throw light on how the potential for member states to *self-impose* transformative, neoliberalizing reforms gradually emerged and became ascendant, with
highly significant consequences.

THE ESTABLISHMENT AND
GRADUAL HARDENING OF 'SOFT' LAW

Before discussing the emergence and hardening of mechanisms such as the
OMC, it is worth briefly outlining what 'soft' law is broadly taken to mean.
Soft law refers to policymaking processes and institutional procedures which
do not have any legally binding force, as in 'hard' law. Nevertheless, it does
specify objectives, priorities, targets and standards which have been agreed
by those that are covered by the processes and procedures. As such, soft law's
potential power is not rooted in traditional, formal understandings of governing but instead in the roles played by symbolism, knowledge paradigms, peer
pressure and principles underpinning negotiations. In the EU this is particularly important, because it is a set of institutions which are defined by the differentiated distribution of legal power (for example, between member states
and EU institutions and also between different EU institutions), overlapping
jurisdictions (both spatially and institutionally), and a post-territorial conception of statehood which nevertheless bases membership on territorial nation-
states. Additionally, how the EU is defined by these three characteristics has
evolved over time, in accordance with Treaty and other law.

Soft law became more prominent from the 1990s onwards, as a means
of managing the growing size and complexity of the EU plus some of the
controversies over 'national sovereignty' that emerged during this period (for
instance, the United Kingdom's opt-out from the Social Chapter, the Danish
referendum rejecting the Maastricht Treaty). Hence soft law was often associated with the notion of subsidiarity, which states that in those areas where
it does not have exclusive competence the EU does not take action, unless
such action is agreed to be more effective than action taken at a national or
local level. As such, soft law in the EU can be understood as referring to
those processes and procedures which develop EU-level goals and objectives
but leave the corresponding formulation and implementation of policies and
institutional changes to member states.

As can hopefully be seen, both of these notions contain within them the
potential for a harder and more hierarchical understanding of policymaking to
emerge. For example, should it be considered that (1) more needs to be done
to achieve the commonly agreed objectives, priorities, targets and standards;
and (2) part of the solution involves greater coordination above the national

level, then soft law provides a useful platform upon which to develop new, more coercive legal mechanisms. If this proves to be the case, then the legal architecture moves closer to a more formal and explicit 'codification of both prohibitions and positive injunctions ... [organized] not only as repression of acts forbidden by law, but also as *repression of a failure to do what the law prescribes*' (Poulantzas 1978: 83, emphasis added). As will be detailed in the following pages, this is precisely what happened from the 1990s onwards, with important implications for the 'social' facets of the EU gemstone and thus for how we understand the gemstone as a whole.

The genesis of the OMC lies in the emergence of soft law in association with the principle of subsidiarity, but more formally it lay in the establishment of the European Employment Strategy (EES). The EES itself was developed out of the European Council summit in Essen in 1994, which called for a coordinated and integrated employment strategy across the EU:

> The European Council urges the Member States to transpose these recommendations in their individual policies into a multiannual programme having regard to the specific features of their economic and social situation. It requests the Labour and Social Affairs and Economic and Financial Affairs Councils and the Commission to keep close track of employment trends, monitor the relevant policies of the Member States and report annually to the European Council on further progress on the employment market, starting in December 1995. (European Council 1994: 2)

The legal basis for the EES was institutionalized by the 1997 Treaty of Amsterdam, which declared that a labour market which is more responsive to economic change was henceforth a matter of common interest across the EU. In response, the Luxembourg Jobs Summit in 1997 (which established the EES) announced four pillars to base common objectives and targets on: employability, entrepreneurship, adaptability and equal opportunities.

Therefore, although the growing presence of social concerns in EU treaties, strategies and agendas appeared to indicate the possibilities for economic and social goals to have parity with one another, there was a repeated emphasis on the need for social policy to complement already-established economic objectives and thus for it to be assessed not in terms of its social content but its economic utility (see also Wöhl 2007, 2011, especially on the framing of gender equality as gender mainstreaming). For instance, the European Commission's 'Standardisation Policy' for the Single Market states: 'Due to their role in protecting health, safety, security, and the environment, standards are important to the public. The EU has an active standardisation policy that promotes standards as a way to better regulat[e] and enhance the competitiveness of European industry' (European Commission 2016). As such, the focus of most EU literatures on whether initiatives such as the EES were driven by member states or the EU was/is missing the point. Instead, it ought to be acknowledged that the legal capacities for fundamentally redefining the ESM, *in the name of the ESM*, were now part of EU governance practices through how they established explicit connections between: individual member states and common EU objectives; and social aspirations and economic necessities. In other words, the ongoing marginalization of the ESM as traditionally conceived actually intensified the glow given off by the EU's social facets, making them increasingly central to analysis because of how they threw light on a wider range of domains and mechanisms via their growing entwinements with other (often economic) aspects of the gemstone.

This allows us to appreciate more appropriately the significance of the famous 2000 Lisbon Strategy. Much discussion has understandably centred on the goal for the EU to become the world's most dynamic economic region within a decade, with much of the renewed vitality coming from emergent industries rooted in the so-called Knowledge-based Economy (KBE). This, combined with the collapse of the dotcom boom in 2001, the criticisms of the Strategy articulated in the midterm Kok report of 2004, plus the uneven and often sluggish economic performance across the EU during the 2000s, led many (academically and politically) to conclude that the Strategy was a failure. Nevertheless, we see something else once we place the Strategy in the context of legal developments up to that point (see also Jessop 2006). For instance, whereas the centre of gravity in the 1994 White Paper and the EES was still within the national realm, that is, for social policy goals at the EU level to be tailored to the diversity found across the continent, the OMC was formalized as the instrument of the Lisbon Strategy as a means of

> spreading best practice and achieving greater convergence towards the main EU goals ... fixing guidelines for the Union combined with specific timetables for achieving the goals which they set in the short, medium and long terms ... establishing, where appropriate, quantitative and qualitative indicators and benchmarks ... translating these European guidelines into national and regional policies by setting specific targets and adopting measures ... periodic monitoring, evaluation and peer review organised as mutual learning processes. (European Council 2000: 7)

From this point forward, a ratcheting process was put in place. This has had four key dimensions: (1) any perceived failures in social policy terms, for instance on unemployment, are of common concern for the EU as a whole; (2) these failures are of common concern mainly in terms of their economic utility; (3) in consequence, social policy continues to be subordinated and is increasingly connected to broader economic objectives; but (IV) in terms of taking action through the OMC, the failures are not understood in this broader context but, crucially, as the absence of sufficient political will to implement 'necessary' and 'appropriate' social policy reforms. Why else would this be one of the main recommendations of the Kok report? 'The European Commission should deliver, to the Spring European Council in the most public manner possible, an annual league table of Member State progress towards achieving the 14 key indicators and targets. Countries that have performed well should be praised, those that have done badly castigated' (High Level Group 2004: 44).

The Kok report was not implemented fully, but nevertheless its call for greater simplicity catalyzed the integration of economic and social policy guidelines, kept formally separate in the original Strategy. Hence, from the mid-2000s onwards, the articulation-cum-subordination of social to economic concerns was explicit, with 'best practice' increasingly positioned within the Commission's understanding of the situation rather than emergent out of dialogical interaction between a range of political and social actors such as member states, the Commission, the European Council, trade unions, employers' associations and NGOs (Zeitlin 2008; Amable, Demmou and Ledezma 2009; van Apeldoorn 2009). Nevertheless, the *responsibility* for any perceived failures still lay with social policy at the member state level. As the Commission stated in July 2008, just two months before the collapse of Lehman Brothers:

> In order to make full use of the potential of the Social OMC, the present Communication has set out a number of areas where the method can be improved, reinforced or further developed. These measures revolve around four objectives: first, *increasing political commitment* and the visibility of the process; second, strengthening the positive *interaction with other EU policies* [IB: economic objectives]; third, reinforcing the analytical tools underpinning the process, with a view to moving towards the definition of *quantified targets* and enhancing evidence-based policymaking [IB: note the absence of qualitative indicators mentioned in the 2000 Strategy]; fourth, increasing ownership in Member States, by *boosting implementation* and enhancing mutual learning. (European Commission 2008: 8, emphases added)

POST-2010 DEVELOPMENTS

This all laid the basis for the Europe 2020 strategy announced in early 2010, which essentially continued in the same direction: a hardening and neoliberalizing of EU legal mechanisms in the area of social policy. For instance, the integrated guidelines were now formally organized into an annual European Semester cycle of surveillance, policy/institutional recommendations and implementation. Even though the warning signs were present in the 1990s, what was in that decade a relatively open, dialogical, horizontal and 'best practice' set of mechanisms had now hardened into a relatively closed, punitive, hierarchical and '*the* best practice' set of procedures. Moreover, this evolution was characterized by the abandonment of an ESM as traditionally conceived, sometimes even rhetorically.

It should hopefully be clear that all of these developments took place *prior* to the emergence of the sovereign debt crisis in Greece in 2010. In other words, post-2010 developments should *not* be viewed purely in terms of a response to exceptional and largely economic crises. While there is an important element of this, the outbreak of the Eurozone crises signified much more—by virtue of the aforementioned integration of economic and social policy guidelines, the subordination of social concerns to economic objectives, the responsibility for 'failure' being placed at the door of social policy at the member state level and the more general hardening of 'soft' law. Therefore, for the purposes of this chapter it is less important to know of the details of the different post-2010 developments—such as the Euro Plus Pact, the Six-Pack, the Two-Pack, and the Treaty on Stability, Coordination and Governance—than to understand that they accelerated and intensified *in the same direction of travel* as what took place up to 2010.

As is noted throughout the book, processes of neoliberalization do not merely entail the smooth substitution of one set of policy/institutional preferences or paradigms for another. This is of particular relevance for the EU, for (as stated earlier) it is a set of institutions which are defined by the differentiated distribution of legal power, overlapping jurisdictions, and a post-territorial conception of statehood which nevertheless bases membership on territorial nation-states. Hence, the EU as a totality will always be defined by some degree of diversity across a range of domains, for example within and between its member states and also within and between different policy and institutional fields. As a result, the dissatisfaction expressed in the Kok report and the subsequent initiatives aimed at restructuring the social policy architecture (at the EU and member state levels) will never be fully addressed, save for every EU member state being placed under conditions of permanent emergency and executive powers being transferred fully from member states to the EU (which is highly unlikely).

Therefore, and in keeping with the earlier points made by Brenner et al. and Poulantzas on law's role in evolving institutional landscapes, it is essential to examine both the content and form of these processes. On the content of post-2010 developments in the EU, the thrust has been towards the following: often drastic austerity in the rush towards balanced budgets and possibly even fiscal surpluses, primarily through the reduction in the size of the welfare state and the public sector, the significant loosening of labour market regulations to promote the growth of atypical employment—that is, not of full-time and/or permanent jobs—and reductions in unit labour costs in the name of greater 'competitiveness', achieved primarily through austerity, atypical jobs, but also legally mandated wage freezes or reductions.

On the form taken by the changes, they are part of the ongoing construction of a permanent, continent-wide conditionality regime that is aimed at all states, regardless of their economic performance.[8] In contrast to 'traditional' structural adjustment programmes in Africa, Latin America and Asia, which were reactively imposed on specific crisis-hit countries, in the EU the attempt is to formalize the requirement to *preemptively self-impose* such measures. In recognition of the intrinsic diversity of the EU, attempts at repressing the failure to do what is prescribed include the 'Reverse Majority Rule', which states that Commission proposals are accepted as valid if they are not prevented within 10 days by the European Council's veto with a simple majority. Additionally, member states are expected to respond to Commission suggestions for budget consolidation (which overwhelmingly focus on austerity measures) before their respective national parliament is consulted. There is the strengthening of the Commission's executive authority as well, to not only monitor closely member states but also propose/impose sanctions on them such as fines of up to 0.2% of GDP. It is not yet clear how much time will be given to make the 'necessary' adjustments, but the underlying principle is that member states could be forced via financial sanctions to implement austerity measures against the will of their citizens. Moreover, it is highly likely that social policy will be the main target of such measures, in the name of further enhancing its economic utility.

None of this could be said to reflect the values embodied in a traditional conception of the ESM. Yet, in Autumn 2013 the European Commission published a document entitled 'Strengthening the Social Dimension of the Economic and Monetary Union' (European Commission 2013), and in early 2016 the Commission President Jean-Claude Juncker announced a wide-ranging consultation on the development of a European Pillar of Social Rights aimed at reinforcing the social dimension more generally. One could conclude from this that the notion of an ESM has become little more than attempted 'means of legitimizing the European institutions' (Jepsen and Serrano Pascual 2005: 243). While this is certainly a good part of the story, we must always keep in mind that authoritarian responses to capitalist crises are 'partially responsible for new forms of popular struggle' which seek to create and live in a different kind of world to the one being imposed on them (Poulantzas 1978: 246).

In other words, the revival of references to the ESM is a good indication that the social and political polarization witnessed across Europe over the last decade still threatens to manifest itself in dramatic and potentially transformative ways, and that the hardening of EU law has left it more brittle and stressed. Yet again, this has shown how the EU's social facets continue to glow luminously, perhaps more than ever before—they are now central to *both* the rise of distinctively European forms of authoritarian neoliberalism and the resistance which has emerged in opposition to these developments.

THE LATENT FRAGILITY OF THE NEW REGIME

The EU's disastrous economic performance since 2007—by 2015, EU and Eurozone GDP were only slightly higher than the pre-recession peak (EuroMemo Group 2016: 9)—means that, after two decades of exhortations to 'reform', it is unsurprising that the arguments in favour of further neoliberalization in the name of 'necessity' ring increasingly hollow. One cannot argue that the wrenching changes have 'worked' even when assessed against a narrow set of criteria for 'success', a case in point being the continued extension of 'exceptional' programmes such as Quantitative Easing. I have argued previously that a key aspect of the rise of authoritarian neoliberalism is 'the more immediate appeal to material circumstances as a reason for the state being unable, despite "the best will in the world" to reverse processes such as greater socioeconomic inequality and dislocation' (Bruff 2014: 115). Nevertheless, when such appeals are made year after year, with at best no improvement in material circumstances and, in many instances, significant deterioration, it is unsurprising that the negative consequences of austerity and neoliberalization become viewed less as exceptional necessities and more as avoidable options.

A well-publicized Oxfam briefing in 2013 laid this bare. Already by that point in time, Oxfam was able to report: mass unemployment in many parts of Europe, especially among young people; rising poverty rates for people in and out of work, the former due to falling real wages and rocketing numbers in precarious jobs and the latter because of social security cuts; growing levels of inequality; and the continued expansion of Europe's luxury goods market (Oxfam 2013: 10–13). In addition, it ought to be stressed that these trends are not exclusive to the most crisis-hit countries such as the so-called PIIGS or the Baltic states. Germany has a current international profile of stability, strong economic performance and emphasis on social concerns, yet up to the onset of global crisis in 2008 income inequality and poverty had risen faster since 2000 than in any other OECD country, surpassing the EU average in the process (Lehndorff 2011: 345).[9] And since then, food bank use (a key indicator of the failure of social policy) has continued to rise (Kleinhubbert 2014).

For both of these reasons—the abandonment of traditional notions of 'social Europe' and the invisibility of benefits to wider society accruing from the measures—the task of gaining societal consent for such changes has been and is likely to be, at best, only partially successful. This has already helped generate numerous new forms of social and political instability. Such developments are multiform, ranging from radical Right populism to those favouring a return to classical social democracy and again to autonomous movements seeking to prefigure a better world. On the first group of struggles, political parties such as the Party for Freedom in the Netherlands, the National Front in France and the True Finns in Finland have taken advantage of the above and, more recently, the refugee and migration crises, to argue for a collectively oriented definition of citizenship in nationalistic and sometimes racist terms. Moreover, by drawing on some traditional Left arguments for a national economic strategy which rebuffs international (capitalist) forces, they are positioning themselves in novel ways compared to earlier forms of Right nationalism/populism.

This is partly because many social democratic parties neoliberalized substantially over the past two decades, with many becoming enthusiastic supporters of the reconceptualization of the ESM (indeed, the Lisbon Strategy was agreed by mainly social democratic governments). Nevertheless, the emergence of new parties such as Podemos in Spain, Syriza in Greece and the dramatic reorientation of the British Labour Party have given rise to the possible revival of more traditional social democratic notions about how to run the economy. This revival is partly associated with, but also outrun by, the strong upsurge in autonomous movements since 2008. Most obviously this manifested in Occupy and related protests across Europe, but there have also been 15-M in Spain, the Indignant Citizens Movement in Greece, and the more general growth of locally organized struggles and community provisioning (see, for example, the remunicipalization movement in Germany).

These three examples of social and political instability are feeding into an increasing crisis of legitimation across the continent. This is also taking a number of forms, but common factors include rising voter volatility from election to election, the gradual decline in the share of the vote taken by traditional 'catchall' political parties (most recently, falling from 79 per cent in 2007 to 57 per cent in 2016 in Ireland, a seismic change) and a more general mistrust of the political elite. A significant outcome is the increasing tendency for new governments to look quite different to their predecessors, with two paths being taken where this is the case. The first is formal or informal alliances between historic political enemies (e.g. Sweden, Germany and Ireland), which for the time being reinforces the status quo yet risks further unravelling of the system of political representation in the future. The second is new configurations of political forces (e.g. Greece, Portugal and Slovenia). Furthermore, future watershed elections currently seem possible (e.g. the Netherlands, France and Austria).

What this all means for the EU in social policy terms is that, for all of its hardening and increasingly hierarchical nature, it is still formally governed by a set of soft law mechanisms. Outside the transformative conditions for countries receiving bailouts, whereby drastic reforms were simply imposed as a condition of the release of funds, member states are still responsible for implementing social policy changes even if the Commission is now central to the policy formulation process. Important here is the fact that, up to now, member state governments have been *part of* and not *resistant to* the processes and developments that I discussed earlier in this chapter. Yet, as shown in Summer 2015, when the EU strongly contemplated removing Greece from the Eurozone in preference to acceding to the Syriza government's request for modified bailout terms (see Bruff 2016), it will become increasingly difficult to regularly bring the system to breaking point before a fracturing does take place. This recently happened with the widespread abandonment of both the Schengen arrangements and the Dublin Regulation in response to the refugee and migrant crises and to populist pressures in a number of countries.

Perhaps this explains the re-emphasis on the ESM and social concerns more generally, as mentioned at the end of the previous section. In addition, the broad consultation promised on the proposed Social Pillar means that the work of advocacy groups such as the EU Semester Alliance for a more democratic, social and sustainable Europe 2020 Strategy is more explicitly recognized. The alliance is a coalition of numerous major civil society and trade union organizations that is coordinated by the European Anti-Poverty Network. Initiatives include the development of a toolkit for engaging with the Semester process and the Europe 2020 Strategy, to help formulate independent assessments of policy developments and alternative proposals for consideration. Yet, as Daniel Seikel (2016) has outlined, the Social Pillar will not be enshrined in Treaty law; it is intended to complement rather than amend the existing set of legislations, directives and regulations, and the ultimate purpose is to operationalize existing individual social rights (i.e. not collective social rights such as the right to strike).

Given the trends and developments discussed throughout the chapter, this is probably not surprising. But it does mean that two outcomes are increasingly coming into view: the fracturing of the system by way of the social and political instabilities that it has helped produce, with a whole host of unanticipated consequences being possible (e.g. the breakdown of the OMC, the exit from the Eurozone or even the EU by one or more countries); and, in an attempt to ward off this threat, the 'socializing' of the system in a way which repudiates the neoliberalizing processes of the previous three decades. Both scenarios are currently unlikely, but it also seems unrealistic to expect that the continuation of existing strategies will last forever (see Jäger and Springler 2015). Nevertheless, if the 'Five Presidents' report from 2015 is anything to go by, this is what to expect for the foreseeable future (Juncker et al. 2015).

CONCLUSION

This chapter has argued that the notion of an ESM is central to the distinctively European forms of authoritarian neoliberalism that have emerged over the past decade. By showing how even governance practices seemingly far removed from what we associate with the term 'authoritarianism' can be part of the rise of authoritarian neoliberalism, the chapter also indicates that there is still plenty of scope for exploration of the concept and of the current conjuncture. Additionally, I have sought, through my discussion of facet methodology, to outline a method of enquiry which enables us to acknowledge the complex and always-evolving nature of the EU without being intimidated by it either. It is inevitable in all areas of research for different scholars to consider different aspects of the topic to be worthy of attention, but this is especially the case for the EU. The key is to be open about this, and show why and how it matters. For example, in this chapter I have argued that the EU's social facets have become more luminous over time because of how they have been increasingly entwined with other (often economic) facets, in the process throwing more light on the EU as a whole.

Accordingly, there is plenty of scope for future research to focus on themes that are covered more implicitly in the above discussion. For example, the role of workfare reforms in the reconceptualization of the ESM, the connection between authoritarian neoliberalism and 'Third Way' politics, the position of the ESM within discourses and practices of resistance, and the lived experiences of authoritarian neoliberalism on an everyday basis. There will be more areas and topics, too, and it is hoped that this chapter (along with this book) has contributed to the development of an increasingly diverse set of contributions on authoritarian neoliberalism.

So can we say that the ESM has now ceased to exist? Certainly, that is becoming an increasingly popular point of view (see various chapters in Menz et al. 2015), challenging the more traditional positions which focus on whether the ESM is, or how it could be, inscribed into EU governance practices. From this chapter's perspective, the ESM *as traditionally conceived* is of increasingly devalued relevance when thinking about the EU. However, the ESM's 'social' heritage is still important symbolically, enabling it to potentially become the focus of struggles which re-emphasize the rights of trade unions, the values of social solidarity and equality plus a form of politics which represents the interests of a broad swathe of social groups. Nevertheless, for such a scenario to arise the long-term trends would need to not just be halted but also reversed. For this to happen, there would have to be a reconceptualization of the ESM which clearly detaches it from the legacies of the past 30 years.

NOTES

1. This chapter has benefited from comments on an earlier draft by Cemal Burak Tansel, plus Gemma Edwards, Rasmus Hovedskov Hansen, Susanne Soederberg and Stefanie Wöhl. Additionally, the writing of the chapter has benefited from earlier conversations on the topic with Mònica Clua-Losada, Eva Hartmann, Ian Lovering, Lukas Oberndorfer, Reecia Orzeck, Adrienne Roberts, Christian Scholz and Angela Wigger. I would also like to thank those who attended my seminar talk 'Neoliberalism and authoritarianism: always intertwined, contemporary manifestations', University of Sheffield, 16 March 2016, when some ideas for this chapter were articulated for the first time.

2. See the otherwise excellent collection edited by Manners and Whitman (2016).

3. For the founding statement, see Mason (2011a). See also Mason (2011b); Davies and Heaphy (2011); Marine and Lewis (2014).

4. As can hopefully be seen, the facet methodology approach makes it possible for us to focus on our own set of research concerns without claiming to cover all aspects of the object of enquiry (indeed, as I have noted, this would be impossible with the EU). This means I am happy to acknowledge that other scholars, with different research concerns, may well posit other elements of the EU gemstone as shining particularly brightly. Examples from current debates would include migration and refugees, identity politics, geopolitics and external relations, and economic crisis.

5. See, for example, Scharpf (2010); Wickham (2012); Whyman, Baimbridge and Mullen (2012) and Hermann (2014).

6. For example, see Cafruny and Ryner (2003); van Apeldoorn et al. (2009); Nousios, Overbeek and Tsolakis (2012).

7. See Holland (1993) and Strange (2006). For an overview, see Whyman, Baimbridge and Mullen (2012).

8. For more on this, see Bruff and Wöhl (2016) and Oberndorfer (2015).

9. See also Bruff (2015) on the neoliberalization of the German political economy.

BIBLIOGRAPHY

Albert M (1993) *Capitalism Against Capitalism*, Haviland P (trans). London: Whurr.
Amable B, Demmou L and Ledezma I (2009) The Lisbon Strategy and structural reforms in Europe. *Transfer* 15(1): 33–52.

Brenner N, Peck J and Theodore N (2010) Variegated neoliberalism: Geographies, modalities, pathways. *Global Networks* 10(2): 182–222.

Bruff I (2014) The rise of authoritarian neoliberalism. *Rethinking Marxism: A Journal of Economics, Culture & Society* 26(1): 113–129.

Bruff I (2015) Germany and the crisis: Steady as she goes? In: Westra R, Badeen D and Albritton R (eds) *The Future of Capitalism After the Financial Crisis: The Varieties of Capitalism Debate in the Age of Austerity.* Abingdon: Routledge, 114–131.

Bruff I (2016) Neoliberalism and authoritarianism. In: Springer S, Birch K and MacLeavy J (eds) *The Routledge Handbook of Neoliberalism.* Abingdon: Routledge, 107–117.

Bruff I and Wöhl S (2016) Constitutionalizing austerity, disciplining the household: Masculine norms of competitiveness and the crisis of social reproduction in the Eurozone. In: Hozić AA and True J (eds) *Scandalous Economics: The Spectre of Gender and Global Financial Crisis.* Oxford: Oxford University Press, 92–108.

Cafruny AW and Ryner M (eds) (2003) *A Ruined Fortress? Neoliberal Hegemony and Transformation in Europe.* Lanham, MD: Rowman & Littlefield.

Davies K and Heaphy B (2011) Interactions that matter: Researching critical associations. *Methodological Innovations Online* 6(3): 5–16.

Delanty G and Rumford C (2005) *Rethinking Europe: Social Theory and the Implications of Europeanization.* Abingdon: Routledge.

Dunn B (2009) *Global Political Economy: A Marxist Critique.* London: Pluto.

Esping-Andersen G (1990) *The Three Worlds of Welfare Capitalism.* Princeton: Princeton University Press.

EuroMemo Group (2016) EuroMemorandum 2016: Addressing Europe's multiple crises: An agenda for economic transformation, solidarity and democracy. Available at: http://www.euromemo.eu/euromemorandum/euromemorandum_2016/index.html

European Commission (1993) *Growth, Competitiveness and Employment: The Challenges and Ways Forward into the 21st Century.* Brussels: European Commission.

European Commission (1994) *European Social Policy: A Way Forward for the Union.* Brussels: European Commission.

European Commission (2008) *Renewed Social Agenda: Opportunities, Access and Solidarity in 21st Century Europe.* Brussels: European Commission.

European Commission (2013) *Strengthening the Social Dimension of the Economic and Monetary Union.* Brussels: European Commission.

European Commission (2016) Standardisation policy. Available at: http://ec.europa. eu/growth/single-market/european-standards/policy/index_en.htm

European Council (1994) European Council Meeting on 9 and 10 December 1994 in Essen: Presidency conclusions. Available at: http://www.europarl.europa.eu/sum mits/ess1_en.htm

European Council (2000) Lisbon European Council 23 and 24 March 2000: Presidency conclusions. Available at: http://www.europarl.europa.eu/summits/lis1_en.htm

Gramsci A (1971) *Selections from the Prison Notebooks,* Hoare Q and Nowell-Smith G (eds and trans). London: Lawrence & Wishart.

Gramsci A (1985) *Selections from Cultural Writings*, Forgacs D and Nowell-Smith G (eds), Boelhower W (trans). London: Lawrence & Wishart.

Hay C, Watson M and Wincott D (1999) Globalisation, European integration and the persistence of European Social Models. Working Paper 3/99. Birmingham: ESRC One Europe or Several Research Programme.

Hermann C (2014) Crisis, structural reform, and the dismantling of the European Social Model(s). *Economic and Industrial Democracy* (Online). DOI: 10.1177/0143831X14555708.

High Level Group (2004) *Facing the Challenge: The Lisbon Strategy for Growth and Employment. Report from the High Level Group Chaired by Wim Kok*. Luxembourg: European Communities.

Hill S (2010) *Europe's Promise: Why the European Way is the Best Hope in an Insecure Age*. Berkeley, CA: University of California Press.

Holland S (1993) *The European Imperative: Economic and Social Cohesion in the 1990s: A Report to the Commission of the European Communities*. Nottingham: Spokesman Press.

Jäger J and Springler E (2015) Conclusions and possible futures. In: Jäger J and Springler E (eds) *Asymmetric Crisis in Europe and Possible Futures: Critical Political Economy and Post-Keynesian Perspectives*. Abingdon: Routledge, 224–233.

Jepsen M and Serrano Pascual A (2005) The European Social Model: An exercise in deconstruction. *Journal of European Social Policy* 15(3): 231–245.

Jessop B (2006) State- and regulation-theoretical perspectives on the European Union and the failure of the Lisbon Agenda. *Competition & Change* 10(2): 141–161.

Juncker JC (with Tusk D, Dijsselbloem J, Draghi M and Schulz M) (2015) *Completing Europe's Economic and Monetary Union*. Brussels: European Commission.

Kleinhubbert G (2014) Storming the food banks: Charities struggle with growing demand. *Spiegel Online International* (3 January). Available at: http://www.spiegel.de/international/germany/german-food-banks-and-soup-kitchens-struggle-with-demand-a-941661.html

Lehndorff S (2011) Before the crisis, in the crisis, and beyond: The upheaval of collective bargaining in Germany. *Transfer* 17(3): 341–354.

Manners I and Whitman R (2016) Special issue: Another theory is possible: Dissident voices in theorising Europe. *Journal of Common Market Studies* 54(1): 3–212.

Marine SB and Lewis R (2014) 'I'm in this for real': Revisiting young women's feminist becoming. *Women's Studies International Forum* 47(A): 11–22.

Mason J (2011a) Facet methodology: The case for an inventive research orientation. *Methodological Innovations Online* 6(3): 75–92.

Mason J (2011b) Knowing the in/tangible. Working Paper #17. Manchester: Morgan Centre.

Menz G, Crespy A and Bjorgo T (2015) (eds) *Social Policy and the Eurocrisis: Quo Vadis Social Europe*. Basingstoke: Palgrave Macmillan.

Nousios P, Overbeek H and Tsolakis A (2012) (eds) *Globalisation and European Integration: Critical Approaches to Regional Order and International Relations*. Abingdon: Routledge.

Oberndorfer L (2015) From new constitutionalism to authoritarian constitutionalism: New economic governance and the state of European democracy. In: Jäger J and Springler E (eds) *Asymmetric Governance and Possible Futures: Critical Political Economy and Post-Keynesian Perspectives*. Abingdon: Routledge, 186–207.

Oxfam (2013) *A Cautionary Tale: The True Cost of Austerity and Inequality in Europe*. Oxford: Oxfam.

Poulantzas N (1978/2014) *State, Power, Socialism*. London: Verso.

Rifkin J (2004) *The European Dream: How Europe's Vision of the Future is Quietly Eclipsing the American Dream*. Cambridge: Polity.

Scharpf FW (2010) The asymmetry of European integration, or why the EU cannot be a 'social market economy'. *Socio-Economic Review* 8(2): 211–250.

Seikel D (2016) The European pillar of social rights: No 'social triple A' for Europe. *Social Europe* (24 March). Available at: https://www.socialeurope.eu/2016/03/european-pillar-social-rights-no-social-triple-europe/

Strange G (2006) The Left against Europe? A critical engagement with new constitutionalism and structural dependence theory. *Government and Opposition* 41(2): 197–229.

Thompson EP (1995) *The Poverty of Theory: Or an Orrery of Errors*, new edition. London: Merlin Press.

van Apeldoorn B (2009) The contradictions of 'embedded neoliberalism' and Europe's multi-level legitimacy crisis: The European project and its limits. In: van Apeldoorn B, Drahokoupil J and Horn L (eds) *Contradictions and Limits of Neoliberal European Governance: From Lisbon to Lisbon*. Basingstoke: Palgrave Macmillan, 21–43.

van Apeldoorn B, Bruff I and Ryner M (2010) The richness and diversity of Critical IPE perspectives: Moving beyond the debate on the 'British School'. In: Phillips N and Weaver C (eds) *International Political Economy: Debating the Past, Present and Future*. New York: Routledge, 215–222.

van Apeldoorn B, Drahokoupil J and Horn L (eds) (2009) *Contradictions and Limits of Neoliberal European Governance: From Lisbon to Lisbon*. Basingstoke: Palgrave Macmillan.

Vaughan-Whitehead D (2015) The European Social Model in times of crisis: An overview. In: Vaughan-Whitehead D (ed) *The European Social Model in Times of Crisis: Is Europe Losing its Soul?* Cheltenham: Edward Elgar, 1–65.

Whyman P, Baimbridge M and Mullen A (2012) *The Political Economy of the European Social Model*. Abingdon: Routledge.

Wickham J (2012) Europe's crisis: Market competition instead of social bonds. TASC Discussion Paper. Available at: http://www.tascnet.ie/upload/file/James WickhamEurope.pdf

Wöhl S (2007) *Mainstreaming Gender? Widersprüche europäischer und nationalstaatlicher Geschlechterpolitik*. Königstein: Taunus.

Wöhl S (2011) Gender mainstreaming in European employment policies. *Critical Policy Studies* 5(1): 32–46.

Zeitlin J (2008) The open method of co-ordination and the governance of the Lisbon Strategy. *Journal of Common Market Studies* 46(2): 436–450.

Chapter 9

The Authoritarian and Disciplinary Mechanism of Reduced Sovereignty in the EU

The Case of Greece

Panagiotis Sotiris

Since 2010 Greece has been synonymous with economic crisis, recession, unemployment and monumental debt. It has been regarded as either the *bête noire* of the European Union, a country that is not in a position to comply with the norms of the European integration project, or the *victim* of the aggressive neoliberal policies and the lack of solidarity coming from the other member states. The 'Memoranda of Understanding' Greece signed with its creditors—namely the EU, the IMF and the ECB—have not only created a condition of limited sovereignty, but also acted as a disciplinary mechanism, whereby the constant supervision and evaluation of the Greek economy and state functions are regulated through loan payments. Yet, not enough attention has been paid to the mechanism behind this extreme condition and, in particular, to the disciplinary aspects of the reduced sovereignty inherent in the European integration process, which is indicative of the broader disciplinary, authoritarian and undemocratic character of contemporary neoliberalism. Accompanying the authoritarian and disciplinary aspect inscribed at the heart of the European integration process is an increased authoritarian turn inside Greece, which includes a growing disdain for parliamentary procedure and discussion, the constant use of *extraordinary* parliamentary procedures and a situation where the representatives of the 'Troika' (EU–IMF–ECB) practically dictate policies. Accordingly, this chapter argues that Greece is the testing ground for a new aggressive version of European integration in a period of 'permanent economic emergency'. The Greek case is not the exception but rather the 'new normal' in Europe. This realization accentuates the necessity of rethinking a strategy of ruptures as a means to recuperate popular sovereignty and democracy.

EUROPEAN INTEGRATION AS A CLASS PROJECT: MONETARY UNION, REDUCED SOVEREIGNTY AND NEOLIBERALISM

European integration is not just a set of common agreements defining a range of policies inside the European Union. Nor is it just a common currency and the lifting of controls to the flow of commodities and capitals. Above all, it is a class strategy that represents the combined efforts of European capitalist classes to respond to the global economic crisis and to the particular crisis of the European 'social model' by means of an offensive neoliberal strategy of capitalist restructuring.[1] As Bastiaan van Apeldoorn has stressed, the embedded neoliberalism of the EU makes European integration not just an economic process but a *hegemonic project* constructed by the forces of capital in Europe. In such a view, European integration

> may be understood in terms of ... 'embedded neoliberalism', reflecting a *hegemonic project* or what we could also call a *comprehensive concept of control* articulated and propagated by—and reflecting as well as mediating the interests of—social and political forces bound up with transnational European capital. ... Embedded neoliberalism is here seen as a *hegemonic* project inasmuch as it seeks to advance neoliberalism through a strategy of incorporating, and ideologically neutralizing, rival projects. (van Apeldoorn 2009: 22, original emphases)

Although, nominally, the European integration process was a combination of liberal, neo-mercantilist and social democratic aspirations, as it was coming out of the different post–Second World War European political traditions, in the end it was neoliberalism that became the dominant aspect of integration. As van Apeldoorn continues, 'At the heart of Lisbon we find an articulation of neoliberal competitiveness with concerns of the transnational social democratic projects in ways that effectively subordinate the latter to the former. However, Lisbon at the same time also reflects the incorporation of the neo-mercantilist project' (2009: 29). Consequently, 'the neoliberal restructuring, set in by the relaunched European integration project through the internal market programme and monetary union, reinforced by the marketization drive culminating in the Lisbon "competitiveness" agenda, and further locked in by the Eastern enlargement, has subordinated the objective of social cohesion to that of a logic of commodification' (van Apeldoorn 2009: 33).

The crucial aspect in the entire European integration process is the ceding of essential aspects of sovereignty in favour of the institutions of the European Union, to a degree without precedent in recent global history. Member states of the Eurozone have no control over monetary policy; they are required to coordinate their state-borrowing practices, accept rigorous budgetary norms or face 'automatic' penal mechanisms from the supervising European Union institutions, to fully open their internal markets—including state procurements—and to comply with European regulations regarding the free movement of European citizens, which also necessitates accepting rules regarding the equivalences of degrees and qualifications. Moreover, privatizations of essential infrastructure were made obligatory already in the 1990s. There are also common rules for agricultural policy, since there are no forms of subsidies other than those of the Common Agricultural Policy. As Drahokoupil, van Apeldoorn and Horn stress, 'European governance had above all become a supranational form of neoliberal governance' (2009: 4), leading to a transfer of the decision-making process regarding the regulatory functions from the member states to the EU institutions:

> Within Europe it is no longer the national states that exclusively provide the regulatory framework that allows the capitalist market economy to function— rather, increasingly, a key role here is played by the EU and by the process of European integration. ... In its institutional set-up, as well as its practices, the Commission is considerably autonomous from political accountability to broader societal interests; at the same time it constitutes a crucial site for the realization of political projects driven by social forces in the struggle for hegemony in the European Union. (Drahokoupil, van Apeldoorn and Horn 2009: 12–13)

The single currency—the euro—has been a particularly important aspect of this mechanism of reduced sovereignty. Although initially designed as a mechanism to enhance the common market and create a unified economic space that would enable the free flow of commodities and capitals, and thus counter regional imbalances, it had from the beginning faced the problem of large divergences in competitiveness and productivity. At the same time, it was endowed from the beginning with a very German conception of monetary discipline as a means to avoid inflation with its traumatic memory from the past (Moss 2005b; Lordon 2015). Moreover, the non-federal character of the European Union meant that the main option to counter the divergences in productivity and competitiveness, namely strong regional redistribution, was excluded from the outset. The principal premise of the monetary project was that the member states, including those of the periphery, would cede sovereignty, refuse the protective mechanisms they were accustomed to—in order to take advantage of the competitive pressure induced by the exposure to foreign competition—and promote capitalist restructuring and labour cost reduction, thus leading, gradually, to a more balanced monetary area, helped in this process by the access to cheaper credit. As Sotiropoulos, Milios and Lapatsioras have underscored regarding the European Monetary Union:

> Pressures from the functioning of the EMU are focused on the core of capitalist exploitation and create the preconditions for the continual restructuring of labor. The EMU puts into effect an extreme variant of the strategy of exposure to international competition, which can continue to exist only through the continual 'adjustment' of labor. It follows from this that the *EMU strategy is a specific mode of organization for capitalist power.* (2013: 192, original emphasis)

It is this particular aspect of the authoritarian and disciplinary character of European integration that accounts for another paradox of this process: the adherence of peripheral countries, with serious productivity and competitiveness gaps with the core European countries, to an aggressive regime of accumulation and exposure to huge and pervasive competitive pressures. I argue that the crucial aspect of this orientation is exactly the attempt to make use of this competitive pressure as a means to get rid of whatever compromises had been made in the past with segments of the subaltern classes and, at the same time, to make use of the legitimacy offered by the 'European Idea'. Although, in most cases, this was presented as a way to get rid of backwardness and to achieve modernization (a key hegemonic discursive element in the European South), it was, in fact—at least in the case of Greece—aimed at the gains made by the subaltern classes in the 'Metapolitefsi' period, namely the period after the fall of the dictatorship which was marked by increased radicalism and movement mobilization. As such, this disciplinary aspect, even if it is presented as a way to modernize the entire fabric of society, was pointed against the subaltern classes with the aim of forcing them to accept an aggressive neoliberal regime of accumulation.

The entire mechanism of the euro requires closer scrutiny. The main thrust behind the logic of the unique currency, with an independent supranational central bank instead of simple currency coordination—as it was the case in the first stages of the EMU—was that a unified economic area required monetary stability in order to facilitate the movements of capitals and goods, which also acquired a new impetus as part of the broader processes of financialization in the 1980s and 1990s. In this sense, the EMU is a 'key moment of the financialisation of Europe' (Durand 2013: 43). The idea was that an independent European Central Bank will offer safeguards against currency attacks and costly defences, exemplified in Britain's forced exit from the EMU after 1992 and the South East Asia crisis of 1997–1998 which showed the dangers of artificially pegging currencies to the dollar in order to boost the influx of investment (Krugman 2009). For this strategy to work and to avoid inflationary tendencies, strict restrictions were put in place with regards to deficits, public debt and inflation. However, seeing the evolution of the euro as simply an evolution of technocratic approaches, or even of an excessive obsession with inflation, runs the risk of underestimating the extent to which it has functioned as a mechanism for the erosion of democracy in Europe. As Wolfgang Streeck has stressed:

> Monetary union, initially conceived as a technocratic exercise—therefore ex-
> cluding the fundamental questions of national sovereignty and democracy that
> political union would entail—is now rapidly transforming the EU into a federal
> entity, in which the sovereignty and thereby democracy of the nation-states,
> above all in the Mediterranean, exists only on paper. Integration now 'spills
> over' from monetary to fiscal policy. The *Sachzwänge* of the international
> markets—actually the historically unprecedented empowerment of the profit
> and security needs of financial-asset owners—is forging an integration that has
> never been willed by political-democratic means and is today probably wanted
> less than ever. (2012: 67)

At the same time, this logic of an independent central bank immune to any interference from social demands or even from the electoral process was also part of a broader tendency to safeguard strategic capitalist interests against the demands and aspiration of the subaltern classes. As Demophanis Papadatos has highlighted:

> The inflationary crises of the 1970s and 1980s represented failure to defend
> the value of credit-money. That failure had social and political implications,
> at the very least because rapid inflation meant losses for creditors and because
> wage-bargaining was disrupted as workers attempted to obtain compensating
> increases in money-wages. The adoption of inflation targeting and central-bank
> independence was a sign of the ability of the capitalist class to learn from this
> experience. (2012: 133)

In a certain way, with strong anti-inflationary benchmarks in place—which practically meant a reduction in public spending and subsidy—along with the lifting of any protective mechanism against cheaper imports, what was formed was an 'iron cage' of capitalist modernization. For the economies of the less productive countries to survive and grow in this highly competitive environment there was no other way than labour cost reduction and increased productivity by means of capitalist restructuring, aided by the access to relatively cheaper credit. The problem, however, was that for peripheral countries this could also lead to a constant loss of competitiveness that could not be countered by rising productivity. This is where the idea of an internal devaluation, namely a reduction not only of real wages but also of nominal wages, was introduced by Olivier Blanchard, the IMF's chief economist from 2008 to 2015, in order to help competitiveness in single-currency economic areas such as the Eurozone. Here is Blanchard's argument:

> Given Portugal's membership in the euro, devaluation is not an option however (and I believe getting unilaterally out of the euro would have disruption costs which would far exceed any gain in competitiveness which might be obtained in this way). The same result can be achieved however, at least on paper, through a decrease in the nominal wage and the price of non-tradables, while the price of tradables remains the same. This clearly achieves the same decrease in the real consumption wage, and the same increase in the relative price of tradables. (Blanchard 2007: 15)

It is interesting that this idea was not introduced with Greece in mind but with Portugal and its slugging economic situation after the introduction of the euro. However, it was only in Greece that it was actually implemented, as a means to answer to the Greek crisis. Yet we should note that, in a certain sense, it was inscribed from the beginning into the logic of integration.

If we were to put this in Foucauldian terms (Foucault 2003, 2008), we can see the emergence of a fully functioning neoliberal governmentality at the European level through the construction of the Eurozone and the social consequences it has wrought within individual member states. This governmentality operates through a *dispositif* of budgetary rules and fiscal constraints as well as of competition within the single-currency area, and reinforces norms of productivity, discipline and neoliberal subjectivity within European societies. As such, the Eurozone is a combination of disciplinary practices and neoliberal biopolitics.

THE GREEK CRISIS AND THE
VIOLENCE OF THE MEMORANDA POLICIES

So far we have only described the workings of the Eurozone in its 'normal functioning'. However, when the economic crisis erupted the contradictions of the financial and monetary architecture of the Eurozone came to the fore. The Greek economic crisis was not just an expression of the global economic crisis and a combination of the actualization of the tendency of the profit rate to fall, of the extended financialization of the economy and of the crisis of neoliberalism as a regime of accumulation.[2] It was also a crisis of the particular Greek developmental paradigm, which was, to a large extent, determined by the contradictions of the Eurozone and, in particular, by the ways that the constant exposure to the competitive environment exacerbated trade imbalances and eroded the productive base of the country.[3] Without this reference to the imbalances of the Greek trade inside the Eurozone and the constant lagging in terms of competitiveness it is impossible to understand the extent of the Greek debt crisis.

The answer of the EU and the IMF to the crisis explicitly revealed the authoritarian and disciplinary character of contemporary neoliberalism. Essentially, the EU adopted the methodology of the IMF's structural adjustment programmes, namely the exchange between new loan financing and the obligation of the indebted country to implement painful austerity measures and neoliberal reforms. However, in the Greek case this was implemented with a cynical twist, to a large degree imposed by the EU: contrary to the IMF's traditional practice, the Greek structural adjustment programme was not from the beginning accompanied with debt restructuring—the partial lifting of the debt burden that would enable the economy to take off again—in contrast the 2012 PSI debt restructuring programme came in the background of an already increased debt burden. This meant that the Greek economy would enter into a vicious economic cycle of debt, recession and unemployment from which it has yet to exit.

However, what is more important is exactly the imposition of the Memoranda mechanism. The condition of limited sovereignty here took an even more aggressive form. Practically, the Memoranda operated on the principle that the Greek government would receive generous loans—which would then help it cover for bank refinancing and for debt payments—and in return it will have to undertake a total make-over of the entire fabric of society, a series of deep reforms that would make it conform to a certain 'norm' of neoliberal policies. Loans in return for austerity and neoliberal structural reforms, this was and still is the idea of the Memoranda.[4]

What was also important was the aggressive character of this attempt towards bringing Greece back into neoliberal 'normality' in the sense that we are no longer dealing with simply expecting the effects of the compliance with the EU regulatory legislation or with the effects of the common market and the unique currency—the two mechanisms designed to enhance the neoliberal transformation of European societies. Here, we are dealing with demands for reforms that go further beyond the *acquis communautaire*. From labour law and pension reform to higher education legislation, these are demands for deep changes that are not being directly linked to EU directives and which bring forward the enhanced neoliberal direction EU policies are beginning to take.

The basic disciplinary process imposed upon Greece has been that of evaluation and review. Representatives of the EU, the IMF and the ECB—the infamous 'Troika'—established themselves inside ministries and demanded a say in most policy choices while simultaneously scrutinizing the entire mechanism of Greek public administration and finance. At the same time, the loans were given in doses, each dose conditional upon positive evaluation of the progress made in implementing the Memoranda. Each round of evaluation was a hard negotiation with the representatives of the government usually ending up with offering new concessions to the Troika. Texts like the IMF country reports on Greece exemplify the character of this reviewing process, with their detailed descriptions and estimates regarding the Greek economy and the implementation of the measures included in the Memoranda (IMF 2013):

> Every EU summit, every round of negotiation between debtors and creditors led to a long series of 'bailouts' accompanied by draconian 'memoranda', endless austerity packages and 'shock therapies' fully conforming to the standard IMF models previously applied to the South, with entire countries placed under regimes of 'limited sovereignty'. The crisis of the Eurozone opened the way for 'disaster capitalism' moving now westwards, to the edges of the Old Continent which has become a laboratory of policies which will eventually be implemented, if only in a modified and possibly softer ways, elsewhere. (Lapavitsas 2012 et al.: XVII)

This also led to an extremely undemocratic process of decision-making with complete disregard for due parliamentary process and democratic deliberation. Basically, legislation was drafted under the demands of the Troika representatives; it was then passed through parliament in an extremely swift fashion as 'urgent laws'. This, in some instance, meant that huge pieces of reforms—with all the proposed reforms being incorporated in one single article (because spreading all these reforms in multiple articles run the danger of some being rejected)—were passed into legislation in the quickest possible way. As some of the members of parliament admitted, they did not even bother to read the pieces of legislation they had voted on. This kind of parody of parliamentary process enhanced the idea that there was no escape from austerity and the Memoranda. The Truth Committee on Public Debt, an initiative of the Greek Parliament in 2015, provided in its preliminary report ample evidence regarding the authoritarian, illegal and socially devastating character of the Memoranda mechanism (Truth Committee 2015).

What was missing in this process was any sense of consideration of popular will. These measures were strongly rejected by the Greek people and the rejection was evident in the massive waves of protests that followed the implementation of the Memoranda, especially in the 2010–2012 period, when social protests took an almost insurrectionary form, using all the repertoire of protest and contestation available—from peaceful mass gatherings to violent confrontations with the forces of order to the electoral revolt of May–June 2012. However, the answer of the Troika representatives was to overlook all these protests despite the fact that the rejection of the measures was the will of the majority of the Greek population, something that was proved beyond any possible doubt in the 2015 referendum.

Of particular importance was the attitude towards referenda. When in 2011 the then Prime Minister George Papandreou suggested that a referendum be held regarding the imposed policies, the Troika, fearing a massive negative expression from the population, not only practically forbade the referendum, but also forced the formation of a government of 'national unity', strong arming the centre-right New Democracy, which until then was opposed to the Memoranda, to participate in a government led by Lucas Papademos, former governor of the Bank of Greece and former vice president of the ECB. In a way, this rejection of a democratic procedure and the imposition of a government of national unity led by a banker was the first example of a European coup d'etat (Sotiris 2011). The emphasis on 'grand coalitions' in support of austerity and the Memoranda has been a constant feature of EU policies. The main objective of these coalitions is not about creating consensus; rather it is about projecting the image that there is no alternative, no actual political choice since all political parties are equally responsible and culpable for these neoliberal policies.

The same undemocratic attitude was made evident in the occasion of the July 2015 referendum. Not only was there a very negative Troika reaction to the referendum announcement after the collapse of the negotiations between the Troika and the Greek government, but also a series of direct interventions, such as the ECB not raising the cap on injections of liquidity to the Greek banking system which led to closed banks for the entire pre-referendum period, and open threats for even more aggressive measures. In fact, a statement made by Jean-Claude Juncker a few months before encapsulated this hatred of democratic procedures: 'There can be no democratic choice against the EU treaties' (quoted in Soudais 2015). This conception of EU treaties and consequently of the entire process of constitutionalization of neoliberalism in the EU is inherently undemocratic and disciplinary. It does not only reveal a distrust of popular will and sovereignty but also of ordinary parliamentary process and deliberation that was expressed in this entire sequence.

Although the Greek debt was supposedly the reason for the bailout programme, the programme not only further increased the Greek burden but it also created the conditions for debt to become a disciplinary mechanism itself, especially since the Greek government was practically blackmailed into accepting extra measures in order to receive the next part of the bailout agreement. Of particular importance was the question of bank liquidity. As a result of the crisis the Greek banking system saw a constant outflow of deposits, running the danger of insolvency. This meant that it needed the injections of liquidity from the ECB as life support and, thus, that not raising the cap on ECB liquidity injections, which would probably bring the banking system on its knees, became the main mechanism of pressure. This mechanism was first used in Cyprus in 2013, as part of the road to the rescue of Cypriot banks, who had found themselves in deep crisis mainly as a result of their dependence upon the Eurosystem (Lapavitsas and Lindo 2014), and then, to a much larger extent, on the eve of the Greek referendum in 2015, which led to closed banks during the entire run-up to the referendum.

AUTHORITARIAN EUROPE

Cédric Durand and Razmig Keucheyan offer a very compelling description of the inherently authoritarian and anti-democratic character of European integration in their analysis of the 'bureaucratic Caesarism' of the EU. This is a 'Caesarism [that is] not military but financial and bureaucratic. A political entity with a fragmented sovereignty, Europe can only see its unity guaranteed by the bureaucracy of Brussels and the structural immixture of international finance in its functioning' (Durand and Keucheyan 2013: 90–1). In a creative use of Gramscian notions, they consider the role of finance as that of a 'pseudo-historical bloc' compensating for the absence of any actual political unification (Durand and Keycheyan 2013: 101). It is this particularly European bureaucratic Caesarism that accounts for the increasingly disciplinary character of the interventions of European institutions and the process of de-democratization:

> Since 2011, the 'Europlus' pact, the reform of the Stability and Growth Pact and the 'European Semester' have increased constraints on budgets and economic policies: sanctions regarding recalcitrant countries are from now on automatic, budget drafts are examined at the European level even before their discussion by national parliaments and the reform of pension systems and the liberalization of labour markets become European objectives. (Durand and Keucheyan 2013: 108)

This perspective can help us understand that the mechanism imposed upon Greece was not exceptional. Although the entire imposition of the Troika mechanism does indeed seem like a series of exceptional measures, what is, in fact, deployed is exactly the condition of limited sovereignty that is inscribed at the heart of the European integration process. In fact, we can argue that the Greek experiment is the first full expression of the inner logic of the European integration project. In this sense, Greece is not the exception; rather it is the new normal.

Of particular importance, and a crucial aspect of this disciplinary functioning, is the way European integration represents a form of neoliberal constitutionalism without democracy. By this I mean that although there is indeed a set of constitutionalized institutions and policy directions in an aggressive neoliberal orientation—a certain European neoliberal rule of law—this is in no way combined with any reference to either a European people or a European civil society or even a European polity. To this we must also add the ways in which the principle of complementarity underpins the relation between European and national legislation. Although those aspects which are considered as parts of the cultural core of nationhood seemed to have been left out of the reach of European legislation—such as the content of education—all the significant aspects of socioeconomic conditions have been delegated to the primacy of European regulation. In a way, this delegation has offered the possibility for European capitalist classes and their political representatives to avoid processes of negotiation and confrontation with the subaltern classes in the name of the necessity to conform to the EU guidelines regarding privatization, pension reform and even certain aspects of labour reform. All these attest to the fact that the disciplinary aspects of the Memoranda mechanism have their corollary in the disciplinary character of the constitutionalization of neoliberalism in the entire EU institutional fabric, and the constant undermining of democratic procedure and popular sovereignty because of the inherently undemocratic character of the version of 'rule of law' performed at the EU level and of the entire process of integration. On this point, it is worth returning to the analyses of the European integration process such as the one offered by Giandomenico Majone, who has stressed the need to distinguish between constitutionalism and democracy when we discuss the European Union (Majone 2005). In a sense, there can be a European constitutional order, a set of ultra-neoliberal supranational guaranties without resorting to any form of democratic decision or democratic legitimacy. Moreover, as Wolfgang Streeck has shown, this is also part of a broader process, namely the erosion of democracy by neoliberalism and the mechanism of debt, and the substitution of the figure of the citizen by the figure of the creditor:

> The democratic state, ruled and (qua *tax state*) resourced by its citizens, becomes a democratic *debt state* as soon as its subsistence depends not only on the financial contributions of its citizens but, to a significant degree, on the confidence of creditors. In contrast to the *Staatsvolk* of the tax state, the *Marktvolk* of the debt state is transnationally integrated. They are bound to national states purely by contractual ties, as investors rather than citizens. Their rights vis-à-vis the state are of a private rather than public character, deriving not from a constitution but from the civil law. Instead of diffuse and politically expandable civil rights, they have claims on the state that are in principle enforceable before a court of law and come to an end with the fulfilment of the relevant contract. As

creditors, they cannot vote out a government that is not to their liking; they can, however, sell off their existing bonds or refrain from participating in a new auction of public debt. The interest rates that are determined at these sales—which correspond to the investors' assessment of the risk that they will not get back all or some of their money—are the 'public opinion' of the *Marktvolk*, expressed in quantitative terms and therefore much more precise and easy to read than the public opinion of the *Staatsvolk.* (Streeck 2014: 80)

At the same time, we can also say that the authoritarian and disciplinary aspects of the erosion of sovereignty by European integration are also the full expression of what Poulantzas defined as authoritarian statism (Poulantzas 1978, see Tansel in this book). According to Poulantzas, the basic aspects that characterized authoritarian statism, such as the decline of parliamentary democracy, the increased decision-making role of the executive and of the state bureaucracy and the insulation of decision-making processes from democratic control, also appear in exacerbated form at the level of the EU. In this sense, the process of European integration, exactly because it has, from the beginning, been devoid of any interference from popular sovereignty, is the optimal condition for the full materialization of the tendency towards authoritarian statism.

There is also an ideological aspect to this authoritarian and disciplinary mechanism. This had to do with the entire negative perception of Greek society. I am not referring to the persistence of borderline racist stereotypes—the famous myth of the 'lazy Southerner'. I am referring to an almost 'orientalist' perception of Greek society's lack of modernization. This gives to the disciplinary voluntarism of the Memoranda the air of a moral crusade to bring a country back to its 'normal path', a position also shared by many Greek intellectuals that support the Memoranda (see Kalyvas, Pagoulatos and Tsoukas 2012). However, there is also another aspect to this ideological legitimization. Presenting Greece as an 'exceptional case' in need of equally exceptional measures and interventions distorts a crucial aspect of the entire Memoranda period, namely the very fact that Greece is not an exception; that austerity and attacks upon whatever is left of the welfare state are an integral aspect of EU policy in all member states; that this mechanism of violent suspension of sovereignty, democratic deliberation and due parliamentary process is being implemented all over Europe (see Bruff in this book).

THE CHALLENGE OF RECLAIMING POPULAR SOVEREIGNTY

All of these considerations present us a broader challenge that is not only theoretical but also political. If this mechanism of reduced sovereignty is a basic aspect of both the neoliberal and the authoritarian and disciplinary character of European integration, then the question of reclaiming popular sovereignty both in the sense of a rupture from the financial, monetary and institutional architecture of the Eurosystem, and of the deepening of democratic processes becomes a central political imperative.

The deeply embedded neoliberalism and authoritarianism of the EU as a class project means that we have to move beyond thinking in terms of 'another EU' and overcome the 'epistemological obstacle' of Europeanism in order to actually think of alternatives (Kouvelakis 2012). In concrete terms, this suggests a strategy of ruptures with the EU, beginning with the necessary exit from the Eurozone as the starting point for any policy that is actually in favour of the subaltern classes (Flassbeck and Lapavitsas 2015). This should not be seen just as a 'technical' question of monetary policy, but as part of a broader process of recuperation of popular sovereignty. Consequently, we have to admit that today the question of sovereignty becomes a class issue, a question around which we can see the condensation of the antagonistic class relations. Reclaiming sovereignty implies a recuperation of a democratic control against the systemic and institutionalized violence of internationalized capital in general and of the embedded neoliberalism of the EU in particular (Lordon 2015).

We all know the problems associated with the notion of sovereignty, in particular its association with nationalism, racism and colonialism. However, here we are talking about a form of sovereignty based upon a social alliance that is different from that of bourgeois 'sovereignty': an alliance rooted in the shared condition of the subaltern classes, their solidarity and common struggle. Echoing Fréderic Lordon, 'democracy and popular sovereignty: one and the same idea, that a community masters its own destiny' (Lordon 2013). In this sense, the recuperation of sovereignty is the necessary condition for a profound change in the relation of forces and represents the collective and emancipatory effort towards another road, an alternative narrative for a potential hegemony of the working classes.

What about the nation? It is obvious that the institutional aspects of national sovereignty are necessary in order to address many of the problems associated with the violence of globalized capital. At the same time, we understand that the crucial question has to do with social alliances and the class strategy behind this recuperation of sovereignty. Does this mean that we have to revisit the lines of nationalism? Does this recuperation of sovereignty necessarily lead to nationalism, ethnic exclusion and racism, the dark sides of the modern democratic state? I think we need to go beyond and rethink both the people and the nation in a 'post-nationalist' and postcolonial way as the emerging community of all the people that work, struggle and hope on a particular territory, as the reflection of the emergence of a potential historical bloc. This is not just a recuperation of the 'national reference' (cf. Bauer 2000). Rather it is a way to rethink the possibility of a new unity and a common reference point for the subaltern classes. The following phrase from Gramsci exemplifies this point:

> The modern prince must be and cannot but be the proclaimer and organiser of an intellectual and moral reform, which also means creating the terrain for a subsequent development of the national-popular collective will towards the realisation of a superior, total form of modern civilisation. (Gramsci 1971: 132–133; Q13§1)

What is interesting in this passage, one of the most dense of the Notebooks, is that it combines the reference to the modern political party or front, the organization of 'intellectual and political reform'—a phrase that signals not only a dialogue with Croce but also with the notion of cultural revolution in the late texts of Lenin—and the notion of a superior and modern civilization which in a certain way reminds us of the references to communist civilization (*civiltà comunista*) in texts from the youth of Gramsci.[5] In this sense, the national-popular element is not a remnant of nationalism, but rather the result of a hegemonic project created by the subaltern classes.

CONCLUSION

The mechanism imposed upon Greece is going to be a constant feature of European integration in the coming future. Despite the obvious crisis of the European project, exemplified in many aspects of the current conjuncture—such as the inability to deal with the economic crisis, the cynicism displayed in the refugee crisis, the widespread distrust towards the political establishment—there does not seem to be a move towards a different direction. Germany's reluctance to mitigate the burden of integration further leads to a greater emphasis upon 'automatic' economic 'brakes' which necessitate Troika-style negotiations for struggling member countries. However, this can also be the greatest problem of the European Union. The capitulation of the Greek government after the referendum and the signing of the third memorandum should not be read as the proof of the success of the strategy pursued by dominant forces in Europe. In fact, we are dealing with a certain crisis of neoliberal European governmentality, exemplified in the widespread distrust of European institutions—a distrust that, most recently, gave rise to the Brexit vote in the United Kingdom. This is what gives a broader significance to developments in Greece. At the same time, it is obvious that any attempt at rethinking democracy, justice and social emancipation cannot be successful without confronting the embedded neoliberalism and authoritarianism of the European integration project.

NOTES

1. See Bruff in this book; van Apeldoorn (2003); Cafruny and Ryner (2003) and Moss (2005a).

2. See Duménil and Lévy (2011); Lapavitsas (2012) and Mavroudeas and Paitaridis (2015).

3. See Sakellaropoulos and Sotiris (2014); Economakis, Androulakis and Markaki (2015) and Mavroudeas and Paitaridis (2015).

4. For the texts of all the Memoranda and their revisions and updates, check the relevant repository at: http://crisisobs.gr/en/repository/?ct=98&st=103.

5. 'The workers will carry this new consciousness into the trade unions, which in place of the simple activity of the class struggle will dedicate themselves to the fundamental task of stamping economic life and work techniques with a new pattern; they will elaborate the form of economic life and professional technique proper to communist civilization' (Gramsci 1977: 101).

BIBLIOGRAPHY

Bauer O (2000) *The Question of Nationalities and Social Democracy*, O'Donnell J (trans). Minneapolis: University of Minnesota Press.

Blanchard O (2007) Adjustment within the Euro: The difficult case of Portugal. *Portuguese Economic Journal* 6(1): 1–21.

Cafruny AW and Ryner M (eds) (2003) *A Ruined Fortress? Neoliberal Hegemony and Transformation in Europe*. Lanham, MD: Rowman & Littlefield.

Drahokoupil J, van Apeldoorn B and Horn L (2009) Introduction: Towards a Critical Political Economy of European governance. In: van Apeldoorn B, Drahokoupil J and Horn L (eds) *Contradictions and Limits of Neoliberal European Governance: From Lisbon to Lisbon*. Basingstoke: Palgrave Macmillan, 1–17.

Duménil G and Lévy D (2011) *The Crisis of Neoliberalism*. Cambridge, MA: Harvard University Press.

Durand C (2013) Introduction: Que est-ce que l'Europe ? In: Durand C (ed) *En finir avec l'Europe*. Paris: La Fabrique, 7–47.

Durand C and Keucheyan R (2013) Un césarisme bureaucratique. In: Durand C (ed) *En finir avec l'Europe*. Paris: La Fabrique, 89–113.

Economakis G, Androulakis G and Markaki M (2015) Profitability and crisis in the Greek economy (1960–2012): An investigation. In: Mavroudeas S (ed) *Greek Capitalism in Crisis: Marxist Analyses*. Abingdon: Routledge, 130–152.

Flassbeck H and Lapavitsas C (2015) *Against the Troika: Crisis and Austerity in the Eurozone*. London: Verso.

Foucault M (2003) *Society Must Be Defended: Lectures at the Collège de France, 1975–76*, Macey D (trans). New York: Picador.

Foucault M (2008) *The Birth of Biopolitics: Lectures at the Collège de France, 1978–79*, Burchell G (trans). Basingstoke: Palgrave Macmillan.

Gramsci A (1971) *Selections from the Prison Notebooks*, Hoare Q and Nowell-Smith G (eds and trans). London: Lawrence & Wishart.

Gramsci A (1977) *Selections from the Political Writings (1910–1920)*, Hoare Q (ed), Mathews J (trans). London: Lawrence & Wishart.

IMF (2013) Greece: Fourth review under the Extended Arrangement under the Extended Fund Facility. IMF Country Report 13/241 (July). Available at: http://www.imf.org/external/pubs/ft/scr/2013/cr13241.pdf

Kalyvas S, Pagoulatos G and Tsoukas H (eds) (2012) *From Stagnation to Forced Adjustment: Reforms in Greece, 1974–2010*. London: Hurst & Co.

Kouvelakis S (2012) Introduction: The end of Europeanism. In: Lapavitsas C, Kaltenbrunner A, Labrinidis G, Lindo D, Meadway J, Michell J, Painceira JP, Pires E, Powell J, Stenfors A, Teles N and Vatikiotis L (eds) *Crisis in the Eurozone*. London: Verso, XIV–XXI.

Krugman P (2009) *The Return of Depression Economics and the Crisis of 2008*. New York: W.W. Norton.

Lapavitsas C (ed) (2012) *Financialisation in Crisis*. Leiden: Brill.

Lapavitsas C, Kaltenbrunner A, Labrinidis G, Lindo D, Meadway J, Michell J, Painceira JP, Pires E, Powell J, Stenfors A, Teles N and Vatikiotis L (2012) *Crisis in the Eurozone*. London: Verso.

Lapavitsas C and Lindo D (2014) Cypriot banks: A pernicious dependence upon the Eurosystem. RMF Occasional Policy Paper 4. Available at: http://www.researchonmoneyandfinance.org/images/occasional_policy_papers/RMF-OPP-4-Lapavitsas-Lindo.pdf

Lordon F (2013) Ce que l'extrême droite ne nous prendra pas. *Le Monde diplomatique* (8 July). Available at: http://blog.mondediplo.net/2013-07-08-Ce-que-l-extreme-droite-ne-nous-prendra-pas

Lordon F (2015) *On achève bien les Grecs: Chroniques de l'euro 2015* Paris: Éditions les liens qui libèrent.

Majone G (2005) *Dilemmas of European Integration: The Ambiguities and Pitfalls of Integration by Stealth*. Oxford: Oxford University Press.

Mavroudeas S and Paitaridis D (2015) The Greek crisis: A dual crisis of overaccumulation and imperialist exploitation. In: Mavroudeas S (ed) *Greek Capitalism in Crisis: Marxist Analyses*. Abingdon: Routledge, 153–175.

Moss BH (ed) (2005a) *Monetary Union in Crisis: The European Union as a Neoliberal Construction*. London: Palgrave Macmillan.

Moss BH (2005b) From ERM to EMU: EC monetarism and its discontents. In: Moss BH (ed) *Monetary Union in Crisis: The European Union as a Neo-liberal Construction*. London: Palgrave Macmillan, 145–169.

Papadatos D (2012) Central banking in contemporary capitalism: Inflation-targeting and financial crises. In: Lapavitsas C (ed) *Financialisation in Crisis*. Leiden: Brill, 119–141.

Poulantzas N (1978/2014) *State, Power, Socialism.* London: Verso.

Sakellaropoulos S and Sotiris P (2014) Postcards from the future: The Greek debt crisis, the struggle against the EU–IMF austerity package and the open questions for Left strategy. *Constellations* 21(2): 262–273.

Soudais M (2015) Juncker dit «non» à la Grèce et menace la France. *Politis* (29 January). Available at: http://www.politis.fr/articles/2015/01/juncker-dit-non-a-la-grece-et-menace-la-france-29890/

Sotiris P (2011) Rethinking the notions of 'People' and 'Popular Sovereignty'. *Greek Left Review* (15 November). Available at: http://bit.ly/1SvjUO9

Sotiropoulos DP, Milios J and Lapatsioras S (2013) *A Political Economy of Contemporary Capitalism and its Crisis: Demystifying Finance.* Abingdon: Routledge.

Streeck W (2012) Markets and peoples: Democratic capitalism and European Integration. *New Left Review* 73: 63–81.

Streeck W (2014) *Buying Time: The Delayed Crisis of Democratic Capitalism.* London: Verso.

Truth Committee on Public Debt (2015) Preliminary report. Athens: Greek Parliament. Available at: http://www.hellenicparliament.gr/UserFiles/f3c70a23-7696-49db-9148-f24dce6a27c8/Report_web.pdf

van Apeldoorn B (2003) *Transnational Capitalism and the Struggle over European Integration.* London: Routledge.

van Apeldoorn B (2009) The contradictions of 'embedded neoliberalism' and Europe's multi-level legitimacy crisis: The European project and its limits. In: van Apeldoorn B, Drahokoupil J and Horn L (eds) *Contradictions and Limits of Neoliberal European Governance: From Lisbon to Lisbon.* Basingstoke: Palgrave Macmillan, 21–43.

Chapter 10

Antinomies of Authoritarian Neoliberalism in Turkey

The Justice and Development Party Era

Barış Alp Özden, İsmet Akça and Ahmet Bekmen

The complex relationship between globalization and authoritarianism has been much debated. Nicos Poulantzas, who offered one explanation for this relationship, warned us about the usage of his own conceptualization of authoritarian statism: 'Given the deepening division between dominant and dominated countries of the imperialist chain—a result of the internationalization of capitalist relations—we cannot engage in general theorization about the contemporary State covering transformations in these countries as a whole' (Poulantzas 1978: 204). It can be argued that following the enormous extension of financial globalization after Poulantzas's death, authoritarian statism has become a global phenomenon, thus overcoming the distinction between 'dominant and dominated countries'. The rules, procedures and mechanisms of 'new constitutionalism', 'disciplinary neoliberalism' (Gill 2008) or 'economic constitutionalism' (Jayasuriya 2001) are not only enforced exclusively in the global South, but are also permeating the global North in the aftermath of the 2007–2008 global economic crisis (Gill 2011).

This transformation has also triggered various conflicts in the social formations on the received end of neoliberal reforms which has resulted in the rise of various forms of authoritarian statisms, as illustrated by Turkey's recent history. Our main argument in this chapter is that the conceptual tools we use to analyze the rise of authoritarianisms fall short of satisfactorily explaining the shifts, cracks and conflicts emerging during the integration of peripheral or semi-peripheral countries into globalization. We argue that the Justice and Development Party (*Adalet ve Kalkınma Partisi*, henceforth AKP) period in Turkey should be studied within the context of Turkey's integration into neoliberal globalization, which has generated specific conflicts within its social and political structures (see Akça et al. 2014a). Thus, instead of discussing how authoritarian statism, disciplinary neoliberalism or economic constitutionalism has been realized in Turkey, we will offer an understanding of AKP politics as both a response to and a factor in deepening these crises by focusing on the crises exploding at socioeconomic and political levels. In doing so, we hope to shed light on the relationship between neoliberalism and the specific form of authoritarianism emerged recently in Turkey.

HISTORICAL TRAJECTORY OF AUTHORITARIAN NEOLIBERALISM IN TURKEY

Turkey is among a group of countries whose transition to neoliberalism has been facilitated through a military coup. In Turkey's case, the 1982 constitution enabled the introduction of practices of authoritarian neoliberalism that encompass the technocratization of economic and social issues, centralization of decision-making processes, and domination of the executive over the legislative and judiciary (Akça 2014a: 14–18). In this regard, the 1980s—during which the labour movement was suppressed and the economic administration became isolated from public needs—was a period in which the economic and political crisis of the late 1970s was resolved in favour of order and capital. Although the labour movement saw a moment of revitalization in the late 1980s, trade unions, through practices of suppression and absorption, were neutralized shortly after (Doğan 2014). The resultant absence of an influential labour movement in Turkey was critical for the shape of the neoliberal hegemony to come.

The 1990s saw the culmination of fractures that would emerge within the social and political structures into a total crisis of hegemony. Three key issues stand out vis-à-vis the crisis of hegemony. The first relates to the rise of medium-scale, Islamic-conservative Anatolian capital, which grew throughout the 1990s, especially by engaging in global production chains. Historically, the monopolization of access to financial resources by Turkey's big capital groups had been the main hindrance for Anatolian capital since the late 1960s. Having no financial background, this faction had remained dependent on bank-owning big capital groups. However, thanks to its specific role in post-1980 industrialization, it has become a much more influential social actor in proportion to its economic capacity. Recently, alongside Istanbul and the Marmara region, new manufacturing centres have emerged in many Anatolian cities, due to the establishment of Organized Industrial Districts. Thus, the transformations of these cities have been accompanied by a simultaneous new phase of proletarianization and the rise of Islamic capital. In this sense, an organic hegemony has been constructed via practices in both workplaces and living spaces (Doğan and Durak 2014; Öngel 2014; Durak 2013).

The second issue concerns the weakening of the centrist parties by the assaults of political Islamism and the Kurdish political movement. Against the rise of these centrifugal political powers, the military extended its claim regarding its duty of defending Turkish nationalism and secularism—two main elements of the Kemalist Republic. Having fortified its legitimacy and power over the low-intensity war in the Kurdish region, the military then became, from the viewpoint of secular powers, the protector of the existing regime against the emerging political Islamists. Its claim on the political sphere peaked with the military intervention of 28 February in 1997, targeting both the then-ruling Welfare Party and Islamist capital. After the intervention, the situation developed into a crisis of representation with all its ideological and political dimensions in that the masses mobilized and represented by political Islam and the Kurdish movement were either partially or fully excluded from the political system, while the rest gradually lost their confidence in it (Akça 2014a: 23–9; Öngen 2002).

The third issue concerns the management of the economy. Throughout the 1990s, the inflow of hot money—encouraged by increasing interest rates—made borrowing increasingly expensive, which further increased the public deficit. Taking advantage of Turkey's poorly regulated banking system, commercial banks started to buy large amounts of government bonds at high interest rates by borrowing from abroad at lower interest rates. Throughout the 1990s, almost all commercial banks benefited from such arbitrage profits, while lending expensively to the public by borrowing cheap credit from abroad became the main method of capital accumulation for almost all capital groups. However, Turkish capitalism also underwent a transformation during this era. The 1995 Customs Union agreement with European Union motivated big capital groups to build on their manufacturing base in order to take advantage of freer access to European markets. Big capital groups, especially those more deeply integrated with global business networks, began complaining about the existing conduct of the economy based on financial rentierism and demanded reform. However, it proved impossible to form a strong and stable government capable of undertaking such radical economic reforms, mainly due to the reasons mentioned above. Thus, there was a crisis of representation for Turkey's big bourgeoisie too (Bekmen 2014).

Overall, by the end of the 1990s, Turkey was experiencing a crisis of hegemony due to the lack of a political centre capable of reconciling tensions within the power bloc, producing broad-based consent and laying the basis for sustainable capital accumulation. This impasse was finally resolved through a series of economic crises. The global economic crisis of 1997–1998 hit Turkey in two successive waves, in November 2000 and February 2001, with the second being particularly devastating (Aybar and Lapavitsas 2001). The 2001 crisis was not just a critical moment for the economic reforms to come; it also almost completely restructured the political sphere. In the subsequent 2002 elections, all three of the parties that had governed during the crisis failed to enter parliament, with only one of them managing to survive as a party.[1] The new parliament consisted of just two parties; one of them, the AKP, founded mainly by Islamist cadres who had just split with the Felicity Party under the name of 'reformers', won the election with 34 per cent of the vote—a share that increased to just over 50 per cent in subsequent elections.

EXPANSIVE HEGEMONY UNDER AKP RULE

It is commonly agreed that there has been a radical change in the last five or six years in the AKP's mode of rule. Although many liberal and left-liberal commentators interpret this as a transition from a liberal-democratic to an authoritarian phase (cf. Keyman and Öniş 2007; Öniş 2013, 2016), the AKP's hegemonic project has always been authoritarian for two main reasons. First, the party did not dismantle the authoritarian neoliberal state form established in the post-1980 period. Second, it has continued the majoritarian and monolithic understanding of democracy it inherited from Turkey's conservative right-wing tradition, which has resulted in intolerance of any kind of political criticism, collective public action, or social and political opposition (Akça 2014a). Therefore, by focusing on the constitutive elements of hegemony and their transformations, we prefer to contextualize the AKP's 'shift' as a change from an *expansive* to a *limited* hegemonic strategy. In expansive hegemony, 'a hegemonic group adopts the interests of its subalterns in full, and those subalterns come to "live" the worldview of the hegemonic class as their own'. In a limited hegemony, 'the hegemonic class fail[s] to genuinely adopt the interests of the popular classes and simply neutralize[s] or "decapitate[s]" them through depriving them of their leadership' (Jones 2006: 52–53; for the Turkish case see Bozkurt 2015; Akça 2014b). Expansive hegemony during the AKP era can be characterized by three different aspects: (1) a neoliberal economic policy capable of reconciling the interests of different capital sections; (2) a populist social policy targeting the incorporation of new sections of the working class and urban poor; and (3) a political reformism aimed at enhancing the sphere of civil rule vis-à-vis the military-controlled tutelary regime. These three elementary aspects will be explored and discussed in detail throughout the chapter.

Economic Orientation and the Power Bloc During the Early AKP Period

Contrary to the initial suspicions and reservations of Turkey's big capital groups about the policy orientation of its cadres, the AKP largely continued the preceding coalition government's post-crisis macroeconomic strategy, including the establishment of independent regulatory institutions, inflation targeting and central bank independence, floating exchange rates and liberalized capital movements. Moreover, the party adhered strictly to the prescriptions of the ongoing IMF programme, especially with regards to the primary surplus target and privatization (Cizre and Yeldan 2005). As such, its reform agenda aimed to integrate the main premises of economic constitutionalism by imposing neoliberal discipline on both the institutional and fiscal designs of the state apparatus. Supplementary to these reforms were a series of industrial development measures and labour market adjustments that aimed to improve the global competitiveness of Turkish economy through production based on higher technology and labour productivity (Oğuz 2012). Undoubtedly helped by a favourable global economic climate, which emerged on the back of high global liquidity and low international interest rates, the new government was able to stabilize the economy, reduce inflation and fuel growth.[2] While the trade-driven growth surge rested on high current account deficits, it did not particularly worry decision-makers or capital groups as long as it was smoothly financed by massive foreign capital inflows. This economic environment provided the opportunity for the AKP to open new paths for private capital accumulation, at least until the global financial crisis began to take its toll on European markets after 2008.

In political terms, this new orientation towards global integration based on productive capital accumulation represented the expansion of the bourgeois base in support of neoliberalism. That is to say, for the first time since political Islamists split from the centre-right mainstream in the early 1970s, the AKP managed to forge an alliance between the economically dominant and politically hegemonic sector—comprising big financial capital and the Istanbul-based Western-oriented big bourgeoisie (organized under TÜSİAD)—and the economically improving but politically subordinated faction which comprised a large group of enterprises that manifest a much greater diversity of size and geographic location (predominantly but not exclusively MÜSİAD members). The political consequence of this alliance was to deepen neoliberal hegemony in Turkey. Through mergers, joint ventures with local capital groups and direct investments that reached a record level in mid-2000, foreign capital, too, acquired a prominent place within the new configuration of the power bloc.

This by no means implies that relations between these capital factions were always conciliatory and cooperative during the early years of AKP rule. Since the capital groups organically linked to the AKP government were ideologically and politically rising within the power bloc, they could renegotiate their position, forms of participation and share of surplus value appropriation vis-à-vis Istanbul-based monopoly capital. Intra-class contradictions became prominent in a number of areas, including the distribution of public tenders and procurement auctions. Since public procurement in Turkey comprises a substantial part of government spending and GDP, procurement auctions are all the more important for distributing public rent. Thus, big business circles have been a vocal critic of the fact that 170 amendments were made on the Public Procurement Law between 2003 and 2014, signifying the 'repoliticization' of the procurement process in favour of domestic capital closely connected to the AKP (Nar 2015). Likewise, MÜSİAD has been particularly critical of financial sector regulations and the growing power of independent regulatory agencies. Unlike TÜSİAD, it opted for a more flexible implementation of budgetary discipline, which it considered to be curbing the growth prospects of small businesses (Hoşgör 2015: 206). Notwithstanding these conflicts between bourgeois factions, the AKP successfully articulated different intra-class interests until the global economic crisis by utilizing a vibrant economic environment, which itself was predicated on the availability of virtually limitless foreign financial resources, complemented with a major privatization boom after 2002 and a new labour regime that has generated more exploitative work relations.

Disarticulation of the Working Class and the Populist Appeal

The various techniques and methods that AKP utilized to launch its hegemonic project would not be much of use if the forces of neoliberalism had not successfully disarticulated the working classes and representational forms that have historically been associated with them. Since 1980—following the liberalization of Turkish economy and its full integration into the global economy—the country has undergone extensive proletarianization, which has significantly changed its social class structure. The fundamental factor underlying this transformation was the dissolution of Turkey's existing agrarian structures, which had supported rural livelihoods until the mid-1980s (Buğra and Keyder 2006). Neoliberal market reforms, which have gained new momentum in the AKP era, precipitated the disintegration of small-scale peasant agriculture and undermined the complex safety networks that many immigrants to Turkey's cities had previously relied on in times of hardship. Exacerbating these changes was the forced expulsion of around two million Kurdish villagers in the early 1990s during the most heated period of armed conflict between the PKK (Kurdistan Workers' Party) and the Turkish armed forces. This drove many young Kurdish men and women into the informal labour markets that had been growing in the peripheries of major urban centres (Alpman 2016). Consequently, the share of agricultural employment in total employment fell from nearly 50 per cent in 1988 to 30 per cent in 2005 and then to 25 per cent in 2010 (TURKSTAT 2010).

The new working class accumulating in major cities has become more and more precarious, disorganized and distrustful of structures of representation that have proved to be increasingly ineffective. The most visible effect of Turkey's neoliberal reorientation in the last three decades has been the impact of adjustment on employment and labour market structures. As real wages have stagnated and the gap between rising manufacturing productivity and wage growth has widened, a sharp class divide has emerged as one of the most important characteristics of contemporary Turkish society (Yeldan 2006). After two decades of privatization of state industries and labour shedding as the main strategies deployed to absorb the shocks of economic crises, the rate of non-agricultural unemployment rose to 14.5 per cent (5 per cent above the 2001 crisis level) in 2002 and remained at around 13 per cent until 2009, when the global financial crisis drove it up to 17.4 per cent. Simultaneously, the proportion of workers without social security reached a peak of 53 per cent in 2004 (World Bank 2009: 13). In the face of these challenges, the AKP government's major policy approach was promoting labour market reforms to expand flexible work forms and promoting the replacement of job security with 'flexicurity' in Turkey's employment regime (Çelik 2015).

These deep-seated transformations have produced a new working class dominated by young, low-paid and poorly trained subcontracted workers with little chance to access stable jobs in the formal sector. With this change in the social composition of workers, it may well be argued, a new form of subjectivity has emerged that is corroding the prospect of class solidarity and collective self-identification. This class is more atomized than ever and is relatively inexperienced in collective action (Özden and Bekmen 2015). Decades of neoliberal restructuring have undermined workers' power to organize through trade unions or left-wing parties, as well as the transformative capacity of the labour movement. The institutional changes caused by neoliberal reforms have dramatically eroded Turkish trade unions' membership figures and their political and ideological influence over society at large (Doğan 2014).

This is the social basis on which the AKP has built its neoliberal and authoritarian hegemonic project. Successive AKP governments have managed to gain the support of broad sections of the working class in three ways: (1) extension of welfare programmes to previously excluded individuals and the implementation of new assistance programmes aimed at ensuring the most basic levels of social protection; (2) integration of low-income households into the financial sector through the booming consumer credit market; (3) the use of symbolic/ideological sources that successfully appeal to the lifeworld of the lower classes. Concerning social welfare, the AKP has created a complex and expansive web of social assistance, involving public poverty reduction programmes, local municipalities, faith-based charitable organizations and other private initiatives. The number of families benefiting from the numerous cash transfer programmes have multiplied many times since 2002 to over 3 million by 2014 (Kutlu 2015: 165). The AKP-controlled local governments and Islamic-oriented charitable organizations channel millions of dollars in donations, thereby representing the state's subcontracting of some of its social responsibilities. Although such social assistance programmes have been inconsistent, unreliable and poorly coordinated, their populist reach and scope has enabled them to appeal directly to the poor and earn the consent of a wide cross-section of public opinion for neoliberal economic policies, including the privatization of some social services and health care (Eder 2010; Özden 2014).

Another aspect of the period that forms a crucial source of the expansive AKP hegemony is the growing indebtedness of working class households due to the significant transformation of banking sector activities in the post-2001 crisis period. While financing the public sector deficit and providing loans to enterprises dominated banking activities in the 1990s, there has been a rapid shift towards financializing households over the last decade. Given stagnating wage incomes and the new consumer culture fed by mushrooming shopping malls and increased advertising, consumer credit, which once had been the privilege of middle- and upper-class families, has increasingly penetrated into the daily lives of low-income households, to cover the gap between their incomes and expenditure (Bahçe and Köse 2010). Consequently, the ratio of household debt to disposable income rose from 7.5 per cent to 49 per cent between 2003 and 2012 (Karaçimen 2014: 163). This growing personal indebtedness of workers not only changed their values and attitudes towards markets and financial institutions, but also shaped their collective psychology, moved by fear of disorder and a belief that only strong leadership could ensure political and economic stability.

The authoritarian neoliberal project is not only constituted through populist policies and the financialization of workers as savers and consumers but also through cultural/ideological sources that the AKP cadres, its organic intellectuals and the Islamic bourgeoisie have manipulated to establish direct links to society. Given that the working class has become disarticulated and class-based discourses and institutions are increasingly excluded from politics, the void is filled by a complex amalgam of Islamism, conservatism and nationalism (Bozkurt 2013). Government institutions have been actively involved in the promotion of conservative values in various areas of social life, as well as facilitating the growth of Islamic capital, which tends to establish informal relationships with workers based on different kinds of social ties, including shared religious values and loyalty to national identity. On this basis, conservative–Islamic discourse has stressed harmony and cooperation while rejecting class conflict. A central theme of conservative–Islamic thought in Turkey has been the denouncing of class and class struggle as an alien cultural construct imported by the leftist-minded established elite. Hence, Islamist labour relations characterize the worker as respectful and hardworking (Durak 2013), rejecting the need for strikes and strike-like actions as fundamental mechanisms to defend the interests of labour vis-à-vis capital. This line of thought is also shared by many trade unionists, particularly the leaders of Islamist labour union confederation Hak-iş (Buğra 2002).

The Political Battle against the Military

As previously outlined, the pre-AKP period was characterized by a state form dominated by the military. This state form materialized more concretely in conjunction with the dynamics of neoliberal capitalism and militarism after the military intervention in 1980. It could reproduce itself under the conditions of the crisis of hegemony and internal warmongering of the 1990s, which enabled the military to increase its political power and capacity to control the political regime. Although the AKP claimed to have broken with its Islamist past, the military, which had previously struggled against political Islamist parties in the 1990s, continued to have strong suspicions about the AKP once it gained power in 2002. Hence, the political battle against the military was the only way for the AKP to establish its hegemony at the state level too. Consequently, under the strategy of expansive hegemony, one of the most important pillars of the AKP's hegemonic project was to promise political reform and democratization. The latter was depicted within the AKP's neoliberal populist strategy as a struggle against bureaucratic power, as civilianization against a military-controlled tutelary regime that had been institutionalized in the following state apparatuses: the military itself, the Presidency of the Republic, the senior judiciary organs (such as the Constitutional Court, Supreme Court of Appeal, Council of State, and High Council of Judges and Public Prosecutors), and the Higher Education Council (Akça 2014a: 33, 37–38, 40–44). This depiction, which garnered support for the AKP not only from conservatives but also from liberals and some leftists, was critical in forging the AKP's expansive hegemony at the ideological level.

Accordingly, the AKP period witnessed important reforms of civilianization. Between 2002 and 2005, the AKP government engaged in, to use Gramsci's term, a 'war of position' against the military especially by using Turkey's EU candidacy as leverage. Through many constitutional and legal reforms—the most important being the National Security Council restructuring—the AKP government curbed the military's political power. The de-militarization of the Kurdish question through some limited reforms on cultural rights and the promise for further democratization, together with consecutive ceasefires declared by the PKK, were also critical in implementing these reforms. In response, hardliners made several coup attempts in 2003 and 2004, but they were unsuccessful because they lacked international and domestic support (Akça and Balta-Paker 2013). As the AKP did not feel itself strong enough to publicly deal with these coup attempts at that time, the military continued to challenge the party. Instead, the AKP's search for some kind of alliance with the military on the basis of remilitarizing Kurdish question and the establishment of new authoritarian measures such as the amendments in the Counterterrorism Law ended up conjuncturally re-empowering the military. The military then vetoed Abdullah Gül's candidacy for the Presidency of the Republic, with the General Staff publishing an e-memorandum in April 2007 that implicitly accused Gül of disloyalty to the main principles of the Republic. Furthermore, in the spring of 2007, there was strong anti-AKP popular mobilization in the 'Republic Protests' organized in major cities (Akça and Balta-Paker 2013).

All these developments pushed the AKP to shift its strategy towards, again to use Gramsci's term, 'a war of manoeuvre' against the military. The day after the e-memorandum, the AKP government harshly criticized the military's move, and following the crisis in the parliament, which impeded the election of the president, it then rescheduled the general elections for 22 July 2007. AKP's subsequent electoral victory with 46 per cent of the votes gave it the political power to continue its political battle against the military. It should also be noted that the AKP's gradually increasing control over the police and judiciary, especially over special courts for serious crimes (*Özel Yetkili Mahkemeler*) was crucial. In October 2008, after a period of preparation by police investigators, the Ergenekon trial began, followed in February 2010 by another trial called Balyoz, which were both based on allegations of military-inspired plots to overthrow the government. Many high-ranking serving and retired military officials—including the former chiefs of general staff of the air, naval and land forces together with many journalists, lawyers, politicians and academics were tried and sentenced to imprisonment. By the end of 2012, the AKP had already won this political battle (Akça and Balta-Paker 2013). During this process, the AKP also gradually gained control over the state apparatuses of the so-called tutelary regime. First, Abdullah Gül became President of the Republic in August 2008. Then, using the power of appointments of the president recognized in the 1982 Constitution, AKP took control over higher education. Finally, it dominated the senior judicial institutions, especially the Constitutional Court and High Council of Judges and Public Prosecutors, after the referendum of 2010. This opened the way for the executive to exert control over these juridical apparatuses and ensure their takeover by pro-AKP cadres.

THE AKP'S SHIFT TO LIMITED HEGEMONY

As previously mentioned, this chapter argues that the late AKP period should be considered as a transition from an expansive to a limited hegemonic strategy which took place within a broader process of reconfiguring the social and political relations of class forces and of restructuring the authoritarian state form. However, it is difficult to separate the two phases by defining a key moment since, as will be revealed below, various factors resulted in a gradual but radical shift within the AKP era. These include the global economic crisis of 2007–2008, the Gezi Revolt in 2013, protracted struggles among various intra-state actors that entered a new phase at the end of 2013, the complex conditions of the conflicts in the Middle East and the trajectory of the Kurdish question after 2010. To the extent that these developments eroded AKP's capacity to reproduce its hegemony over various sectors of Turkish society—especially the big bourgeoisie, urban, secular middle classes, precarious young professionals, Kurds, Alevis and international actors—it shifted its hegemonic strategy in an exclusionist way. This shift to limited hegemony also corresponded to a shift from a conservative populism to an Islamist political strategy, which polarized the political sphere based on *kulturkampf* and aimed at consolidating and mobilizing its own mass of voters through an Islamist political discourse. However, this should not be taken as a merely discursive shift. Rather, it should be interpreted as an attempt to forge a new historical bloc under the leadership of Islamic bourgeoisie (Akça 2014b).

Global Economic Crisis and the Changing Balance of Forces within the Power Bloc

The global economic crisis of 2007–2008 plainly revealed the long-standing fault lines of the Turkish economy. The global competitiveness of Turkey's exporting industries vis-à-vis their East Asian counterparts remained weak since the projected structural change in the composition of industry had been hardly achieved. A tripling in Turkish exports between 2002 and 2008 was overshadowed by a quadrupling of imports due to the heavy dependence of exports on imported intermediate and capital goods. The surge in foreign direct investments (FDIs) had only a limited effect on improving productivity since FDI flows were directed largely towards privatizations or mergers. Thus, the Turkish economy proved to be structurally incapable of sustaining growth without continuously high foreign inflows, thereby reinforcing high interest rates and currency overvaluation. Consequently, when the global crisis reached the so-called emerging markets, Turkey was among the most affected, with a collapse of growth and a wave of closures, especially of small and medium-size manufacturing enterprises. GDP shrank by 4.7 per cent in 2009 while the cost of the contraction fell heavily on the shoulders of the most disadvantaged. Sectors such as construction, textiles, automotive and retail, which were the locomotive of economic growth before 2008, were hard hit by plunging consumer demand (Bakır 2009).

The AKP's expansive hegemonic project during its initial years in power largely rested on the party's ability to maintain the unity and cohesion of the power bloc, which was very much dependent on maintaining rapid economic growth. The global economic crisis, therefore, considerably changed and transformed relations within the power bloc, and between the AKP and each capital faction composing the power bloc. Once the era of rapid economic growth was perceived to be over, the AKP's policy concerns shifted. One indicator of this shift was the government's decision to loosen its public spending regime, a move seen by the big bourgeoisie as well as international capital as very detrimental and destabilizing to macroeconomic balances. Despite continuous calls from TÜSİAD, the government refused to sign a precautionary IMF standby agreement in 2009, preferring temporary cuts in consumption taxes to stimulate consumption. The government presented its decision to postpone the IMF programme as a sign of national autonomy and economic strength (Öniş and Güven 2011: 603). However, behind this populist rhetoric lay the policy choice of prioritizing the interests of those capital groups that are more dependent on perpetual expansion of domestic demand vis-à-vis big financial capital, for which suppression of inflation and maintaining monetary stability is essential.

Another crucial response of the government to the crisis involved its asser-tive foreign policy, including a strategic shift towards the Middle East and in-creasingly Africa. The key driving force underlying this imperial orientation, which came to be known as neo-Ottomanism, was the Islamic capital faction through its business associations of TUSKON and MÜSİAD, which initially launched the process as a search for new markets and economic opportuni-ties in Turkey's immediate neighbourhood. The share of Middle Eastern and African countries in Turkish exports climbed rapidly to 43 per cent in 2012 from 23 per cent in 2006 (Tanyılmaz 2015: 99). However, it may well be argued that this initiative was motivated not only by economic needs but also represented a desire to assert the faction's dominance over the power bloc (Özden 2015). Given increasing economic problems and escalating political contradictions during this period, it became all the more crucial for this fac-tion to augment its control over the use of political power.

The fissures in the power bloc became more visible as TÜSİAD intensified its attacks on the government for decreasing the primary surplus, increasing allocations for local administrations and undermining the autonomy of regulatory institutions. Yet MÜSİAD also continuously urged the government to take new measures to revive the domestic market via grandiose public investments and increasing the amount of loans available to consumers and private companies (Hoşgör 2015). As the AKP's hegemonic appeal has increasingly shrunk as a result of its weakening ability to represent the economic-corporate interests of all constituents of the power bloc, it had to rely more heavily on authoritarian forms of governing. One example of this authoritarianism in the economic realm has been the continuous attacks and symbolic coercion that target private banks owned by large conglomerates. Erdoğan personally accused these banks of forming an 'interest rate lobby', being envious of Turkey's economic and political rise, and aiming to plot against the government. Political disaffection between Erdoğan and the bankers has gone so deep that the chief economic adviser to the President of the Republic recently declared that the government should seize İş Bankası, the largest private bank in Turkey (Karakaya 2016).

One motive behind the pressure on banks is the government's increasing need for private loans to finance large construction projects. Speculative construction initiatives have become a crucial field of activity to ensure the expansion of capitalist accumulation, particularly since the outbreak of the crisis. The government has promoted the construction sector via consumer credits, mass housing projects and government spending on major public sector projects. The spectacular influence of the construction sector during the AKP era is also promoted by increasing the initiatives of particular state institutions, such as the Mass Housing Development Administration (TOKİ) and the Privatization Administration (Türkün 2011; Di Giovanni in this book). These institutions have been given the authority of top-down decision-making on urban and housing policy and, as such, illustrate the concentration and centralization of power. The economic decision-making power is being increasingly delegated to the executive branch as important economic and social decisions have been made through cabinet decrees (Hoşgör 2015: 220). Urgent expropriation decisions have become the principal way of distributing public tenders, which not only allow the state to suppress the people's reactions to the negative consequences of brutal neoliberal practices but also enable the AKP to open up new venues of accumulation for its supportive capital groups.

Restructuring the Authoritarian State Form and the Protracted Crisis of the State

As the clashes within the power bloc intensified, control over state apparatuses became more and more vital. The AKP era became heavily marked by struggles for the restructuring of and control over the state. The civilianization process did not bring about a democratization of the state in Turkey since the AKP did not change the authoritarian nature of the state but restructured it to establish total control over the state apparatuses. It simply replaced the military-centred authoritarian state form with a police- and judiciary-centred one (Akça 2014a: 38), which was already very effective in its political battle against the military. However, it was not the AKP per se but mostly the Gülen Community, a powerful religious brotherhood, which controlled the most critical apparatuses of this new state form (Ertekin, Özsu and Şakar 2014; Şık 2012). Gülen's influence became one of the most important dynamics of the intra-state clashes in the due course.

The new police- and judiciary-centred state form has both global and local characteristics. The first global characteristic is that it corresponds to the neoliberal restructuring of police forces, the shift from 'a post- to a pre-crime society' and the new punitive practices of the 'penal state' in order to control new potentially dangerous social and political groups (Neocleous 2008, 2014; Zedner 2007; Wacquant 2009; Briken and Eick in this book). Second, after the 9/11 attacks, such a security-based political rationality gained new momentum. The war on terror, the doctrine of preemptive war and the anti-terror laws constructed a new state of exception, which has been deployed both globally and nationally to control social and political discontent. Now, the terrorist and the enemy could be anyone. Political crimes are redefined as terror crimes and normal legal procedures are suspended (Neocleous 2014; Paye 2004).

Accordingly, on the one hand, the AKP period has witnessed the acceleration of global structural trends within Turkey. On the other hand, the new state form has developed its Turkish peculiarities too since it was at the centre of harsh political struggles among competing state and political elites trying to eliminate political adversaries. This new authoritarian state form was constructed through a series of legal changes in the Penal Code (2005), the Criminal Procedure Code (2005), the Counterterrorism Law (2006), and Police Powers and Duties Law (2007) (Berksoy 2010, 2013). In 2005, the new Penal Code redefined terror crimes in a way to include many legitimate acts of political and social protest while special courts for serious crimes (*Özel Yetkili Mahkemeler*) replaced the old State Security Courts. A broad range of crimes has been included within the purview of exceptional trial processes and these legal changes have given extraordinary discretionary power to specially authorized prosecutors. A penal system has emerged that creates a monumental state of exception, allowing the police and the judiciary to operate on the idea of engaging with an 'enemy' as if they are at war (İnanıcı 2011). The definitions of terror and terrorist in the Counterterrorism Law are so broadly defined that a wide spectrum of issues, actors and acts are deliberately and arbitrarily treated as linked to terror or terrorists (Göktaş

2012), which has allowed the AKP's political opponents to be criminalized as 'terrorists'. Besides socialists, Kurds and the Kurdish movement, who have always been defined as 'internal enemies', first the Kemalist elites (civil and military bureaucrats, journalists, academic scholars, etc.) and later on the Gülenist bureaucratic cadres have also been treated as enemies of the state. Many trials have been opened by the special serious crimes courts in order to eliminate or deactivate political opponents. This juridico-political structure has also severely damaged freedoms of the press, speech, assembly and association in Turkey.

This new neoliberal security state was effective not only in the political battle against the military in controlling all state apparatuses but also in dealing with all kinds of social and political opposition since the AKP's hegemonic capacity started to contract steadily in the aftermath of the global economic crisis. In that sense, the Gezi revolt was a critical threshold. Having established its control over all state apparatuses and gained another victory in the 2011 elections, the AKP set about constructing a new Turkey in its own image in a fashion that was increasingly indifferent to and inconsiderate of oppositional groups. It introduced a kind of biopolitics distinguished by its articulation of neoliberalism and religious conservatism, including the increasing control of social life by means of a myriad of policies imposed in authoritarian ways. Those policies were related to the control of women's bodies, the Islamization of national educational system, limitations imposed on the sale and consumption of alcohol, various unwarranted interventions in cultural and artistic fields, numerous urban renewal schemes, severe pressure on the media, and harsh police violence against social protests and street politics. The mass popular revolt, known as the Gezi movement, came as a response to those policies (Akça et al. 2014b).

In order to deal with this popular revolt, the AKP had to resort to the use of harsh police violence and Islamist discourse. More critically, however, the AKP decisively shifted its political strategy from an expansive to a limited hegemony, which aimed at consolidating and mobilizing its own mass of voters. This also corresponded to a shift from a Turkish centre-right style populism to a more Islamist discourse. While describing the Gezi revolt as a coup attempt endorsed not only by the 'pro-tutelage bloc' and 'marginal, terrorist, illegal organizations' but also by the nebulous 'interest rate lobby' and 'external forces', it redefined the anti-AKP bloc to include international and national monopolistic capital and world powers (implicitly the United States and the European Union). This marked a return to the classical political line of Turkey's political Islamist movement (*Milli Görüş*). Thus, it was not merely a conjunctural ideological turn but rather reflected the increasing clashes within the power bloc, as part of a new hegemonic strategy aimed at forging a new historical bloc under the leadership of the Islamic bourgeoisie. The disarticulated working class—over which the AKP had successfully established the hegemony of the capitalist class through neoliberal populist policies—continued to be the critical social base of this new historical bloc. In order to increase its capacity of control over this social base, the AKP refashioned its populist political discourse by emphasizing its Sunni-Muslim identity (Akça 2014b). However, two consecutive critical events revealed that this new political strategy was more fragile than anticipated, which led the AKP to respond with new measures of authoritarianism. The first was the police operations and trials that started at the end of 2013 concerning a huge corruption case which implicated four ministers and the son of the then prime minister Erdoğan. This was the peak of the clash between the AKP and the Gülen community over their different views concerning the control of the state, the Kurdish question and Turkey's Middle East policy. From the sidelines, the Turkish public watched these competing groups within different state apparatuses, including the police, judiciary, national intelligence and the ministry of internal affairs, engage in a fierce struggle. Not only were the AKP and Erdoğan insufficiently powerful to control these critical state apparatuses but there was also a deep crisis of the state. AKP responded to these developments both by more extensively using the police-centred neoliberal security state and by increasing control over the police and judiciary, especially by purging the Gülenist cadres. Accordingly, in the first months of 2014, the government introduced several new regulations concerning senior judicial institutions and the National Intelligence Organization which aimed at increasing control and domination of the executive over these state apparatuses (Yazıcı 2014).

The second critical event was the street protests that began on 6–7 October 2014, mainly by Kurds, in reaction to the AKP's policy in Rojava. The AKP's Sunni/Islamist foreign policy in Syria (and more generally in the Middle East), its support for radical Islamist groups and its prioritization of curbing the power of the Kurdish movement in Syria passed a threshold during the resistance of Kurdish fighters in Kobane against ISIS. In support of the resistance in Kobane and against the AKP's pro-radical Islamist and anti-Kurdish policies in Syria, thousands of Kurdish people participated in street protests. The harsh police violence in response to the protests led to the death of 50 people. A new package of legislation, publicly known as the 'Internal Security Package', was presented to the parliament in November 2014 and ratified in April 2015 by Erdoğan, now President of the Republic, after long and harsh parliamentary debates. The new regulations included more restrictions on basic and political rights, increased police discretionary powers—including sanctions to use firearms—and enhanced the scope of exceptional trials.

CONCLUSION: IN SEARCH OF THE
PRESIDENTIAL SYSTEM

The results of the general election held in June 2015 were surprising for two reasons. For the first time in its history, the Kurdish movement succeeded in passing the 10 per cent election threshold to enter parliament as a party while the AKP failed to win enough votes to form a single-party government. This situation only tantalized the political opposition for a short time. The countercoup, this time, came in a civil guise, staged by Erdoğan. In July, the negotiation process conducted with the Kurdish movement was stopped with the war restarting shortly after. In August, Erdoğan declared the coup himself: 'Whether one accepts it or not, Turkey's administrative system has changed. Now, what should be done is to update this de facto situation within the legal framework of the constitution' (*Hürriyet* 2015). With these words, Erdoğan confirmed that he would bypass the existing constitution and act as a de facto president.

Beyond doubt, what rendered this civil coup possible was the consensus Erdoğan reached with the military to restart the war with the Kurds. Factors such as the strengthening of the Kurdish party, HDP (Peoples' Democratic Party) in Turkey, the rise of the PKK as an internationally recognized actor in the war against ISIS, and the declaration of autonomous regions by its Syrian ally, PYD (Democratic Union Party) in Northern Syria neighbouring Turkey established this unexpected consensus. This enabled the de facto regime to strengthen itself through the new war in the Kurdish regions—which has gone far beyond the one conducted in the 1990s—and through the practices of a police state in the rest of Turkey. These two aspects of repression were combined by the regime under the umbrella of the 'war against terror', conducted mainly against the PKK and the Gülen community, which is now declared a terrorist organization by law.

The most explicit feature of this era is the increasing autonomy of Erdoğan and his close circle, the *Palace*, from the existing political system. From Erdoğan's viewpoint, even his own party and the government have become parts of the state apparatus that should be kept under strict control. Two main motives have underpinned almost every action of Erdoğan: first, keeping the state apparatus under as much control as possible; second, in order to do this, protecting and even increasing his plebiscitary capacity. His prolonged insistence on shifting to the presidential system corresponds with these two motives. In fact, from the 1980s onwards, a presidential system has become a suggestion presented by protagonists of neoliberalism within the context of 'efficient government' while various important capital groups have declared their support for a presidential system based on rule of law and check and balance mechanisms. Poulantzas suggests authoritarian statism is 'neither the new form of a genuine exceptional State, nor, in itself, a transitional form on the road to such a State: it rather represents the new 'democratic' form of the bourgeois republic in the current phase of capitalism' (Poulantzas 1978: 208–209). It seems that the presidential system proposed by Erdoğan and his followers under the name of 'Turkish-style presidential system' would go even beyond the form of authoritarian statism Poulantzas has identified.

NOTES

1. Democratic Left Party (DSP), Motherland Party (ANAP) and Nationalist Action Party (MHP)—the three parties that comprised the previous coalition government— all failed to surmount the national 10 per cent threshold, thus were unable to win representation in the new parliament.
2. Average annual GDP growth was 7.5 per cent between 2002 and 2005. During the same period inflation fell to a single digit, 9 per cent, for the first time in decades and by 2008, exports reached $134 billion dollars, 90 per cent of which consisted of manufactured goods (Öniş and Şenses 2009).

BIBLIOGRAPHY

Akça İ (2014a) Hegemonic projects in post-1980 Turkey and the changing forms of authoritarianism. In: Akça İ, Bekmen A and Özden BA (eds) *Turkey Reframed: Constituting Neoliberal Hegemony*. London: Pluto, 13–46.

Akça İ (2014b) Gezi ve siyasal iktidar üzerinde etkileri: Yaygın hegemonyadan sınırlı hegemonyaya. In: Abat E, Bulduruç E and Korkmaz F (eds) *Bizim Bir Haziranımız: Haziran Ayaklanması Üzerine Notlar*. İstanbul: Patika, 127–147.

Akça İ and Balta-Paker E (2013) Beyond military tutelage? Turkish military politics and the AKP government. In: Canan-Sokullu E (ed) *Debating Security in Turkey: Challenges and Changes In The Twenty-First Century*. Lanham, MD: Lexington Books, 77–92.

Akça İ, Bekmen A and Özden BA (eds) (2014a) *Turkey Reframed: Constituting Neoliberal Hegemony*. London: Pluto.

Akça İ, Bekmen A and Özden BA (2014b) A postscript: #resistturkey. In: Akça İ, Bekmen A and Özden BA (eds) *Turkey Reframed: Constituting Neoliberal Hegemony*. London: Pluto, 247–260.

Alpman PS (2016) *Esmer Yakalılar: Kent-Sınıf-Kimlik ve Kürt Emeği*. İstanbul: İletişim.

Aybar S and Lapavitsas C (2001) The recent Turkish crisis: Another step toward free market authoritarianism. *Historical Materialism: Research in Critical Marxist Theory* 8(1): 297–308.

Bahçe S and Köse AH (2010) Krizin teğet geçtiği ülkeden krize bakış: Teorinin naifliği, gerçekliğin kabalığı. *Praksis* 22: 9–40.

Bakır C (2009) Wobbling but still on its feet: The Turkish economy in the global financial crisis. *South European Society and Politics* 14(1): 71–85.

Bekmen A (2014) State and capital in Turkey during the neoliberal era. In: Akça İ, Bekmen A and Özden BA (eds) *Turkey Reframed: Constituting Neoliberal Hegemony*. London: Pluto, 47–74.

Berksoy B (2010) The police organization in Turkey in the Post-1980 period and the re-construction of the social formation. In: Khalili L and Schweler J (eds) *Policing and Prisons in the Middle East: Formations of Coercion*. London: Hurst & Co., 137–155.

Berksoy B (2013) *Military, police and intelligence in Turkey: Recent transformations and needs for reform*. İstanbul: TESEV.

Bozkurt U (2013) Neoliberalism with a human face: Making sense of the Justice and Development Party's neoliberal populism in Turkey. *Science & Society* 77(3): 372–396.

Bozkurt U (2015) AKP rule in the aftermath in the Gezi protests: From expanded to limited hegemony? In: David I and Toktamış KF (eds) *'Everywhere Taksim': Sowing the Seeds for a New Turkey at Gezi*. Amsterdam: Amsterdam University Press, 77–88.

Buğra A (2002) Labour, capital, and religion: Harmony and conflict among the constituency of political Islam in Turkey. *Middle Eastern Studies* 38(2): 187–204.

Buğra A and Keyder Ç (2006) The Turkish welfare regime in transformation. *Journal of European Social Policy* 16(3): 211–228.

Çelik A (2015) Turkey's new labour regime under the Justice and Development Party in the first decade of the twenty-first century: Authoritarian flexibilization. *Middle Eastern Studies* 51(4): 618–635.

Cizre Ü and Yeldan E (2005) The Turkish encounter with neo-liberalism: Economics and politics in the 2000/2001 crises. *Review of International Political Economy* 12(3): 387–408.

Doğan AE and Durak Y (2014) The rise of the Islamic bourgeoisie and the socialisation of neoliberalism: Behind the success story of two pious cities. In: Akça İ, Bekmen A and Özden BA (eds) *Turkey Reframed: Constituting Neoliberal Hegemony*. London: Pluto, 219–233.

Doğan MG (2014) The deradicalisation of organised labour. In: Akça İ, Bekmen A and Özden B A (eds) *Turkey Reframed: Constituting Neoliberal Hegemony*. London: Pluto, 188–202.

Durak Y (2013) *Emeğin Tevekkülü: Konya'da İşçi-İşveren İlişkileri ve Dindarlık*. İstanbul: İletişim.

Eder M (2010) Retreating state? Political economy of welfare regime change in Turkey. *Middle East Law and Governance* 2(2): 152–184.

Ertekin OG, Özsu F and Şakar M (2014) *Yargıda Kumpasın Köşe Taşları: AKP ve Cemaat*. İstanbul: Tekin.

Gill S (2008) *Power and Resistance in the New World Order*, 2nd edition. Basingstoke: Palgrave Macmillan.

Gill S (2011) Who elected the bankers? *Iskra* (18 December). Available at: http://stephengill.com/news/2011/12/who-elected-the-bankers.html

208   *Barış Alp Özden, İsmet Akça and Ahmet Bekmen*

Göktaş K (2012) Yeni yargı: Kurumsallaşma ve pratik. *Birikim* 275: 18–22.
Hoşgör E (2015) The question of AKP hegemony. In: Balkan N, Balkan E, and Öncu A (eds) *The Neoliberal Landscape and the Rise of Islamist Capital in Turkey*. New York: Berghan, 201–234.
Hürriyet (2015) 'Türkiye'nin yönetim sistemi fiilen değişmiştir'. *Hürriyet* (15 August). Available at: http://www.hurriyet.com.tr/turkiyenin-yonetim-sistemi-fiilen-degismistir-29815380
İnanıcı H (2011) *Parçalanmış Adalet: Türkiye'de Özel Ceza Yargısı*. İstanbul: İletişim.
Jayasuriya K (2001) Globalisation, sovereignty, and the rule of law: From political to economic constitutionalism? *Constellations* 8(4): 442–460.
Jones S (2006) *Antonio Gramsci*. Abingdon: Routledge.
Karaçimen E (2014) Financialization in Turkey: The case of consumer debt. *Journal of Balkan and Near Eastern Studies* 16(2): 161–180.
Karakaya K (2016) Will government seize Turkey's largest bank? *Al-Monitor* (11 April). Available at: http://www.al-monitor.com/pulse/originals/2016/04/turkey-can-government-confiscate-largest-bank.html
Keyman F and Öniş Z (2007) *Turkish Politics in a Changing World: Global Dynamics and Domestic Transformations*. Istanbul: Bilgi University Press.
Kutlu D (2015) *Türkiye'de Sosyal Yardım Rejiminin Oluşumu*. İstanbul: Notabene.
Nar M (2015) The committed changes within Public Procurement Law in Turkey (2003–2014). *International Journal of Business and Social Research* 5(2): 1–20.
Neocleous M (2008) *Critique of Security*. Edinburgh: Edinburgh University Press.
Neocleous M (2014) *War Power, Police Power*. Edinburgh: Edinburgh University Press.
Oğuz Ş (2012) Türkiye'de kapitalizmin küreselleşmesi ve neoliberal otoriter devletin inşası. *Mesleki Sağlık ve Güvenlik Dergisi* 12(45/46): 2–15.
Öngel S (2014) Flexible and conservative: Working-class formation in an industrial town. In: Akça İ, Bekmen A and Özden BA (eds) *Turkey Reframed: Constituting Neoliberal Hegemony*. London: Pluto, 203–218.
Öngen T (2002) Political crisis and strategies for crisis management: From 'low intensity conflict' to 'low intensity instability'. In: Balkan N and Savran S (eds) *The Politics of Permanent Crisis: Class, Ideology and State in Turkey*. New York: Nova Science Publishers, 55–83.
Öniş Z (2013) Sharing power: Turkey's democratization challenges in the age of the AKP hegemony. *Insight Turkey* 15(2): 103–122.
Öniş Z (2016) Turkey's two elections. The AKP comes back. *Journal of Democracy* 27(2): 141–154.
Öniş Z and Güven AB (2011) Global crisis, national responses: The political economy of Turkish exceptionalism. *New Political Economy* 16(5): 585–608.
Öniş Z and Şenses F (2009) Turkish economy at a new stage of integration into the global economy. In: *Turkey and the Global Economy: Neoliberal Restructuring and Integration in the Post-Crisis Era*. Abingdon: Routledge, 304–314.
Özden BA (2014) The transformation of social welfare and politics in Turkey: A successful convergence of neoliberalism and populism. In: Akça İ, Bekmen A and

Özden BA (eds) *Turkey Reframed: Constituting Neoliberal Hegemony*. London: Pluto, 157–173.

Özden BA (2015) Ustanın çırakları alt-emperyalistler: Politik bir emperyalizm analizi denemesi. In: Bekmen A and Özden BA (eds) *Emperyalizm: Teori ve Güncel Tartışmalar*. İstanbul: Habitus, 113–156.

Özden BA and Bekmen A (2015) Rebelling against neoliberal populist regimes. In: David I and Toktamış KF (eds) *'Everywhere Taksim': Sowing the Seeds for a New Turkey at Gezi*. Amsterdam: Amsterdam University Press.

Paye JC (2004) *La fin de l'Etat de droit: La lutte antiterroriste, de l'état d'exception à la dictature*. Paris: La Dispute.

Poulantzas N (1978/2014) *State, Power, Socialism*. London: Verso.

Şık A (2012) *Pusu (Devletin Yeni Sahipleri)*. İstanbul: Postacı.

Tanyılmaz K (2015) The deep fracture in the big bourgeoisie of Turkey. In: Balkan N, Balkan E and Öncü A (eds) *The Neoliberal Landscape and the Rise of Islamist Capital in Turkey*. New York: Berghan, 89–116.

TURKSTAT (2010) *The Summary of Agricultural Statistics*. Ankara: Turkish Statistical Institute.

Türkün A (2011) Urban regeneration and hegemonic power relationships. *International Planning Studies* 16(1): 61–72.

Wacquant L (2009) *Punishing the Poor: The Neoliberal Government of Social Insecurity*. Durham, NC: Duke University Press.

World Bank (2009) Informality in Turkey: Size, trends, determinants and consequences. Available at: http://siteresources.worldbank.org/TURKEYEXTN/Resources/361711-1277211666558/bpg_SizeTrendsDeterminantsAndConsequences.pdf

Yazıcı S (2014) Türkiye'nin son on yılı: Avrupa demokrasisinden otokrasiye. *Perspectives* 10: 24–27.

Yeldan E (2006) Neo-liberal global remedies: From speculative-led growth to IMF-led crisis in Turkey. *Review of Radical Political Economics* 38(2): 193–213.

Zedner L (2007) Pre-crime and post-criminology? *Theoretical Criminology* 11(2): 261–281.

Chapter 11

Resistance and Passive Revolution in Egypt and Morocco

Brecht De Smet and Koenraad Bogaert[1]

The notion of 'authoritarian neoliberalism' indicates a loss of neoliberalism's 'hegemonic "aura"' and a shift towards 'extraordinary' modes of governance (Bruff 2014: 115). Recent developments of securitization, debt discipline, constitutionalization of austerity and coercive policies towards migrants, trade unions and other social actors illustrate a shift from traditional bourgeois democracy to a 'nondemocratic state' in the West. It is hard to deny the increasing authoritarian policies of governments in the face of the political, economic and social problems that flow from the contemporary crisis of capitalism. However, in order to understand the nature and direction of the development of the state at this juncture, the concept of 'authoritarianism' has to be grounded in a long-term historical and class-based analysis. If one takes the Western post-war period as the norm of capitalist accumulation and bourgeois state formation, contemporary neoliberal politics indeed appear as an extraordinary, authoritarian deviation. Yet, the history of capitalist development since the nineteenth century suggests that revolutions both in the global North and in the global South have always showed the limits of bourgeois democracy and a tendency towards more authoritarian forms of state power (Amin 2011). Gramsci, for example, understood the rise of Fascism and authoritarianism in the 1920s and 1930s as the 'normal' political forms of that capitalist epoch (De Smet 2016: 98–99). Instead of the norm, the post–Second World War class compromise, democratization and welfare state were the unique outcomes of 'extraordinary' economic and (geo)political conditions. This transition represented a 'counter-revolution in democratic form', which displaced demands for radical change by far-reaching reforms of the bourgeois state. A similar argument could be made with regard to the postcolonial developmentalist projects in the global South (see below).

Since the 1970s, neoliberal transformations within global capitalism represented an evolving and variegating 'restoration of class power' (Harvey 2006), revealing capitalism's inner susceptibility to crisis and the coinciding loss of hegemonic consensus. However, class power was restored differently in the global South as it was in Europe or in the United States. In this chapter we investigate the emergence of new forms of authoritarianism in 'revolutionary' Egypt and 'reformist' Morocco during the neoliberal age to demonstrate how pre-existing forms of authoritarianism are transformed in relation to and converged with structural shifts in global capitalism. In other words, how neoliberal reform created new forms of capitalist class power in articulation with 'older' forms of authoritarianism (e.g. neo-patrimonialism, clientelism, state repression, etc.).[2] We argue that, despite a shared global condition of crisis and neoliberal restructuring in the 1970s, divergent national historical trajectories and hegemonic policies determined these two countries' respective vulnerability and resistance to revolutionary upheaval. This perspective not only debunks mainstream assumptions linking 'economic liberalization' to 'political democratization', but also rejects the very idea of an 'impure', 'crony' capitalism in the global South, for authoritarian accumulation in these spaces is closely connected to capitalist transformation and state reconfiguration in Western liberal democracies.

Furthermore, a closer look at the trajectories of Egypt and Morocco sheds light on the varying hegemonic success of neoliberal reform. A shift towards more authoritarian policies does not *necessarily* entail a hegemonic crisis. The difference between domination and hegemony is not the quantitative *proportion* between coercion and consent needed to maintain class power, but the extent to which force is successfully *grounded* in popular consent (Thomas 2009: 162–165). An authoritarian regime can be quite hegemonic if its use of violence, coercion and exclusion is accepted by broad layers of the population. Hence, the implementation of neoliberal policies within different national contexts provoked different forms of resistance and produced particular political and economic trajectories.

We use Gramsci's notion of *passive revolution* as a comparative concept to understand the different capacities of Egyptian and Moroccan elites in exploiting changes in global capitalism and adapting to popular pressures. Passive revolution refers to the capacity of dominant classes in periods of crisis and societal transformation to preempt, deflect or absorb revolutionary struggles 'from below' and reconfigure the state and the economic structure 'from above' to their advantage (De Smet 2016; Gramsci 1971; Morton 2010: 317–318). Postcolonial state formation could be interpreted as such, as a new elite coming out of the liberation movements took over power and neutralized more radical revolutionary aspirations, resulting in the developmentalist and national bourgeois projects of the Third World (Amin 2011: 102).

When used as a comparative concept, passive revolution is both *encompassing* and *individualizing* (see Tilly 1984). An encompassing comparison explains the Egyptian and Moroccan cases in terms of their relation to the whole: neoliberal transformation. The different cases are presumed to exist not in isolation from each other, displaying independent similarities and differences, but are considered part of a shared historical process of global and regional reconfiguration and contestation. Such a method of 'incorporated comparison ... views comparable social phenomena as differentiated outcomes or moments of an historically integrated process, whereas conventional comparison treats such social phenomena as parallel cases' (McMichael 1990: 392).

The comparison between Egypt and Morocco leads us to the conclusion that (1) the pace, intensity and momentum of the neoliberal assault; (2) the sources and strength of the elites' hegemony; and (3) the extent and character of organized discontent were directly and coherently interrelated, determined the capacity of dominant groups to contain popular discontent, and produced different political outcomes.

THE END OF DEVELOPMENTALISM AND THE REARTICULATION OF AUTHORITARIANISM

In the wake of the decolonization struggles, national liberation movements in the global South radically reconfigured the colonial states. Ideologically, these postcolonial societal projects shared the outlook of Western Fordism–Keynesianism, which espoused that the state was the main motor of capitalist 'modernization', that political loyalty had to be assured through some form of class compromise and wealth redistribution, and that extreme economic liberalism had to be rejected (Amin 2011: 101–102). In the MENA region, even though Arab nationalist and socialist regimes expressed this project most saliently, both monarchical and republican states could be labelled as developmental states with authoritarian yet redistributive policies.

The global economic crisis of the 1970s and the subsequent Third World debt crisis spelled the end of developmentalism and opened the door to neoliberal restructuring. Under the flag of short-term 'stabilization' and long-term 'structural adjustment', the IMF and the World Bank pushed through the neoliberal restructuring of Third World economies. Privatization became *the* dominant 'development' strategy. Within neoclassical and neoliberal discourses this was presented as a necessary instrument to 'roll back' highly inefficient public enterprise. In addition, privatization was also presented as an efficacious weapon against corruption and clientelist networks as the process dismantled the personal 'cash cows' of rent-seeking state elites (cf. Walton and Seddon 1994: 334–336).

Economic liberalization would then empower new social groups and bring forth a *political* liberalization (cf. Springborg 2011).

However, the project of global neoliberalism failed to live up to its universalist promises of freedom, welfare and individual empowerment. Instead, the dismantlement of welfare and developmentalist state projects and the unrestricted movement of global finance capital entailed a growing gap between possessors and dispossessed, a switch from class compromise to confrontation and new forms of authoritarianism. A new accumulation strategy emerged, based on the deregulation of markets, prices and goods; on the flexibility of labour and production; on increased transnational competitiveness and on the disintegration of collective bargaining in favour of meritocratic individualism which effectively undermined the position and strength of labour vis-à-vis capital.

Especially in the MENA region, the move towards privatization was often inspired by the severe decline of public revenues, rather than by the inefficiency of public enterprises and the superior efficiency of private ones (Ayubi 1997). One of the key actors in the neoliberal passive revolution was not the elusive market, but state institutions, which actively 'regulated deregulation'. Those who controlled the state also controlled the specific implementation of privatization policies. Consequently, structural adjustment has reinforced, rather than weakened, the position of ruling classes. At the same time, the conditions were created for foreign capital and new local elites to participate in economic restructuring and seize important parts of previously state-dominated economic sectors. Authoritarianism in the region was fundamentally transformed by a convergence of interests of domestic ruling classes and (global) economic elites (Bogaert 2013).

This aggressive confrontation between capital and its discarded social base—industrial labour, public sector workers, peasants—did not take place without a fight (Walton and Seddon 1994). Social struggle was at the heart of these restructurings, and the political future in those days was still very open, uncertain and undecided. From the late 1970s onwards, 'new waves' of protest emerged in the MENA and in the rest of the global South. Urban mass protests and riots were among the first expressions of popular discontent with the new neoliberal policies (Bayat 2002).

The reconfiguration of authoritarianism in the region was determined not only by structural adjustment policies imposed 'from outside' by international creditors, but also by the particular adoption of these schemes by incumbent elites and by the social struggles they provoked in different countries. The cases of Egypt and Morocco illustrate how the global neoliberal 'passive revolution' became articulated in quite different national trajectories of political and economic struggle and transformation, respectively provoking and blocking revolutionary outcomes.

EGYPT'S STALLED NEOLIBERALISM

Looking at Egypt's history of colonization and decolonization through the lens of passive revolution, crucial ruptures appear as attempts by domestic ruling groups to reorganize both state and economy in order to reproduce their social existence in a context of mass struggle. The 1919 revolution led to an unstable compromise between revolutionary actors, domestic elites, especially landlords, and British capital. The failure of the ruling coalition to 'modernize' Egypt—that is, achieve full independence and political democracy, redistribute land and industrialize—led to a persistent crisis of hegemony, which was forcefully resolved by a military coup in 1952. In the face of a mass uprising the 'Free Officers' led by Colonel Gamal Abdel Nasser took over control of the state institutions. By leaning on the resistance of nationalists, workers and peasants against domestic and foreign elites, Nasser was able to conquer state power, but the mobilization of these subaltern forces also generated a political debt. In the next two decades a new form of authoritarian class rule developed, which, despite the lack of political participation and the reliance on state violence, control and surveillance, was strongly grounded in popular consent (cf. De Smet 2016). It was generated by social reforms, distributive policies, state-led corporatism and a strong nationalist and anti-imperialist stance—being at the forefront of the anti-colonial struggle in the MENA and the global South offered Egyptians a new sense of dignity and prestige.

However, already from the second half of the 1960s, discontent among workers and students was fomenting over the lack of democracy and failing development goals. A falling rate of profit in the second half of the 1960s limited the capacity of the Egyptian public sector to redistribute surplus. Consequently, prices and taxes were increased and absolute surplus-extraction increased (lengthening of the workweek without compensation, cancellation of paid holidays, etc.) (Posusney 1996: 219). Egypt's defeat in the 1967 Six Day War against Israel delivered the fatal blow to the authoritarian project of 'Arab socialism'. Increasing subaltern contestation, partly stimulated by the May '68 students' and workers' revolt elsewhere, expressed and stimulated the emerging hegemonic crisis of authoritarian Nasserism, years before the rise of Islamism in the 1970s (al-Bendary 2008). This leftist turn from below was as much a pressing factor for the ruling groups to transform the developmentalist accumulation strategy and its class alliances as the continued economic malaise.

When in 1970 Anwar Sadat succeeded Nasser as president, he tried to solve the economic and hegemonic crisis by an increased integration of Egypt into the Western-dominated global economy. This reorientation came at a time when the West itself was struggling to solve the problems of Fordist-Keynesian accumulation. Therefore, together with Pinochet's Chile, Sadat's Egypt became a laboratory of neoliberalism in the global South (Callinicos 2011). The *Infitah*, the opening up of Egypt's economy to increased foreign investment, required sweeping changes to existing class coalitions and consent-generating mechanisms, prompting a confrontation with workers, students and other subaltern groups. Sadat tried to deflect this conflict in a passive-revolutionary way by presenting his changes as a top-down 'democratic revolution' against the authoritarian Nasserist state (Tucker 1978: 6). However, despite the establishment of a multiparty system and free elections, the 'deep state' of the military, bureaucratic and security apparatus remained firmly in power—albeit cleansed of Nasserist and Marxist elements. By the end of the 1970s, the National Democratic Party (NDP) emerged as the new dominant political apparatus of the ruling class coalition. Fundamentally, what changed was not the authoritarian character of the state, but its class base, excluding subaltern forces such as workers and peasants in favour of new layers of private capitalists, consumerist middle classes, international capital and transnational actors such as the IMF.

However, the confrontational restructuring of Egypt's state and economy only added to the existing economic and hegemonic crisis. Privatization and liberalization of state companies, combined with a high inflation, led to deindustrialization, jobless growth, unemployment and a fall of real wages (Farah 2009: 39–41). Increasing labour resistance and strikes against these measures, temporarily halted due to the 1973 October War, culminated in a general uprising or 'bread riot' in January 1977 following IMF-imposed austerity measures. Industrial workers in Helwan demonstrated in Tahrir Square. Their protests were joined by students and people from the urban lower and middle classes.

Sadat's attempt to present the capitalist class offensive as a process of democratization failed to produce a new imaginary that could replace the project of Arab nationalism. He increasingly relied on a politicized Islam to offer an ideological counterweight to Nasserism. Yet, the repression of the 1977 uprising and the Camp David negotiations with Israel after the 1973 October War alienated the president's Islamist allies as well. Sadat's failure to forge a new hegemony would eventually lead to his assassination by Islamists in 1981.

Under Hosni Mubarak, a much more protracted and appeasing process of passive revolution would take place, at least in the 1980s. A new 'post-populist' class compromise was reached, one which was negotiated on a purely material base, without the ideological prestige and mobilization of the Nasserist era. Redistributive policies were rooted in an emerging rentier economy. From the second half of the 1970s onwards, a stream of revenues from migrant workers' remittances from the Gulf countries; foreign loans and diplomatic, military and economic aid; the re-opened Suez Canal; oil and gas; and tourism rendered a full confrontation with industrial labour unnecessary to drive up the rate of profit. Despite a process of deindustrialization the public sector continued to expand until the mid-1980s (Richards and Waterbury 2008: 190; Roccu 2013). The accumulation of external rents was not the result of smart strategy by Egypt's elites, but the contingent outcome of global and regional processes. The geopolitical position of Egypt and its new relation with Israel, combined with the rise of the Gulf as an economic powerhouse, temporarily created unique opportunities for the dominant groups to reproduce their social existence without far-reaching transformations in the economic and political structures of the nation.

Mubarak's early presidency heralded a softening of the coercive dimension of state power. Political prisoners were released, civil rights such as freedom of press and of association were reinstated to a limited degree and elections were held. Liberal commentators praised the country for its gradual 'democratization', but this shift soon proved to be a 'grand delusion' (Kienle 2001). Although oppositional politics were tolerated in clearly delineated spaces in civil and political society, they remained subordinated to the interests of the new class coalition that had been established in the 1970s. The relatively successful co-optation and subjugation of opposition groups such as the leftist al-Tagammu party, the liberal al-Wafd and the Muslim Brotherhood marked the consolidation of the Mubarak dictatorship, rather than its undermining. Industrial workers, for their part, still associated with Nasserist hegemony and continued to interpellate the state as an independent power that defended public interest by maintaining a just class equilibrium. They displayed their economic productivity and political loyalty to the state in exchange for material concessions (Posusney 1996: 233). The state, for its part, could no longer rely on a strong hegemony and primarily maintained power by keeping the subaltern classes in a fragmented, disorganized and clientelist condition.

The process of gradual neoliberal restructuring in Egypt, moving back and forward between measures of economic liberalization and state control, highlights that the emerging global neoliberal passive revolution was not a homogenizing force, able to simply copy its political, economic and ideological structures onto the fabric of Egyptian society. Firstly, the initial speed, intensity and confrontational character of the passive revolution provoked a strong reaction from subaltern groups who were already revolting against authoritarianism and austerity in the late 1960s. Economic concessions to avert social explosions such as the 1977 insurrection slowed down the transformative process. Secondly, the influx of windfall rents at the end of the

1970s provided the ruling elite with opportunities to actually slow down the dismantlement of populist redistribution and maintain the public sector as a key economic actor until the 1990s (Bayat 1993: 76–78; Beinin 2001: 157). However, new rents were not invested in industry or agriculture, but they were spent on imports and subsidies of consumer goods (Richards and Waterbury 2008: 223). A fall in rentier income from 1984 onwards necessitated a new accumulation strategy. In the 1990s and 2000s the Mubarak clique returned to Sadat's confrontational policies and aggressively reconfigured the post-populist bloc through economic dispossession and state violence.

MOROCCO'S ROYAL PASSIVE REVOLUTION

Morocco did not follow the political path of many of the other states in the region (cf. Leveau 1997; Catusse 2008). Whereas the Egyptian pre-capitalist landowners played the role of a 'comprador' elite, often allying themselves with British imperialism against local nationalist forces, the Moroccan sultanate was drawn into a confrontation with French imperialism, leading to the exile of Mohammed V in 1953. As a result, the nationalist party *Istiqlal* (Independence) allied itself with the monarchy in a concerted struggle for independence and used the popularity of King Mohammed V to gain popular support.

In the power struggle that evolved afterwards, the monarchy eventually gained the upper hand. Deploying its traditional and anti-colonial prestige and instigating the fragmentation of nationalist forces through the formation of a multiparty system, the monarchy was able to position itself symbolically above party politics, supervising the political scene as a 'supreme arbiter' (Waterbury 1970). The monarchy did not construct a mobilizing myth around regionalist or universalist notions of Arab nationalism or socialism, but presented itself as a particular, Moroccan institution that was at the heart of the nation and the religion of its people—an authentic, historical institution with the king as the 'Commander of the Faithful' (Hinnebusch 2014: 14; Waterbury 1970).

While most Arab countries implemented policies to promote rapid industrialization often at the expense of the agricultural sector, the monarchy actively developed and prioritized the agricultural sector. The palace saw a stable rural landowning class as one of the essential foundations of its power base (Pennell 2000: 306). As such, it also tried to limit the political weight of the cities and the urban nationalist movement. Similarly, as the army personnel consisted mainly of soldiers from rural and Berber descent, the military declared its allegiance to the monarchy instead of the mostly urban Arab nationalists (Vermeren 2002).

Whereas regional heavyweights such as Egypt, Syria, Algeria, Libya and Iraq eventually turned to the Soviet Union for support, Morocco aligned itself to the West from the start. The United States and especially France became its most important allies. In contrast to other Arab countries that ended up with some form of state-led accumulation, Hassan II preferred a controlled liberal economic system. State intervention in the Moroccan economy during the 1950s and 1960s was dictated more by neo-patrimonial strategies, clientelism and the structural weakness of the domestic private sector than by a populist developmentalist strategy (Ben Ali 1997; Kaioua 1996; Waterbury 1970).

However, at the end of the 1960s a slackening rural economy, increasing popular discontent and several cracks within the ruling bloc forced the monarchy to change its political strategies and its social base (Joffé 1988). The urban riots of 1965 in Casablanca marked a first turning point in authoritarian rule. They could be considered as a precursor of the austerity protests of the 1980s. The riots were severely repressed and prompted King Hassan II, who succeeded his father in 1961, to dissolve parliament and install a five-year state of emergency. However, two failed military coups in 1971 and 1972 rooted in the increasing political and economic tensions in the country demonstrated that mere repression was not going to be enough (Hinnebusch 2014: 16).

Economic windfalls (notably a rise in the export prices for phosphate), foreign aid (including from Saudi Arabia) and international bank loans eventually gave the monarchy leverage to develop and expand developmentalist policies in order to establish a more stable political equilibrium with the working classes, the emerging urban middle class and a growing group of educated youth in the cities (Glasser 1995; Richards and Waterbury 2008: 201–202, 243–248). Especially the oil boom of 1973 caused a strong increase in the international export prices of phosphates and provided the government with considerable resources for public spending. With the 1973–1977 Economic Plan, the monarchy gradually shifted its priorities from rural to urban regions. Economic rents were invested in the expansion of the public sector and redistributed some of the national wealth through public employment. Moreover, the monarchy also tried to strengthen the private sector, which was still considered the backbone of the economy. Apart from the implementation of several protectionist measures (e.g. import taxes and licences), a *Moroccanization law* was issued in order to secure at least 50 per cent of Moroccan ownership in domestic firms and promote an emerging corporate class (Cherkaoui and Ben Ali 2007). With the Moroccanization of the economy, the monarchy explicitly sought to deepen and strengthen its ties with the urban bourgeoisie while it encouraged the controlled emergence of a capitalist elite under the wings of a guardian state. As a result, access to the state apparatus and state favours became a necessary condition for success in business (Ben Ali 1997; Cammett 2007). Finally, foreign-owned agricultural property was to be expropriated and distributed among Moroccan landowners—however, only those with high connections within the state administration benefitted from the agrarian reform (Swearingen 1987).

These economic transformations were reinforced by a reconfiguration of state power, developing new forms of coercion and consent. A new security chief was appointed as Minister of Interior, the civilian Driss Basri. He became the main architect behind the infamous 'years of lead'. Until the early 1990s, Hassan II leaned on his civil security apparatus to violently repress the political opposition, leading to the arrest, torture, imprisonment, disappearance and murder of tens of thousands of political activists. At the same time, the king also realized the importance of active consent for the stability and effectiveness of his rule. Parliament and a multiparty system were reinstated, which granted a democratic legitimacy to the monarchy's reforms and created a space where loyal opponents could be recruited and disloyal forces isolated. Hassan II turned to the nationalist movement, including the leftist UNFP (which was severely repressed during the 1960s), to include them in a new political consensus.

Last but not the least, the monarchy's hegemony and prestige were strengthened through a renewal of its historical anti-colonial leadership. In 1975, Hassan II called for a peaceful mass march to 'liberate' the Spanish Sahara, which resulted in the famous 'Green March', mobilizing almost half a million people and effectively winning the support of the nationalist opposition parties (Pennel 2003: 173). The campaign resulted in a war with the Popular Front for the Liberation of the Sahara and the Rio de Oro (POLISARIO), which was partly concluded in 1979 with a very costly occupation. Despite the devastating effect on the national budget, the political gains were pivotal for Hassan II. The political opposition was effectively neutralized at a time when the economic and social conditions were worsening. Consequently, when the first austerity measures were introduced at the end of the 1970s, the 'locus of contestation shifted to the streets, where it has remained ever since' (Maghraoui 2002: 26).

While Egypt was leaving the path of state-driven accumulation in the 1970s, Moroccan state intervention increased throughout this decade. However, the absence of durable and extensive rent revenues limited the monarchy's capacities to bind public loyalties on the basis of a rentier social contract (Leveau 1997). Already in 1975, the rentier aspect of the Moroccan economy was largely exhausted. The sharp fall in export earnings from phosphates and the crisis in the agricultural sector led to a sharp increase of the public deficit.

Despite the introduction of the first austerity measures at the end of the 1970s, foreign public debt increased from 19.6 per cent of GDP in 1975 to a staggering 85 per cent in 1983 (Cohen and Jaïdi 2006: 37). In 1983, Morocco turned again to the IMF for support and a structural adjustment programme was implemented. The following neoliberal restructurings of the 1980s and 1990s coincided with a decline in real and relative incomes and put further pressure on the stability of the royal bloc. As the material dimension of hegemony crumbled, neoliberal restructurings prompted massive protests. 'Bread-riots' broke out in 1981 in Casablanca, after a general strike organized by one of the most powerful trade unions in the country. They were heavily repressed. Nevertheless, a new countrywide wave of protests followed in 1984, starting in Marrakech due to another rise in consumer goods prices. The revolts quickly spread to more than 50 cities. Six years later, a new general strike on 14 December 1990 set the beginning of another violent explosion. This time it originated in Fez and then spread to the cities of Tangiers, Kenitra and Meknes.

Despite the fact that the monarchy successfully managed to weaken the influence of the trade unions through repression and co-optation, especially after the 1981 riots (Clément and Paul 1984), protests persisted in massive numbers and the state was confronted with another opponent: a rapidly growing Islamist movement (Pennel 2003: 175–180). In order to maintain the monarchy's rule, a new process of passive revolution was needed, forcing Hassan II to start a gradual political 'reform' process in the 1990s.

MUBARAK'S NEOLIBERAL OFFENSIVE

In Egypt, from the second half of the 1980s onwards, due to a fall in rental income and unproductive distributive policies, national debt rose to more than $38 billion in foreign obligation and the budgetary deficit increased to over 20 per cent (Richards and Waterbury 2008: 225). The combination of a domestic crisis of rent-based accumulation with foreign pressure by the United States, IMF and World Bank shifted the state's gradual and careful molecular passive revolution back to a confrontational strategy (Farah 2009: 41). In 1991 Egypt accepted an Economic Reform and Structural Adjustment Program (ERSAP), which aimed to contain and decrease foreign debt and inflation, by cutting state subsidies on consumer goods, privatizing public companies, liberalizing markets and prices, freezing wages, commercializing agricultural lands and implementing a flat tax.

Such neoliberal policies required the further exclusion of subaltern forces from wealth redistribution and the subduing of recalcitrant factions of the capitalist class (Roccu 2013). However, the capitalist offensive was not grounded within new forms of hegemony; on the contrary, the aggressive class confrontation went hand in hand with a decrease in leadership and prestige of the dominant groups. The ruling class coalition was restricted instead of expanded, and already co-opted allies and opponents were alienated. Firstly, bureaucratic layers in the NDP and the public sector and the higher echelons of the armed forces felt a deep resentment towards the rising faction of neoliberal 'cronies' around Gamal Mubarak, the President's son. Secondly, workers, peasants and young graduates were increasingly excluded from the neoliberal class alliance. The ERSAP restored economic growth and the rate of profit by decreasing wages and benefits, by exploiting workers in the private sector, and by expropriating farmlands and increasing the prices of land rent. (Farah 2009: 41, 44; Mitchell 1999: 463). Thirdly, the limited spaces for opposition within the political and civil spheres were further restricted. From 1990 onwards, direct state regulation of political and civil society increased: parties' internal affairs were supervised, professional syndicates were put under direct state control, NGOs were closely scrutinized and newspapers faced stricter rules of censorship. Ironically, such measures severely restricted the capacity of the state to absorb and regulate political opponents, making them search for other ways to wage opposition.

Moreover, neoliberal policies did not solve Egypt's economic problems; on the contrary, their implementation worsened an already existing crisis of capital accumulation. In the countryside, the state sought the support of wealthy landowners in the realization of the free trade policies backed by the IMF and World Bank by promoting the production of cash crops that could be sold on the world market (Abdin and Gaafar 2010: 14). However, as rural capitalists were loath to make high-risk, capital-intensive investments in the productivity of agriculture, they were more interested in low-risk, inexpensive and often violent methods to drive up the rate of exploitation (Mitchell 2006).

In the industrial sector, the privatization of the public sector aimed to establish an ensemble of competitive and productive private entrepreneurs. However, the combination of global neoliberalism with collapsing state-driven capitalism resulted in a strengthening of oligarchic and monopolistic tendencies. State elites became investors in large private sector enterprises or used state power to favour their friends and families in the subcontracting sector, realizing huge profits. Public holding companies remained the largest shareholders in many of the privatized enterprises. State holding companies set up private corporations or joint ventures, and in 1998 the state bought back shares in most of its privatized enterprises (Mitchell 2002: 280–282). Neoliberal reform in Egypt did not at all entail a retreat of an abstract 'state' from an abstract 'market', but a redirection of state power and resources towards an increased accumulation of capital achieved by an aggressive policy of dispossession, which benefitted only a small clique within the ruling classes (Mitchell 1999: 461–462; Naguib 2011).

A crucial element in maintaining hegemony is the perception that the state and the ruling group are capable of realizing the 'common good'. Oligarchic economic reform, everyday state violence against ordinary citizens, faltering support for the Palestinian cause, and feeble opposition against the Afghanistan, Iraq and Lebanon wars discredited the Mubarak regime in the eyes of a majority of the population. The state undermined the material base of its consent-generating class compromise while at the same time restricting access to the ruling coalition and dissolving spaces where opposition forces could be regulated and co-opted. Hence, the 25 January Revolution was rendered possible by a deep crisis of hegemony in combination with the existence of protest movements that already operated outside the state.

Broadly three forms of resistance emerged. Firstly, throughout the 1980s and 1990s, there was a steady growth of a diversity of Islamic movements, ranging from puritanical Salafist organizations, over jihadist cells, to the Muslim Brotherhood. In the 1990s the threat of Islamic fundamentalism was appropriated by the Egyptian state as a defensive raison d'être. Western governments and the enfeebled domestic secular opposition were invited to support the Mubarak regime as the lesser evil against a radical theocratic enemy. Attacks and assassinations by terrorist organizations such as the Islamic Group gave the government an excuse to repress the Brotherhood. From 1995 onwards, Brotherhood activists, student leaders and members of parliament were systematically arrested, intimidated, detained and tortured. However, despite its illegal status and its continuous harassment by the security forces, the Brotherhood was allowed not only to run its candidates in the sham elections, but also to become the biggest opposition in parliament, especially during the elections of 2000 and 2005 (Zemni and Bogaert 2009). Apart from constituting a form of resistance, Islamism functioned as the state's 'negative hegemony', reminding the population of the fundamentalist alternative to the Mubarak regime.

A second movement focused on universal civil and human rights and the issue of democratization. The rise of independent NGOs defending civil and human rights and hosting meetings of political movements and parties in the 1990s resulted in a hub of democratic opposition. From the year 2000 onwards this civil-democratic movement entered its second phase. Students organized massive demonstrations in Cairo in support of the Second Palestinian Intifada—collective actions 'from below' that ended two decades of political demobilization. These mobilizations became a platform for political discussion, coordination and cooperation between leftist, Nasserist and Islamist

activists (Abdelrahman 2009: 42–44). The war in Afghanistan and the loom-
ing intervention in Iraq gave a new impetus to the development of the existing solidarity networks. At the end of 2004 the first explicitly anti-Mubarak
demonstration was organized with the central slogan of free and democratic
presidential elections. In February 2005 *Kefaya* (Enough) was established
as a unitary movement of existing committees and campaigns. At first, the
state attempted to co-opt the movement, but as the protests grew in numbers
and militancy, it reverted to a violent repression of democratic activists.
Moreover, the state preempted one of the chief demands of the movement
by changing the constitution itself so the president could be elected directly.
This minor correction to the political system effectively took the wind out of
Kefaya's sails. Moreover, the civil-democratic movement failed to construct
a hegemony of its own and forge structural connections between its core of
students, intellectuals and urban middle-class groups, and other subaltern
agents: workers, farmers and the urban poor. Nevertheless, the experience
had laid the foundations of a network of democratic activists that would grow
over the years and initiate the first protests of the 25 January Revolution in
2011 (De Smet 2015).

A third movement consisted of social protests around class- and commu-
nity-based problems. In the countryside, by the mid-1990s, half of the rural
population lived in poverty, an increase of 10 per cent in comparison to 1990
(Mitchell 1999: 463). Neoliberal reform stimulated a rise in land rents and
the concentration of landed property. Landless and small landholding farmers
reacted with numerous land occupations and protests over the next decade,
which were violently repressed by landowners and security forces (Bush
2007). Similarly, the process of privatization and deterioration of workers'
livelihoods induced a surge of labour conflicts, but until the mid-2000s these
protests remained short lived and could not forge connections between different workplaces. The 2003 cabinet of Ahmed Nazif further intensified the
privatization and liberalization process, stimulating not only an increase in
labour protests, but also a development of workers' actions towards independent trade unionism, which constituted one of the pillars of the 25 January
Revolution (De Smet 2015; Zemni, De Smet and Bogaert 2013).

MOROCCO'S PREEMPTED REVOLUTION

This deep crisis of hegemony contrasted sharply with Morocco's efforts to
build a new one in the 1990s and 2000s. Confronted with budgetary and
financial constraints, growing social unrest and personal illness, King Hassan II set out on a path of gradual political reforms during the 1990s. This

process of 'democratization from above' intended to expand the base of the ruling bloc and reinvigorate the monarchy's hegemony by reasserting its position as the supreme arbiter over the nation's politics. First of all, Hassan II started a personal campaign around human rights. He liberated political prisoners, closed 'secret' detention centres, founded a state-sponsored Council on Human Rights in May 1990 and installed a Minister of Human Rights in 1993 (Brand 1998; Zemni and Bogaert 2006). These measures were inspired not only by the need to address internal unrest and political instability, but also by a drive for greater respectability in the international community—especially in Europe and the United States. By the end of the 1990s, Amnesty International and Human Rights Watch reported that Morocco dramatically improved its human rights record, while the World Bank lauded the country as being one of the 'success stories' of reform in the region (Zemni and Bogaert 2006).

The second and more crucial constituent of what became known as the *alternance* process was the inclusion of the historical opposition into the government after the parliamentary elections in 1997. On 4 February 1998, the leader of the USFP, Abderrahman Youssoufi, was appointed prime minister. The USFP formed a government together with the *Istiqlal* and other political parties. This political opening sparked the hope, not only among foreign observers, but also among many Moroccans themselves, that a genuine process of democratization was under way.

Mohammed VI, who ascended the throne in 1999, further expanded the political reform process. He immediately proved his willingness to reform by getting rid of the widely despised and hated minister of interior, Driss Basri, and acknowledging the government's responsibility during the 'years of lead' (Vermeren 2002). Mohammed VI launched several social development initiatives and repeatedly stressed the importance of good governance, human rights, economic development and citizen participation. This sudden change in style, compared with the more repressive image of his father Hassan II, even earned him the reputation of 'king of the poor'.

These careful policies of co-optation and negotiation constituted a crucial difference with the confrontational capitalist offensive in Egypt. The Moroccan monarchy established a radical break with the 'years of lead', creating a new hegemonic momentum centred on gradual democratic reform and just kingship, winning over domestic and international support. Although the optimism of a 'Moroccan exception' experienced a setback after the suicide bombings in Casablanca in May 2003, many observers still praised the country's economic openness to the rest of the world (Zemni 2006; Cavatorta 2007). They believed, for example, that the implementation of important social policies such as the National Initiative for Human

Development (INDH) and the Cities Without Slums Program testified that there was still evidence of a real transition towards more political liberalization (e.g. Navez-Bouchanine 2009).

Despite these reform efforts, protest in Morocco did not cease or even diminish. Quite similar to Egypt, three intertwined forms of resistance can be distinguished. First, the Islamists grew stronger, both the legalized Party for Justice and Development (PJD) and the unrecognized, but tolerated, movement *Al-Adl wal-Ihsan* (Justice and Charity). The Islamists demonstrated that, if necessary, they were capable of mobilizing a massive crowd. At demonstrations in solidarity with Palestine, against the invasion of Iraq or in opposition to the reform of the Family Code in 2004, Islamist movements, especially *Al-Adl wal-Ihsan*, mobilized close to a million people each time (Cavatorta 2007).

Second, as in Egypt, Morocco witnessed the growth of civil and human rights movements. The process of *alternance*, the increasing attention given in the West to issues of democratization and the role of civil society and the accession of Mohammed VI to the throne opened up political space for human rights movements, neighbourhood associations and women's movements to become active and offered many secular and leftist activists—who had experienced repression during the 'years of lead'—a way to be politically active outside party politics and militant trade unionism. A salient example was the Moroccan Association of Human Rights (AMDH). The AMDH has gathered older leftist militants that were active in radical student movements, trade unions and leftists parties in the 1970s and 1980s, and younger activists, many of whom were/are active in the 20 February Movement. Today, the organization has approximately 12,000 listed members and over 90 local sections spread over the country.

Finally, ever since the urban riots of the 1980s, the country has been confronted with economic protests and struggles around class issues. From the early 1990s onwards, unemployed graduates mobilized on a regular and structural basis, and since the establishment of the Moroccan National Association of Unemployed Graduates (ANDCM) in 1991, unemployed graduates have become a permanent and highly visible feature of the social protest landscape in Morocco. Many activists within ANDCM were and are closely connected to the left, and they consider their economic situation and unemployment as the economic dimension of authoritarianism and the result of a 'class policy' (Emperador 2013: 5). Other groups of unemployed graduates, more prominent in the bigger cities, have taken a more pragmatic stance and mobilized around the notion of a 'right to work'. They demand their 'right' to be employed in the public sector, reinvigorating the old developmentalist social contract granting university graduates access to the public sector (Bogaert and Emperador 2011).

Furthermore, there was a significant increase in local economic protests all over the country in the mid-2000s (Bogaert 2015). These protests were diverse and demonstrators expressed demands particular to their predicament, for example, access to public jobs, better infrastructure (roads, houses, etc.) and lack of support after natural disasters (earthquakes, floods), or they denounced the continuous price hikes of consumption goods like water and electricity. Yet, these struggles were not merely 'socioeconomic' but also about public services, the question of ownership over national resources and the redistribution of wealth; in other words, about fundamental political questions.

There was an attempt, from the mid-2000s onwards, to bring these scattered protests together in a more structured coordination: the 'movement against the high cost of living'. AMDH, one of the movement's protagonists, managed to set up more than 80 active local committees or *tansikiyat* spread around the country. Both AMDH and the local *tansikiyat* actively supported the 20 February movement in 2011, and together with the Islamists of *Al-Adl wal-Ihsan*, they guaranteed its success during the first months. The monarchy's 'benign' passive revolution entailed a calculated retreat from its explicitly dominating position in certain spheres of civil and political society since the 1980s. By creating and delimiting the terrain for oppositional politics, the monarchy was able to channel discontent along lines it could control. While these passive revolutionary policies were generally successful in absorbing the traditional opposition parties and trade unions into the monarchy's coalition, they also opened up space for organizations and movements that escaped the royal hegemony, such as *Al-Adl wal-Ihsan*, the AMDH and, eventually, the 20 February Movement. In the wake of the revolutions in Egypt and Tunisia, the 20 February movement succeeded in organizing regular mass demonstrations in more than 50 cities and towns throughout the country, especially during the first months of its existence.

However, in comparison with Egypt and Tunisia, the response of the general population to the anti-regime protests was rather gradual and cautious (Molina 2011). One of the reasons was that the monarchy, instead of repressing these mobilizations, appropriated popular initiative by announcing constitutional reform on 9 March, less than three weeks after the first nationwide protests. This was one of the main demands of the movement. A new constitution was implemented only a few months later through a national referendum. Nevertheless, despite the fact that the monarchy managed to drown the 20 February movement in its politics of consent and restore political stabilization in the short term, in the long run the movement might have planted the seed of a more profound counter-hegemonic project. In this regard, the 20 February Movement did not represent an actual parallel to Egypt's revolutionary mass uprising, but rather its '*Kefaya* moment'. And even though it equally failed to forge connections with the broader society (e.g. unemployed graduates, workers, farmers, the urban poor, etc.), the movement dared to question the political, economic and moral dimensions of the 'royal hegemony'.

REFORM AND REVOLUTION IN NEOLIBERAL TIMES

This chapter set out to investigate the histories behind the different outcomes of the Arab uprisings in Egypt and in Morocco. Whereas by 2011, relatively large protest movements were still nibbling at Morocco's royal hegemony, Egypt's state was falling into an organic crisis, in which almost all state institutions, except for the armed forces and the judiciary, had been discredited in the eyes of the masses. We suggested that an explanation for this dichotomy is to be found in the different pace, intensity and character of national articulations of a global neoliberal history. Studying the impact of neoliberal reform in relation to authoritarianism and the uprisings implies that we understand how 'the global' is always grounded and how authoritarianism—capitalist state power—is transformed in relation to global shifts, on the one hand, and particular interests, specific balances of power, struggle and resistance, on the other.

Our analysis shows that there was an important difference between the position of the Moroccan monarchy and the Egyptian presidency, the two core institutions of state power in these countries. In Egypt the post-1919 process of passive-revolutionary decolonization was largely unsuccessful, leading to a second rupture in 1952, which led to a more complex authoritarianism rooted in a broad social base.[3] Conversely, the Moroccan case represents a more gradual, negotiated process of decolonization: a successful passive revolution in which the colonial domestic elites—the sultan and the rural landlords—remained the dominant groups within the postcolonial state. While Nasser had to ground his hegemony in a myth of revolution and discontinuity with the 'feudal' past and 'imperialist' present, Mohammed V personified the continuity of the Moroccan nation—even in the face of postcolonialism. The Moroccan king was able to combine 'modern' anti-colonial legitimacy with his 'traditional' political and religious prestige and leadership of the king as the Commander of the Faithful.

Both states embarked on a project of developmentalism after their decolonization. In Egypt, during the heydays of the Nasserist regime, the state became the primary agent of capital accumulation through the development of a large industrial public sector. State-led industrialization and redistribution was, besides the development of an impressive security apparatus, a core element within the construction of a developmentalist and Arab social-ist hegemony. The economic crisis in the second half of the 1960s and the defeat in the Six Day War undermined the material and ideological base of Nasserism. In order to attract foreign capital, ruling elites led by President Sadat forcefully reconfigured the dominant class alliances and accumulation strategy along neoliberal lines. The implementation of IMF austerity mea-sures in 1977 provoked a general uprising, the first bread riots in the region. Throughout the 1980s, President Mubarak was able to slow down neoliberal reform and its concomitant confrontational politics, by leaning on the largely 'external' factor of geopolitical and economic rents. Yet, the fiscal crisis of the second half of the 1980s forced the state to go back on the offensive, de-ploying an aggressive strategy of accumulation by dispossession in the 1990s and 2000s. Combined with intensified oppression and exclusion of political opponents and subaltern groups, these policies further undermined the hege-mony of the ruling classes, leading to the buildup of the revolutionary process and the uprising in January and February 2011.

In Morocco, the hegemony of the ruling bloc was never constructed around a universalist socialist or developmentalist myth, but around the monarchy as a particular, Moroccan institution representing the nation and its religion. Furthermore, the Moroccan state never became the primary motor of capital accumulation—only its facilitator. *Moroccanization* did not entail a large-scale nationalization of foreign firms, as happened in Egypt after the Suez War in 1956 and with the Socialist Decrees of 1961, but a strategy to support the private sector and tie it to the regime. The state transferred surpluses and profits to the private sector and absorbed most of the investment risks. This was both out of necessity, due to a weak private sector, and to integrate dif-ferent groups of elites into royal patronage. Thus, the monarchy was able to regulate economic life and reap its benefits, while largely escaping from the need to take responsibility for its shortcomings. Conversely, an economic cri-sis did not *automatically* endanger the hegemonic position of the monarchy.

When confronted with severe social unrest and a succession of nationwide riots and protest in the 1980s, the monarchy fell back on harsh repression to restore order and political stability. Recognizing the long-term dangers of such confrontational politics for the royal *institution*, Hassan II embarked on a gradual reform process: *alternance*. This 'benign' passive revolution restored the monarchy's hegemony and cleared the path for Mohammed VI to succeed his father. Mohammed VI predominantly focused on economic reform and provided the monarchy, for the time being, with a sufficiently strong hegemonic position to prevent the 20 February Movement and other protests to turn into a revolutionary mass movement.

In the end, Egypt's 'revolution against neoliberalism' (Armbrust 2011) was successfully deferred in Morocco, not necessarily because neoliberalism's 'objective' social consequences were less harsh or protests were less numerous or strong, but because the monarchy managed to maintain hegemonic power, generating sufficient consent among the population to continue its rule. In Egypt, the power of the presidency was undermined by its failure to maintain the material (redistribution), political (broad class alliances) and ideological (moral and cultural leadership) dimensions of hegemony. This, in Trotsky's words, 'did not exclude the possibility of revolution, but, on the contrary, made revolution the only way out' (Trotsky 2007: 30).

NOTES

1. An earlier version of this paper with the title 'Kings, Pharaohs and Neoliberalism: Passive Revolution and Resistance in Egypt and Morocco' was presented at the conference Contentions Against Neoliberalism: Reconstituting the Social Fabric in the Developing World at the Oxford Department of International Development (ODID), 27–28 June 2013, Oxford University, UK.
2. See also Özden, Akça and Bekmen; Springer; and Lim in this volume.
3. See De Smet (2016) for an extensive discussion.

BIBLIOGRAPHY

Abdelrahman M (2009) With the Islamists?—Sometimes. With the state?—Never! Cooperation between the Left and Islamists in Egypt. *British Journal of Middle Eastern Studies* 36(1): 37–54.

Abdin AE and Gaafar I (2010) Rational water use in Egypt. In: El Moujabber M, Mandi L, Liuzzi GT, Martin I, Rabi A and Rodriguez R (eds) *Technological Perspectives for Rational Use of Water Resources in the Mediterranean Region*. Bari: CIHEAM, 11–27.

al-Bendary A (2008) Recalling 1968 (Interview with Hossam Issa). *Al-Ahram Weekly* (May #898). Available at: http://weekly.ahram.org.eg/2008/898/fe2.htm

Amin S (2011) *Global History: A View from the South*. Cape Town: Pambazuka Press.

Armbrust W (2011) The revolution against neoliberalism. *Jadaliyya* (23 February). Available at: http://www.jadaliyya.com/pages/index/717/the-revolution-against-neoliberalism

Ayubi N (1997) Etatisme versus privatization: The changing economic role of the state in nine Arab countries. In: Handoussa H (ed) *Economic Transition in the Middle East. Global Challenges and Adjustment Strategies*. Cairo: The American University in Cairo Press, 125–166.

Bayat A (1993) Populism, liberalization and popular participation: Industrial democracy in Egypt. *Economic and Industrial Democracy* 14(1): 65–87.

Bayat A (2002) Activism and social development in the Middle East. *International Journal of Middle East Studies* 34(1): 1–28.

Beinin J (2001) *Workers and Peasants in the Modern Middle East.* Cambridge: Cambridge University Press.

Ben Ali D (1997) Economic adjustment and political liberalization in Morocco. In: Handoussa H (ed) *Economic Transition in the Middle East. Global Challenges and Adjustment Strategies.* Cairo: The American University in Cairo Press, 183–217.

Bogaert K (2013) Contextualizing the Arab Revolts: The politics behind three decades of neoliberalism in the Arab World. *Middle East Critique* 22(3): 213–234.

Bogaert K (2015) The revolt of small towns: The meaning of Morocco's history and the geography of social protests. *Review of African Political Economy* 42(143): 124–140.

Bogaert K and Emperador M (2011) Imagining the state through social protest: State reformation and the mobilizations of unemployed graduates in Morocco. *Mediterranean Politics* 16(2): 241–259.

Brand L (1998) *Women, The State and Political Liberalization: Middle Eastern and North African Experiences.* New York: Columbia University Press.

Bruff I (2014) The rise of authoritarian neoliberalism. *Rethinking Marxism: A Journal of Economics, Culture & Society* 26(1): 113–129.

Bush R (2007) Politics, power and poverty: Twenty years of agricultural reform and market liberalisation in Egypt. *Third World Quarterly* 28(8): 1599–1615.

Callinicos A (2011) The return of the Arab revolution. *International Socialism* 130. Available at: http://isj.org.uk/the-return-of-the-arab-revolution/

Cammett MC (2007) *Globalization and Business Politics in Arab North Africa: A Comparative Perspective.* Cambridge: Cambridge University Press.

Catusse M (2008) *Le temps des entrepreneurs? Politique et transformations du capitalisme au Maroc.* Paris: Maisonneuve & Larose.

Cavatorta F (2007) Neither participation nor revolution: The strategy of the Moroccan Jamiat al-Adl wal-Ihsan. *Mediterranean Politics* 12(3): 381–397.

Cherkaoui M and Ben Ali D (2007) The political economy of growth in Morocco. *The Quarterly Review of Economics and Finance* 46(5): 741–761.

Clément JF and Paul J (1984) Trade unions and Moroccan politics. *MERIP Middle East Report* 127: 19–24.

Cohen S and Jaidi L (2006) *Morocco: Globalization and Its Consequences.* Abingdon: Routledge.

De Smet B (2015) *A Dialectical Pedagogy of Revolt: Gramsci, Vygotsky, and the Egyptian Revolution.* Leiden: Brill.

De Smet B (2016) *Gramsci on Tahrir: Revolution and Counter-Revolution in Egypt.* London: Pluto.

Emperador M (2013) Does unemployment spark collective contentious action? Evidence from a Moroccan social movement. *Journal of Contemporary African Studies* 31(2): 194–212.

Farah NR (1986) *Religious Strife in Egypt: Crisis and Ideological Conflict in the Seventies*. New York: Gordon and Breach.

Farah NR (2009) *Egypt's Political Economy: Power Relations in Development*. Cairo: The American University in Cairo Press.

Glasser BL (1995) External capital and political liberalizations: A typology of Middle Eastern development in the 1980s and 1990s. *Journal of International Affairs* 49(1): 45–73.

Gramsci A (1971) *Selections from the Prison Notebooks*, Hoare Q and Nowell-Smith G (eds and trans). London: Lawrence & Wishart.

Harvey D (2006) *Spaces of Global Capitalism: Towards a Theory of Uneven Geographical Development*. London: Verso.

Hinnebusch R (2014) Change and continuity after the Arab Uprising: The consequences of state formation in Arab North African states. *British Journal of Middle Eastern Studies* 42(1): 12–30.

Joffé G (1988) Morocco: Monarchy, legitimacy and succession. *Third World Quarterly* 10(1): 201–228.

Kaioua A (1996) *Casablanca, l'industrie et la ville*. Tours: Urbama.

Kienle E (2001) *A Grand Delusion: Democracy and Economic Reform in Egypt*. London: I.B. Tauris.

Leveau R (1997) Morocco at the crossroads. *Mediterranean Politics* 2(2): 95–113.

Maghraoui A (2002) Depoliticization in Morocco. *Journal of Democracy* 13(4): 24–32.

McMichael P (1990) Incorporating comparison within a world-historical perspective: An alternative comparative method. *American Sociological Review* 55(3): 385–397.

Mitchell T (1999) No factories, no problems: the logic of neo-liberalism in Egypt. *Review of African Political Economy* 26(82): 455–468.

Mitchell T (2002) *Rule of Experts: Egypt, Techno-Politics, Modernity*. Berkeley, CA: University of California Press.

Mitchell T (2006) The properties of markets: Informal housing and capitalism's mystery. Cultural Political Economy Working Paper Series #2. University of Lancaster Institute for Advanced Studies in Social and Management Sciences.

Molina IF (2012) The monarchy vs. the 20 February movement: Who holds the reins of political change in Morocco? *Mediterranean Politics* 16(3): 445–441.

Morton AD (2010) The continuum of passive revolution. *Capital & Class* 34(3): 315–342.

Naguib S (2011) Egypt's unfinished revolution: Egypt since the fall of Mubarak. *International Socialist Review* 79 (September–October). Available at: http://isreview .org/issues/79/feature-egyptianrevolution.shtml

Navez-Bouchanine F (2009) Evolution of urban policy and slum clearance in Morocco: Successes and transformations of 'social contracting'. *International Social Science Journal* 59(193/194): 359–380.

Pennell CR (2000) *Morocco since 1830: A History*. New York: New York University Press.

Pennell CR (2003) *Morocco: From Empire to Independence*. Oxford: One World.

Posusney MP (1996) Collective action and workers' consciousness in contemporary Egypt. In: Lockman Z (ed) *Workers and Working Classes in the Middle East: Struggles, Histories, Historiographies*. Albany, NY: New York State University Press, 211–246.

Richards A and Waterbury J (2008) *A Political Economy of the Middle East*. Boulder, CO: Westview Press.

Roccu R (2013) *The Political Economy of the Egyptian Revolution: Mubarak, Economic Reforms and Failed Hegemony*. Basingstoke: Palgrave Macmillan.

Springborg R (2011) The political economy of the Arab Spring. *Mediterranean Politics* 16(3): 427–433.

Swearingen WD (1987) Morocco's agricultural crisis. In: Zartman W (ed) *The Political Economy of Morocco*. New York: Praeger, 159–172.

Thomas P (2009) *The Gramscian Moment: Philosophy, Hegemony and Marxism*. Leiden: Brill.

Tilly C (1984) *Big Structures, Large Processes, Huge Comparisons*. New York: Russell Sage.

Trotsky L (2007) *The Permanent Revolution & Results and Prospects*. London: Socialist Resistance.

Tucker J (1978) While Sadat shuffles: Economic decay, political ferment in Egypt. *MERIP Reports* 65 (March): 3–9+26.

Vermeren P (2002) *Histoire du Maroc depuis l'indépendance*. Paris: La Découverte.

Walton J and Seddon D (1994) *Free Markets and Food Riots*. Oxford: Blackwell.

Waterbury J (1970) *The Commander of the Faithful: The Moroccan Political Elite— A Study in Segmented Politics*. New York: Columbia University Press.

Zemni S (2006) Islam between jihadi threats and Islamist insecurities? Evidence from Belgium and Morocco. *Mediterranean Politics* 11(2): 231–253.

Zemni S and Bogaert K (2006) Morocco and the mirages of democracy and good governance. UNISCI Discussion Papers #12: 103–120.

Zemni S and Bogaert K (2009) Egyptian Muslim Brotherhood and competitive politics. In: Salih M (ed) *Interpreting Islamic Political Parties*. New York: Palgrave Macmillan, 149–166.

Zemni S, De Smet B and Bogaert K (2013) Luxemburg on Tahrir Square: Reading the Arab Revolutions with Rosa Luxemburg's *The Mass Strike*. *Antipode: A Radical Journal of Geography* 45(4): 888–907.

Chapter 12

Klepto-Neoliberalism

Authoritarianism and Patronage in Cambodia

Simon Springer

In response to the financial crisis of the 1970s the Wall Street–Treasury nexus, in concert with the World Bank and the International Monetary Fund, sought to reconstruct the global power (im)balance by attempting to eliminate any inklings of collectivism in the global South through the imposition of brutal forms of economic discipline. For some this represents the heart of neoliberalism, which has been considered as a class reaction (Harvey 2005). Yet to focus our attention exclusively on the external forces at play in the constitution of neoliberal ideas risks contributing to an overgeneralized account of a universal and singular political economic idea, which insufficiently accounts for the abundance of local variations that currently comprise the neoliberal project as a series of articulations with existing institutional contexts and cultural forms. The nascent language of 'neoliberalization' (England and Ward 2007) responds to this ubiquitous view by instead encouraging a geographical understanding that recognizes neoliberalism's hybridized forms as it shape-shifts along its travels around our world. This more nuanced interpretation was first advanced by Peck and Tickell (2002), who insisted that neoliberalism is not merely an end-state, but rather a varied series of processual, protean and promiscuous phenomena that occur both 'out there' and 'in here', with diverging and irregular effects, yet still recalling an overarching 'logic' owing to its spatial diffusion. With such an appreciation of neoliberalization in mind we can better understand the consequences of inherited historical contexts, institutional frameworks, geographical landscapes, policy regimes, regulatory practices and ongoing political struggles as repeatedly reconstituting neoliberalism through unfolding processes of articulation (Peck 2001; Smith 2007).

Cambodia offers a useful example of neoliberalization insofar as this transitional process to a free market economy was actually a predetermined outcome of the United Nations peace agreement of the early 1990s (UN 1991).

The country's transition was predated by three decades of war during the latter part of the twentieth century and a genocide that resulted in the deaths of 1.5 million people at the hands of the Khmer Rouge regime (Kiernan 1996). Less well known is that another nightmare of comparable magnitude preceded the Pol Pot holocaust. In an effort to ostensibly flush out Viet Cong forces thought to be operating within Cambodian territory, between October 1965 and August 1973, the United States carpet-bombed Cambodia despite the country's proclaimed neutrality (Owen and Kiernan 2006). The protracted bombing campaign killed approximately 600,000 Cambodians (Kiljunen 1984), and in the hindsight of history, it served as the most effective recruiting tool of the Khmer Rouge, who promising to end the bombing and liberate the country from American imperialism seized power on 17 April 1975. When Pol Pot's troops finally fell to Vietnamese forces on 7 January 1979, 10 long years of silence followed at the international level (Chandler 2008). Throughout the 1980s Cambodia was effectively under the suzerain control of Hanoi, which ran the country as a client state. As Cold War geopolitics were central to the foreign policy objectives of global North governments at the time, Cambodia and its genocide were ignored. It was not until the Iron Curtain fell in 1989 and the global political climate shifted that the Cambodian question could finally be answered, as the Khmer Rouge continued to terrorize the population from their stronghold along the Thai border. The United Nations Transitional Authority (UNTAC) was tasked with presiding over a 'triple transition' from a brutal state of war to a tenuous peace, from overt authoritarianism to an unconsolidated 'democracy' and from a command economy to a particular version of free market neoliberal economics.

Elsewhere across the global South, neoliberal economics were initially promoted as a series of nostrums that, once implemented by unleashing market forces, would supposedly improve the lives of people from all walks of life. In spite of the obvious character of imposition in Cambodia's neoliberalization, this particular context also clearly reveals that powerful elites were all too happy to accommodate the entrance of markets. Neoliberalism frequently initiates opportunities for well-connected government officials to informally manipulate material and market rewards, thus enabling them to easily enrich themselves in the process. It is precisely with respect to this sense of the local appropriation of neoliberal ideas that we must move beyond conceptualizing a 'neoliberalism-in-general'. Neoliberalism never represents a singular or fully realized policy regime, regulatory framework or ideological form, and so we must necessarily work towards conceiving a multiplicity of 'actually existing neoliberalisms' with particular characteristics ascending from shifting geohistorical consequences that are entrenched within regional, national and local process of market-driven socio-spatial change (Brenner and Theodore 2002). What constitutes 'neoliberalism with Cambodian characteristics' as distinctly Cambodian are the ways in which patronage has enabled local elites to transform, co-opt and (re)articulate neoliberal reforms through a framework that has focused on 'asset stripping' public resources (Springer 2010). As a system of hierarchical relations that are woven through the political economy of Cambodia starting with the Prime Minister and extending down through every level of government to the village, the patronage system offers rewards for those who capitulate and punishments for those who refuse its logic. The result has been to increase Cambodians' exposure to corruption and violence, as neoliberalism works in concert with authoritarian means. While some scholars have insisted on focusing exclusively on an extraneously convened neoliberalism as a means of critique (Thavat 2010), they risk ignoring the local geographies of existing institutional frameworks and political economic circumstances, where internal constitution, individual agency, variability and societal influences all play a role in facilitating, circulating and (re)producing neoliberalism. Indeed, neoliberalization in Cambodia has been characterized by considerable contestation, inconsistency and concession. It is to such a notion of relationality and struggle that this chapter is attuned, where, in addition to offering empirical context to some of my more theoretical work on the violence of neoliberalism (Springer 2012, 2016), the local circumstances of individual neoliberalizations are understood as connected with global processes of neoliberalism.

I begin this chapter by considering the Royal Government of Cambodia's (RGC) discursive positioning of populism vis-à-vis international 'enemies' inasmuch as it presents a convenient pretext for the tensions of neoliberal development. This discussion critiques the frequent suggestion that the RGC maintains a 'communist' outlook rather than recognizing the kleptocratic 'shadow state' practices that have been modified to accommodate a neoliberal modality. I then turn my attention more specifically to the mechanisms of Cambodia's patronage system via an analysis of privatization and primitive accumulation. I assess these developments through a critique of the purview that legal reform will somehow serve as cure-all for development, contrasting this idea with the realities of a judiciary firmly entrenched within patron relations. The degree of political patronage in Cambodia reflects a certain nepotism, or what I am calling '*nepoliberalism*' to reflect a particular application of neoliberalism that is never without the influence of patron politics. The enduring impunity of those with connections to power is the concentration of the final section before the conclusion, where I assess the continuing constraints of the poor with regard to patronage and the inequality and precarity it affords. It is here, in the question of (in)security, that Cambodia's neoliberalization alongside patronage demonstrates the depth of kleptocracy and violence in the country.

THE ENEMY INSIDE: NEOLIBERAL
DISCOURSES IN THE SHADOW OF THE STATE

In positioning itself as a populist government, the RGC frequently uses the tightly controlled Khmer language media (LICADHO 2008) as a vehicle for criticisms of the international financial institutions (IFIs) and bilateral donors, which it often depicts as 'enemies' to Cambodian interests.[1] This discourse recalls the same general premise that existed in Cambodian politics under the Khmer Rouge, when paranoia for 'enemies of the revolution' was widespread and became one of the key ideas in the resultant genocide (Kiernan 1996). When employed against local opponents, the notion of 'enemy' (*khmaang*) has offered a rationale for much of the overt political violence that has marred elections and democratic process. In contrast, when this idea is used against the international community, the language of 'enemy' (*setrov*) is less accusatory, only ever voiced in Khmer, and does not suggest that this opponent will be stamped out.[2] Those reservations about the donor community that are conveyed in the local media are largely representative of the bravado of Prime Minister Hun Sen, where his intended audience is homegrown. This approach helps his government maintain a certain degree of popularity with its electorate, but also mobilizes a useful scapegoat when the strains of neo-liberalization become particularly acute.

The rural population represents the primary power base of the ruling Cambodian People's Party (CPP), even though this is also the location that benefits least from neoliberalizing processes as uneven development proceeds. This geography is explained by the fact that those limited state provisions and benefits of development that do 'trickle down' to rural areas are not considered by many Cambodians to have been sourced from the state. Instead, such development is often confused as originating from the ruling party, and particularly as having come from Hun Sen. This conflation of the CPP and the state is not incidental as major infrastructure projects almost always bear the monogram of Hun Sen and a CPP party sign, even when the money originates from state coffers (Hughes 2003). The enmeshment of the CPP within the RGC has been so thorough that many Cambodians have difficulty identifying a difference between the two. This strategy of confusion works well with respect to the RGC's symbolic hand-washing from the negative effects of neoliberalization. The idea of neoliberal reform being an imposition spearheaded by foreign geopolitical interests and foreign corporate greed that works in concert with the mediations of Cambodian elites is avoided, as Hun Sen and the CPP instead present themselves as benevolent benefactors and the champions of Cambodia's development, even as they are able to misappropriate state revenues through the 'shadow state' (Reno 1995). Such an arrangement is obviously advantageous for Cambodian elites because it obscures the way in which neo-liberalism's ideological formation evolves through a variety of spatial settings, including its articulation with local political economic circumstances, in this case the patronage system. In my other work I have attempted to show how Cambodian donors, and indeed many scholars of Cambodia, use a reflection of the discourse mounted by Cambodian elites when they suggest that the tensions of neoliberalization are outcomes of explicitly 'local' political economic conditions, and in particular a 'culture of violence' (Springer 2015). Within this discourse there is little consideration afforded to 'global' political economic circumstances, giving us an incomplete picture that is reductionist with respect to the political economic complexity that comprises neoliberalization in 'actually existing' circumstances of articulation.

Adding to the discursive misperceptions, Cambodians often describe Cambodia's state form as communist, a claim repeated by some scholars who point to the country's historical legacy and swollen bureaucracy. For example, Craig Etcheson (2005: 143) has argued that although the CPP 'publicly abandoned socialism along with command-and-control economic policies [in 1989] … [it] did not … abandon its internal Leninist structures and procedures, which it retains to this day'. Yet Cambodia's bloated bureaucracy and internal party structures are not enough to suggest that they are 'Leninist', a problematic characterization that is assumed rather than actually explained by Etcheson. Instead, they are distinctly Cambodian and they should be considered as one of the key characteristics of neoliberalism in the country, contrasting with notions of 'small government' that are typically connected with neoliberalism in other contexts. These structures speak to Cambodia's patronage system, which offers the underpinning to the government's 'legitimacy'. While neoliberal ideology would have us believe that such patronage will be eroded as the mechanism of the market comes to dominate social relations, the Cambodian experience instead actually shows how patronage becomes strengthened and entrenched (Slocomb 2010). The adoption of a neoliberal configuration by high-ranking government officials in Cambodia is largely owing to its latent potential to provide them not only with enrichment, but also with the ability to influence the monetary channels of investment and privatization in ways that only those embedded within their systems of patronage can receive any direct benefit. This condition is essentially a question of how power is oriented in Cambodia, which rather than being an open and transparent system of exchange, neoliberalization in the country is caught up in the murkiness of shadow state politics, where kickbacks are a mandatory component of its substantive 'rollout'.

The case of the homegrown company Sokimex is demonstrative of the shadow state in Cambodia. Founded in 1990 to coincide with the country's transition towards a free market economy by a close associate of Hun Sen and local tycoon, Sok Kong, Sokimex is Cambodia's largest business conglomerate, repeatedly receiving preferential treatment in obtaining lucrative government contacts under a veil of secrecy and non-disclosure on its accounts (Cain 2009). The company is notable in terms of its diversity, maintaining a broad portfolio that includes business ventures in petroleum importing, import-export services, construction, garment manufacturing, a service station chain, hotels, property development, transportation industries, a domestic airline, an exclusive contract to supply the Cambodian military with fuel and clothing, rubber plantations and the concession to manage ticket sales to Angkor Wat (Cain 2009). Sam Rainsy, official leader of the opposition, has publicly chastised the relationship between Sokimex and the ruling party, calling it the 'financial pillar for the ruling CPP', where 'you cannot make the distinction between Sokimex, the CPP, and the State. The CPP apparatchik is inextricably intertwined with the State. Sokimex was doing business not only for, but in the name of the State' (quoted in *Phnom Penh Post* 2000). Such questions are not new; for example, in early 2000 four MPs aligned to Sam Rainsy sent a letter to Hun Sen requesting clarification about the government's relationship with Sokimex. In their response, the RGC indicated that the only reason it appears to favour Sokimex is the company's proven track record, praising them as being highly competent and always fulfilling contractual obligations. Yet this sanguine assessment is questionable given Sokimex's history of shoddy construction projects (*Phnom Penh Post* 2000). While the transfer of ownership from the public to the private sector maintains the ostensible goal of making public holdings more efficient, capable and profit generating, the Cambodian characteristics of neoliberalization modify this idea through the country's patronage system. Instead, efficiency and competency are of little concern, and the primary motivation becomes profit for well-connected power brokers (Barton and Sokha 2007b; Un and So 2009).

The overarching contextualization of policy response in Cambodia is framed by ongoing poverty in a country having only recently emerged from decades of war and genocide. This violent geohistorical context is effectively the initial 'shock' (Klein 2007) that enabled neoliberalization to emerge as the supposed panacea for Cambodia's problems, while the Paris Peace Accords and UNTAC established the general legal framework in an attempt to ensure an 'idealized' state form through which later neoliberal reforms could be realized (UN 1991).[3] The institutions and agencies engaged in the evaluations of policy are multiple in Cambodia, including ministries, local and international NGOs, as well as multilateral and bilateral donors. While the relevant Cambodian ministries are usually responsible for oversight, the direction of programme and policy orientation primarily flows from the wishes of the international donor community, only to be revaluated and reinterpreted by Cambodian elites as they invent ways to guarantee their privileged positions remain unobstructed. As neoliberalization is increasingly viewed as an opportunity to secure both political and monetary power, the motivating logic of any given reform policy must follow the general principle that it offers something of 'value' to established elites.

NEPOLIBERALISM: PRIVATIZATION, RULE OF LAW AND ACCUMULATION BY PATRONAGE

The ability of the Cambodian elite to cement their positions of privilege is demonstrated by the leasing of the rights to collect admission on national monuments such as Angkor Wat and Choeung Ek to private ventures (Kea 2006) and the abundant land swap deals involving central Phnom Penh and Siem Reap locations where institutional facilities, such as ministries and police headquarters, are exchanged for cash and privately held lands on the periphery of these cities (Wasson and Yun 2006). While the NGO community has criticized transfers of public holdings to private investors as examples of unpopular policies where corruption of the neoliberalization process has occurred (Lesley and Sam 2005; Ghai 2007), such practices continue unabated. Unsurprisingly, as these processes unfold, the bulk of financial remuneration mysteriously disappears from state ledgers and the value of public assets are purposefully underestimated, which is effectively theft from the commons. Land speculation in particular has been haunted by the spectre of primitive accumulation under Cambodia's neoliberalization, where over the past 20 years private investors have either purchased or leased an astonishing 45 per cent of the country's total land area (Global Witness 2009). Opposition leader Sam Rainsy is broadly in support of a pro-market orientation, yet he has also stated publicly that should he be elected as Prime Minister he will nationalize the millions of hectares of land that has been illegally acquired by businesspeople through land swaps and land grabs (Sokchea 2008). In contrast, Cambodia's donors have long advocated that a cadastral property system be put in place, which means a bounding and ordering of all of the country's available space into the structures of private ownership backed by legal rights and obligations. Rather than calls for redistribution of the land that has been acquired through questionable means, the emphasis in Cambodia is on further legal reform. The RGC has facilitated this focus inasmuch as it provides an enormous opportunity for enrichment through the networks of patronage, as this system's circuits have infiltrated the judiciary, guaranteeing that legal processes are always understood in ways that advantage well-connected power brokers (Ghai 2007; LICADHO 2007a).

Conditions of patronage in Cambodia produce considerable violence, as those without its securities are often forcibly removed from their lands where and when speculation establishes a monetary value. Speculation alone triggered a major eviction in Mittapheap District, Sihanoukville, when 105 families were violently removed from their village on 20 April 2007. The land they had lived on uncontested for the previous two decades—thus granting them legal ownership rights under Cambodian law—was now an area demarcated as a 'development zone' (LICADHO 2007b). Tourism in the area had increased substantially around that time, and prior to the global financial crisis that began in 2008, offshore oil exploration had threatened to turn Sihanoukville into a boomtown economy, heightening speculative activities even further (McDermid and Sokha 2007). I interviewed evictees from this village in June 2007, and people complained of the complicity that local CPP officials had in their precarious situation, pointing to the patronage system as the root of the problem since the local village and commune chiefs were aligned to the CPP and blamed the villagers for their own evictions. They noted how there was support from local officials around election time when they needed something from the villagers, but outside of the campaign period officials were otherwise absent, unavailable and disinterested. Villagers also noted how they felt the village and commune chiefs were profiting from their eviction. Given the significant media attention that has been placed on land grabbing, one would be inclined to think that investor ethics would slow the pace of violent evictions. Yet the reality is that evictions are taking place under the pretexts of 'beautification' and 'development' (Brickell and Springer 2016; Springer 2015), where local tycoons initially acquire the land in question and only subsequently offer it for lease or sale to private foreign companies (Amnesty International 2008). Nevertheless, the drive for profits outstrips concerns for human well-being as at least 10,000 families have been evicted from Phnom Penh over the last decade to make way for various development projects. As for the residents, they usually never receive any money in compensation for the loss of their homes and are only occasionally offered resettlement (*Phnom Penh Post* 2008).

Companies frequently exploit the services of the military and police as private armies to carry out evictions. In response the donor community has made repeated calls for respect of legal norms, and a deepening of the rule of law so that less 'dubious' investors (meaning foreign) will want to become involved in the country. Unfortunately, the problem with this emphasis is that the protections offered by law primarily revolve around securing the stability of a property system, where human security is relegated to a secondary concern. Elsewhere I have argued that the property system in Cambodia can be understood as a mechanism that affords legitimacy to processes of violent accumulation (Springer 2013). In effect, respect for the rule of law in accordance with donor standards would only function to entrench the violence of Cambodia's evictions by obscuring its underlying character of primitive accumulation through rendering this process legitimate. The fundamental difference with the current situation is that adherence to the rule of law, and the dissolution of the patronage system that neoliberals theorize such respect would engender, levels the playing field between Cambodian elites and their foreign counterparts with respect to access to the means of accumulation by dispossession. This is the crux of neoliberalization's desired objective from the standpoint of donors, while neoliberal reform is something Cambodian elites will accept only when it is clear that they alone stand to gain.

When the condition of financial reward is not met or somehow jeopardized, there is usually a prolonged stalling process on legislation in Cambodia. The adoption of Cambodian children by foreigners offers a case in point, where obstruction tactics by the RGC are very clear. In 2001, while investigating adoptions, Cambodian officials at the highest levels of government were accused by US immigration officials of complicity in scams that involved hundreds of babies and millions of US dollars (Cochrane and Sam 2005). The result was that a number of counties placed moratoriums on adoptions from Cambodia, while members of Cambodia's international donor community such as the United States, Canada and France had been pressuring the RGC to adopt legislation that will regulate adoptions in light of fears over human trafficking. Aside from concerns over children being bought and sold, another major goal of an adoption law on the part of the donor community was to build confidence in Cambodia's legal system and the rule of law, conditions that would work to enhance investment (Development Partner's Consensus Statement on Governance 2008). For years the RGC stalled on this issue based on the requirement by donors that a 'fixed price' on adoption processing be established. Depending on the connections of the individual facilitating the adoption, processing fees range from being essentially free up to tens of thousands of US dollars. International agencies are charged higher rates than local facilitators, while prospective parents negotiating the process themselves are not required to pay, but must instead navigate much longer wait times and fend off repeated requests for bribes from officials to see that their paperwork makes its way through the Cambodian ministries.[4] With respect to neoliberalization in Cambodia, the broader implication is that policies that attempt to circumvent the patronage system's ability to accumulate capital are obstructed, while those that facilitate the accumulation of capital within the patronage system are pushed through.

Cambodia is a country that remains heavily dependent on aid, where international donors have provided over half of the government's annual budget for more than a decade now (Global Witness 2009). Accordingly, the intended audience for Cambodia's privatization, liberalization and deregulation policies is primarily the donor community that is requesting them. Yet there are nuances to this as it is not as simple as donor demands being fully implemented wherever and whenever they are requested. The donor community often criticizes the lack of transparency in the mechanisms through which policies are being implemented. In particular, bidding processes on government contracts and the sale of public holdings are routinely critiqued as being corrupt. Consequently, policy reform proceeds in a veiled way, whereby the substantive acts of neoliberalization that are occurring at centre stage are witnessed and applauded, while the role of patronage is still partially obscured and out of view. What this means is that 'neoliberalism with Cambodian characteristics' is an extremely secretive affair, and the linkages within the patronage system that inform neoliberalization in Cambodia can only be speculated upon. Yet because the same small group of individuals always seems to receive the reward of a contract or newly privatized asset, the top of the patronage system is actually quite apparent and well documented (ADHOC 2008; Global Witness 2009). What occurs below the top rungs of patron power is unclear and not well mapped out, although evidence has begun to emerge that suggests that they operate along familial lines (Global Witness 2007; *Phnom Penh Post* 2007). What this suggests is that neoliberalism in Cambodia proceeds as a form of nepotism, or what we might call '*nepoliberalism*'.

What can be determined from Cambodia's patronage system is that as a hierarchical, secretive and long-standing mode of power relations in the country, it provokes significant violence (Slocomb 2010), which carries over into the contemporary political economy of neoliberalization. This violence is operationalized through particular channels as it keeps important mediators of social relations (i.e. judges, high-ranking military and police officials, top monks, commune chiefs, and journalists and media outlets) on an unofficial 'payroll'. In the past this payroll was not simply orchestrated by the ruling CPP as a whole, but rather through two rival patronage systems within the party, where the two key players were Hun Sen and former Party Chairman, President of the Senate and Acting Head of State, Chea Sim (Global Witness 2009). These adversarial factions were never on equal footing, as Chea Sim was much less involved in corruption than the Prime Minister, and accordingly he had fewer supporters and a much smaller roll call than Hun Sen, who has control over both the military and the police. Conflicts between these two opponents have been numerous over the years, culminating in July 2004, with Chea Sim fleeing Cambodia after apparently refusing to sign controversial legislation to allow a new government to be formed following the 2003 national elections (Rand and MacIssac 2004). He returned ten days later, citing that he required medical treatment in Thailand, but no explanation was ever offered as to why military forces surrounded his home on the day of his departure, suggesting Chea Sim and Hun Sen had come to an agreement concerning their differences and the conditions of his return to Cambodia (Yun 2004). More recently, following the death of Chea Sim in 2015, Hun Sen's consolidation of power within the CPP has been profound, as he now also serves as Party Chairman, giving him even greater control over the two existing patronage networks, which are now surely being combined.

TRADING (IN)SECURITIES: INVESTMENTS OVER HUMANS, PROFITS OVER PEOPLE

Cambodia's patronage system puts considerable pressure on individuals to conform, which as the case of Heng Pov revealed, often entails being an accomplice or agent in the killing of political adversaries, or at least a participant in an ongoing conspiracy of silence. Heng Pov is the former Undersecretary of State and assistant to the Minister of the Interior, as well as former police commissioner of Phnom Penh and a personal adviser to Hun Sen. He had amassed considerable wealth through his long-standing connection to the Prime Minister's patronage circuits. What has not been proven is Heng Pov's role in any violence. After a falling-out with the Prime Minister, a warrant for Heng Pov's arrest was issued by Cambodian authorities on 21 July 2006, accusing him of involvement in the 2003 assassination of Municipal Court judge Sok Sethamony and linking him to a number of other serious crimes (Barton 2006). Heng Pov fled Cambodia on 23 July 2006 and raids on his home apparently uncovered weapons and $1 million in cash. Heng Pov responded by accusing government officials of involvement in the 30 March 1997 grenade attack on a peaceful protest outside the National Assembly. He also claimed that a government official ordered the 7 July 1999 murder of actress Piseth Pilika, and the 7 July 1997 assassination of then Secretary of State in the Ministry of the Interior, Hor Sok, both of whom were vocal critics of corruption within the ruling party (Gillison and Ana 2006). Which side is to be believed in this dispute on who murdered who is anyone's best guess, but what is clear is that the patronage system engenders violence and by providing the necessary framework of concealment to ensure that it proceeds with impunity. The violence of such political rivalry in Cambodia has to some extent transitioned alongside neoliberalization. This particular form of violence now focuses its malignant powers on those who oppose the logic of neoliberalization in the country, where it is journalists like Youk Tharidh, union leaders like Chea Vichea, outspoken monks like Bun Thoeun, and deforestation activists like Chut Wutty who are now targeted, whereas in the past it was primarily opposition politicians who faced threats and intimidation. Since neoliberalism now forms the backbone of political economic power in Cambodia, this shift in who is being targeted is owing to the kinds of challenges that are being raised, which directly address the questionable accumulation practices of the country's elites.

Within Cambodia's NGO community there is a growing awareness of the rising tide of inequality in the country, which is viewed as an outcome of Cambodia's transitional political economy. Piled on top of increasing socio-economic disparity is the country's historical legacy of genocide and war, where people continue to operate with a survival mentality (Hayman 2007). Human security in Cambodia is fragile as people are often more concerned with what they are going to have for dinner than they are with the patterns of wealth disparity, except when it directly threatens their livelihoods through the threat of violent evictions. What Cambodia's historical context in concert with ongoing poverty and inequality means in terms of neoliberal governmentality is that most individuals in Cambodia are already adept at fending for themselves. They have never known state provisions of social welfare, and continually look to the patronage system as their only available security net. On the other hand, their subjectivation to neoliberalism in terms of its ability to foster an entrepreneurial spirit is mixed (Springer 2015). Individuals know how to make ends meet and often engage in the informal sector, but this does not always convert into sophisticated economic knowledge, and Cambodians are increasingly struggling with the scourge of microfinancing and high debt loads that they can never escape from. This dire situation is exacerbating homelessness as property is routinely leveraged against the predatory loans that Cambodians take on. Neoliberal governmentality in Cambodia thus ensures that individuals are caught between a Scylla and Charybdis of violence. The poor must either look to the domination of the patronage system to ensure their livelihoods, or seek semi-official economic channels as an alternative, wherein they become easy prey to usury through private moneylenders or microfinance institutions. Cambodia's donor community and the IFIs are quick to make excuses for this particular form of accumulation by dispossession, pointing to the implementation of rule of law as the solution inasmuch as it can provide enforcement on the repayment of loans so that the formal banking sector is more willing to offer loans to everyday Cambodians. In other words, in order to repeal the violence of ongoing primitive accumulation in the form of predatory lending practices, Cambodia must replace it with a new form of violence, a 'force' that will provide security on investments called 'law'. In effect, this is a call for a different form of concealed violence. Should one fail to make payments on a loan due to economic hardship or otherwise, the law will step in to dispossess the individual of whatever limited means he or she has left, or simply incarcerate them. Neoliberalization in this sense becomes a form of criminalizing the poor (Wacquant 2001), by 'legitimizing' the means of accumulation by dispossession through a legal framework.

'Neoliberalism with Cambodian characteristics' is a ticking time bomb; one that may result in a repeat of the violent revolution of the 1970s should the discontent that boils just beneath the surface continue unaddressed. The ongoing epidemic of violent dispossessions may very well trigger an explosion (Sokha 2007; Lempert 2006), something Hun Sen well recognizes, as he has repeatedly addressed the Cambodian media with paranoid invocations of his firm grip on political and military power (Soenthrith and Yun 2004; *Koh Santepheap* 2008). Even more revealing was his proclamation in March 2007, when he publicly declared 'war on land-grabbing' to symbolically illustrate his concern, not for the people of Cambodia, but for his own position of power (Yun 2007). For now, what can be witnessed are the growing number of cracks in the structure of Cambodian neoliberalism as murders, rapes and assaults have become a common lived experience for the poor as marginalization and minor differences are magnified, resulting in a pattern of societal conflict (Uvin 2003).[5] In contrast, elites have worked hard to insulate themselves from potential reprisal through a ratcheting down of Cambodia's security regime, utilizing the apparatus of the state, such as authoritarian clampdowns on public space, as well as private measures visible in the landscape, such as fenced properties monitored by armed guards (Springer 2009, 2010). Similarly, there is growing evidence to suggest that domestic violence is also on the rise (Brickell 2015). Although the government eventually responded to this phenomenon by acknowledging it as a social problem, the push to see a law on domestic violence passed through the National Assembly represents yet another exercise in bureaucratic foot-dragging, not only because Cambodian elites had little to gain by passing the law but also that such a law would counteract the male-dominated, masculine interests of the elite.

In stark contrast to the slow pace of progress on the domestic violence law, the establishment of a pseudo-legal framework for oil and gas exploration was rapid (Un and So 2009). In the 1990s oil exploration was only speculatively on the country's radar, yet petroleum legislation was quickly passed in 1991 (Council of Ministries 1991), coinciding with the structural changes that would ensue as Cambodia transitioned to a free market economy under the Paris Peace Accords signed that same year. Throughout the 1990s discreet amendments were made to the existing petroleum legislation, clearing the way for the questionable founding of the Cambodian National Petroleum Authority (CNPA) in 1999, without primary legislation passed by the National Assembly. This placed direct control of the institution into the hands of Hun Sen and his deputy, Sok An, making the institution highly politicized from the outset as exercise of this power sidelined those who were supportive of Chea Sim prior to his death (Carmichael 2003). The CNPA's establishment by royal decree means that, to this day, it operates without oversight from the Cambodian parliament or other relevant ministries. By 2006, the Council for the Development of Cambodia, the body in charge of foreign investment, had approved $403 million worth of investment initiatives to facilitate the exploitation of mineral resources. Global Witness (2009) has charged that concession allocations have occurred under a blanket of secrecy, where financial bonuses, totalling millions of dollars, paid to secure concessions do not show up in the 2006 or 2007 revenue reports from the Ministry of Economy and Finance. Once again and unsurprisingly, Sokimex is the company that stands to profit the most from these developments, having entered the petroleum business in May 1996 through its purchase of state-owned oil company Compagnie Kampuchea des Carburants as part of the RGC's market-oriented privatization programme. As part of the deal, Soximex was tasked with the storage, distribution and import of petroleum in Cambodia, giving the company a stranglehold on the industry with a market share of approximately 40 per cent. The deal obviously led to further speculation of Sok Kong's close ties to Hun Sen and the CPP (Cain 2009), and led many observers to anticipate a 'resource curse' scenario (Barton and Sokha 2007a). These patterns of patronage and corruption within Cambodia's extractive industries are repetitions of what happened in the 1990s, when the country's political elite focused their energies on resource exploitation in Cambodia's forest sector (Global Witness 2007; Le Billon and Springer 2007). In short, 'neoliberalism with Cambodian characteristics' is shaped by a kleptocratic system of nepotism, where 'legitimacy' is conferred through partisan control of the military, a quasi-legal framework with a thoroughly corrupt judiciary (Sam and Poynton 2007), and a labyrinthine system of patronage that extends down to the lowest levels of government in the village.

CONCLUSION

Understanding neoliberalism requires that we appreciate its nuances with respect to the complexity of exchanges between local and extra-local forces operating within the global political economy. Crucially, we must acknowledge and account for the traction of neoliberalization as it moves around the globe into different contexts by attending to how neoliberalism is always necessarily co-constituted with existing political circumstances and economic frameworks. Likewise, it is imperative to recognize that an excessive focus on either external or internal phenomena to the exclusion of relational connections across space is inadequate in addressing the relevant features and significant articulations of neoliberalism as a series of 'glocal' processes. Dismissing neoliberalism as a mere 'bogeyman' figure (Thavat 2010) demonstrates a lack of understanding for the processes of articulation, whereby existing institutional frameworks and economic conditions are altered as variable societal influences circulate and thereby transform neoliberalism into its 'actually existing circumstances' of neoliberalization. Even more problematic is that such disregard actively ignores or serves to retrograde the theoretical gains that critical scholars have made over the past decade by returning neoliberalism to an ill-conceived and ageographical 'bulldozer effect' through an insistence that it is a monolithic and static phenomenon. Yet most harmful of all is that accounts that do not adopt a relational perspective of neoliberalism make no consideration for how retaining the abstraction of neoliberalism as a 'global' project—even as we recognize that its connections to particular contexts come with a high degree of specificity—enables geographically diffuse phenomena like inequality and poverty to find a point of similarity (Springer 2008). In other words, it allows us to identify how the structural violence of capitalism operates in diverse settings. Such disarticulation of the scope of neoliberalism effectively paralyzes attempts at constructing and supporting solidarity beyond the micro-politics of the 'local', thereby weakening a potentially liberatory basis among the world's poorest and most vulnerable peoples.

In theorizing neoliberalization as a processual, hybridized, variegated and protean phenomenon—as is the cutting edge in the critical literature today (Brenner et al. 2010)—the particularity of the Cambodian context suggests that the four-way relationship between neoliberalism, violence, kleptocracy and patronage is necessarily infused with characteristics that are unique to this location. My argument is thus not to construct a metanarrative that suggests that the practical effects of neoliberalism are everywhere and always the same. Instead, I only want to draw attention to some of the relations that neoliberalism has produced or facilitated—in this case violence, kleptocracy and patronage— by locating these intersections within the specificity of a particular context. As the Cambodian state is increasingly neoliberalized in its decision-making, economic orientation, planning agencies and developmental agenda, as each of these becomes more intensively embedded within transnational circuits of capital and expertise (Sneddon 2007), violence becomes gradually more woven into the fabric of Cambodian life through the existing patronage system. While patron politics undoubtedly predate Cambodia's adoption of neoliberal ideas, it is clear that patronage has since become intimately tied to neoliberalization. While 'neoliberalism with Cambodian characteristics' points to a distinctive geohistorical set of power relations operating in combination with a broader hegemonic ideological project, this does not mean that this argument can only be considered as relevant to the Cambodian context. The 'in here' implications of Cambodia's particular imbrications between patronage, kleptocracy, violence and neoliberalism have wider 'out there' relevance owing to the similarities of experience that countries on the losing end of colonialism have weathered and continue to endure under global capitalism. Establishing how far such theorizations can be extended requires comparative analysis and detailed empirical research in other countries where klepto-neoliberalism, or *nepoliberalism*, is unfolding. While I can speculate that patterns characterizing the relationship between neoliberalism, kleptocracy, patronage, and violence would emerge in (post)colonial locales like many African states and particularly other Southeast Asian nations with analogous political legacies and cultural histories, this would always be marked with contradictions and contingencies that are dependent on the context in question. The stark brutality of neoliberalism may ultimately prove to be less or perhaps even more intense than is currently found within the Cambodian context.

NOTES

1. I refer particularly to 'Western' donors, as the RGC has been largely uncritical of money arriving from Asia and China in particular, which has risen considerably in recent years.
2. The first sense of 'enemy' (*khmaang*) is used to refer to adversaries in a battle or war, while the second sense (*setrov*) is used in a more general sense of opposition.
3. Cambodian elites were not oblivious to this 'shock'. De facto privatization spread across the country throughout the 1980s. Prior to UNTAC, the RGC had shown itself to be committed to economic reform including through revisions to marketing, land tenure, investment and taxation legislation designed to attract foreign capital, as well as the privatization of state holdings and reductions on subsidies (Slocomb 2010).
4. These observations are based on my family's own experience of adopting a Cambodian child in early 2007.
5. A reading of the 'police blotter' section in any issue of the *Phnom Penh Post* will confirm this claim.

BIBLIOGRAPHY

ADHOC (2008) Human Rights Situation 2007 Report. Cambodian Human Rights and Development Association (February). Available at: http://www.adhoc-cambodia .org/?p=367

Amnesty International (2008) Rights Razed: Forced Evictions in Cambodia (11 February). Available at: http://www.amnesty.org/en/library/info/ASA23/002/2008/en

Barton C (2006) Crooked cop or whistle-blower? *Phnom Penh Post* (11 August). Available at: http://www.phnompenhpost.com/national/crooked-cop-or-whistleblower

Barton C and Sokha C (2007a) Donors put spotlight on petro cash. *Phnom Penh Post* (20 April). Available at: http://www.phnompenhpost.com/national/donors-put-spotlight-petro-cash

Barton C and Sokha C (2007b) Private profit versus public gain. *Phnom Penh Post* (18 May). Available at: http://www.phnompenhpost.com/national/private-profit-versus-public-gain

Brenner N, Peck J and Theodore N (2010) Variegated neoliberalism: Geographies, modalities, pathways. *Global Networks* 10(2): 182–222.

Brenner N and Theodore N (2002) Cities and the geographies of 'actually existing neoliberalism'. *Antipode: A Radical Journal of Geography* 34(3): 349–379.

Brickell K (2015) Towards intimate geographies of peace? Local reconciliation of domestic violence in Cambodia. *Transactions of the Institute of British Geographers* 40(3): 321–333.

Brickell K and Springer S (2016) An introduction to contemporary Cambodia. In: Brickell K and Springer S (eds) *The Handbook of Contemporary Cambodia*. Abingdon: Routledge.

Cain G (2009) Sokimex in line for black rewards. *Asia Times* (6 February). Available at: http://www.atimes.com/atimes/Southeast_Asia/KB06Ae01.html

Carmichael R (2003) A volatile, high-octane blend. *Phnom Penh Post* (15 August). Available at: http://www.phnompenhpost.com/national/volatile-high-octane-blend

Chandler D (2008) *A History of Cambodia*, fourth edition. Boulder, CO: Westview Press.

Cochrane K and Sam R (2005) Adoption gumshoe gives detailed report on baby-scam payoffs. *Phnom Penh Post* (20 May). Available at: http://www.phnompenh post.com/national/adoption-gumshoe-gives-detailed-report-baby-scam-payoffs

Council of Ministries (1991) Petroleum Regulations (28 September). Archived by Asia Pacific Centre for Environmental Law, Faculty of Law, National University of Singapore. Available at: http://sunsite.nus.edu.sg/apcel/dbase/cambodia/regs/carpet.html

Development Partner's Consensus Statement on Governance (2008) Official statement prepared for the Cambodian Development Cooperation Forum, 19–20 June 2007. Available at: http://www.cdc-crdb.gov.kh/cdc/first_cdcf/session1/sonsensus_statement.htm

England K and Ward K (eds) (2007) *Neoliberalization: States, Networks, Peoples*. Oxford: Wiley-Blackwell.

Etcheson C (2005) *After the Killing Fields: Lessons from the Cambodian Genocide*. Westport, CT: Praeger.

Ghai Y (2007) Report of the Special Representative of the Secretary-General for human rights in Cambodia (A/HRC/4/36). Available at: http://www.ohchr.org/EN/countries/AsiaRegion/Pages/KHIndex.aspx

Gillison D and Ana P (2006) Statement in Heng Pov's name details allegations. *Cambodia Daily* (16 August): 1–2.

Global Witness (2007) *Cambodia's Family Trees: Illegal Logging and the Stripping of Public Assets by Cambodia's Elite*. London: Global Witness. Available at: https://www.globalwitness.org/en/reports/cambodias-family-trees/

Global Witness (2009) *Country For Sale: How Cambodia's Elite Have Captured the Country's Extractive Industries*. London: Global Witness. Available at: https://www.globalwitness.org/en/reports/country-sale/

Harvey D (2005) *A Brief History of Neoliberalism*. Oxford: Oxford University Press.

Hayman A (2007) The rich, the poor and the income gap. *Phnom Penh Post* (1 June). Available at: http://www.phnompenhpost.com/national/rich-poor-and-income-gap

Hughes C (2003) *The Political Economy of Cambodia's Transition, 1991–2001*. London: Routledge Curzon.

Kea P (2006) 'Privatized' Killing Fields site tries to quiet critics. *Japan Times* (13 January). Available at: http://search.japantimes.co.jp/cgi-bin/nn20060113f2.html

Kiernan B (1996) *The Pol Pot Regime: Race, Power, and Genocide in Cambodia under the Khmer Rouge, 1975–79*. New Haven, CT: Yale University Press.

Kiljunen K (ed) (1984) *Kampuchea: Decade of the Genocide*. London: Zed.

Klein N (2007) *The Shock Doctrine: The Rise of Disaster Capitalism*. Harmondsworth: Penguin.

Koh Santepheap (2008) Hun Sen: Nobody can topple Hun Sen. Translated from Khmer by Vong Socheata. Available at: http://ki-media.blogspot.com/2008/03/hun-sens-speech-points-to-internal.html

Le Billon P and Springer S (2007) Between war and peace: Violence and accommodation in the Cambodian logging sector. In: de Jong W, Donovan D and Abe K (eds) *Extreme Conflict and Tropical Forests*. New York: Springer, 17–36.

Lempert D (2006) Foreign aid: Creating conditions for the next civil war. *Phnom Penh Post* (29 December). Available at: http://www.phnompenhpost.com/national/foreign-aid-creating-conditions-next-civil-war

Lesley E and Sam R (2005) Public land deals flaunt intentions of law. *Phnom Penh Post* (28 January). Available at: http://www.phnompenhpost.com/national/public-land-deals-flaunt-intentions-law

LICADHO (2007a) *Human Rights in Cambodia: The Charade of Justice* (December). Cambodian League for the Promotion and Defense of Human Rights. Available at: http://www.licadho-cambodia.org/reports.php?perm=113

LICADHO (2007b) *Illegal Forced Eviction of 105 Families in Sihanoukville Fact Sheet* (July). Cambodian League for the Promotion and Defense of Human Rights. Available at: http://www.licadho-cambodia.org/reports.php?perm=108

LICADHO (2008) *Reading Between the Lines: How Politics, Money & Fear Control Cambodia's Media 2008* (May). Cambodian League for the Promotion and Defense of Human Rights. Available at: http://www.licadho-cambodia.org/reports.php?perm=119

McDermid C and Sokha C (2007) Islands in the stream of cash. *Phnom Penh Post* (9 August). Available at: http://www.phnompenhpost.com/national/islands-stream-cash

Owen T and Kiernan B (2006) Bombs over Cambodia. *The Walrus* (October): 62–69.

Peck J (2001) *Workfare States*. New York: Guilford Press.

Peck J and Tickell A (2002) Neoliberalizing space. *Antipode: A Radical Journal of Geography* 34(2): 380–404.

Phnom Penh Post (2000) All that glitters seems to be... Sokimex. *Phnom Penh Post* (28 April). Available at: http://www.phnompenhpost.com/national/all-glitters -seems-be-sokimex

Phnom Penh Post (2007) It's a family affair. *Phnom Penh Post* (23 February–8 March): 8–9.

Phnom Penh Post (2008) Phnom Penh's decade of land evictions. *Phnom Penh Post* (3 October). Available at: http://www.phnompenhpost.com/national/timeline-phnom-penhs-decade-land-evictions

Rand N and MacIssac V (2004) In Cambodia, Hun Sen is in the driver's seat. *Asia Times* (20 July). Available at: http://www.atimes.com/atimes/Southeast_Asia/ FG20Ae01.html

Reno W (1995) *Corruption and State Politics in Sierra Leone*. Cambridge: Cambridge University Press.

Sam R and Poynton D (2007) Judicial reform 2007: an iron fist gone limp. *Phnom Penh Post* (26 January). Available at: http://www.phnompenhpost.com/national/ judicial-reform-2007-iron-fist-gone-limp

Slocomb M (2010) *An Economic History of Cambodia in the Twentieth Century*. Singapore: NUS Press.

Smith A (2007) Articulating neoliberalism: Diverse economies and everyday life in postcolonial cities. In: Leitner H, Peck J and Sheppard ES (eds) *Contesting Neoliberalism: Urban Frontiers*. New York: Guilford Press, 204–222.

Sneddon C (2007) Nature's materiality and the circuitous paths of accumulation: Dispossession of freshwater fisheries in Cambodia. *Antipode: A Radical Journal of Geography* 39(1): 167–193.

Soenthrith S and Samean Y (2004) Hun Sen says opposition plans revolt. *Cambodia Daily* (19 July). Available at: https://www.cambodiadaily.com/archives/hun-sen-says-opposition-plans-revolt-41951/

Sokchea M (2008) Sam Rainsy vows to confiscate lands from Tycoon if he wins in election. *Phnom Penh Post* (2 June). Available at: http://www.phnompenhpost .com/national/sam-rainsy-vows-confiscate-lands-tycoon-if-he-wins-election

Sokha C (2007) Rights groups echo PM's fear of farmer revolution. *Phnom Penh Post* (9 February). Available at: http://www.phnompenhpost.com/national/rights-groups-echo-pms-fear-farmer-revolution

Springer S (2008) The nonillusory effects of neoliberalisation: Linking geographies of poverty, inequality, and violence. *Geoforum* 39(4): 1520–1525.

Springer S (2009) The neoliberalization of security and violence in Cambodia's transition. In Peou S (ed) *Human Security in East Asia: Challenges for Collaborative Action*. New York, Routledge, 125–141.

Springer S (2010) *Cambodia's Neoliberal Order: Violence, Authoritarianism and the Contestation of Public Space*. Abingdon: Routledge.

Springer S (2012) Neoliberalising violence: Of the exceptional and the exemplary in coalescing moments. *Area* 44(2): 136–143.

Springer S (2013) Violent accumulation: A postanarchist critique of property, dispossession, and the state of exception in neoliberalizing Cambodia. *Annals of the Association of American Geographers* 103(3): 608–626.

Springer S (2015) Postneoliberalism? *Review of Radical Political Economics* 47(1): 5–17.

Springer S (2016) The violence of neoliberalism. In: Springer S, Birch K, and MacLeavy J (eds) *The Handbook of Neoliberalism*. Abingdon: Routledge, 153–163.

Thavat M (2010) The neoliberal bogeyman of Cambodia. *New Mandela* (27 July). Available at: http://asiapacific.anu.edu.au/newmandala/2010/07/27/the-neoliberal-bogeyman-of-cambodia/

UN (1991) Agreement on a Comprehensive Political Settlement of the Cambodia Conflict. Available at: http://www.usip.org/sites/default/files/file/resources/collections/peace_agreements/agree_comppol_10231991.pdf

Un K and So S (2009) Politics of natural resource use in Cambodia. *Asian Affairs* 36(3): 123–138.

Uvin P (2003) Global dreams and local anger: From structural to acute violence in a globalizing world. In: Tetreault MA, Denemark RA, Thomas KP and Burch K (eds) *Rethinking Global Political Economy: Emerging Issues, Unfolding Odysseys*. London, Routledge, 147–161.

Wacquant L (2001) The penalisation of poverty and the rise of neo-liberalism. *European Journal on Criminal Policy and Research* 9(4): 401–412.

Wasson E and Yun S (2006) Council of Ministers approves sub-decree to manage state land. *Cambodia Daily* (13 December): 16.

Yun S (2004) Chea Sim, CPP healthy, party claims. *Cambodia Daily* (30 July): 1–2.

Yun S (2007) This is war, Hun Sen tells land-grabbers. *Cambodia Daily* (6 March): 1–2.

Chapter 13

Variegated Neoliberalization as a Function and Outcome of Neo-authoritarianism in China[1]

Kean Fan Lim

When the former US Treasury Secretary, Timothy Geithner, proposed to his G20 counterparts in a November 2010 meeting that their respective governments adopt current account deficit or surplus targets of less than 4 per cent of GDP, it drew an intriguing response from the then Vice-Foreign Minister of China, Cui Tiankai: 'The artificial setting of a numerical target cannot but remind us of the days of a planned economy' (*Bloomberg* 2010). At one level, Cui was probably offering a witty counterpoint: indeed, it was China that had operated as—and some might argue it still *is*—a centrally planned economy. On closer reading, however, there might be a more profound underlying meaning to Cui's remarks that exemplifies a new dimension to the Communist Party of China's (CPC) politico-economic ideology: freedom of financial and commodity flows across the global economy is strongly preferred, while the notion of 'a planned economy' at this scale—led by a hegemonic US government that heavily influences the terms of market exchange—is deemed an *un*desirable barrier to capital accumulation. This outlook strongly suggests China is not unlike what Harvey (2005: 64) terms a 'neoliberal state', within which 'the freedom of businesses and corporations (legally regarded as individuals) to operate within [an] institutional framework of free markets and free trade is regarded as a fundamental good' (see also Lim 2010; Nolan 2012).

Juxtaposed against this perspective, however, is the fact that the CPC continues to weave egalitarian principles of 'common affluence' (*gongtong fuyu* 共同富裕) and 'harmonious society' (*hexie shehui* 和谐社会)—or what Deng Xiaoping (1982) refers to as the 'universal truth of Marxism'[2]—in tandem with its policies to deepen market-like rule. As the CPC more recently puts it, these principles could be attained only through a government that is 'big' and 'good', features that 'fundamentally distinguish the Chinese path from neoliberalism, which takes the capitalist political system and private ownership as its basic political and economic foundations, and which advocates "small government," that is governments that do not intervene in the economy' (*Qiushi* 2014).[3] Quite clearly contradicting Cui Tiankai's unwillingness to remember 'the days of a planned economy', this claim raises a theoretically significant question that remains unaddressed in politico-economic studies of China: What is the *function* of neoliberalization in the CPC's long-standing political commitment to social egalitarianism?

To address this question, it is necessary first to understand that neoliberalization in and through China does not occur in a post-ideological or ahistorical vacuum. Neoliberalization, as Zhang and Ong (2008: 10) observe, has taken on the appearance of 'an inexorable process that renders all national spaces intelligible or commensurable in accord with predetermined universal norms'. This perception of inexorability, in turn, engendered formalistic conceptualizations in the social sciences that 'assess whether particular nation-states are more or less "neoliberal" in terms of a preconceived collection of attributes', assessments that 'tend to give short shrift to the role of situated phenomena in shaping outcomes' (ibid.). In China, however, the increasing influence of neoliberal logics within Chinese policymaking circles is entwined with—if not subsumed under—the seemingly incommensurable political strategy to control the means and social relations of production in the name of socialism. For this reason, the willingness of senior CPC cadres to embrace the logic of a self-regulatory 'free' market at the global scale does not—or, indeed, cannot—translate into a wholesale adaptation of neoliberal logics at the national scale.

This multifaceted development corresponds to a key point discussed in Cemal Burak Tansel's introductory chapter: the relationship between authoritarianism and neoliberalism need not be novel or mutually incompatible. The strategies to effect market-like rule in China are first and foremost a legacy of authoritarian capacities and policies instituted *prior* to the launch of marketization in the 1980s. Of particular significance is the connection between this legacy, the 'big and good' government celebrated by the CPC today and the intensifying integration of the Chinese political economy within the global system of capitalism. Taking the constitutive role of this 'situated phenomenon' into account, this chapter raises an equally plausible proposition: geographically variegated neoliberalization, driven and repurposed by the Chinese state through a range of intrinsically discriminatory policies, have become at once *a precondition and an outcome of/for the CPC's long-standing attempt to secure perpetual rule.*

The subsequent discussion will be arranged in two parts. Part one provides an overview of the development of authoritarian capacities before the CPC launched market-oriented reforms. This overview will be followed by the second part, wherein two approaches that constitute authoritarian neoliberalism in post-Mao China will be presented. This section first explores how the engagement with neoliberal logics in China is expressed through unilateral, state-driven territorial reconfigurations. Second, it foregrounds how the transition to market-like rule and export-oriented growth over the past three decades have been predicated on the retention of one Mao-era institution—the *hukou* (household registration 户口) mode of demographic control instituted during the 'socialist high tide' of 1958. The concluding section examines the conceptual implications of the drive for a socialist future on the premise of inherently authoritarian and discriminatory measures.

THE CONSTRUCTION AND CONSOLIDATION OF AUTHORITARIAN CAPACITIES SINCE 1949

Chinese policymakers' engagement with neoliberal reason in the post-Mao era (1976 to the present) could arguably be traced to the late University of Chicago economist Milton Friedman. Friedman is largely accepted as the leading proponent of the neoliberal ideology in the 1970s and, together with a group of like-minded economists known as the 'Chicago Boys', worked at formulating a set of policies to actualize this ideology (see Klein 2007; Peck 2010). While the first wave of these policies was implemented with mixed success in South America in the 1970s, it came to historical prominence worldwide through the policies of Margaret Thatcher and those of Ronald Reagan. Friedman advised both leaders. Less known but no less important was the fact that Deng Xiaoping, another of Thatcher and Reagan's contemporaries and then newly appointed leader of China, *also* received a crash course from Friedman in 1980.

Crucially, the Deng administration opted not to go down the path of Latin American economies by selling off state-owned assets and opening up the entire national territory to the transnational flows of capital. Underpinning this decision was a long-standing political campaign, beginning in the 1930s, against imperialism. The CPC's academic organ, *Qiushi* (2014), recently reiterated the importance of this agenda within the contemporary context of global economic integration: 'With its powerful state-owned sector and capacity for macro control, China is able to prevent developed countries from taking control of its economic lifelines, thereby maintaining the independence and autonomy of its political and economic development.' What ensued, instead, was a gradual path of policy experimentation and selective reforms of institutions developed during the Mao era. For this reason, China's national-scale developmental trajectory after 1978 is an appropriate platform from which to theorize how neoliberalism works as a flexible developmental ideology across different geographical-historical contexts. Specifically, the Chinese case demonstrates how neoliberal logics were selectively integrated within and subsequently reinforced authoritarian capacities that were *already* an integral part of the Chinese party-state.

The rationale of Chinese state authoritarianism could arguably be traced to the CPC's pre-1949, militaristic attempt to overcome the nascent state structure established by its political nemesis, the incumbent Nationalist party (or Kuomintang). To attain political dominance over an unstable China, the peasantry was mobilized in an often-violent revolt against what was known as 'landlord tyrants and evil gentry' (*tuhao lieshen* 土豪劣绅). Underpinning this attempt was a commitment to socio-spatial egalitarianism: equitable re-distribution of land was promised to the peasants if the revolution succeeded. Yet it was clear from the outside that egalitarianism would be a fluid concept. As Mao Zedong told fellow cadres at the 1946 launch of mobilization directives, what he really required of the peasants was a *willingness* to rebel, *not* egalitarianism per se: 'The peasants' egalitarianism is revolutionary prior to the land redistribution, do not object to that; what should be objected is the egalitarianism *after* the land redistribution' (Mao 1993: 78–9; author's translation and emphasis). This emphasis echoes Bianco's (2001: 233) influential interpretation that the 'peasant revolution' was in fact 'a peasant movement without peasants': the peasants' human agency was procured primarily for political ends, and what counted as 'egalitarianism' in one period could—and did—easily expire in another (cf. Zhang 2001, 2003).

Indeed, while land was redistributed between 1950 and 1952, egalitarian landownership was soon subsumed under a major collectivization drive—which also included means of production and, crucially, the labour power intrinsic to the peasants—in the mid-1950s. No political options were available to resist this unilateral, top-down injunction, and by 1958 around 80 per cent of the national population was residing in what was termed the 'People's Communes' (*renmin gongshe* 人民公社). Associated with this authoritarian collectivization was the implementation of a discriminatory and still function-ing policy to preserve strict demographic control—the previously mentioned *hukou* institution. Modelled after the 'internal passport' system of the Soviet Union, this institution classified each Chinese citizen as either an 'agricul-tural' (*nongmin* 农民) or a 'non-agricultural' resident (*fei nongmin* 非农民). Along with this classification came a certain set of rights (and prohibitions), the primary of which was severely restricted movement between (rural) com-munes and/or (urban) industrial units.[4]

It was on the premise of this enforced demographic separation that a dis-tinct mode of capital accumulation—the 'price scissors'—was instituted.

Each commune was responsible for delivering specific products to the state; migratory restrictions produced a *spatially inelastic* labour market that ensured full state control over labour costs. Rural demand was also state managed through a quasi-subsistence distribution of daily supplies. Input and output prices were therefore completely determined by the state, and the CPC opted to price agricultural outputs below value when these were sold to urban industrial units. In short, the *hukou* institution and the ability of the Chinese party-state to determine the territorial allocation of means of production jointly enabled for the enforced absorption of surplus value from rural residents.

These regulatory policies instituted in the name of socialistic development after 1949 were patently paradoxical: the Mao administration was built upon the very contingency—uneven socioeconomic development—it sought to extinguish through fresh forms of stratification based fully on political power. The outcome was a new regulatory structure that underminded the socio-spatial egalitarianism promised to the peasants prior to the 1949 revolutionary victory. Yao Zhongqiu (hereafter his pen name Qiu Feng), a prominent public intellectual in China, puts this development into perspective:

> This is a hierarchical society, Mao-era society toppled the equal-rights society that existed in China since the Qin Dynasty, it totally toppled what was originally an equal-rights social structure. Why do we say so? This kind of social structure is an unequal society produced by a relatively unique governance logic of the Communist Party, it definitely is not equal, and practically it is a new modern form of hierarchical society. Its criterion of differentiating hierarchical position is power. If you have power, you will stand at the highest point; if you don't, you have nothing. (Qiu Feng 2010, author's translation)

As such, Whyte (2005: 6) correctly problematizes the conventional account that portrays Deng Xiaoping as trading off social equality for economic efficiency: this account 'diverts attention from other features of the stratification system of Mao-era China, many of which were decidedly not egalitarian either in intent or consequences'.[5] Rather, Whyte (2005: 6) adds:

> In China the combination of virtually total suppression of markets in favor of bureaucratic allocation as well as of voluntary changes in residence and employment makes the dominance of one's bureaucratic location rather than one's individual human capital or other social background traits (and one's resulting 'market position') much greater as a general rule.

As the next section will elaborate, market-oriented reforms instituted by Deng and his successors may have led to changes in pricing and migratory mechanisms; however, the suppressive effects of territorial and demographic control not only persisted, but have also been *repurposed* to facilitate authoritarian neoliberalism in and through contemporary China.

THE CONDITIONS AND CONTAINMENT OF NEOLIBERALIZATION IN/THROUGH CHINA

Authoritarian Spatial Planning, Surplus Generation and Social Displacement

There are good reasons for fast-paced economic growth in post-Mao China—GDP expanded an average of 9 per cent annually between 1979 and 2015—to be associated with the shift to market-like rule. After all, the CPC was increasingly receptive to the engagement of/with foreign capital, which led in turn to China's current position as the 'world's factory' (Naughton 2010). This engagement began with Deng's two-pronged approach to 'down scale' rural production to the individual household and to gradually enrol Chinese state space into the production networks of transnational capital. Underpinning these reforms is still the goal of capturing surplus value, albeit in the form of foreign currencies, in order to purchase foreign technologies and goods. This was to be realized through increased production in town-village enterprises (TVEs) in the rural hinterland, the reforms of state-owned enterprises (SOEs) and the facilitation of public–private joint ventures (particularly with large TNCs).

The incorporation of market-like regulatory logics generated a (still) recurring series of territorialized re-institutionalization in city-regions (cf. Brenner, Peck and Theodore 2010; Li and Wu 2012). This began with gradual foreign capital inflow in the Special Economic Zones (SEZs) in southeastern China in 1980 and subsequent openness to foreign capital in 14 other cities in 1984. It soon became clear by the mid-1980s that there was a coastal bias to the engagement with foreign capital. In one sense, this was not surprising: the primary corollary of free market capitalism is, after all, acute uneven economic-geographical development (Smith 1984; Harvey 2006). The challenge for the Deng administration was to make this ideologically and politically palatable.

In the first decade of reforms, Deng Xiaoping publicly demonstrated his willingness to accept *temporary* interprovincial development as a trade-off for opening Chinese borders to transnational capital flows. The spatial expression of Deng's economic policies was guided by a distinct geographical theory—the 'ladder step' approach (*tidu tuiyi lilun* 梯度推移理论). First introduced by the Shanghai-based academics Xia Yulong and Feng Zhijun (1982), this prescriptive 'theory' attracted the attention of a senior CPC member, Bo Yibo, and subsequently permeated central policymaking circles.

It was instituted as a policy blueprint during the 7th Five-Year Plan (1986–1990). Specifically, the blueprint delineated the Chinese political economy into three economic-geographical belts: the eastern (coastal), central and western. The Deng administration gave one belt (the eastern seaboard) the priority in ascending the development 'ladder'. It assumed that the fruits of development in the 'first mover' belt would diffuse downwards to other rungs of the ladder. This template of *instituted uneven development* became the basis for market-oriented reforms.

At the discursive level, Deng was more explicit than Mao in stating how uneven development was only a short-term means to an egalitarian future. In a 1988 speech entitled 'Two Big Pictures' (*liangge dajü* 两个大局), Deng summed up his time-oriented theoretical approach to economic-geographical development:

> The coastal area must accelerate its opening up to enable this broad region of 200 million people to first develop, from which it will stimulate even better development in the interior. This is a matter that involves a big picture. The interior must understand this big picture. (Deng 1993: 277–278; author's translation)

Deng, however, identified an equally important 'big picture', which entailed people in the coastal provinces to reciprocate the state's decision to first implement reforms in their provinces by accepting the subsequent redistribution of accumulated value accruing from economic liberalization for the development of the interior:

> Upon attaining a certain level of development, the coastal areas are requested to give more energy to assist in the development of the interior, this is also a 'big picture'. ... It is an obligation for economically advanced areas to help those that are more backward, and it is also a major policy. (Deng 1993: 277–278; author's translation)

Interestingly, Deng and his successors retained one Mao-era institution—the *hukou* institution—as they facilitated export-oriented, urban-based industrialization along the eastern seaboard. The interaction of inherited and new policies of/for instituted uneven development engendered widening economic-geographical disparities at multiple scales—coastal–interior, interprovincial, urban–rural, intra-urban—over the past two decades (Wang 2008; *The Economist* 2011). As will be elaborated shortly, this generated a new form of surplus capture from the rural hinterland: the capture of surplus rural labour power.

Challenges generated by the 'ladder step' policy have become increasingly clear. As means of production were concentrated in city-regions such as Shenzhen and Guangzhou in the Pearl River Delta and Suzhou and Shanghai in the Yangtze River Delta, significant inflationary pressures on wage costs, consumer goods and real estate emerged. These pressures are in part an outcome of what Oi (1992: 101–102) refers to as 'local corporatist states', each of which 'coordinates economic enterprises in its territory as if it were a diversified business corporation'. The corporatization of decentralized governance manifests itself at the macro level through land-use changes: local state cadres try to enrol prime agricultural land into (urbanizing) circuits of capital, in turn producing a 'great urban transformation' at significant social and environmental costs (Harney 2009; He and Wu 2009; Hewitt 2008; Lin 2009a; Tsing 2010). Yet change was not just occurring within the cities.

An expanding literature reveals how primitive accumulation, a distinct precondition and expression of neoliberalization, has become a prevalent driver of rural transformation in China. Looking at transformations in the Shanghai rural landscape, Buck (2007) shows how primitive accumulation is related to the subsumption of labour to capital. Lin (2009b: 441) highlights how major city governments in Guangdong province 'scaled up' their development policies through the 'forceful annexation of suburban cities and counties'. While Webber (2008a, 2008b) states that there are economic and non-economic logics that underpin the primitive accumulation process, Walker (2006: 1) views the violent capture of rural space and resources, which have triggered 'a tidal wave of peasant protest' over the past two decades, as a clear reflection of 'gangster capitalism' at work. Against these varied interpretations of the causes and implications of primitive accumulation across China, one pattern is clear: Deng's (1993: 64) fear that post-1978 Chinese social formations would split into distinct 'haves' and 'have-nots' (*liangji fenhua* 两极分化) was certainly not unfounded.[6]

To overcome the growing social tensions associated with marketization and economic liberalization, the Chinese state launched three broad regional development programmes, namely the Great Western Opening Up (*xibu dakaifa* 西部大开发), the Northeast Revitalization (*dongbei zhenxing* 东北振兴) and the Rise of the Central (*zhongbu jueqi* 中部崛起). While funds have been redistributed to the provinces involved to launch concrete developmental projects, these programmes entailed no specific institutional (re)formulations at the provincial level.[7] The more crucial goal of these programmes appears to be the production of cross-provincial geographical imaginations. This goal is to materialize through a discursive-ideological strategy: the name of each programme began to be included in individual provinces' policy documents, while the mass media began to discuss province-specific economic development policies in relation to the broader regional strategy (e.g. how the urbanization of capital and labour power in Chongqing is connected to and helps drive the Great Western Development programme).

Geographically targeted (re)institutionalizations were more recently implemented at the intra-urban level, with six 'nationally strategic new areas' (*guojia zhanlüe xinqu* 国家战略新区) identified as bordered zones within selected cities to 'move first, experiment first' (*xianxing xianshi* 先行先试). The 'new area' concept is actually not novel, although its scale of implementation has widened considerably since 2006. Following the success of the first four SEZs, the world-renowned Pudong New Area in Shanghai was approved for development in 1990, and has since been transformed into a city-regional 'motor' of China's economic growth. This intra-urban (re)institutionalization was not extended elsewhere in China for 14 years until the Binhai industrial region adjacent to the northeastern city of Tianjin was designated China's second 'nationally strategic new area' in 2006. From 2009 to 2012, four more 'new areas' were demarcated. Two 'new areas' are in the western interior, namely Liangjiang New Area in the city of Chongqing and Lanzhou New Area, which overlaps with the city of the same name in Gansu province. The other two are located along the coast, namely Zhoushan Archipelago New Area, based offshore in Zhejiang province, and Nansha New Area, strategically positioned between two specialized new zones (Hengqin, in Zhuhai, and Qianhai, in Shenzhen) in the Pearl River Delta. It appears that several more of these 'nationally strategic new areas' will be identified across the country in the coming years (*Xinhua* 2012).

The evolving range of state-mandated (re)territorialization is summarized in Figure 13.1. In one sense, this proactive spatial reorganization is part of what Wu (2015) aptly terms 'planning for growth'. The ability to reconfigure means of production—finance, land and labour power—is central to this process. At the same time, however, this unilateral approach to planning exemplifies neo-authoritarianism in three aspects: (1) it takes place without public input and yet involves large amounts of direct and indirect public financing; (2) it often involves contentious requisitions of land that lead to forced evictions; and (3) it leaves unchanged key institutions of Mao-era state authoritarianism. The remaining part of this section will examine the rationale of one long-standing aspect of this authoritarianism, the enforced urban–rural separation.

The 1958 *Hukou* Institution, A-Social Low-Wage Labour Power and the 'China Price'

Just as the National People's Congress (NPC), China's top legislature, and the national committee of the Chinese People's Political Consultative Conference (CPPCC), the country's top political advisory body, were preparing for their annual meetings in 2010 (known locally as 'the two meetings', or

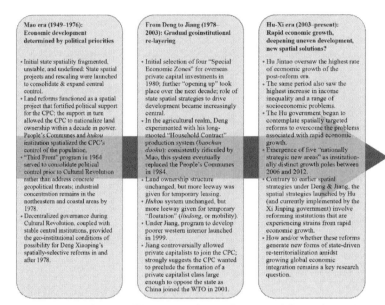

Mao era (1949–1976): Economic development determined by political priorities	From Deng to Jiang (1978–2003): Gradual geoinstitutional re-layering	Hu-Xi era (2003–present): Rapid economic growth, deepening uneven development, new spatial solutions?
• Initial state spatiality fragmented, unstable, and undefined. State spatial projects and rescaling were launched to consolidate & expand central control. • Land reforms functioned as a spatial project that fortified political support for the CPC; the support in turn allowed the CPC to nationalize land ownership within a decade in power. People's Communes and *hukou* institution spatialized the CPC's control of the population. • "Third Front" program in 1964 served to consolidate political control prior to Cultural Revolution rather than address concrete geopolitical threats; industrial concentration remains in the northeastern and coastal areas by 1978. • Decentralized governance during Cultural Revolution, coupled with stable central institutions, provided the geo-institutional conditions of possibility for Deng Xiaoping's spatially-selective reforms in and after 1978.	• Initial selection of four "Special Economic Zones" for overseas private capital investments in 1980; further "opening up" took place over the next decade; role of state spatial strategies to drive development became increasingly central. • In the agricultural realm, Deng experimented with his long-mooted "Household Contract" production system (*baochan daohu*): consistently ridiculed by Mao, this system eventually replaced the People's Communes in 1984. • Land ownership structure unchanged, but more leeway was given for temporary leasing. • *Hukou* system unchanged, but more leeway given for temporary "floatation" (*liudong*, or mobility). • Under Jiang, program to develop poorer western interior launched in 1999. • Jiang controversially allowed private capitalists to join the CPC; strongly suggests the CPC wanted to preclude the formation of a private capitalist class large enough to oppose the state as China joined the WTO in 2001.	• Hu Jintao oversaw the highest rate of economic growth of the post-reform era. • The same period also saw the highest increase in income inequality and a range of socioeconomic problems. • The Hu government began to contemplate spatially targeted reforms to overcome the problems associated with rapid economic growth. • Emergence of five "nationally strategic new areas" as institutionally distinct growth poles between 2006 and 2012. • Contrary to earlier spatial strategies under Deng & Jiang, the spatial strategies launched by Hu (and currently implemented by the Xi Jinping government) involve reforming institutions that are experiencing strains from rapid economic growth. • How and/or whether these reforms generate new forms of state-driven re-territorialization amidst growing global economic integration remains a key research question.

Figure 13.1.   China's rolling series of state-driven spatial transformations

lianghui 两会), 13 newspapers from across China issued an unprecedented joint call to the Chinese government for *hukou* reforms. 'China has long suffered from the *hukou* system,' the deliberately timed editorial said. 'We think that citizens are born free and should have the right to freedom of movement. We urge delegates to do everything possible to propose a *hukou* reform timetable' (*The Economic Observer*, 1 March 2010, see Figure 13.2). This high-profile entreaty followed claims and attempts to reform this institution, which suggests the CPC was fully cognizant of its negative social impacts (see, for example, Chan and Buckingham 2008; Lim 2014). No full timetable was published at the time of writing, however, and research continues to demonstrate the social exclusionary effects of this institution (Zhang, Zhu and Nyland 2014; Song 2016). These developments explicitly suggest that there remains a strong impetus to retain this discriminatory system of social control, that any engagement with marketization in China necessarily negates the principle that 'citizens are born free'.

As the urbanization of capital intensifies across China, there appears little logic why this institution remains socially relevant. Indeed, following China's accession to the WTO in 2001, there has been a surge in rural migrant labour to the cities. The average for the past decade has exceeded 200 million 'floating' migrants, with the 2014 total recorded at 253 million (Chinese National Health and Family Planning Commission 2015). City-regions along the

Figure 13.2.   Unprecedented: a joint public call by 13 major newspapers across China for *hukou* reforms. The headline translates to 'Plea to representatives of the "Two Meetings" to press for accelerated *hukou* reforms'.
Source: Reproduced from *The Economic Observer* (1 March 2010); English caption by the author

coastal seaboard, primarily Guangdong, Fujian, Jiangsu and Zhejiang, are the most targeted destinations (Chinese State Council 6th Population Census Office 2012). Negating benefits for these migrants would only reinforce the tensions between 'locals' (*bendi ren* 本地人) and 'non-locals' (*waidi ren* 外地人); by extension, it generates an undesirable social cost in the CPC's quest for a 'harmonious society'.

Perhaps the most plausible reason, then, is economic. Not having to provide social welfare to incoming migrants meant municipal governments could divert fiscal resources to capital-friendly projects (building industrial parks, offering tax breaks, etc.) and hence drive down the costs of production. This is an indirect aspect of what Harney (2009) has shown elsewhere as the 'China price'.[8] It would also be politically feasible to mandate migrants to return to their rural residences during economic downturns, in turn precluding localized social instability. In this sense, the *hukou* system has paradoxically become the basis of a 'small' government in the cities; it is, in short, an enabler of an emergent 'neoliberal urbanism' in China (He and Wu 2009).[9]

The treatment of rural migrant workers as *a-social* and *spatially elastic* labour power reveals, in turn, a sustained absorption of rural resources—land, labour power, monetarily defined surplus value—for urban-based industrialization. As Qiu Feng (2010, author's translation) puts it, the retention of the rural–urban demographic control has to be understood within this Mao-era framework of unequal power relations:

> Currently the political framework in China remains institutionally hierarchical, such that when people discuss urban–rural disparity, it should not even be called 'disparity', it should be called urban–rural institutional segregation [*fenge zhidu*, 分割制度]. The city and the village are two different worlds, these two worlds do not enjoy mutual engagement, in every aspect the city is emplaced in a position to plunder and pillage. You can simply say there are two different types of citizens, or say that farmers are basically not even considered citizens. Originally I used a more provocative term, called 'internal colonialism'. To the peasant, the Communist Party's institutionalization of the urban–rural divide is essentially a form of colonial institutionalization. Power is used to establish this institutionalization, with the village treated as a colony, its resources relentlessly plundered, even now it is like this.

This account of 'plunder and pillage' is incisively noted by one anonymous commentator on China's influential social critique website, *Wuyouzhixiang* (乌有之乡), in relation to the history of post-Mao reforms. Specifically, s/he puts forth a detailed explanation of how successive rollbacks in redistributive functions—another interesting exemplar of neoliberal governance—in the post-Mao era contributed to the growth of peasant migrant workers into cities where, paradoxically, they could access no social welfare:

> The Chinese economy already entered a cul-de-sac at the beginning of the 1990s, an irrevocable depression was set in motion. But the authorities decided to take risks in order to conceal the erroneous trajectory, they adopted the so-called 'investment-driven economic growth' strategy and engaged in all sorts of elementary construction. Such malignant investments, with no concerns about production output, did not move the Chinese economy out of its entrapment. As such, to preclude the possibility of total collapse, the authorities had no choice but to consecutively implement a series of 'developmental policies' that transferred the economic burden to the ordinary citizens. One example is the different sorts of additional taxation, which led to 20 per cent annual increases in tax revenues. Even so, [these policies] could not sustain a national economic turnaround, because of this, the authorities then began to ask the people to shoulder costs that should have been covered by tax revenues, such as education capital, medical capital, pension capital, housing capital, all of these [costs] were pushed to society. This is the first reason why there are so many peasant migrant workers. (*Wuyouzhixiang*, 19 November 2012, author's translation)

Two important characteristics are highlighted by this observation. First, it establishes the interrelationship between Deng's rural reforms, which rolled back the redistributive function previously in place in the People's Communes, and the urban bias that undergirds post-Mao developmental strategies as discussed in the previous part. A weakening of state-driven redistribution was thus a precondition of the market exchange of *a*-social labour power in the urban-based industrial zones and service sectors. Second, it opens up the idea that post-Mao Chinese economy was and remains 'entrapped'. The crucial question that extends from this idea is the role of pre- and post-reform spatial projects in this 'entrapment' process. As this anonymous author intimates, it was the concentration of reforms at the urban scale that further entrenched the economy in a 'cul-de-sac':

> After this phenomenon [of peasant outflows], almost every new form of 'policy' is to foot the bill of earlier policies, even by the end of last century, there was no sign of a turnaround and many local governments already had their eyes set on pension budgets. Faced with no choice, the central government had to allow local governments to sell land [i.e. re-lease land-use rights in open markets] in order to derive funds. All of a sudden, the transfer of land became prevalent. In order to enable the expropriated land to fetch good prices, local governments used 'policies' to assist developers to raise property prices, it is against such a backdrop that 'urbanization' took on its deformed character. ... The state virtually used all its funds on large-scale urbanization and so-called industrialization while it consistently reduced its commitment to construct new villages and irrigation works. Add to this local governments' continuation of land-based financing [*tudi caizheng* 土地财政], leading to all ways and means to expropriate peasants' living resources through land requisition, in turn literally producing an 'asset-less class' [*wuchan jieji* 无产阶级] that, having no operational base, would be free to enter every single 'city'. This way, it provides the new capitalist class and compradors a limitless supply of cheap labour power. Presented before us is a clear trajectory: that is, the obliteration of villages, land dispossession, the extraction of the cheapest labour power, environmental degradation, all to work for the US, to work for the world. Pollution is retained domestically, enjoyment gets exported abroad, we end up subsidizing the use of our resources. Is this the 'fundamental agenda' of the beautiful lie that is industrialization and urbanization? (ibid.)

Viewed collectively, the accounts by Qiu and the anonymous observer reveal a distinct pattern of post-Mao reforms that arguably also engendered the rolling series of primitive accumulation, territorial re-institutionalization and entrenched socio-spatial disparities discussed in the previous part—the lack of a coherent reform agenda throughout the shift to market-like rule. Zheng Yongnian, a prominent analyst of Chinese politico-economic change, views this approach to reform as 'firefighting':

> The cause of social splits and antagonism in China is due to the lack of significant reforms over the past many years. Or it could be said the reforms were not

precise, to the extent that people were saying some phenomena not only did not experience any reform, they have instead regressed. There is an impression that our reforms lack initiative, a large part of reforms seems to be passive. These kinds of reforms cannot be called reforms, they are only firefighting measures. That is because you are led by the situation, you are running along with society, and you can't even run faster than society, while true reform should guide society towards progressive development. Because [reforms were] to cope with emergencies, because [reforms were] passive, therefore more and more social problems have accumulated. (Interview with *International Herald Leader*, 9 September 2013; author's translation)

It is ironic, then, when *Qiushi* (2014), the online journal of the Central Committee of the CPC, proclaimed 'it is fair to say that the global spread of neoliberalism has been the cause of bitter suffering in many developing countries'. Social problems have caused 'bitter suffering' across post-Mao China *because* of the incoherent engagement with market-like rule, with the most prominent and long-lasting being the unequal treatment of rural migrants (Hinton 1990; Chan 2009). In response, *more* coercive measures have been implemented, leading to what political analyst Zhu Jiaming (2013) terms 'the advancement of the state and the retreat of the people' (*guojin mintui* 国进民退). If anything, Chinese neoliberalism can be defined by this entwinement between political authoritarianism, enabled by the hierarchical society established during the Mao era, and the ad hoc incorporation of market-like rule in different territories.

CONCLUSION

The CPC's engagement with neoliberal logics has been driven by contradictions that manifest at different geographical scales. At the global level today, it is very easy to mistake the Chinese government as a firm advocate of US-led neoliberalism. After all, China-based firms, particularly the national sovereign wealth fund (China Investment Corporation) and large SOEs (e.g. CNOOC and SINOPEC), are lobbying national governments for the 'freedom' to expand into new markets and successfully fulfil the CPC's 'Go Abroad' market expansion programme. Yet even this push for global free trade and investments is in itself an *outcome* of domestic authoritarianism. In spite of accession to the WTO, the CPC has not succumbed to US-led pressures to alter its fixed exchange rate regime, an arrangement which ensures China-based producers enjoy propitious terms of trade and economic stability since the inception of market reforms. Paradoxically, this very regime has led to the accumulation of large amounts of reserves that need to be reinvested to preclude devaluation (Lim 2010). Contrary to popular zero-sum conceptions of Sino-US relations, then, US (neoliberal) hegemony is in fact not unwelcomed by the Chinese state. If anything, US hegemony has, in a most intriguing twist, become the *sine qua non* of capital accumulation and economic stability in China.

The picture becomes more complicated when it is assessed at the national and subnational scales. Underpinning the CPC's relationship with neoliberal logics is an emphasis on 'the role of macro control, laying emphasis on exerting the strengths of both planning and market forces' (*Qiushi* 2014). To be sure, there has been a clear move towards a market society at the national level: individual production is now not only tolerated, but increasingly celebrated, as demonstrated by the co-optation of private capitalists within the party-state after 2001 (see Dickson 2008). Accompanying this process is a recurring series of spatial planning that creates more liberal, place-specific institutional domains to engage with transnational circulatory capital. That being said, the paradox of this process is obvious: what are meant to be 'free' subnational spaces of/for market-based transactions *have to be* unilaterally planned and instituted.

As this chapter has shown, the relationship between the Chinese state authoritarianism and the global neoliberal hegemony has been one of *simultaneous* containment and constitution (contra *Qiushi* 2014). The CPC relies on free market logics at the global scale while it aims to contain these logics domestically through a series of administrative (territorially differentiated regulatory measures and control of rural labour power) and economic measures (direct control of market exchange through SOEs and the financial system). Conceptually, these developments demonstrate how state authoritarianism drives and cushions the global-scale neoliberalization process. If the market is self-regulatory anywhere, there should not be proactive state intervention at the intra- and inter-state levels. As the aforementioned 'Geithner Proposal' indicates, neoliberalization is an impossibility without proactive state intervention. It is even plausible to suggest that states are inherently anti-market because they do not believe in self-regulating markets in the first place; what counts as 'markets'—and, indeed, as 'free' markets—to individual states is thus open to interpretation. Peck (2010: 7) sums up this dialectic incisively: 'Neoliberalism ... has only ever existed in "impure" form, indeed can only exist in messy hybrids. Its utopian vision of a free society and free economy is ultimately unattainable.' Then again, it is important to note that neoliberalization in and through China has never been premised on the attainment of a utopian 'free society' and 'free economy' (Nonini 2008; Wang 2009; Wu 2010). Indeed, absolute socioeconomic freedom would dismantle the current hierarchical society so painstakingly constructed by the Mao administration and, more crucially, call into question the raison d'être of the CPC. It would be hard to imagine the authorization of this prospect any time soon.

NOTES

1. This chapter is a significantly revised version of a paper previously published in *Progress in Human Geography* 38(2): 221–247.

2. While the existence of 'universal' truths in Marxism remain moot per se, three characteristics are certainly not 'universalized' by Karl Marx and Friedrich Engels: (1) the design of a Marxist state apparatus that holds power over the proletariat within the contemporary international system of nation states; (2) the specific temporal moment when this state apparatus hands over power absolutely to the proletariat; and (3) strategies to address recurring uneven economic-geographical development. As such, it is arguable that the 'Chinese characteristics' that accompany the putative 'universal truths' of Marxism are these three contingent characteristics: precisely because these characteristics are contingent, there is a degree of policy flexibility for the CPC to justify its existence as the leader of the Leninistic 'dictatorship of the proletariat', and by extension, to use state space strategically to further legitimize the perpetuity of a one-party governance system.

3. Of China's Top 500 Enterprises for 2015 (based on 2014 revenue), 293 were SOEs (guoqi 民企) while 207 are privately owned (*minqi* 民企). SOE-ownership is differentiated by place: they are either central government-owned (*zhongyang qiye* 中央企业) or provincial government-owned (*difang guoqi* 地方国企). While there is an increase in the number of *minqi* (from 169 in 2009), it is important to note that the top 19-ranked are SOEs, while the first *minqi* to make the ranking—Ping An Insurance—was placed 20th. Perhaps more important is the economic influence of these SOEs in spite of the growing *minqi* numbers: the 293 firms account for 78.3 per cent of income, own 90.2 per cent of assets, and account for 81 per cent of total employment. For the full statistical overview (published in Mandarin), see Sina.com (2015). This interesting information points to two potential research directions: (1) how the Chinese party-state continues to influence domestic and global economic growth through the SOEs; and (2) the extent to which private enterprises are allowed to wield influence in the domestic economy.

4. For a historical overview of the *hukou* system, see Cheng and Selden (1994); Chan (2009).

5. For a full review on entrenched uneven development during and after the Mao era, see Lim (2016).

6. The need to redress economic-geographical inequality, as recent statistics suggest, is pressing: the average income in 2010 of a resident in the province-level cities of Shanghai, Beijing and Tianjin is at least five times more than a resident in the three provinces with the lowest per capita GDP, namely Yunnan, Gansu and Guizhou (*The Economist* 2011). A report by the Chinese Household Finance Survey Center of Chengdu's Southwestern University of Finance and Economics put China's 2010

Gini coefficient at 0.61, which, according to World Bank figures, is substantially above the average of 0.44 for all countries (*Caixin Online* 2012).

7. For a detailed overview, see Li and Wu (2012); Liu et al. (2011).

8. This refers specifically to an artificially low price relative to what it would have been if negative environmental and social externalities are taken into account.

9. This is also a process that has specific gendered effects. As Tamara Jacka (2005: 221, 105) highlights, for example, 'Female migrants generally earn less than male migrants and there are significant differences in the experiences of the two groups ... [housing conditions of migrant women] very often [leave] them highly vulnerable to physical and sexual violence and other forms of abuse.'

BIBLIOGRAPHY

Bloomberg (2010) China says Fed stimulus risks hurting global recovery. *Bloomberg* (5 November). Available at: http://www.bloomberg.com/news/articles/2010-11-05/china-says-u-s-fed-must-explain-bond-buying-or-endanger-global-confidence

Brenner N, Peck J and Theodore N (2010) Variegated neoliberalism: Geographies, modalities, pathways. *Global Networks* 10(2): 182–222.

Buck D (2007) The subsumption of space and the spatiality of subsumption: Primitive accumulation and the transition to capitalism in Shanghai, China. *Antipode: A Radical Journal of Geography* 39(4): 757–774.

Caixin Online (2012) China's Gini Index at 0.61, University report says. *Caixin Online* (11 December). Available at: http://english.caixin.com/2012-12-10/100470648.html

Chan KW (2009) The Chinese *Hukou* system at 50. *Eurasian Geography and Economics* 50(2): 197–221.

Chan KW and Buckingham W (2008) Is China abolishing the *Hukou* system? *The China Quarterly* 195: 582–606.

Cheng T and Selden M (1994) The origins and social consequences of China's *Hukou* system. *The China Quarterly* 139: 644–668.

Chinese National Health and Family Planning Commission (2015) *Zhongguo liudong renkou fazhan baogao 2015* [Development report of China's floating population 2015]. Beijing: China Population Press.

Chinese State Council 6th Population Census Office (2012) *Major Figures on 2010 Population Census of China* [in Mandarin]. Beijing: China Statistics Press.

Deng X (1993) *Deng Xiaoping wenxuan*, Vol. 3. Beijing: People's Publishing House.

Dickson B (2008) *Wealth into Power: The Communist Party's Embrace of China's Private Sector*. Cambridge: Cambridge University Press.

Harney A (2009) *The China Price: The True Cost of Chinese Competitive Advantage*. London: Penguin.

Harvey D (2005) *A Brief History of Neoliberalism*. Oxford: Oxford University Press.

Harvey D (2006) *Spaces of Global Capitalism: Towards a Theory of Uneven Geographical Development*. London: Verso.

He S and Wu F (2009) China's emerging neoliberal urbanism: Perspectives from urban redevelopment. *Antipode: A Radical Journal of Geography* 41(2): 282–304.

Hewitt (2008) *Getting Rich First: Life in a Changing China*. London: Vintage.

Hinton W (1990) *The Great Reversal: The Privatization of China, 1978–1989*. New York: Monthly Review Press.

Jacka T (2005) *Rural Women in Urban China: Gender, Migration and Social Change*. London: M.E. Sharpe.

Klein N (2007) *The Shock Doctrine: The Rise of Disaster Capitalism*. Harmondsworth: Penguin.

Li H (2006) *Mao and the Economic Stalinization of China, 1949–1953*. Lanham, MD: Rowman & Littlefield.

Li Y and Wu F (2012) The transformation of regional governance in China: The rescaling of statehood. *Progress in Planning* 78(2): 55–99.

Lim KF (2010) On China's growing geo-economic influence and the evolution of variegated capitalism. *Geoforum* 41(5): 677–688.

Lim KF (2014) Spatial egalitarianism as a social 'counter-movement': On socio-economic reforms in Chongqing. *Economy and Society* 43(3): 455–493.

Lim KF (2016) On the shifting spatial logics of socioeconomic regulation in post-1949 China. *Territory, Politics, Governance* (Online). DOI: 10.1080/21622671.2015.1099466

Lin GCS (2009a) *Developing China: Land, Politics and Social Conditions*. Abingdon: Routledge.

Lin GCS (2009b) Scaling-up regional development in globalizing China: Local capital accumulation, landcentred politics and reproduction of space. *Regional Studies* 43(3): 429–447.

Liu W, Jin F, Liu Y, Liu H, Zhang W and Lu D (2011) *Zhongguo Quyu Fazhan Baogao*. Beijing: Shangwu Yinshuguan.

Mao Z (1993) *Mao Zedong Nianpu (1893–1949), Xiajuan*. Beijing: Zhongyang Wenxian Chubanshe.

Naughton B (2010) China's distinctive system: Can it be a model for others? *Journal of Contemporary China* 19(65): 437–460.

Nolan P (2012) *Is China Buying the World?* Cambridge: Polity.

Nonini DM (2008) Is China becoming neoliberal? *Critique of Anthropology* 28(2): 145–176.

Oi JC (1992) Fiscal reform and the economic foundations of local state corporatism in China. *World Politics* 45(1): 99–126.

Peck J (2010) *Constructions of Neoliberal Reason*. Oxford: Oxford University Press.

Qiu F (2010) Liqing pingjunzhiyi, xiaolü, he gongping de misi. *Aisixiang* (27 March). Available at: http://www.aisixiang.com/data/34114-4.html

Qiushi (2014) The Chinese path: An answer to a series of problems developing countries face in modernization. *Qiushi Journal* 6(3). Available at: http://english.qstheory.cn/2014-08/14/c_1111963549.htm

Smith N (1984) *Uneven Development: Nature, Capital and the Production of Space*. Oxford: Basil Blackwell.

Song Y (2016) *Hukou*-based labour market discrimination and ownership structure in urban China. *Urban Studies* 53(8): 1657–1673.

The Economist (2011) All the parities in China. *The Economist* (24 February). Available at: http://www.economist.com/node/18233380

Tsing Y (2010) *The Great Urban Transformation: Politics of Land and Property in China*. Oxford: Oxford University Press.

Walker KLM (2006) 'Gangster capitalism' and peasant protest in China: The last twenty years. *Journal of Peasant Studies* 33(1): 1–33.

Wang H (2009) *The End of the Revolution: China and the Limits of Modernity*. London: Verso.

Webber M (2008a) Primitive accumulation in modern China. *Dialectical Anthropology* 32(4): 299–320.

Webber M (2008b) The places of primitive accumulation in rural China. *Economic Geography* 84(4): 395–421.

Whyte MK (2005) Rethinking equality and inequality in the PRC. Paper presented at the 50th Anniversary conference for the Fairbank Center for East Asian Research, Harvard University, 9–11 December. Available at: http://www.wcfia.harvard.edu/sites/default/files/1068__MKW_rethinkingequality.pdf

Wu F (2010) How neoliberal is China's reform? The origins of change during transition. *Eurasian Geography and Economics* 51(5): 619–631.

Wu F (2015) *Planning for Growth: Urban and Regional Planning in China*. Abingdon: Routledge.

Xia Y and Feng Z (1982) Tidu lilun yu quyu jingji. *Shanghai Kexue Yanjiusuo Qikan (Yanjiu yu jianyi)* 8: 21–24.

Zhang H (2010) The *Hukou* system's constraints on migrant workers' job mobility in Chinese cities. *China Economic Review* 21(1): 51–64.

Zhang L and Ong A (2008) *Privatizing China: Socialism from Afar*. Ithaca, NY: Cornell University Press.

Zhang M (2001) *Xiangcun Shehui Quanli he Wenhua Jiegou de Bianqian, 1903–1953*. Nanning: Guangxi Renmin Chubanshe.

Zhang M (2003) Huabei diqu tudi gaige yundong de yunzuo (1946–1949). *21shiji* 76 (April): 32–41.

Zhang M, Zhu CJ and Nyland C (2014) The institution of *Hukou*-based social exclusion: A unique institution reshaping the characteristics of contemporary urban China. *International Journal of Urban and Regional Research* 38(4): 1437–1457.

Zhu J (2013) *Zhongguo gaige de qilu*. Taipei: Linkingbooks.

Postscript

Cynthia Enloe

CCTV cameras have become part of the urban landscape—they are features of neighbourhood street corners—yet privatized security guards patrol the supermarket. State intelligence agencies are expanding, yet the state is outsourcing the management of the local water supply. Each is among the most common of contemporary markers of civic life. As Cemal Burak Tansel and his contributors have revealed here, they seem to be pulling the state in two quite different directions. The quantum leap in the number of public CCTV cameras and the dramatic expansion of governments' intrusive intelligence powers have vastly increased the powers of the state. Simultaneously, many governments today are energetically shedding their responsibilities, in the name of economic austerity and/or alleged operational efficiency. Farming out formerly state responsibilities to private contractors or terminating them altogether today passes as governance.

Given these expansions and sheddings, to live as a responsible citizen in many states today calls for extraordinary initiative. Under what conditions can the state intrude on one's personal spaces without a formal warrant? Do all employees in all sectors have a state-ensured right to organize? Who is actually responsible for cleaning the subway stations or for interpreting the hours of digital images on the states' omnipresent CCTV cameras? To uncover definitive answers to any of these crucial civic questions, a citizen now has to become a resourceful sleuth.

One key question posed by this book's authors concerns the disciplinary state, not in the older sense of the 'nanny state', the (patriarchally cartoonish) notion of a welfare state that exchanges public benefits for patronizing interference, but, instead, a disciplinary state that consciously denies its citizens their rightful due. Is this latter sort of disciplinary statism on the rise in the early twenty-first century? If so, where exactly? As a corollary, one is prompted to ask: Is the chief cause of this sort of disciplinary statism the growing commitment of state officials in certain sorts of states to do the bidding of profit-maximizing private economic actors?

Cemal Burak Tansel and his co-authors go further, however. They challenge us, their readers, to ask ourselves: What actions can we take—or which actions by others can we support—that will effectively challenge such a profit-maximizing disciplinary statism in this distinctive sort of contemporary state?

Comparative analysis can yield valuable insights, but, as these contributors have shown us, it is a tricky enterprise. The major category of states selected here for comparative investigation is one that groups together in one analytical corral those present-day states which base their legitimacy on fair and open competitive elections to choose genuine representatives who are empowered to effectively oversee all arms of the state's executive branch. Such qualifying states must also effectively protect the equal rights of women and men, as well as of people of all economic means and of all racial and ethnic identities, so that they might appeal to the state for protection and campaign and cast secret ballots. In addition, to qualify for the analytical category featured here, a given contemporary state must already have instituted a substantial legislatively required, state-administered social safety net and a dense fabric of labour rights. Such a net and its accompanying fabric must have been designed—and enforced by state officials—to ensure reasonable standards of care for the young, the ill and elderly, decent working conditions for paid workers, the right of paid workers to organize and the construction of a material floor below which citizens, in the name of social solidarity, must not be allowed to fall.

This is a tall order. Not many states fully meet these criteria. Ask women in any of these seemingly qualifying states. Ask members of any of the racially or ethnically marginalized groups in any state selected for this distinctive category of states. They each will raise flags of caution. Nonetheless, into this comparative category by, say, 2017 one might include, for instance, the admittedly flawed states of Japan, Chile, Netherlands, Germany, Britain, France, Iceland and Norway.

Other states would clearly not qualify for this comparative analytical category. They may have electoral rituals, a quasi-market economy and faux labour unions; these excluded states may also make gestures towards social solidarity, as well as gender and ethnic equality; they may even have constitutional guarantees of judicial independence and legal due process. In practice, however, such states do not analytically qualify: for instance, the states of contemporary Turkey, China, Russia and Egypt.

Yes, one could spend hours debating what other countries today have state systems that qualify for or that should be excluded from this comparative category. The point is that one needs to craft an explicit category of states in order to meaningfully conduct the present enquiry. Not surprisingly, I would contend that the qualifying criteria should include gender-smart understandings of social democracy-in-practice.

The value of constructing such an admittedly arguable category of states is that it enables one to track those particular states which have 'made the cut' over time. That is what the creators of this book set out to do.

As they launched their ambitious comparative project, they spelled out their collective hunch: something significant was happening in those states, states which were characterized in the post-2000 era by both genuine (if not full) democratic politics plus state-ensured economic rights and social safety nets (if not well-enough stitched) for their society's paid workers and vulnerable citizens. That is, Cemal Burak Tansel and his contributing researchers think that there is good reason to believe that the ties between those states and their national citizenries are loosening. They believe, as well, that that loosening is due to those states' officials pursuing the construction of a disciplinary state whose objectives are no longer to sustain individual rights and social solidarity, but are to protect and enhance the interests of the major wielders of private capital.

These authors mean to provide us with a handbook. Having read their findings and their explanations closely, we should be able to conduct our own trackings of our own chosen qualifying states.

To do this well, however, we will need to be crystal clear about our research into state officials' (including the state's popularly elected representatives') intensions. This will not be easy. Over the past 45 years, for instance, feminists around the world have taught us not to collapse state officials' patriarchal goals into state officials' capitalist goals. For instance, state officials in these allegedly socially responsible democratic states who do not take seriously women employees' charges of persistent unequal pay or rampant workplace sexual harassment may be motivated in their denials and their neglect by goals quite distinct from just protecting employers' profits. They may be motivated by a desire to sustain what still remains of their society's patriarchal social order.

Likewise, we now know that state officials who do not energetically oversee those police officials who routinely disproportionately stop, frisk and arrest more members of racial and ethnic minorities than they do members of the socially privileged communities may not themselves be motivated in their hands-off actions mainly or only by their desire to ensure that policing works for the controllers of capital. Their enabling of such police abuses may be chiefly fuelled by racially and ethnically infused myths and anxieties.

Intensions are always difficult to expose. Why do officials of any state individually or collectively do what they do? It can be tempting to dismiss such a question, to argue or indirectly imply instead that 'the state' is its own creature, that hence, any individual official or group of officials has no agency of their own: their ideas, actions and in-actions are determined simply by mega-forces and macro-structures beyond their control and beyond even their own critical understanding. I am, I confess, rather wary of such a presumption. I think it is a weak guiding light for investigating and tracking any social democratic state as it may be transformed into a disciplinary state.

We have learned that even people who have been brutally victimized might exercise some modicum of agency, if only to sustain their elemental sense of selfhood. Thus, to pick up the analytical baton that this provocative book's authors have handed us, we need to ask what has been happening to the values, alliances, ambitions and fears of senior, mid-level and bottom-rung officials—those inside the labour, welfare, commerce, natural resources, policing, treasury, immigration, gender equity and judicial bureaucracies of these chosen states.

The authors of this book have presented us with a comparative research and activist challenge that is meant to stretch us. It is up to each of us to take up their demanding challenge.

Index

Notes on Contributors

İsmet Akça is a member of the Department of Political Science and International Relations at Yıldız Technical University. His research areas include the political sociology of Turkey, military and politics, military and economy, theories of state and neoliberalism. He most recently edited with Ahmet Bekmen and Barış Alp Özden *Turkey Reframed: Constituting Neoliberal Hegemony* (2014).

Ahmet Bekmen is a member of the Faculty of Political Science at Istanbul University. His research interests include theories of state and power, neoliberalization and Turkish politics. He is one of the co-editors of *Turkey Reframed: Constituting Neoliberal Hegemony* (2014).

Koenraad Bogaert is Post-doctoral Assistant at the Department of Conflict and Development Studies, Ghent University.

Kendra Briken is Lecturer in Human Resource Management at the University of Strathclyde.

Ian Bruff is Lecturer in European Politics at the University of Manchester, UK. He has published widely on capitalist diversity, neoliberalism and social theory. He recently completed a large cross-country project on the diversity of contemporary capitalism(s) with Matthias Ebenau, Christian May and Andreas Nölke, which produced two German-language collections in 2013 plus an English-language special issue in 2014 and an English-language volume in 2015. He is currently researching the political economy of authoritarian neoliberalism in Europe and is Managing Editor of the *Transforming Capitalism* book series.

Mònica Clua-Losada is Associate Professor in Global Political Economy at the Department of Political Science at the University of Texas Rio Grande Valley. She is also an executive board member of the Johns Hopkins University–Universitat Pompeu Fabra Public Policy Center in Barcelona. Her research focuses on the contestation, subversion and resistance of labour and other social movements to capitalist relations of domination. She has written on the effects of the current financial crisis on the Spanish state. Her work has been published in different languages and outlets, the most recent work can be found in *New Political Economy* and *Comparative European Politics*. She is currently working on a manuscript (forthcoming in the RIPE series) with David Bailey and Nikolai Huke entitled *Beyond Defeat and Austerity: Disrupting (the Critical Political Economy of) Neoliberal Europe*, which offers an autonomist Marxist reconsideration of European Integration.

Brecht De Smet is Post-doctoral Lecturer and Researcher at the Department of Conflict and Development Studies, Ghent University, and the author of *Gramsci on Tahrir: Revolution and Counter-Revolution in Egypt* (2016) and *A Dialectical Pedagogy of Revolt: Gramsci, Vygotsky, and the Egyptian Revolution* (2015).

Annalena Di Giovanni is a PhD candidate in the Department of Geography at the University of Cambridge.

Volker Eick is Political Scientist at the Faculty of Law, Center of European Law and Politics at the Universität Bremen and co-editor of *Urban (In)Security: Policing the Neoliberal Crisis* (2013).

Cynthia Enloe is Research Professor in the Departments of International Development, Community and Engagement; Women's and Gender Studies; and Political Science at Clark University in Worcester, Massachusetts. She is the author of 14 books, including *Maneuvers: The International Politics of Militarizing Women's Lives* (2004), *The Curious Feminist* (2004) and *Globalization and Militarism* (new edition, 2016), as well as *Nimo's War, Emma's War: Making Feminist Sense of the Iraq War*, (2011), *The Real State of America: Mapping the Myths and Truths about the United States* (co-authored with Joni Seager) (2012), *Seriously! Investigating Crashes and Crises as if Women Mattered* (2013). Her new, updated and revised second edition of *Bananas, Beaches and Bases* was published in June 2014.

Wendy Harcourt is Associate Professor at the International Institute of Social Studies of the Erasmus University, The Hague. She received the

2010 Feminist and Women's Studies Association's Prize for her book on *Body Politics in Development: Critical Debates in Gender and Development* (2009). She has edited five books including *Women and Politics of Place* with Arturo Escobar (2005).

Kean Fan Lim is Assistant Professor in Economic Geography at the School of Geography, University of Nottingham, UK. He adopts an interdisciplinary approach to understand and explain the political-economic processes driving institutional continuity and change in East Asia, with current emphasis on China. Working from multiple locations in China, Kean studies how place-specific policy experimentation in China is complicated by different, if at times contradictory, developmental approaches. He has published widely in key journals in geography and across the social sciences, and is currently working on two monographs.

Luca Manunza received his PhD in Sociology from the University of Genoa and has been collaborating with the Department of Sociology at the University Suor Orsola Benincasa and with the Department of Urban Planning at the University Federico II in Naples since 2005. He is a member of URiT (The Social Topographies Research Unit) and an editorial member of *Social Cartographies*. His research focuses on social control, migration, urban and social transformation. He has also worked for Italian and foreign broadcasters as a freelance filmmaker and is a member of independent Neapolitan telestreet Insu^TV.

Barış Alp Özden is a member of the Department of Political Science and International Relations at Yıldız Technical University. His research focuses on labour history, political economy and social policy in Turkey. He is co-editor of *Turkey Reframed: Constituting Neoliberal Hegemony* (2014) and *Emperyalizm: Teori ve Güncel Tartışmalar* (2016).

Olatz Ribera-Almandoz is a PhD candidate at the Department of Political and Social Sciences at Universitat Pompeu Fabra, Barcelona. She is also a visiting scholar at the University of Manchester and a member of the Johns Hopkins University–Universitat Pompeu Fabra Public Policy Center. Her doctoral research investigates the interaction between social movements and the state in contexts of multilevel political arrangements with special focus on the (new) demands for social justice, reproduction and welfare in Spain and the United Kingdom. She also worked as a researcher in public policy analysis in a variety of public and private institutions, including the Institute of Government and Public Policy (IGOP) and the Barcelona Institute of Regional and Metropolitan Studies (IERMB).

Sébastien Rioux is Canada Research Chair in the Political Economy of Food and Wellbeing and Assistant Professor in the Department of Geography at the Université de Montréal, Canada.

Panagiotis Sotiris holds a PhD from Panteion University, Athens. He has taught social and political philosophy and social theory at the University of Crete, Panteion University of Athens and the University of the Aegean. In 2004, he published a monograph on Althusser in Greek titled *Communism and Philosophy: The Theoretical Adventure of Louis Althusser* (2004). He has published widely on Althusser, Marxist philosophy, modern social theory and current social and political developments in Greece.

Simon Springer is Associate Professor in the Department of Geography at the University of Victoria, Canada. His research agenda explores the political, social and geographical exclusions that neoliberalization has engendered, particularly in post-transitional Cambodia, where he emphasizes the spatialities of violence and power. He cultivates a cutting edge theoretical approach to his scholarship by foregrounding both poststructuralist critique and a radical revival of anarchist philosophy. Simon's books include *The Anarchist Roots of Geography: Towards Spatial Emancipation* (2016), *The Discourse of Neoliberalism: An Anatomy of a Powerful Idea* (2016), *Violent Neoliberalism: Development, Discourse and Dispossession in Cambodia* (2015), and *Cambodia's Neoliberal Order: Violence, Authoritarianism, and the Contestation of Public Space* (2010). Simon serves as a co-editor of *ACME: An International E-Journal for Critical Geographies* and for the *Transforming Capitalism* book series.

Cemal Burak Tansel is Anniversary Postdoctoral Research Fellow in the Department of Politics at the University of Sheffield. His research focuses on the historical sociology of state formation and capitalist development in the Middle East and the political economy of development. His peer-reviewed research articles have appeared in the *European Journal of International Relations*, *Review of International Studies* and *Journal of International Relations and Development*.

Printed in Great Britain
by Amazon